A Reader's Guide
to the Short Stories of

NATHANIEL HAWTHORNE

*A*
*Reference*
*Publication*
*in*
*Literature*

*Hershel Parker*
*Editor*

# A Reader's Guide
## to the Short Stories of

# NATHANIEL
# HAWTHORNE

## LEA BERTANI VOZAR NEWMAN

G.K.HALL&CO.

70 LINCOLN STREET, BOSTON, MASS.

**Library of Congress Cataloging in Publication Data**

Newman, Lea Bertani Vozar.
　　A reader's guide to the short stories of Nathaniel Hawthorne.

　　(A Reference publication in literature)
　　Bibliography: pp. 349–80
　　1. Hawthorne, Nathaniel, 1804–1864—Criticism
and interpretation.　　I. Title.　　II. Series:
Reference publication in literature.
PS1888.N4　　813'.3　　79–20100
ISBN 0–8161–8398–8

*This publication is printed on permanent/durable acid-free paper*
MANUFACTURED IN THE UNITED STATES OF AMERICA

# Table of Contents

# Foreword

Hawthorneans have often seemed hellbent on making the facts about the Man of Mosses as nebulous as the airiest of his tales and sketches. Lacking a collected edition of Hawthorne letters, lacking a chronology such as Jay Leyda constructed for Melville, scholars and critics have often been frustrated when trying to run down the simplest facts. Those bedeviled souls will rejoice at Lea Newman's *A Reader's Guide to the Short Stories of Nathaniel Hawthorne*, the most helpful compendium about the stories ever assembled. The sections on "Publication History" are a godsend to anyone wanting to lay hand on reliable information quickly, and the sections on "Circumstances of Composition, Sources, and Influences" are also extremely useful. These sections are greatly indebted to quotations from previously unpublished letters in volumes of the Ohio State University Centenary Edition. Critics will find much pertinent information in the sections on "Relationship with Other Hawthorne Works" and "Interpretations and Criticism." Lea Newman has put at our fingertips an extraordinary quantity of information hitherto unavailable.

HERSHEL PARKER

# Preface

The purpose of this book is to provide a compendium of historical and critical data for each of Nathaniel Hawthorne's fifty-four short stories. The book is intended to serve both as a practical, self-contained guide for general readers and as a review and research tool for readers with a special interest in Hawthorne's fiction. The pages that follow transform an unwieldy body of factual and theoretical information, never before assembled in one place, into a coherent and convenient overview designed to help the average intelligent reader to understand and appreciate Hawthorne's stories more fully. The following pages also direct the specialist to sources and other works where he may further explore the tales for scholarly or pedagogic purposes.

Each of the fifty-four chapters that follow is devoted to one of the fifty-four pieces in Hawthorne's canon that most readers call short stories. While ordinarily the short-story genre is not difficult to define, in the case of Hawthorne's work the distinction is not always clear-cut. Hawthorne himself uses the terms *sketch* and *tale* interchangeably in his prefaces and letters so that his own statements cloud the issue. Readers have found some pieces impossibie to classify. Hyatt Waggoner says, "No sharp separation can be made between the allegorical 'processions,' the sketches with some narrative ingredients, and the 'tales proper,' as we think of the short story today" (*Hawthorne: A Critical Study*, rev. ed. [Cambridge, Mass.: Belknap Press, 1963], p. 253). It is, of course, the second of Waggoner's categories that presents the most difficulties. Three pieces, all of which I classify as short stories, will serve to illustrate the problem. Waggoner unhesitatingly includes "The Celestial Rail-road" among the sketches (p. 17), calls "The Canterbury Pilgrims" a "sketchlike story" (p. 39), and dismisses "Wakefield" as a story that "never expands much beyond anecdote" (p. 98). On the other hand, another reader, in an admittedly minority position, argues that "Wakefield" is an essay that follows the "illustrated idea" pattern of many of Hawthorne's sketches (Thomas F. Walsh, Jr., " 'Wakefield' and Hawthorne's Illustrated Ideas: A Study in Form," *Emerson Society Quarterly*, 25 [1961], 29–35). Neal F. Doubleday deals with a classification similar to mine in his excellent study, *Hawthorne's Early Tales: A Critical Study* (Durham, N.C.: Duke Univ. Press, 1972). For his purpose, he defines the tales as "pieces of some considerable narrative interest." He distinguishes between pieces with an interest in event and pieces with little or none, and he limits his discussion to "pieces that do have an interest of event" (p. 3).

Because my compendium aims to be a guide and a tool enabling the reader who enjoys a short story to more completely enjoy Hawthorne's short stories, my working definition is similar to Doubleday's. If a piece has an identifiable narrative pattern, what Aristotle calls plot and the "soul" of tragedy, I have included it in my survey. Such pieces as "Fancy's Show Box" and "The Christmas Banquet" are thus classified as stories, in spite of their discursive and essaylike style, because they do have a viable narrative thread. They engage the reader, emotionally and aesthetically, in a series of events that involve fictional characters who participate in and are affected by those events. Other pieces, such as "Main Street" and "The Custom-House," are not included because, although a form of fictional characterization is involved (the showman in the first, the narrator in the second), a climactically developed narrative pattern is not readily identifiable. The only acknowledged short works by Hawthorne which fit this definition that I have not included are the short stories written for children, because they fall out of the scope established for this study.

Although the children's stories, and the sketches and novels, are not assigned chapters by name, all of them, and everything else in Hawthorne's canon, are a significant part of this work. They are used wherever and whenever they inform in any way the fifty-four stories that are its direct concern. Because the short stories often deal with the same themes and concepts as do the essays, and because both the tales and the sketches contain the germs for the full-length romances, all of Hawthorne's works are involved in the analyses that follow.

I have used the Centenary Edition of Hawthorne's work, published by the Ohio State University Press, for my texts. Each of the stories reviewed appears in one of the three volumes devoted to the tales: Volume IX, *Twice-told Tales*; Volume X, *Mosses from an Old Manse*; and Volume XI, *The Snow-Image and Uncollected Tales,* all edited by J. Donald Crowley. The other completed volumes in the Centenary Edition have also been used wherever they were relevant.

The analysis of each story is divided into four parts. The first subdivision of each chapter covers the publication history, including pertinent details of Hawthorne's often unhappy relations with his publishers and of his pay—or lack of it—for each story. Much of the publication data comes from Crowley's "Historical Commentary," which is part of the editorial appendixes in Volumes IX, X, and XI of the Centenary Edition.

The second subdivision deals with the circumstances of composition: when and where each story was written, what sources inspired it, and what influences, direct and indirect, helped to shape it. The most common source for story "germs" is Hawthorne's own notebook, with earlier stories and sketches a close second. Hawthorne's personal experiences and relationships, his reading, and his letters provide background material and additional insights. The first of these—the stockpile of observations and story ideas that Hawthorne kept in his notebooks to draw on when he was ready to write something for publication—makes up a sizable portion of the second subdivision. The entries come from Volume VIII of the Centenary Edition, *The American Notebooks,* edited by Claude M. Simpson.

Unfortunately, Hawthorne's letters, which are an equally valuable primary source of information, are not as readily available. A definitive collection still awaits publication, although a volume in the Centenary Edition has long been slated for it. The work is under way, however, and the Centenary editors were able to draw from the correspondence data on file for the commentaries in Volumes VIII through XI. I have relied heavily on the background provided in the Centenary Edition, but I have also used a variety of other sources to provide additional correspondence, other kinds of personal documents, and recollections of acquaintances, friends, and relatives. These sources include a wide assortment of biographies, book-length critical studies, and journal articles that explore every conceivable aspect of Hawthorne's life from how, at the age of four, he was given his first book, Bunyan's *Pilgrim's Progress,* to how he consistently arranged to be "out" whenever Emerson called at the Old Manse.

The third subdivision of each chapter surveys the relationship of the story to other works in Hawthorne's canon. Because Hawthorne's writings reveal an obsession with a few themes—guilt, isolation, the nature of illusions—the interrelationships are close and complex as well as extraordinarily illuminating. Here, as in each of the sections, I take into account what others have said. It is the fourth subdivision, however, that is devoted primarily to published explications and criticism. This final section of each chapter reviews all the significant interpretations that the story has generated and presents a profile of its critical status.

All four sections are indebted to the host of scholars who have advanced Hawthorne criticism despite the lack of a good edition of the letters. The seminal studies and landmark essays of the Hawthorne enthusiasts of the early twentieth century have been followed by an avalanche of criticism. Without the kind of analytical survey I have provided, a reader who would be familiar with the published critical commentary on any story would find his task time-consuming in the extreme. I have made full use of the pioneering efforts of such leaders as Stewart, Turner, Warren, Fogle, and Male and the subsequent work of Crews, Doubleday, Martin, Pearce, and Baym, to mention but a few of the outstanding Hawthorne scholars. My survey is an attempt to treat all the significant publications related to the short stories, beginning with reviews by Hawthorne's contemporaries and moving up through 1975, with the addition of studies of special import that appeared in 1976 and a few in 1977.

In reporting on the accumulated critical material, my objective has been the maximum completeness compatible with optimum conciseness. The aim is to present each interpretation succinctly enough to introduce the general reader to its main thesis with dispatch, yet thoroughly enough and with sufficient representative detail to allow the specialist to judge its worth or promise. In the case of the much-written-about stories, I define the possible approaches by establishing a frame of reference that subsumes the otherwise unmanageable number of individual interpretations. This method synthesizes the shared concepts of several critics into a position statement and keeps repetition at a minimum. Where this practice is used, as with the historically-minded or the Freudian-oriented readers, variations on the theme worthy of note follow the aggregate view. In the countless exercises in discrimination that every synopsis and every analyses represent, my intention has always been to include enough detail so that readers will not find it necessary to search elsewhere for an adequate understanding of the significant aspects of the story. Readers may find themselves drawn to explore the original critiques, not because they found the précis unclear or confusing, but because they discovered new and challenging avenues of interest.

Similarly, readers should not find it necessary to shuffle between chapters, because each chapter is designed to be self-sufficient. Occasionally, however, a reader will be directed to another analysis, should he happen to be investigating a particular aspect of a story that is closely related to another story. The publication history of the pieces that are thought to have been part of *The Story Teller* is one example in which such cross-references have been used. A detailed account, including passages from Hawthorne's correspondence with his publishers, is given in the chapter devoted to "The Devil in Manuscript." For the other stories in the projected collection, a minimal background is provided with a cross-reference to the "Devil in Manuscript" chapter. In this way, duplication is held to a minimum without undue inconvenience to the reader. The exception may be the four stories that make up the "Legends of the Province-House." Since they are seldom reprinted as a group and often appear singly in anthologies, individual analysis appear to fit my purpose best; however, the group has a unity that makes it difficult to avoid repetition. My resolution of the difficulty is a more intricate system of cross-reference for these four stories, but here, too, readers interested in one of the stories as an independent work should be able to regard the cross-references as optional and supplementary.

Another objective of this study has been to present an overview of all the disparate positions of any consequence without prejudice or partiality. Because subjectivity is ingrained in the very act of perception, I realize that the objectivity I intend is well-nigh impossible. Nevertheless, this project represents an attempt to move toward this unreachable goal. Eclecticism has been its mode and its aim since its inception. In fact, the rationale for its structure—that is, the arrangement of chapters in alphabetical order—was chosen to avoid any organization that would imply a meaningful arrangement and, thereby, undercut the objectivity.

Part of the uniqueness of this study rests on its eclectic purpose. Whereas other scholars have occasionally provided reviews of earlier criticism for individual stories, they have invariably done so either to confirm their own findings or to set up an adversarial position for attack. In the following pages, each critical contingent has been fairly represented with as much impartiality as possible. For example, due note is made of a linguistic analysis of "The Minister's Black Veil" that uses transformational grammar to establish Hooper's passivity, in spite of my personal opinion that Hooper's retreat into inaction is clearly demonstrable without resorting to linguistic theory. One of the reasons for trying to achieve objectivity is to allow the reader to judge the validity of the proposals on their own merits, always with the understanding that certain established criteria shared by the majority of knowledgeable readers take precedence.

The exercise of judgment is evident in every phase of this project, not least in the ever-present necessity for deciding what constitutes due attention. Some stories merit less attention than others, as the varying lengths of the chapters confirm. The same is true of the published critiques. The essential objectivity of this project is not, I trust, hampered by an occasional word of praise for something especially well done or for the solving of an issue that has long vexed others. Also, I have chosen not to refrain from identifying what is singular or eccentric or plainly absurd when the occasion warrants it, particularly if the proposal appears to be contradicted by the text of the story itself.

In organizing the incredible number of published critical statements on the short stories (the latest bibliography of secondary sources for "Young

Goodman Brown" lists over 400 for that story alone), I have tried to synthesize the multitude of proposed readings into an overview that clearly defines what positions have been adequately defended, what issues have been thoroughly debated, and what aspects have been sufficiently explored. I hope that writers and editors alike will be alerted to what has been exhaustively treated and that the redundancy that has unfortunately marred the growth of Hawthorne criticism will be curtailed. One who has read through the criticism—the valuable and the worthless—must advocate a halt to needless proliferation.

Is there, then, anything new to be said about Hawthorne's tales? Most emphatically, there is. The recent work of such scholars as John J. McDonald and C. E. Frazer Clark, Jr. confirms the viability of contemporary Hawthorne criticism. However, editors must reassure their readers that current Hawthorne publications will be worth reading by exercising discrimination and by insisting that what they call new be truly new.

In the discussions that follow, some "new" insights are offered. The Dantean echo in the description of the procession in "My Kinsman, Major Molineux" is one, but the most original aspect of my work is in the illumination of relationships within Hawthorne's canon—how one story clarifies another, how one character is rooted in an earlier version of a similar character, how one thematic concern is repeated with subtle but significant variations in several pieces. A number of the relationships outlined in the third subdivision of each chapter have been pointed out before; Randall Stewart's introduction to his edition of *The American Notebooks* and Arne Axelsson's detailed classification of character types are notable examples of earlier work in this area. But many of the parallels and contrasts that I suggest have not been published in any of the works listed in the extensive bibliography that concludes this project. Such groupings are useful in helping to establish which works make good companion pieces for others, which stories best exemplify one aspect of Hawthorne's concerns (historical, moral, aesthetic, psychological), or which tales best represent Hawthorne's literary techniques as an allegorist or a symbolist or a writer of romances.

The critical barometer for the short stories of Nathaniel Hawthorne fluctuates, like that of most literary works, with the critical atmosphere of the times. In Hawthorne's day, the short stories were considered apprentice work that prepared the way for his greatest accomplishments as a writer of romances. In many quarters today, the short stories, along with *The Scarlet Letter,* are regarded as Hawthorne's best work. "Young Goodman Brown" and "My Kinsman, Major Molineux" are among the most widely read American short stories of all time. These two and a few others—"The Minister's Black Veil," "Ethan Brand," "Rappaccini's Daughter"—are what many believe to be the best measure of Hawthorne's genius. The question of whether the novels or the short stories are Hawthorne's most important contribution to American literature is not at issue in this study. I believe the project establishes the stories as worthy of attention in and of themselves. My concern has been to make them as available from every perspective as possible.

The pages that follow are the result of a complicated process of collecting, reviewing, assessing, classifying, merging, and distinguishing. Their worth rests squarely on a pragmatic premise. If anyone who reads a short story by Hawthorne can use this guide to experience the story more meaningfully and completely, my project will have succeeded.

\* \* \* \* \*

For the assistance and support contributed toward the successful completion of this book, I am grateful to the staff of the libraries of North Adams State College and Williams College; to my typist, Agnes Carriere; to my mentor, Everett Emerson; and especially to my husband, "Chick" Newman.

To the students in my literature classes at North Adams State College, I am grateful in a less specific yet equally significant way. It was the excitement and enjoyment of sharing Hawthorne's short stories with them that generated the enthusiasm that prompted my interest in Hawthorne's fiction and ultimately in this undertaking.

# A Note on References and Documentation

Because the use of footnotes in a study of this kind would be cumbersome, documentation is incorporated into the text in parentheses. The text for each story is established immediately below the chapter title at the beginning of each segment. Page references to the text of each story are indicated by italic Arabic numerals, followed by a period and an additional set of italic Arabic numerals which indicate line references when such identification is necessary for clarity.

Other references to the Centenary Edition of Hawthorne's works are handled in the same way, except that a *CE* and the volume number in Roman numerals precedes the page and line references. For example, references to the eighth volume of the Centenary Edition, which is *The American Notebooks* and the most frequently cited source, appear thus: (*CE, VIII, 158.3–5*).

Arabic numerals in parentheses and not italicized refer to the secondary sources listed in the bibliography. A colon separates the item number from the specific page citation. When more than one source is involved, a semicolon separates the sources. For example, (11:125–26; 43:26–27) refers to two items in the bibliography under secondary sources, items 11 and 43, and specifically to pages 125 and 126 of the first and pages 26 and 27 of the second.

# I

# Alice Doane's Appeal

*(Centenary Edition, Volume XI, Uncollected Tales, 266–80.)*

## Publication History

This story was first published in the fall of 1834 in the *Token and Atlantic Souvenir* (pp. 84-101) dated 1835, as the work of the author of "The Gentle Boy," an earlier story that had appeared in the same annual gift book three years before (*CE, XI, 432*). No record of Hawthorne's exact pay for "Alice Doane's Appeal" has been found. Estimates range from $13 to $18, depending on whether the 1831 offer of 75¢ per page or the figure of $1 per page is used. Because an earlier version of "Alice Doane's Appeal" was submitted with the four stories that appeared in the 1832 *Token,* a lingering contract on the figure Samuel Goodrich offered in 1831 may have been in force (207), but it has also been argued that Hawthorne was more likely paid at the rate established for the 1836 *Token* contributions (250:109).

Hawthorne tried to make the original version of this story a part of his two earliest collections, *Seven Tales of My Native Land* and *Provincial Tales,* but neither project succeeded in finding a publisher (11:121–30). (See circumstances of composition, below.) The revised version with the frame addition was never collected during the author's lifetime. The fact that Hawthorne's editor, James T. Fields, did not include "Alice Doane's Appeal" in *The Snow-Image* suggests that either he or Hawthorne rejected it. (Its attribution made it easily identifiable when Fields was looking through the old *Token* issues for pieces to fill out the last collection.) In the preface to *The Snow-Image*, Hawthorne refers to a few remaining tales "such as no paternal partiality could induce the author to think worth preserving" (*CE, XI, 6.27–28*). "Alice Doane's Appeal" is probably one of those so disparaged (*CE, XI, 390–91*; 149:215). It was first reprinted in the posthumous collection, *Sketches and Studies,* published in 1883 by Houghton Mifflin, descended from the Ticknor, Reed, and Fields firm (*CE, XI, 397, n.4*).

## Circumstances of Composition, Sources, and Influences

The inner story of Alice Doane may well be Hawthorne's earliest tale, possibly dating back to his college days at Bowdoin before 1825. Elizabeth Hawthorne recollects, in one account, that her brother showed her "a tale of witchcraft" called "Alice Doane" in "the summer of 1825" (233:I, 124); in another, she refers to "Seven Tales of My Native Land," the collection of which it was a part, as having been written "soon after he left college" (458.1:323).

"Alice Doane's Appeal," as published in the 1835 *Token,* appears to be a revision of the early story (11:125). A fictional account of the inner story's history is given by the narrator in the frame story. Its details follow the account in "The Devil in Manuscript": a few pieces that chanced to be "in kinder custody" (*CE, XI, 269.19*) escaped destruction when the author burned his early works in frustration over not being able to get them published. The frame also follows Hawthorne's actual experience, even to identifying the *Token* as the place where several tales in the series were published. When Hawthorne submitted some of his *Provincial Tales* to the *Token*'s editor for advice on getting them published, his letter described one that was "founded upon the Superstitions of this part of the country" as "rather wild and grotesque." That he meant Alice Doane's story is confirmed by Goodrich's response a month later, on January 19, 1830, which singled out "Alice Doane" as the one of the group that he doubted would get "public approbation." The other stories, "My Kinsman, Major Molineux," "Roger Malvin's Burial," "The Gentle Boy," and "The Wives of the Dead," were included in the 1832 *Token* after Hawthorne gave up trying to get them published as a collection, but "Alice Doane's Appeal" did not appear until three years later. The 1835 *Token* version must have been written between 1830, when Goodrich rejected the original, and late spring of 1834, when the 1835 *Token* was being assembled for fall publication (*CE, IX, 486–90*).

The question of what specific changes Hawthorne made, and why he made them, has given rise to several theories. The assumption has generally been that Hawthorne's purpose was to increase the aesthetic and moral effectiveness of the story (483.1:16). What is known about Hawthorne's attempts to publish the earlier version has resulted in another explanation, that is, that Hawthorne "toned down in summarized narrative . . . the incestuous and sexual portions" of the original in order to assuage Goodrich's fear that the genteel readers of the *Token* would find the story offensive (206). Goodrich's criticism, which, according to Gross, "specifies neither a personal dislike nor an artistic failure," provided the impetus for the changes that Hawthorne made, albeit not without resentment. The following passage is cited as an expression of Hawthorne's exasperation at what he had to do in order "to comply with the exigencies of the gift-book trade":

> I kept an awful solemnity of visage, being indeed, a little piqued that a narrative which had good authority in our ancient super- stitions, and would have brought even a church deacon to Gallows Hill, in old witch times, should now be considered too grotesque and extravagant for timid maids to tremble at. (*278.1–6*)

A study of the tales featured in the popular periodicals of Hawthorne's day reveals that a story, "The Hermitess," by Goodrich himself in the 1828 *Token,* involves a strong treatment of incest and is superficially similar to the Alice Doane segment. This suggests another reason for Goodrich's negative appraisal and explains Hawthorne's addition of the extensive frame as an attempt to make his story different from Goodrich's (314:152).

Other explanations for the revisions center on Hawthorne's attitude toward the Gothic mode, a genre he had admired since his youth. When the story appeared in the *Token,* the Gothic effects had obviously been altered. One analysis considers the Gothicism ironically exaggerated and suggests that Hawthorne's revision is evidence of his attempt to get away from the Gothic style (307). A more judicious theory proposes that Hawthorne's revisions are an attempt to rejuvenate the Gothic mode, not to abandon it (40; 43:37–38). According to Baym, Hawthorne sum- marized the Alice Doane portion to balance the length of the manu- script with its new context, not to eliminate the incest, which is still a strong element. His prime concern was to write successful fiction; the finished story chronicles the narrator's discovery that he could more effectively engage his readers' emotions by conjoining his Gothic effects with history.

Hawthorne's extensive reading in colonial history undoubtedly in- fluenced him to add the historically oriented frame (65:127; 483.5:16). In particular, Charles W. Upham's book, *Lectures on Witchcraft* (Boston, 1831), seems to be reflected in the way Hawthorne depicts the unregu- lated imagination and unchecked passion of the Salem witch persecutors (161).

One other literary influence has been credited with shaping this story. The presence of many "concealed borrowings" from Edmund Spenser's *Faerie Queene* has been noted, most specifically the Alice-Leonard- Walter-wizard plot as an elaboration of the Archimago episode (I, i,

29-I, ii, 11) and part of the first Duessa episode (I, ii, 12–30). These Spenserian analogues parallel many of the inner story's motifs:. erotic fantasizing, sexual jealousy, repression, transference, ambivalence, homicidal hatred, and compulsive violence (426:129; 455:1–1i).

The most personal source for the narrator's expression of inherited guilt over the injustices perpetrated in Salem in 1692 is Hawthorne's feelings as the descendant of John Hathorne, one of the presiding judges at the witchcraft trials. Hawthorne refers to him directly—and to the unequivocal acceptance of his ancestor's guilt as his own—in "The Custom House" preface of *The Scarlet Letter*:

> His son, too [John Hathorne, son of William Hathorne, an original settler of Salem], inherited the persecuting spirit, and made himself so conspicuous in the martyrdom of the witches, that their blood may fairly be said to have left a stain upon him. . . . I know not whether these ancestors of mine bethought themselves to repent. . . . At all events, I, the present writer, as their representative, hereby take shame upon myself for their sakes. . . . (*CE, I, 11*)

There can be little doubt that the author was speaking of and for himself when the narrator refers to Gallows Hill as "the high place where our fathers set up their shame" (*267.9–10*).

## Relationship with Other Hawthorne Works

"Alice Doane's Appeal" offers an early example of the primal concerns and primary techniques that contribute to Hawthorne's most effective fiction; at the same time, it incorporates the fragmentation and Gothic excesses that mar the last four romances he attempted but never completed (115:44; 500:49). Turner calls this story "a bridge" between his earliest attempts and the remainder of his works. The inner tale is like his early novel, *Fanshawe*, in that it has no significant historical location (483.5:16) and is heavily dependent on the Gothic conventions (40:107; 181:43). The villains in the two works are also alike, both in their personal appearance and in their evil designs against innocent girls (455:lix; 181:43). The possibility that Hawthorne may have written *Fanshawe* and "Alice Doane" at the same time helps to account for the many parallels in theme and technique (231:82–83). The other early works most often associated with "Alice Doane" as possible survivors from *Seven Tales of My Native Land* are "The Hollow of the Three Hills" and "An Old Woman's Tale" (11:125–26; 43:26–27; 84:8–9; 115:44).

The wizard in "Alice Doane's Appeal" has been called Hawthorne's first witch doctor (181:420), the prototype for a series of variations including Rappaccini and Chillingworth (455:lv) and the mesmerists, Matthew Maule in *The House of Seven Gables* and Westervelt in *The Blithedale Romance*. Leonard Doane is a forerunner of the pale young man bound to the wizard figure, best exemplified by Dimmesdale (181:420). The Faustian nature of the Leonard-wizard relationship makes it an early example of the devil used as a psychological symbol, a mythic image developed more fully in "Ethan Brand" (477:56). "Alice Doane's Appeal" may be considered the first of several attempts to recast the Faust story as a triangle, with "Rappaccini's Daughter" and *The Scarlet Letter* as the more successful examples (181:420–21). Perhaps the closest parallel to the devil-ancestor figure in the closing paragraph of the frame is the devil-father image in "Young Goodman Brown."

The closing paragraph of the story adumbrates Hawthorne's use of history in all his works, that is, as a means of assisting the imagination to engage the reader's heart (500:55–56). Insofar as Hawthorne's depiction of the Puritans from a historical perspective is concerned, Leonard Doane's perverted vision of evil in the graveyard has been deemed analogous to the Puritanical distortion of religious principles characterized by Richard Digby in "The Man of Adamant," Parson Hooper in "The Minister's Black Veil," and "Young Goodman Brown" (46:74). All of these characters, beginning with Doane, reflect their creator's judgment, as expressed in "Main Street," that "the sons and grandchildren of the first settlers were a race of lower and narrower souls than their progenitors had been" (*CE, XI, 86.1–3*).

In its attempt to impute its readers with historical guilt as a moral legacy of a national past, "Alice Doane's Appeal" is like "My Kinsman, Major Molineux" (368:151–52). Both stories can be viewed as psychological parables of the American Revolution, with the conflict between Leonard and Walter, like that between Robin and his uncle, symbolizing the struggle between "Old World and New World sons of the same fatherland, loyalist and colonial" (181:403).

The Alice Doane plot and the Molineux story share some significant similarities with "Young Goodman Brown" (426:134). All three have a common intent (dramatization of perilous unconscious states, among them sexual guilt and patricide), a common structure (question, quest, revelation), and common devices and stage properties (journeys, illusions, visions, devils, crowds of fiends, public illumination). The high rating afforded both "My Kinsman, Major Molineux" and "Young Goodman Brown" by twentieth-century readers offers one explanation for the surprising volume of attention bestowed on "Alice Doane's Appeal"— importance through association.

## Interpretations and Criticism

The nature of the relationship between the Alice Doane story and its frame is a central interpretative question. At first glance, the two plots appear to contradict each other. The inner story, which blames a wizard for the Leonard-Walter-Alice tragedy, seems to confirm the witch-craft charges that the narrator in the frame condemns as unjustified and totally reprehensible. The conclusion that the piece is fragmented, that its strands are loosely tangled rather than woven into a coherent whole (46:68; 500:50), stems partly from this apparent contradiction.

One reader has attempted to eliminate this contradiction by demon-strating, through a close scrutiny of the text, that Hawthorne intended the wizard to be innocent (164). Leonard Doane's "diseased imagina-tion" is, she finds, a counterpart of the delusion and hysteria that con-trolled the witch-hunters of 1692, and conversely, the wizard is analogous to the innocent victims of the Salem witch trials. Such an interpretation establishes a thematic unity between the two segments. However, the ambiguity that Hawthorne creates by mixing seventeenth and nineteenth-century voices in the inner story is misleading; the wizard's absolution, desirable as it may be in thematic terms, remains an unresolved enigma.

Others have explained the disjointed effect in psychoanalytic terms. Even an un-Freudian critic such as Waggoner attributes the story's "tangled" strands to the author's inability to achieve the necessary aesthetic distance between himself and his material (500:50). In Leonard's feelings after he murders Walter, for example, the vision of the dead enemy-father is transparent and forbidden enough to explain the com-pulsive-awakening aura that follows without the benefit of logical or harmonious transition (502: vii-viii). Waggoner's inference that the im-plicit transference of guilt in the passage is a reflection of the early death of Hawthorne's father, the neuroticism of Hawthorne's mother and elder sister, and the unhappy seclusion of his young manhood (500:52) are more explicitly interpreted by the Freudian critics (406).

Crews, for example, sees both of the plots as exercises in displacement, the inner one confirming that Hawthorne's sense of history, expressed overtly in the frame, is rooted in guilt over family conflict (115:44–60). The patricidal overtones with which the narrator depicts the authorial figure of Cotton Mather as the villain responsible for the persecutions is seen as analogous to Leonard Doane's vision of his dead father, who survives in repressed fantasy when he kills Walter Brome. (Cotton Mather functions as a stand-in for Hawthorne's great-great-great-grandfather, John Hathorne.) According to Crews, Hawthorne blames his ancestors for a "guilt and phrenzy" (267.7) associated with unnatural feeling; Leonard

Doane's murder of his projected evil other self is a psychological counter-part to what the New England magistrates did in Salem to the accused witches. The wizard personifies the unconscious compulsion that drives men to commit crimes abhorrent to themselves. In spite of the psychological correlation between the two plots, the conclusion is that Hawthorne's juxtaposition of the idea of moral responsibility for a national past and his repressed incestual and patricidal guilt does not work. The story remains confused and confusing.

Other readers have been able to unify the story by focusing on the two young ladies who are the narrator's audience in the frame. In one critique, their "conversion" becomes Hawthorne's primary motive. The thematic tension between the Oedipal triangle and the Salem witch hangings is part of the "strategy of conversion" that Hawthorne follows to determine "whether truth were more powerful than fiction" (*278.8–9*). The girls' response to the narrator's final exhortation demonstrates that art, through imagination, can help history function as a redemptive force, but in this reading, too, the "wizard-is-to-blame" ending of Alice's story is considered "emotionally and morally irrelevant" (65). Another analysis links the young ladies with Leonard Doane; Walter Brome, as the mirror image of Doane's personal and psychologically repressed past, is equated with the witch-hunting Puritans invoked in the frame as the young ladies' repudiated cultural fathers. The wizard shows the Doanes their heritage as Hawthorne shows the girls theirs (189:13–22). The most negative appraisal of the girls' role in the story accuses them of interfering with Hawthorne's ability to communicate to his larger reading audience. The nineteenth-century plot is "incidental," but the narrator's confusedly sentimental and stern manner, directed at the genteel female readers of the *Token,* impairs the effectiveness of the whole (368:152).

As barometers of reader response, the two young ladies in the frame are important to Baym's interpretation of "Alice Doane's Appeal," too. She sees the story as a chronicle of the narrator's discovery of how to write American Gothic; therefore, the inner story and the frame are designed deliberately to contrast with each other. The innocent Alice Doane is replaced by the innocent victims of the witchcraft delusion, Leonard Doane is superseded by Cotton Mather, and the machinations of the wizard give place to "vices of spirit and errors of opinion, that sufficed to madden the whole surrounding multitude" (*279.26–27*). The contrasting inner and frame plots function as effective foils to underscore the author's newly found method to reach his audience (43:37–38).

By whatever method the disparate elements in "Alice Doane's Appeal" are reconciled, the consensus is that the story is an artistic failure. The one totally approbative reading invents a technique called "dissolving form" to justify what is supposed to be Hawthorne's wizardlike authorial role, intended to convey a world where "everything is continually in the process of becoming something else" (93). By attempting to justify the multiple levels of consciousness that operate in the story as part of Hawthorne's conscious artistry, this reading maintains that the apparently disjointed sections of the tale are organically related and contribute to a coherent whole.

Ingenuity notwithstanding, the prevailing opinion among Hawthorne followers continues to be the more convincing: "Alice Doane's Appeal" is not Hawthorne at his best. However varied the individual areas of emphasis may be, most critics point to this story as important because it documents Hawthorne's discovery of the historical past as a fitting subject for fiction (43:37–38; 46:68–73; 65; 189:13–22; 309:58–59; 368: 151–52; 426:134; 500:55–56; 534:251). In the final analysis, "Alice Doane's Appeal" is more significant for what it reveals about its author in psychological, artistic, and sociological terms than as a literary work of art. The attention bestowed on it is misleading. For those who do not know Hawthorne's works, it makes a poor introduction; for those aficionados who know Hawthorne well enough to take him with rough edges showing, it offers some valuable insights.

# II

# The Ambitious Guest

(*Centenary Edition, Volume IX, Twice-told Tales,* 324–33.)

## Publication History

This story was first published in the *New-England Magazine* in June 1835 (VIII, 425–31) as the work of the author of "The Gray Champion" (*CE, IX, 572*). As one of the seventeen pieces by Hawthorne published anonymously in Park Benjamin's magazine between November 1834 and December 1835, it appears to have been part of *The Story Teller.* (See publication history of "The Devil in Manuscript.") In 1842, Hawthorne included "The Ambitious Guest" in the second volume of the second edition of *Twice-told Tales.*

## Circumstances of Composition, Sources, and Influences

A letter written by Hawthorne to his mother from Burlington, Vermont, on September 16, 1832, which describes his stay at Ethan Crawford's house in the Notch of the White Hills of New Hampshire, establishes the earliest probable date of the beginning of composition for this story. The completion date of early 1834 rests on the theory that the story is one of the tales to be narrated by the protagonist in *The Story Teller,* specifically to his audience at the Notch described in "Sketches from Memory No. I" (*CE, X, 422-38*) in the sections subtitled "The Notch of the White Mountains" and "Our Evening Party among the Mountains" (11:141–42). Since Hawthorne submitted the entire manuscript for his projected book to Samuel Goodrich in the first months of 1834, and since he seldom did any extensive writing during the summer months, he probably wrote "The Ambitious Guest" during the fall of 1832 or the winter of 1833, while his Mount Washington adventures were fresh in his mind (84:57). A later composition date, 1834, has been less convincingly proposed, primarily on the supposition that the New York publication of Bulwer-Lytton's *Last Days of Pompeii* in 1834 encouraged Hawthorne to write his American version of "Vesuvius" (77:27).

The fidelity with which the two mountain sketches and the story parallel Hawthorne's letter about his New Hampshire trip firmly establishes Hawthorne's own experiences in 1832 as a direct source for many elements in

"The Ambitious Guest." In the story, the guest says, "I meant to have been at Ethan Crawford's tonight" (326:12): in the sketch, the group of travelers sit around the fire in Ethan Crawford's parlor the night before their six-mile ride to Mount Washington early in the morning (CE, X, 425–29): and in his letter, Hawthorne describes how he started off at 4:00 A. M. one "showery morning" and "galloped and trotted and tript and stumbled" on a six-mile horseback ride to the foot of Mount Washington (455:283, n.1). Hawthorne also tells "how, when I got up the mountain on one side, the wind carried me a great distance off my feet and almost blew me down the other, and how the thermometer stood at twelve degrees below the freezing point." The guest, too, complains of the wind and the cold in the Notch. Finally, two observations in the sketch are thematically related to the story. The first-person narrator confides to his readers that he feels the Notch "is one of those symbolic scenes, which leads the mind to the sentiment, though not to the conception of Omnipotence" (CE, X, 423). Later in the comment, "Mountains are Earth's undecaying monuments" (CE, X, 424), he foreshadows the guest's desire for an earthly monument and associates it with the mountain's power and endurance, which ironically will destroy his immortality instead of establishing it.

Cameron, tracing the genesis of the story to events before the 1832 trip, suggests that Hawthorne began thinking about writing it not long after reading about the mountain slide at Crawford's Notch that destroyed the Willey family on August 28, 1826. The extensive accounts of the catastrophe published in the New England newspapers and reprinted in the Salem Essex Register were easily accessible to Hawthorne (77:2–22), and he could also have read about it in the Peter Parley books published by his editorial adviser, Samuel Goodrich, in 1831 and 1832 (99:104). The fact that a three-volume work called Collections, Topographical, Historical, and Biographical, relating to New Hampshire was charged to the Hawthornes from the Salem Athenaeum in 1827 and 1829 indicates an interest in New Hampshire years before his 1832 visit (259).

A comparison of the details in Hawthorne's story with those given in most of the factual accounts shows quite clearly that Hawthorne adapted the facts to suit his artistic purpose. In the story, Hawthorne omits the family name of Willey, the dog who survived the disaster and helped locate the bodies, and the two hired men who were also killed in the landslide. He changed the mother's name, added five years to the daughter's age, moved the time of the avalanche from nearly midnight to earlier in the evening, and transformed the traveler Barker, who discovered the empty house the morning after, to the anonymous stranger who arrived the night before. He also chose to leave the bodies unfound. He added the grandmother, but he kept the family's reputation as kind and generous hosts, their emergency retreat, prepared when an earlier landslide had threatened them, and the fatal slide's unpredictable turn that left the house untouched.

Many of these changes are attributable to literary influences. Hawthorne chose the biblical name Esther as a more noble and heroic appellation for the good wife in the story than her actual name, Polly (77:23). Furthermore, the story's theological framework, with its emphasis on man's suffering and bewildered helplessness at the hands of an inscrutable, all-powerful God, echoes the Book of Job (510.5:493–94). Hawthorne's interjection on the futility of human ambition may have been encouraged by the articles featured in the leading periodicals of his day (77:23–26) and by the influence of two of his favorite writers, Samuel Johnson in *Rasselas* (183:193–94) and William Godwin in *St Leon* (458:8). Among the other detected influences on the story are those of Gustav Schwab's "The Thunderstorm" (143), the "school of catastrophe" to which many American writers and painters of the years 1810–45 belonged (122), the Gothic and graveyard school of writers (298:21; 482:556), and the tenth chapter of Increase Mather's *Essay for the Recording of Illustrious Providences* (77:255). Hawthorne's allusion to the "herb, heart's ease" in the opening paragraph, which ironically foreshadows the family's illusory and short-lived happiness, can be traced to Shakespeare's *A Midsummer Night's Dream* (II, i, 169–72).

## Relationship with Other Hawthorne Works

As a tale of New Hampshire, "The Ambitious Guest" shares the general setting of the White Mountains with "The Great Stone Face" and the specific location of Crawford's Notch with "The Great Carbuncle." The two Notch stories are also alike in the earthbound quests they portray (77:29).

One critic finds a psychological affinity between the guest's obsession with fame and the emotional immaturity of such Hawthorne characters as Mr. Hooper in "The Minister's Black Veil," Giovanni in "Rappaccini's Daughter," Aylmer in "The Birthmark," and "Young Goodman Brown" (29:342). These stories have also been grouped with "The Ambitious Guest" as revelations of Hawthorne's faith in an ordered universe where man's duty is submission to divine Providence and love toward his fellow man (345:74). From an ironic perspective, however, the angry Mountain God in this story is not unlike the concept of the Calvinist Jehovah suggested in "Roger Malvin's Burial." In both, an omnipotent power appears to demand and exact expiation for transgressions that are either obscure or imaginary.

The guest bears a strong resemblance to the hero of Hawthorne's first novel, *Fanshawe*, an overly dedicated scholar-idealist who, like the guest, dies prematurely with his potential unfulfilled (455:lxv). The anonymous stranger has also been linked to a less typical Hawthornesque type, the transcendental idealist on the order of "The Artist of the Beautiful" (324:307).

## Interpretations and Criticism

The ambiguity in this story is so pervasive that readers are divided even on the very basic issue of identifying the protagonist. The traditional choice has been the title character; the guest is central to the story. The family's simple and modest ambitions are a foil for his lofty aspirations (99:107–09). In one reading, the response to the catastrophe is measured in direct proportion to the sympathy felt toward the young stranger (324:318). On the other hand, another critic argues that if the tale is guest-centered, no total emotional effect results. Only when the family is recognized as the collective protagonist does the contrast between its initial contentment and its untimely fate become dramatically effective (160:154–55). Still others have lumped the family and the guest together as equally guilty, either of hubris, which makes them tragic heroes (189:246), or of loss of faith, which makes the God who punishes them the protagonist (345).

Although no existential reading of the story has been published, "The Ambitious Guest" is often used in college courses as a corollary to Camus's *The Plague*, Hemingway's "A Clean, Well-Lighted Place," and the Bible's Ecclesiastes. The daughter's statement that "it is better to sit here, by this fire . . . and be comfortable and contented" (*328.24–26*) is much like Candide's conclusion at the end of Voltaire's satire that he must content himself with cultivating his garden. "The Ambitious Guest" has even been proposed as a source for the famous statement by Vanzetti, of the Sacco and Vanzetti trials, beginning, "If it had not been for these things. . . ." The parallels in rhetoric, wording, and concepts between Vanzetti's statement and Hawthorne's depiction of the guest's ironic death are striking (214).

While Hawthorne's ambivalence in this story has made it thematically attractive to a variety of philosophical outlooks, its artistic worth has been consistently questioned. It has been criticized for its "excessive foreshadowing" (77:28), its "insistent irony" (149:145), and its "too direct and unartistic moral" (99:108). It has also been praised, for its "skillful fusion of theme and structure" (99:108), its effectively serious situational irony (156), and its overall complex artistry (77).

In the final analysis, however, what emerges as most memorable about "The Ambitious Guest" is its theme—or rather, its multiplicity of themes, including the paradoxical possibility that ultimately no themes exist and that man's place and role in the universe are essentially meaningless. The event on which the tale turns is, by its very nature, inexplicable. Is the avalanche a natural phenomenon whose erratic pattern is the result of random chance? Or is it the act of an angry God who has not been placated? Or is Providence punishing the wicked? The characterizations are also enigmatic. Is the young guest wrong to want to be remembered on earth? . . . or the father to think about a good farm and a proper gravestone? . . . or the grandmother to have her grave clothes prepared for her burial? Were they all wrong to seek escape from the slide in their "sure place of refuge" (*326.29*)? The daughter's simple and familial desires appear to be the "right" ones, but since she too is destroyed, does her death mean that mankind is indiscriminately and arbitrarily condemned? Or is the contentment she enjoyed during her brief lifetime sufficient, in contrast to the guest's "high and abstracted ambition" (*327.24*)? Each of these alternatives is possible. In a world where nuclear annihilation lurks as another possibility, Hawthorne's nineteenth-century story takes on twentieth-century overtones and becomes shockingly relevant.

# III

# The Antique Ring

(*Centenary Edition, Volume XI, Uncollected Tales*, 338–52.)

## Publication History

This story was first published in *Sargent's New Monthly Magazine of Literature, Fashion, and Fine Arts* in February 1843 (I, 80–86) under Hawthorne's own name (323:20). Epes Sargent solicited it, along with "The Old Apple Dealer," in 1842, but did not send the $10 in payment for the two pieces until early 1846, after Hawthorne had written asking for the tear sheets to prepare copy for *Mosses from an Old Manse* (*CE, X, 503–04*). Hawthorne, however, did not include "The Antique Ring" in the 1846 *Mosses* or in either of his two subsequent collections. The story was finally collected by Sophia Hawthorne in 1876 when she edited *The Dolliver Romance and Other Pieces* for James R. Osgood and Co. of Boston.

## Circumstances of Composition, Sources, and Influences

Although the exact composition date for "The Antique Ring" remains conjectural, the fall of 1842 has generally been accepted (84:61). Recently, a more specific estimate—the first two weeks in November 1842—has been convincingly proposed (323:20). Except for "The Old Apple Dealer," which is essentially a revision of an extended notebook entry, "The Antique Ring" appears to be the first of over twenty stories and sketches written by Hawthorne at the Old Manse in Concord, Massachusetts, after he moved there with his new bride in July 1842 (112; 323).

Although the story-within-a-story is based on the legend about the ring given to Lord Essex by Queen Elizabeth and is essentially historic, the frame story concerns itself, as do most of the Old Manse-period pieces, with Hawthorne's contemporary society. A member of this society, Henry Wadsworth Longfellow, who was a Bowdoin classmate of Hawthorne's and a literary associate and friend, may have served as model for the characterization of Edward Caryl, the narrator. Caryl's literary career and accomplishments parallel Longfellow's, except for Caryl's being a reluctant lawyer, a detail possibly borrowed from the circumstances of another contemporary and mutual friend, George S. Hillard (322). As with many of the fictional characters who are artists, Caryl can also be viewed as a partial self-portrait, especially since he is described as "assisting the growth of American literature," one of the author's perennial concerns.

## Relationship with Other Hawthorne Works

Two other works, "Egotism: or the Bosom-Serpent" and "The Christmas Banquet," also written and published during the stay at Concord, are subtitled "From the Unpublished 'Allegories of the Heart.'" This collection of stories never materialized as such, but "The Antique Ring" and three other pieces written during the Old Manse period—"The Birthmark," "Rappaccini's Daughter," and "Earth's Holocaust"—may all have been related to this project because of their persistent heart imagery (11:146–47). When "The Antique Ring" supposes "the Gem to be the human heart, and the Evil Spirit to be Falsehood . . . ," it qualifies itself as one of the "Allegories of the Heart."

"Egotism" has been likened to "The Antique Ring" in its method as well as its theme. By highlighting one clearly allegorical element—the ring in one, the snake in the other—Hawthorne presents two morally effective tales without following the prescribed allegorical formula of an exact equation between fictional characters and abstract moral qualities (188: 78–80). The ring has also been classified as a talismanic image and its powers viewed as comparable to those of the portrait in the earlier story, "The Prophetic Pictures," and of the works of art in two stories published a year after "The Antique Ring," "The Artist of the Beautiful" and "Drowne's Wooden Image" (185:89, n.28). The birthmark, in the 1846 story by that name, is another parallel to Essex's ring, acquiring the properties of a talisman when Aylmer turns it into a work of artifice in his attempt to remove it (28:x–xiii).

## Interpretations and Criticism

The lack of critical attention directed toward "The Antique Ring" attests to its author's good judgment in choosing not to include it in his collections. In one discussion where it gets some attention, it is used to "best state the case against Hawthorne's allegory" and to illustrate the limitations of his attempt at integrating the two disparate worlds of magic and British political history (188:78–80).

In an anthropological reading that obviously disdains value judgments, Hawthorne's ring and the shields of Achilles and Aeneas as portrayed by Homer and Virgil are considered as examples of cosmic images which inconographically compress history (185:214–19)—exalted company for a story more often compared to the nondescript gift-book fiction of its day (322:625). Because the ring had once belonged to the wizard Merlin and had been endowed with fiendish powers before it was purified "by a deed of unostentatious charity," it effectively demonstrates the ambivalence generated by *kosmoi* (the essential type of allegorical image); like most *kosmoi*, Hawthorne's image is both good and evil at the same time.

"The Antique Ring" is the source for a statement repeatedly quoted as a key to understanding Hawthorne's symbolic method. At the end of his story, when asked to attach a more specific moral, Edward the narrator replies "with a half-reproachful smile. —'You know that I can never separate the idea from the symbol in which it manifests itself'" (*352.19–21*). In his best works, Hawthorne could not either.

# IV

# The Artist of the Beautiful

*(Centenary Edition, Volume X, Mosses from an Old Manse, 447–75.)*

## Publication History

This story was first published in June 1844 in *United States Magazine and Democratic Review* (XIV, 605–17) under Hawthorne's own name (*CE, X, 580*). The only extant record of payment for the seven pieces of Hawthorne's that appeared in the *Democratic Review* in 1844 and 1845 indicates that Hawthorne received $100 on October 1, 1845 from John L. O'Sullivan, who was the magazine's editor and Hawthorne's personal friend. If this is the total remuneration that Hawthorne received for these contributions, his earnings for "The Artist of the Beautiful" on a per-page average would have been a little over $18, or less than one fourth of the standard magazine payment of $5 per page. (See publication history of "The Christmas Banquet.") That Hawthorne was acutely aware of the financial inequities attached to his current occupation is clear from a letter he wrote on March 24, 1844, shortly after he is thought to have begun work on "The Artist of the Beautiful." It reads, "It will never do for me to continue merely a writer of stories for the magazines—the most unprofitable business in the world." For Hawthorne in 1844, however, tale-writing remained the only viable option (*CE, X, 509, 515*).

## Circumstances of Composition, Sources, and Influences

"The Artist of the Beautiful" was written in the spring of 1844, probably between March 12 and May 3 (323:30). Two notebook entries made during October 1837 reveal Hawthorne's long-standing fascination with the question of the relationship between Nature and art: "The reason of the minute superiority of Nature's work over man is, that the former works from the innermost germ, while the latter works merely superficially" (*CE, VIII, 158.3–5*), and "a person to spend all his life and splendid talents in trying to achieve something naturally impossible,—as to make a conquest over Nature" (*CE, VIII, 165.26–28*). An undated story hint in 1840 more specifically anticipates Owen Warland's butterfly, although the use of the word *trifle* suggests a less worthwhile accomplishment than depicted in the story: "To represent a man as spending life and the intensest labor in the accomplishment of some mechanical trifle,—as in making a miniature coach to be drawn by fleas, or a dinner-service to be put into a cherry-stone" (*CE, VIII, 185.26–29*). A final related notebook entry was probably written between December 1843 and the spring of 1844 when he was working on the story: "Allston's picture of Belshazzar's Feast—with reference to the advantages, or otherwise, of having life assured to us, till we could finish important tasks on which we were engaged" (*CE, VIII, 242.12–14*). This idea is elaborated upon in a long digressive paragraph in the story (*466–68*), which also alludes to the painter Washington Allston (1779–1843), who worked on "Belshazzar's Feast" at intervals from 1817 until his death, leaving it unfinished (*CE, VIII, 615*).

In addition to the author's notes, a variety of literary sources have been cited for the automata which foreshadow the butterfly. The details described in the story (*465.15–28*) have been traced to John Beckmann's *History of Inventions and Discoveries* (1817) and William Derham's *Physio-Theology* (1758) (320). Another work, Isaac D'Israeli's *Curiosities of Literature* (1823), not only describes some of the mechanical marvels (such as a brass duck capable of performing the whole process of digestion and excretion), but may also have suggested the story's basic conflict and Owen's apprenticeship as a watchmaker (518). Hawthorne's story may also be indebted to a paragraph in Fanny Kemble's *Journal* (1835), a popular travel account of its day, in which a tiny, mechanical bird that could flutter its wings and fly is called the "realization of fairy-land through machinery" (137).

Several sources for the butterfly as a symbol for the beautiful have been proposed—a Spenserian poem, the myth of Psyche, and Hawthorne's own observation prompted by the butterflies he saw around a salt ship. Edmund Spenser's "Muiopotmos: or the Fate of the Butterflye" presents some striking parallels that support the theory that it may have served as a prototype; Hawthorne's butterfly, like Spenser's, is created by an artist, is an embodiment of the Platonic ideal, is amazingly lifelike, and is destroyed in the end (535). The butterfly is also the form in which the soul is embodied in the myth of Psyche (233:203). Hawthorne's reaction to the sight of butterflies in flight, as recorded in a letter dated October 4, 1840, appears to reflect the symbolism of the Greek myth and, in likening them to the creations of the imagination, to foreshadow Owen's butterfly (483:304). Hawthorne wrote, "I cannot account for them, unless they are the lovely fantasies of the mind" (84:36). Two readers suggest that the life cycle of the butterfly provides the imagery for Owen's characterization and the structural basis for his development from his cocoonlike dormancy to his final burst of insight and "realization" (408; 233:203). Two other myths have also been cited as less direct influences: the Pygmalion legend (233:203; 303) and Diotima's account in *The Symposium* of the ladder of love (233:203–04). The latter helps to explain how Owen can accept the loss of Annie by using his love for her to ascend to a higher ideal of beauty.

For several readers who find no irony in the presentation of Owen and his accomplishment, the influence of Ralph Waldo Emerson is considered a significant factor (324; 431:236). One argues that a close parallel exists between the conclusion of Emerson's essay "The Poet" (1884) and the climax of Hawthorne's story. Emerson warns the poet that he must "pass for a fool and churl for a long season," but with the eventual reward "that the ideal shall be made real to thee, and the impressions of the actual world shall fall like summer rain, copious, but not troublesome, to thy invulnerable essence"; Owen's history of failure and ridicule culminates in his imperviousness to everything except exultation at having risen "high enough to achieve the Beautiful," the same course outlined for Emerson's ideal poet (324:318–19). Affinities between the theory of beauty advanced in the story and Edmund Burke's *Philosophical Inquiry into the Origin of Our Ideas on the Sublime and the Beautiful* (1756) have also been established (140). In direct contrast to these Romantic influences, one reader who finds irony a powerful element in the story turns to Jonathan Swift as a model for what he terms the narrator's satiric stance. The less-than-reliable affirmation of Owen's triumph is attributed in part to Hawthorne's Swiftian attitude toward proliferation of newly invented and useless mechanisms associated with "progress" (121).

According to Stewart, Hawthorne put a good deal of himself into the idealists he created for his fiction; Owen's plight is in some ways an expression of the author's disillusionment with the world's response to his artistic creations (455:xlviii–xliv). During the months Hawthorne spent writing this story, he became a father for the first time. The impact of his new responsibilities and the difficulties he was experiencing with his writing are candidly expressed in a letter to George Hillard, dated March 24. 1844:

> I have business on earth now, and must look about me for the means of doing it. . . . It [writing stories] requires a continual freshness of mind; else a deterioration in the article will quickly be perceptible. If I am to support myself by literature, it must be by what I call drudgery, but which is incomparably less irksome as a business than imaginative writing. (*CE, X, 509*)

In pitting the frail and sensitive Owen against the materialistic forces of society, Hawthorne remarks, "It is requisite for the ideal artist to possess a force of character that seems hardly compatible with its delicacy" (*454.26–28*). Owen's "contact with the Practical" appears to reflect, however obliquely, Hawthorne's own frustrating attempts to use his art as a means of supporting himself and his family in the same kind of unresponsive and uncomprehending world (511:366). That Melville triple-scored this passage in his copy of *Mosses* (315:223) reveals the significance that Owen's dilemma held for a fellow writer who was subject to many of the same pressures that Hawthorne felt. Also implied in Hawthorne's comment, and confirmed by Owen's debilitating encounters with the world, is the danger that the artist can be driven to isolate himself in order to maintain his artistic sensibilities. Hawthorne expresses a similar view outside his fiction in a letter written in 1840:

> So now I begin to understand why I was imprisoned so many years in this lonely chamber, and why I could never break through the viewless bolts and bars; for if I had sooner made my escape into the world, I should have grown hard and rough, and been covered with earthly dust, and my heart would have become callous by rude encounters with the multitude. (458:36)

The context makes it clear that Hawthorne's intent is to qualify himself as a worthy companion for the uncontaminated Sophia to whom he is writing, but the world is represented, as it is in the story, as a crude place that dulls the perceptions. That the author put a part of himself in Owen seems patently clear.

## Relationship with Other Hawthorne Works

As Hawthorne's most direct and sustained study of the artist and his relationship with society, "The Artist of the Beautiful" addresses the same fundamental issues explored in "The Prophetic Pictures," "Drowne's Wooden Image," and "The Snow-Image." At the same time, Owen Warland is one of several idealistic characters who are physically frail and abnormally sensitive. His precursors are the title characters in *Fanshawe* and "The Ambitious Guest," while he is himself a precursor to Dimmesdale in *The Scarlet Letter* and Clifford in *The House of Seven Gables* (172:267; 455:lxvi), as well as a partial model for Holgrave in the latter, Coverdale in *The Blithedale Romance*, and Kenyon in *The Marble Faun* (315:224). Owen is also like the painter of "The Prophetic Pictures," Aylmer of "The Birthmark," and Rappaccini in having placed an ideal objective above human concerns (47:109–10), but, unlike these colder artist-scientist figures, he has not endangered anyone else in his pursuit of the ideal (233:205). Aylmer is the idealist most often associated with Owen (47:96; 191:17; 455:xlvi); Crews classifies them both among Hawthorne's escapists. Like "Young Goodman Brown" and Hooper in "The Minister's Black Veil," they flee from the challenges of normal adult life into either a phobia or a zealous project (115:111).

Peter Hovenden also has several parallels among Hawthorne's characters; he has been likened to the nameless Cynic of "The Great Carbuncle," to Westervelt and to Silas Foster of *The Blithedale Romance* (186:81–83), and to Judge Pyncheon of *The House of Seven Gables* (455:liii). The contrast between Judge Pyncheon and Clifford epitomizes the same unbridgeable chasm between the man of affairs and the artist as that between Robert Danforth and Owen (172:266). Martin has called these conflicting personalities—the Hovenden clan (including the blacksmith) and Owen—"bifurcated" characters because, when considered in the totality of the individual tale, they complement each other. Other pairs who represent the same contrarieties of imagination and practicality are Peter Goldthwaite and John Brown in "Peter Goldthwaite's Treasure," Mr. Lindsey and his wife in "The Snow-Image," and Aylmer and Aminidab in "The Birthmark" (308:25–26).

Thematically, this story has been linked with "The Great Carbuncle" and "The Birthmark" as studies in the pursuit of the ideal (395; 47:96). The transformation motif appears in "Drowne's Wooden Image," written just prior to "The Artist of the Beautiful" (323:30), and reappears in the last two stories Hawthorne wrote, "The Snow-Image" and "Feathertop," and in his final completed novel, *The Marble Faun*, which was originally titled *Transformation* (391).

## Interpretations and Criticism

Hawthorne's characteristic ambivalence has contributed to a widely divergent series of interpretations of this story; the spectrum ranges from an affirmation of the value of art and the triumph of the Romantic idealist over a materialistic society (186:70–90) to a condemnation of the artist and his ignominious defeat by the forces of life (496). A great many middle positions between these two extremes have been taken, some of them defined by the degree of irony that each reader perceives. One sees Owen's personality, his creation, and his supposed victory as deliberately ironic manifestations of the limitations of art and of the egocentric artist (121). Another finds Hawthorne's disapproval expressed in subtle hints rather than ironic barbs, but the conclusion is similar: Owen, as the ideal artist, is an isolated, presumptuous intellectual who attempts to rival God (341). Still another sees no ironies or ambiguities in Owen's portrayal, only a sympathetic understanding of the risks that the dedicated artist confronts (215).

This last, untempered acceptance of Owen's "Romantic" triumph ignores the ambiguous language that Hawthorne uses to describe his characters and their situations. The most convincing interpretations are the ones that take into account not only that Owen is called a "genius" (451.11), "the being of thought, imagination, and keenest sensibility" (466.28–29), but also that he is described as a puny creature (451.13), "full of little petulances" (453.16–17), with nerves that flutter (452.10) and a "morbid sensibility" (458.25). Robert Danforth reveals a crass utilitarianism when he declares that "there is more real use in one downright blow of my sledgehammer, than in the whole five years' labor that our friend Owen has wasted on this butterfly" (472.11–14), but he is characterized as a man of "comely strength" (448.32–33), whose "massive substance [is] thoroughly warmed and attempered by domestic influences" (468.10–12). Even the baby who destroys Owen's masterpiece of "perfect beauty" (470.22) is ambivalently presented as "a little personage who had come mysteriously out of the infinite, but with something so sturdy and real in his composition that he seemed moulded out of the densest substance which earth could supply" (468.34–469.2). Moreover, when the narrator asserts that it is "with good reason" (474.25) that Annie admires her own infant far more than the butterfly, he undercuts his own avowal of Owen's triumph three paragraphs later.

These internal discrepancies are acknowledged by judicious readers of all persuasions. For example, Fogle, who reads the story as a proclamation of the artist's ultimate superiority, nevertheless admits: "Warland does not always show up well in his environment" (186:86). Bell, who reads the story as a revelation of the artist's pathetic limitations, concedes that Hawthorne started out to champion the Transcendental cause and to tell Owen's story "with utter tenderness." She concludes, however, that the author's doubts and disbelief emerged in the telling, ultimately negating the Romantic view (47:94–103). And Stubbs, who believes that Hawthorne endorses the artist but with severe qualifications, emphasizes the tension created between the narrator's pro-Romantic statements and the concrete scenes that present a criticizing countermovement (468:57). He presents a balanced view, recognizing, like Fogle and the proartist camp, Hawthorne's kinship with and compassion for Owen, while acknowledging, like Bell and the more antiartist faction, Hawthorne's reservations.

The factors that form the basis for all these critical positions can be classified into three major areas: philosophical, sociological, and psychological. The two vying ideological forces in the story are Puritanism, with its distrust of art and glorification of useful work, and Romanticism, which conversely glorifies art and disdains all but spiritual values. Some see the creative instinct triumphing over the Protestant work ethic in the finale (255:168; 431:236), but not without some concessions to Hawthorne's Puritan heritage. Hawthorne's deprecation of himself as an artist who does not live up to his ancestors' concept of useful service may be reflected in his portrayal of Owen's shortcomings, especially when they are set against Danforth's "strength" (186:86–87). The story's inherent contradictions are directly related to the author's philosophical dilemma: he could neither accept the Puritans' dismissal of art nor wholeheartedly endorse the Romantic view that art is equivalent to salvation (286:118–19). This vacillation is pervasive enough to make even the narrator's pro-Romantic affirmations suspect. One of these precepts is the veneration of the ideal and the corollary notion that the work of art is an inferior copy of the artist's original version (*458.9–13*). Owen's fulfillment in the "far other butterfly" appears to confirm such an outlook. This denouement has been interpreted as a confirmation of the view that the supreme value of art lies in the enhancement of the artist even if he leaves behind no enduring works (533.5). The dramatic context, on the other hand, supports an anti-Romantic reading: Owen's triumph is a solipsistic delusion (468:57–58) that fails to mask the artist's failure to communicate (47:107). Lewis, for example, insists on an ironic interpretation because the story itself, as a perceptible and indestructible symbol of the artistic imagination, belies Owen's accomplishment; the story's concluding statement is not an endorsement of Emersonian aesthetics, but "a knowing description of the habitual recourse of the thwarted transcendentalizing imagination" (286:118–19).

Inextricably related to these philosophical questions is the issue of the artist and society. While the story clearly dramatizes that Owen is different from everyone else who inhabits his social world, the causes, consequences, and implications of his apartness have been diversely explained. Many blame the unsympathetic environment of a materialistic society for alienating the sensitive artist (32:128–32; 255; 168; 309:74; 477:93–96). Such an outlook has been explained as an expression of Hawthorne's own frustrations in not being able to find a place for himself in his community. The author's milieu is also reflected in Owen's characterization which follows the popularly accepted stereotype of the artist as an ineffectual, effeminate, and neurotic aesthete (172). That these negative connotations are a part of Owen's portrayal is verified by one reader's reaction: he prefers Danforth, an "intelligent, decent workman," over "the insufferable Owen" (52:135). (This reading subsequently faults the story for not reconciling the roles of the artist and the citizen in the context of American society in spite of the story's obvious contention that no such reconciliation is possible.) The obstacles that society interposes between itself and the artist have been interpreted, in a few readings, as challenges which contribute in a positive way to Owen's eventual success and maturity (198; 64). By internalizing the conflict between Owen Warland and society (on the suggestion in his name that he is his own warland), one of the readings envisions Owen as becoming one with the world in the process of rising above it (64). The majority of readers, however, find no such accommodation with social forces. Owen's isolation may be willful and "voluntary" (341) or "enforced" (255:168) and "involuntary" (32:130); he may be "in advance of mankind" (394:123–24) or out of step with it (121); but he is inexorably cut off from society.

The third group of responses enlists the aid of psychology in assessing Owen's predicament. The view is predominantly pejorative: Owen is a "stunted man" (497:32) whose butterfly symbolizes a paranoic narcissism and whose behavior exhibits the classic symptoms which characterize the struggle to sublimate homosexual tendencies (446). He seeks refuge in the pursuit of the ideal because he is impotent, and when his ineffectual advances have been safely set aside by Annie's marriage to Danforth, he returns to accept "Annie-as-mother" for his muse. The final proclaimed victory of pure art coincides with a total failure of manhood and repudiates Hawthorne's often-expressed belief in the primacy of emotional involvement (115:167–70). Von Abele uses the contradictions in this story to explain Hawthorne's artistic disintegration: the difficulty lies in the author's inability to accept himself as both artist and man "without splitting the two and putting them into profound opposition" (497:32–44). This identification with both Owen and Danforth helps to explain the alternately positive and negative images they project.

Most of the readings acknowledge, usually indirectly and in much less clinical language, the same theories that the Freudian-based critics propose. For example, without the disparaging jargon, Erlich describes Owen as one of Hawthorne's men who uses women imaginatively but who avoids contamination from any physical contact with them (168). Annie's effect on Owen raises an issue not so easily resolved, however. The story reads:

> . . . had he [Owen] won Annie to his bosom, and there beheld her fade from angel into ordinary woman, the disappointment might have driven him back, with concentrated energy, upon his sole remaining object. On the other hand, had he found Annie what he fancied, his lot would have been so rich in beauty, that, out of its

> mere redundancy, he might have wrought the Beautiful into many
> a worthier type than he had toiled for. (*464.21–28*)

While one reader takes this to mean that the Beautiful is achieved more readily when normal channels of happiness have been cut off (47:109), another finds in it a happy testament to the writer's marriage and to the belief that the artist can achieve harmony with the material world which he idealizes (64:386). Once again the fictional paradox is Hawthorne's own: the isolation of the artist is as necessary for his creative powers as it is unhealthy for his human development (38).

In 1847, in an overall favorable review of *Mosses*, *Blackwood's Magazine* specifically chided "The Artist of the Beautiful" for its "palpable improbability" (*CE, X, 530–31*). In 1966, these unrealistic aspects again attracted attention, this time as part of what made the story a piece of "science-fiction with a vengeance" (191:15–19). The fantastic in the story is seen by another twentieth-century reader as one of the surrealistic parallels that link the story with Kafka's "The Hunger Artist" (347). Peculiarities notwithstanding, "The Artist of the Beautiful" has become one of Hawthorne's most anthologized and best-known stories, primarily because, as Warren said, it is the best of Hawthorne's few attempts at describing the inner life of the artist (511:366). The ambiguities that have generated the prolific and manifold reactions surveyed here reflect the author's divided allegiance and find a responsive chord in the reader who recognizes the conflicting forces in Owen's warland as his own. "The Beautiful" remains as beguiling—and controversial—as ever.

# V

# The Birthmark

(*Centenary Edition, Volume X, Mosses from an Old Manse, 35–56.*)

## Publication History

This story was first published in March 1843 in *Pioneer* (I, 113–19) under Hawthorne's own name. How much he was paid for it is uncertain. When he submitted "The Hall of Fantasy," which appeared in the February 1843 issue, to his friend, James Russell Lowell, who was a partner in the magazine, Hawthorne reported that Epes Sargent had offered $5 per page, but that *Pioneer* could have it for whatever their "arrangements" would allow. In a February 28, 1843, letter to her mother, Sophia wrote that they were expecting $70 from Lowell; that figure would have covered the $5 per-page rate for both *Pioneer* pieces. However, a March 16 letter from Hawthorne to Sophia reports the failure of Lowell's magazine with the comment, "Not improbably we shall have to wait months for our money, if we ever get it at all." In 1846 "The Birthmark" was collected in *Mosses from an Old Manse,* appearing as the first selection after the opening essay (*CE, X, 503, 573*).

## Circumstances of Composition, Sources, and Influences

This story was probably written between January 13 and February 1, 1843 while Hawthorne and Sophia were living at the Old Manse in Concord during their first year of marriage (323:23). A series of five notebook entries delineates the pattern of development from a rather vague concept to the specific embodiment it ultimately assumes. The first dates back to 1836: "Those who are very difficult in choosing wives seem as if they would take none of Nature's ready-made works, but want a woman manufactured particularly to their order" (*CE, VIII, 20.13–15*). The next two, one immediately following the other, were entered between October 16 and December 6, 1837: "A person to be in possession of something as perfect as mortal man has a right to demand; he tries to make it better, and ruins it entirely," and "A person to spend all his life and splendid talents in trying to achieve something naturally impossible,—as to make a conquest over Nature" (*CE, VIII, 165.23–28*). The latter anticipates the theme of "The Artist of the Beautiful" as well. The fourth, which clearly reveals the noble yet tragic aspects of the protagonist's character, appears in the 1839 segment: "A person to be the death of his beloved in trying to raise her to more than mortal perfection; yet this should be a comfort to him for having aimed so highly and holily" (*CE, VIII, 184.26–28*). This is clearly echoed in Georgiana's dying words: "You have aimed loftily!—you have done nobly! Do not repent, that, with so high and pure a feeling, you have rejected the best that earth could offer" (*44.27–29*). Finally, sometime after June 1, 1842, but before February 1, 1843 when he submitted the story to Robert Carter, Lowell's partner, Hawthorne paraphrased a case he had read about in Andrew Combe's *The Principles of Physiology* (Edinburgh, 1836):

> The case quoted in Combe's Physiology, from Pinel, of a young man of great talents and profound knowledge of chemistry, who had in view some new discovery of importance. In order to put his mind into the highest possible activity, he shut himself up, for several successive days, and used various methods of excitement; he had a singing girl with him; he drank spirits; smelled penetrating odors, sprinkled cologne-water round the room &c &c. Eight days thus passed, when he was seized with a fit of frenzy, which terminated in mania. (*CE, VIII, 235.24–236.8*)

The story incorporates the chemical experiment, the perfumed and secluded retreat, and Aylmer's maniacal frenzy, but the grosser sensual indulgences are eliminated and a loving wife replaces the singing girl (455:xxv; 516:171–72). The particular experiment that Aylmer uses on Georgiana may have been suggested by another section in Combe's *Physiology* entitled "Reciprocal Action beween the Skin and Other Organs" (191:10).

One source study calls Hawthorne's discovery of the Combe case "a felicitous happenstance" that merely parallels some of the circumstances in the history of Sir Kenelm Digby, whose situation and character provide a more exact prototype (390:337–47). Not only is the singing, the prolonged scenting of closed rooms, and the chemical experimentation a part of Digby's story, but his wife's death, in 1633, was allegedly caused by his administering "viper-wine" to her in an effort to preserve or perfect her beauty. Digby's almost fanatic preoccupation with sympathetic birthmarks (his *Power of Sympathy* reports the successful surgical removal of a strawberry mark from a Lady's neck) and his attempts to revive flowers (reported to the Royal Society in *Vegetation of Plants*) are mirrored in Aylmer's obsession with Georgiana's birthmark and in his temporary success in revitalizing a blighted geranium. Furthermore, Digby's allegorical, semifictional account of his relationship with his wife ("Loose

Fantasies" in *Private Memoirs*) reveals the same rivalry between "love of science" and "love of woman" that Hawthorne attributes to Aylmer. In *The Scarlet Letter,* Digby is referred to specifically as one of Chillingworth's famous associates "whose scientific attainments were esteemed hardly less than supernatural" (390:346).

An extensive range of literary sources has been credited with shaping this story. Among them are Book II of Spenser's *The Faerie Queene* as a legend-of-temperance prototype (83); Maturin's *Melmoth the Wanderer,* and the Gothic tradition in general, as precursors of Aylmer's sorcererlike role and occult experiments (152; 298:108); and the Pygmalion myth, primarily as an ironic inversion—that is, Hawthorne has Aylmer compare himself to Pygmalion (*40.30–32*) in order to dramatize the difference between Pygmalion, who wants his perfect work of art to enter the imperfect realm of Nature, and Aylmer, who wants his mortal wife to achieve the perfection of the Ideal (26).

Two other literary sources have been traced to Hawthorne's activities immediately before and during the time he was writing the story. Aylmer's Faustian characteristics may be attributable in part to Goethe's *Faust,* a work much admired by the Peabody circle, with whom Hawthorne became more intimately involved after his marriage to Sophia Peabody (447:91). However, many of the evenings of their first winter together at the Old Manse were spent reading Shakespeare aloud, and two of Shakespeare's plays have been cited as likely analogues. The idea of the birthmark as the cause of the heroine's death and a symbol for human imperfection may have come from *Cymbeline* (516:175–86), while Aylmer's relationship with his laboratory assistant, Aminidab, bears a close resemblance to that between Prospero and Caliban of *The Tempest* (455:xlv; 511:367). The optical phenomena with which Aylmer relaxes Georgiana could also have been suggested by the scene in which Prospero entertains the lovers with a dance performed by spirits (516:186).

The optical phenomena have also been traced to a nonliterary source, three inventions of Hawthorne's day: the diorama, the stereoscope, and the daguerreotype (191:13). In spite of the story's eighteenth-century setting, Aylmer's aspirations appear to be based on mid-nineteenth-century thinking; for example, Benjamin Silliman's *Elements of Chemistry* (1830) holds forth the same promise as Aylmer's natural philosophy (447:91). Hawthorne's decision to set the story in the preceding century has several possible explanations. By using nineteenth-century inventions fifty years before their public discovery, Aylmer would be recognized by the author's contemporaries as a man ahead of his time (191:13); Aylmer could also be linked to Galvani's electrical experiments in Italy in 1786, which had apparently revived organic matter. The opening sentence of the story refers to the "recent discovery of electricity and other kindred mysteries of Nature which seemed to open paths into the region of miracle," and an electrical machine is a part of the fictional laboratory's equipment (304:80–84). Finally, the story could have been set to coincide with the dates of Swedenborg's mystic career (1745–72), principally because Swedenborg's earlier position as the greatest proponent of Cartesian science in the eighteenth century is equivalent to that of Digby in the seventeenth, and also because the Swedenborgian notion of correspondences is equivalent in many ways to nineteenth-century Transcendentalism (491:217–18).

The autobiographical aspects of "The Birthmark" can be made to corroborate the Swedenborg allusion because the tradition of spiritualized matter and the formulations that accompanied it had touched Hawthorne's personal life when his fiancée found her headaches relieved by a mesmerist's influence. The story can be viewed as a fictional restatement of what Hawthorne had earlier expressed in a letter to Sophia:

> And what delusion can be more lamentable and mischievous than to mistake the physical and material for the spiritual? What so miserable as to lose the soul's true, though hidden, knowledge and consciousness of heaven, in the mist of an earth-born vision? (491:218)

Moreover, Aylmer parallels Hawthorne's personal situation and reflects some of his traits. Both are newlyweds, and both have devoted themselves exclusively to their work over a long period of time before marrying (431:226). Aylmer's coldness, curiosity, and egocentric ambition are depicted with a self-irony that is confirmed by the almost literal resemblance between Aylmer's journal and the author's notebooks (280:59–60; 390:347; 431.226; 516:172). In his letters to Sophia during their engagement, Hawthorne expresses the same desire for an ideal love beyond temporal limitations that is implicit in Aylmer's attitude toward Georgiana. Hawthorne wrote, "Do you not feel, dearest, that we live above time and apart from time, even while we seem to be in the midst of time? Our affection diffuses eternity round about us" (39:235–36). This sentiment reappears in the story's final sentence when its author chastises Aylmer for failing "to look beyond the shadowy scope of time, and living once for all in eternity, to find the perfect future in the present." That Hawthorne believed he had found that "perfect future" is reconfirmed in a notebook entry made on August 5, 1842, a month after his wedding and four months before he wrote "The Birthmark"; it reads, "We have been living in eternity, ever since we came to live at this old Manse" (CE, VIII, 315:11–12). Aylmer's tragic inability to live "once for all in eternity" appears to be an inverse reflection of Hawthorne's newly found happiness (516:186).

## Relationship with Other Hawthorne Works

"The Birthmark" has most often been associated with two related groups of Hawthorne stories, those dealing with the scientist and those dealing with the artist. Because Aylmer tries to remove the birthmark, which is "an artiface by negation," he assumes the role of the artist or creator as depicted in "Drowne's Wooden Image" and "The Prophetic Pictures" (28:x-xiii; 123:58; 431:228-29). His artistic vision is closest to Owen Warland's in "The Artist of the Beautiful" (47:182-85; 186:128; 188:46; 455:xlv), especially in their determined efforts to objectify perfect beauty. As idealists in the Emersonian sense (39:237), they exemplify the problems inherent in the inability to separate the world of the ideal from the world of appearance (188:47). "P's Correspondence" illustrates this same difficulty (188:46), while "The Snow-Image" presents an inverse imbalance—instead of spiritualizing matter as Aylmer does, Mr. Lindsey attempts to materialize spirit with equally tragic results (6:187-89). *Fanshawe* and "The Ambitious Guest" are early versions of Aylmer's scholarly-idealist leanings (455:xlv).

The high purpose and dedication that characterize the artist figure are found in the overintellectualized men of science who are also Aylmer's counterparts. Dr. Rappaccini is most like Aylmer (32:71-73; 458:248-49; 333:92-93; 162:50); both are sorcerer types (298:107-08) whose alleged good intentions end in death for the beautiful women in their lives (513; 270:97-98; 447:148). Parallel science-oriented characters inhabit Hawthorne's works, from Dr. Cacaphodel of "The Great Carbuncle" (39:237; 394) to the elixir-searching protagonists of the unfinished romances (186:198-206; 516:173), but "Dr. Heidegger's Experiment" presents the closest analogue, anticipating "The Birthmark" most directly (390:346). "The Birthmark," in turn, is a preliminary model for "Ethan Brand," the most fully developed of Hawthorne's Fausts (31; 333:92-93; 447:103; 458:248-49).

Aylmer's attempt to erase the birthmark of sin has also been linked with the Puritan community in *The Scarlet Letter*, who assume the responsibility of judging and perfecting their fellow man (186:117; 486:65). Chillingworth and Aylmer are secular versions of the Puritans' sanctimonious pretensions (333:92-93; 458:248-49; 486:59).

"The Birthmark" has been collected with "The Artist of the Beautiful" and "Rappaccini's Daughter" as Hawthorne's "three great complete works of science-fiction"; as such, they pre-date the genre of which they are now considered an important part (191:xii, 3–23). ·

## Interpretations and Criticism

While ambivalence is most often recognized as a hallmark of Haw-thorne's fiction, it becomes a central issue in "The Birthmark," a story so delicately balanced that its readers have been unable to reach a con-sensus as to whether its central character is a hero or a villain. Aylmer has been called noble (67:105; 506) and fiendish (333), an idealistic scientist with a spiritual quest (315:254) and a dangerous manipulator with monomaniacal intent (270:94; 513). According to Heilman, Haw-thorne wanted to have it both ways; consequently, he made Aylmer a tragic hero whose urgent good will coincides with inordinate pride and a deficient sense of reality (226:575). Aylmer has also been called a Lucifer who turns into "a tragic Satan"; the paradoxes built into his high-minded yet blasphemous pursuits have thus been interpreted as Hawthorne's subtle way of suggesting that Satan is a part of the Godhead (123:58). The typical reader's assessment of Aylmer is summed up in less esoteric terms by another critic: "Aylmer is to be pitied for his folly, abhorred for his heartlessness, and admired for his aspirations" (191:10–11).

Certainly, Aylmer is favorably portrayed in the contrast that Hawthorne sets up between Aminidab and Aylmer, whether or not one chooses to discount Aylmer's rationale and Georgiana's dying reaffirmation as mis-guided delusions (454:249). Reid extends Aminidab's unfavorable por-trayal to the sound of his name—the short, abrupt vowels terminating in voiced dental and labial plosives suggest his limited, earthbound nature, especially when contrasted with the open vowels combining with liquids and nasals in Aylmer's name to connote the airiness of a lofty spirit. Aylmer as a variant of Elmer, which means "noble," and Aminidab as an anagram on the words *bad in man* further support the contrast between the two (390:349–50). Two other anagrams have been proposed: "bad amina" for Aminidab (492; 139) and "Malrey," meaning "bad king," for Aylmer (139). Van Winkle, after dismissing the biblical source for Aminidab's name, asserts that the assistant is a "bad soul" in name only, while Aylmer's "bad anima" dominates the story (492); De Hayes interprets the name symbolism of both as essentially negative (139).

The nature of Aylmer's folly has been variously interpreted. Heilman's seminal article shows how Hawthorne uses the language of religion (*miracle, votaries, faith, mysteries, holy*) to establish Aylmer as a man who mistakes science for religion and ends up unable to distinguish between spirit and matter (226). A subsequent interpretation extends the apotheosis-of-science theme to include Aminidab as a symbol of religion subverted to the ends of science. As a variant of the biblical Amminidab (a name associated with the priesthood of the Hebrew people), the laboratory assistant typifies the old authoritarian religion; when he says, "If she were my wife, I'd never part with that birth-mark" (*43.32*), he expresses a greater respect for the human personality than that held by amoral science (471). Aminidab's brutish nature, however, contradicts such an endorsement and has led to another, somewhat different conclusion: the dangerous deification of science may not be as basic to Aylmer's tragedy as is his excessive transcendental faith (390:348–49). Representing the unquestioning acceptance of authoritarianism, Aminidab suggests not only an equally undesirable option but also a disillusionment with orthodox theology. Another reader faults the Christian tradition itself for having allowed its once powerful symbols to become iconoclastically defunct, a failure that opened the way for Aylmer to seek religious perfectionism in his scientific endeavors (486:49–59).

It is in this quest for perfection that Aylmer's science and romantic transcendentalism are alike, and it is precisely on that basis that they are censured. Several commentators have emphasized that Hawthorne's attitude is not so much ambivalent as moderate; it is the scientific and romantic extremes that are condemned. The author is as aware of the dangers of nineteenth-century romanticism when its limitations are not acknowledged (47:184; 39:239; 466:64–65) as he is wary of the impersonal and inhuman objectivity of science (447:91–92) and its myopic vision that misleads its proponents into confusing realities (191:13–15). In Hawthorne's assessment, knowledge is not condemned (500:262) nor are the responsible contemporary scientists of his day (174); Aylmer's error lies in attempting to upset the "Great Chain of Being," where every creature is assigned a particular place in nature (313:284), and in disturbing the balanced tension between the ideal and the earthly (162:50). One reader specifically identifies the target as the alchemical tradition of spiritualized matter (491), but whatever nineteenth-century manifestation Aylmer is interpreted as representing, his greatest fault remains his extremism. Those who defend his impatience with imperfection (511:351) and who uphold his love for his wife (39:233) are faced with a tragic denouement that better supports those who find Aylmer guilty of choosing science over woman (309:68–70) and knowledge over love (162:52). None, however, denies that Hawthorne's ideal-seeking scientist errs not so much in kind as in degree and that the middle ground remains Hawthorne's ideal (162).

Georgiana's characterization is affected by the concept of moderation as well. With the birthmark in the shape of a hand to symbolize her human mortality (237), she represents a balance between heaven and earth (390:351). Her imperfection may have been to trust Aylmer (447:81), but when she becomes a "fascinated participant" in his plan to perfect her (304:82), her entrapment is not as significant as is her total conversion to Romantic dynamism (186:130–31). When the birthmark is removed, she is no longer the mediator between extremes that is requisite for human existence (390:351). This balance that Georgiana symbolizes has also been called "harmony," a reference to the reconciliation of opposites discernible in the pattern of union and separation that marks the tale (350). Even her name, combining the masculine George and the feminine Anna, exemplifies this harmony, a marked contrast to Aylmer's compulsive separatism, which destroys her in the end.

In psychological terms, Aylmer has been accused of violating Georgiana's "wholeness," an act that reveals his inability to deal with a psychically unified human (350). Baym, Crews, and Lesser have all equated Aylmer's abhorrence of the birthmark with his revulsion to Georgiana's sexuality and his own sexual inadequacies (41:40–41; 115:126; 277:88–89). Baym believes that Hawthorne's criticism of Aylmer rests primarily on Aylmer's inability "to engage in the fundamental loving relation of husband and wife"; Lesser, on the other hand, views Hawthorne's attitude as neither condemnatory nor indulgent. He explains the story's effectiveness in terms of the sympathetic hearing it gives to ordinarily repressed impulses; the reader's unconscious responds to the integrative activity between ego and superego that the story triggers and the healing of intrapsychic tension that results (277:90–93).

Of special significance to these Freudian-based interpretations is the dream that Aylmer recalls at Georgiana's insistence. Hawthorne explains that Aylmer remembers it "with a guilty feeling" and adds, "Truth often finds its way to the mind close-muffled in robes of sleep, and then speaks with uncompromising directness of matters in regard to which we practise an unconscious self-deception, during our waking moments" (40.24–28). Freud or Jung could hardly have said it better. The importance of this dream passage has repeatedly been emphasized. Melville scored it in his copy of *Mosses* (35:254), and commentaries continue to discuss its relevance to Hawthorne's concept of reality as distinguished from actuality (371:20–21; 500:255).

"The Birthmark" has been suggested as an influence on one of Melville's stories, "The Bell Tower" (493), while the origin of Aylmer's sin in an apparent good has been paralleled to the pattern of *Moby–Dick* (333:101–02), and the concept of original sin as basic human nature (as represented by the birthmark) has been equated with Melville's concern with original sin and depravity in *Billy Budd* (454:81).

In 1847, *Blackwood's Magazine* objected to Aylmer's impossibly unrealistic attitude toward his wife, commenting: "Unfortunately, in Mr. Hawthorne's stories, it is the human being himself who is not probable or possible" (*CE, X, 530–31*). In 1898, Henry James described himself as having been "struck with something stiff and mechanical" in "The Birthmark" (241:51). And in 1968, Shulman called it a "static, schematic, and padded story" (431:227). But in spite of these selected negative responses, admirers have consistently outnumbered detractors. The story has been commended for its complexity of characterization (506) and for its handling of point of view. Fogle admires the universalized yet personal irony that the stress between detachment and sympathy conveys (186: 117). Another reader defines the story's "elusive excellence" in terms of its effectiveness as a carefully wrought history designed to expose the follies of Transcendental thought (491). Psychological critiques continue to affirm its emotional validity (277:87–90; 350; 513), but most of the praise that the story has garnered has been directed at its symbolism (notwithstanding James's complaint about its incongruities). The hand-shaped birthmark has generally been considered a delicate yet masterful symbol; it has been interpreted as an apt emblem for "human imperfection" (454:79–81), for "original sin" (532), for mortality, and, in conjunction with other hand references in the tale, for Aylmer's hand in which Georgiana suffers her fate (270:94; 237).

The paradox of Hawthorne's ambivalence, which is at the same time a virtue, provocative and enriching, and a fault, debilitating and counterproductive, provides the perfectly appropriate vehicle for the paradox of Aylmer, whose virtues and vices are also inextricably mixed. In this respect, the form and content of "The Birthmark" are one, and Hawthorne can be said to have achieved what he did not allow his protagonist to achieve, a measure of aesthetic perfection.

# VI

# The Canterbury Pilgrims

(*Centenary Edition, Volume XI, The Snow-Image*, 120–31.)

## Publication History

This story was first published in 1832 in *The Token and Atlantic Souvenir* (pp. 153–66) dated 1833, as the work of the author of "The Gentle Boy" (*CE, XI, 429*). Two other Hawthorne pieces, the bibliographical sketch "Sir William Pepperell" and "The Seven Vagabonds," appeared in the same issue. Most scholars agree that Samuel Goodrich, the editor, paid Hawthorne an average of $1 per page for his *Token* contributions, which would have made his earnings from "The Canterbury Pilgrims" an approximate $14. When Hawthorne was collecting copy for the second edition of *Twice-told Tales*, he made corrections in both "The Seven Vagabonds" and "The Canterbury Pilgrims" on an 1833 *Token* copy, probably in preparation for the printer's copy, but "The Canterbury Pilgrims" was not included in the revised collection (*CE, IX, 544*). Apparently, he omitted it in favor of his other tale about the Shaker community, "The Shaker Bridal," which appeared in the 1838 *Token* and was included in the 1842 *Twice-told Tales* (149:222). In 1851, "The Canterbury Pilgrims" was finally collected in *The Snow-Image* after Hawthorne's editor, James T. Fields, found it in his search through *The Token* for pieces that could be added to Hawthorne's last collection (*CE, XI, 389–90*). The Centenary Edition follows the annotated 1833 *Token* copy, discovered in 1972 by C. E. Frazer Clark, Jr., as more authoritative than the 1851 alterations, since it represents what Hawthorne wanted in 1841 (*CE, XI, 412–13*).

## Circumstances of Composition, Sources, and Influences

This story was probably written in the fall of 1831, not long after Hawthorne's visit to the Shaker settlement in Canterbury, New Hampshire. In a letter to his sister Louisa dated August 17, 1831, he describes his experiences there in pleasant terms:

> On my arrival, the first thing I saw was a jolly old shaker carrying

an immense decanter full of their superb cider, and as soon as I told
my business, he turned out a tumblerfull and gave me. It was as
much as a common head could cleverly carry. Our dining room
was well furnished, the dinner excellent, and the table was attended
by a middle aged shaker lady, good-looking and cheerful, and not to
be distinguished either in manners or conversation from other well-
educated women in the country. This establishment is immensely
rich. Their land extends two or three miles along the road, and
there are streets of great houses, painted yellow and topt with
red.... On the whole, they lead a good and comfortable life, and
if it were not for their ridiculous ceremonies, a man could not do
a wiser thing than join them. (225:127)

In the story, "the red roofs of the Shaker village" do appear, but otherwise
Hawthorne's depiction is strikingly different. Instead of high spirits, good
food, and a comfortable life, the settlement offers only a "cold and pas-
sionless security" much like "that other refuge of the world's weary
outcasts, the grave" (*131.11–13*).

This disparity between Hawthorne's initial reaction to the Shakers and
his open condemnation of them in his stories has been accounted for in
several ways. Waggoner says that this "radical discontinuity" between
experience and art is typical of the entire first two thirds of Hawthorne's
writing career and that his best work habitually reshapes his direct observations to conform with his essentially moral sensibility. For the purpose of his writing, the question of whether the Shakers' enforced chas-
tity was ethically valid overshadowed his immediate positive response
to the thriving community he visited (500:39–44). Waggoner notes that
Hawthorne uses only three elements from his experience at the Shaker
village in "The Canterbury Pilgrims" and that one of them, the idea of
a Shaker settlement as a retreat from the world, is not strictly a matter
of observation. The other two are the location of the settlement at the top
of a hill and the fountain whose description opens the story, which
Waggoner confirms as still standing, although the spring that supplied it
has gone dry (500:40–41). The absence of all three of Waggoner's "elements" from Hawthorne's letter to his sister Louisa demonstrates one of
the problems involved in using personal correspondence for story sources.

Another critic offers a simpler explanation for the discrepancy between
Hawthorne's immediate reaction to the Shakers and his portrayal of
them in his stories (205). Gross believes Hawthorne was influenced by
a book he withdrew from the Salem Athenaeum ten days after his letter
to Louisa. This book, *An Account of the People Called Shakers* by
Thomas Brown (Troy, 1812), reviews the history of the Shakers and
describes such practices as whippings and public mortifications inflicted
by frigid, self-righteous elders on those they accused of "fleshliness." Al-

though Hawthorne does not include anything like the case of the three Shaker girls who were forced to strip naked and whip themselves because they had been caught "attending to the amour of two flies in the window," he does replace the "jolly old shaker" described in his letter with an elder that could well have come from Brown's account. According to the young Shaker Josiah, "father Job is a very awful man to speak with, and being aged himself, he has but little charity for what he calls the iniquities of the flesh" (*122.29–32*). Gross also cites a possible source for the plot in Brown's story of Reuben Rathbone, who after some years as a Shaker left the settlement with a Shaker maiden whom he loved (205:461, n.12).

That the public attitude toward the Shakers in the 1830s was generally critical is demonstrated by an article in *The Penny Magazine* which describes the settlement in much the same light as does Brown's history (76). Possibly Hawthorne was partially responding to what he thought his readers expected when he discarded his first impression of the Shaker community in favor of a more pejorative view; however, his own reflection is a more probable source, especially since the Shakers' practices of celibacy and repressive communal supervision violated two of his most basic beliefs, the saving power of love and the sanctity of the human heart (274:84–85).

Hawthorne's subsequent visits to Shaker communities, one with Emerson in 1842 to a settlement near Harvard (*CE, VIII, 361–62*) and another with Melville, Evert and George Duyckinck, and Julian in 1851 at Hancock (*CE, VIII, 464–66*), prompted no such lighthearted approval; in fact, the lengthy journal entry devoted to the latter calls the Shakers "a filthy sect . . . hateful and disgusting to think of" and presents a rare display of scatalogical humor. Hawthorne commends Julian, then a boy of five, for "conferring with himself" (a euphemism for urinating) during their visit and then avows that "such a mark of his consideration . . . on the system and establishment of these foolish Shakers" was "the one of which they were most worthy."

## Relationship with Other Hawthorne Works

Although "The Canterbury Pilgrims" was published before Hawthorne began writing *The Story Teller,* it has been linked to the projected collection as one of his earlier stories that might have been incorporated into its framework (11:130; 43:50).

The story to which it is most closely related is "The Shaker Bridal," the only other story about the Shakers that Hawthorne wrote. They have been grouped as thematically alike by Stewart, who sees the two stories as condemnations of a misdirected idealism (458:254), and by Stein, who believes Hawthorne's interest in the Shakers was prompted by their "moral rigorism" and spiritual pride, traits that he associated with dogmatic Puritanism (447:83).

The majority of critics, however, have discussed the Shaker stories as complementary rather than identical (149:138–39, 222; 162:39; 274; 283). Lauber says "The Shaker Bridal" presents a retreat from life; "The Canterbury Pilgrims," its opposite, an acceptance of life (274:83). Levy reads them as two variations on a single theme, the fragility of human hopes that are as easily destroyed by the world at large (in "The Canterbury Pilgrims") as by the Shaker community (in "The Shaker Bridal"). He emphasizes the similarity between the pilgrims and Adam Colburn; he analyzes the narrow margin of faith, nothing more than a "precarious impulse," that separates Josiah and Miriam from Adam and Martha; and although he admits that Martha's anguish exceeds the suffering of the wife in "The Canterbury Pilgrims," he concludes that Hawthorne sympathizes as much with the pilgrims as he does with the young couple (283). This ambivalence, or "middle ground" as Levy call it, is undeniably present in "The Canterbury Pilgrims," but what makes "The Shaker Burial" an illuminating corollary to "The Canterbury Pilgrims" is the resounding condemnation of the Shakers' denial of life that it provides, a condemnation that eliminates all ambiguity. Levy's insistence on Hawthorne's indecisiveness ignores the fact that Miriam's hopes, however precarious, are preferable to Martha's frustration and death. In the closing paragraph of "The Canterbury Pilgrims," Hawthorne equates the Shaker community with the grave; in "The Shaker Burial" he works out that analogy dramatically in Martha's fate. (Lauber points out that the imagery Hawthorne uses in his description of the ritual of the Shaker bridal clearly reinforces a life-in-death motif [274:83]).

"The Great Carbuncle" is another story occasionally grouped with "The Canterbury Pilgrims" primarily on the basis of their allegorical elements (162:38; 500:99); for Doubleday, the type-poet in "The Canterbury Pilgrims," who is a subtle self-parody as well as a burlesque of the romantic outlook, is more trenchantly portrayed than his counterpart in "The Great Carbuncle" (149:223–24).

"The May-Pole of Merry Mount" has also been paralleled with "The Canterbury Pilgrims" because of the similarity between the young couples in both. Eisinger sees them as champions of a middle way: Josiah and Miriam choose a middle way away from the unnatural restrictions of the Shaker life; Edgar and Edith, a middle way between similar Puritan restrictions and the hedonism of the Merry Mounters (162:35). Double-day calls both the Shaker asceticism and the Merry Mount sensuality false Edens of irresponsibility; the last sentence in each of the stories describes two young lovers who are willing to hazard the uncertainties of life in a world without guarantees (149:227).

## Interpretations and Criticism

Waggoner has written the longest and most comprehensive analysis of "The Canterbury Pilgrims." Originally, he called it "very nearly a perfect story" (501:373); his revised version continues to praise its structure, "very like a beautifully constructed piece of music . . . built out of progressively complex explorations of contrasted themes," but he admits that "it is not one of the really great tales." Its type-characters, set speeches, and pageantlike action keep it from being a fully developed piece of fiction (500:78–90).

Most critics agree with Waggoner's reconsidered appraisal, but otherwise, unanimity is rare. Romantic (423) and existential (283) interpretations challenge Waggoner's Christian conclusions, while a thematic reading (283) rejects his structural and symbolic approach. For Waggoner, the fountain, which is both a natural spring and a manmade artifact, is a symbol for "a middle ground" between the "merely" natural world below (represented by the moon and the spring in the opening paragraph) and the "unnatural" renunciation above (represented by the Shaker community at the top of the hill). Both of these extremes are "escapes" from man's humanity; when the couple drink at the fountain, they affirm the "ideal equilibrium" between the temporal and the eternal that they will attempt to follow.

Secor notes that the absurd romantic poet, who also drinks at the fountain, becomes more ridiculously romantic; however, Secor attributes the effect to the summer moon, whose rays upset the equilibrium of the fountain (423). The moon is responsible not only for the poet's increased romanticism, but for the romantic love and hope upon which Josiah and Miriam base their decision to face the harsh reality described by the pilgrims. Waggoner's discussion circumvents such a romantic interpretation: the story's opening sentence, which deliberately connects the summer moon with the false moonshine of the popular romantic tale, gives the romantic trappings an ironic dimension; the failure of the farm couple's "romantic love" dispels the young lovers' romantic hopes. Hawthorne's realistic view of the normal course of married love is confirmed by a notebook entry in which he culminates his description of a display of affection by a newly wed couple with the comment, "It would be pleasant to meet them again next summer, and note the change" (500:87). Waggoner concludes that Hawthorne meant the young couple's chances to rest on their ability to resist pride and to change *eros* to Christian *caritas*.

Levy challenges both Secor's romantic outlook and Waggoner's Christian reading with an existential interpretation: "life justifies itself . . . as a self-existent process" (283). Rejecting their concerns with structure and symbols as conducive to distortions, he undertakes a "close thematic analysis." Levy concludes that with the odds clearly against them, Josiah and Miriam choose "hope . . . in the midst of uncertainty" and "move in the direction of growth despite the absence of assured consequences."

Arvin has given "The Canterbury Pilgrims" an autobiographical dimension by interpreting the young couple's decision to participate in the world as an imaginative foreshadowing of Hawthorne's own resolution to give up the ways of a recluse, a move that would not take place until almost a decade after he wrote the story (27:68–69). Baym's concern is professional autobiography; for her, this story offers evidence of Hawthorne's attempt throughout the 1830s to do socially legitimate writing. By displaying fiction as the vehicle for conservative wisdom, "The Canterbury Pilgrims" made the potential danger of the imagination less dangerous (43:50–51).

Few readers would disagree that this story caters to the conventional reader's expectations. Therein may lie its most significant shortcoming for twentieth-century readers, who generally prefer the unconventional. The "dangerous" moral uncertainties and psychological perplexities that Hawthorne explores in other works are missing in this one. No one doubts for a moment that the forces of good are on the side of Josiah and Miriam as they face their new life together; they are young, pure, hopeful, and in love. It is this unequivocal goodness bathed in sweetness and light that undoubtedly pleased the genteel readers of Hawthorne's day, and that displeases the less genteel sensibilities of most readers today.

# VII

# The Celestial Rail-road

(*Centenary Edition, Volume X, Mosses from an Old Manse, 186–206.*)

## Publication History

This story was first published in May 1843 in *United States Magazine and Democratic Review* (XII, 360–66) under Hawthorne's own name (*CE, X, 576*). In December 1843, Hawthorne received a payment of $100 for the six pieces that appeared in the *Democratic Review* between February and June 1843, which would have made his earnings from this story approximately $17.50, or less than half the standard magazine rate of $5 per page (*CE, X, 505–06*). (See publication history of "The New Adam and Eve" for details of Hawthorne's financial plight in 1843 and his relationship with John L. O'Sullivan, the magazine's editor.) Numerous reprints of "The Celestial Rail-road" were made without Hawthorne's permission (71), a practice that Hawthorne complained of bitterly in a letter to Horatio Bridge dated April 1, 1844: "the pamphlet and piratical system has so broken up all regular literature, that I am forced to work hard for small gains" (*CE, X, 505*). "The Celestial Rail-road" and the other five *Democratic Review* contributions for 1843 were collected in the 1846 edition of *Mosses from an Old Manse*. The original manuscript, in the possession of an anonymous collector, was used as the copy text for the Centenary Edition (*CE, X, 575–76*).

## Circumstances of Composition, Sources, and Influences

This story was probably written in March 1843 while Hawthorne was living at the Old Manse in Concord (323:25). The following undated notebook entry (made after June 1, 1842 but before July 27, 1844) furnishes one of the details used in the description of Vanity Fair in the story:

> An Auction (perhaps in Vanity Fair) of offices, honors, and all sorts of things considered desirable by mankind; together with things eternally valuable, which shall be considered by most people as worthless lumber. (*CE, VIII, 283.21–24*)

The source for this note has been traced to John Bunyan's *Pilgrim's Progress* (*CE, VIII, 613*) although the story's internal evidence is sufficient to establish Bunyan's allegory as Hawthorne's model without additional documentation. In fact, Hawthorne's adaptation of Bunyan is such a crucial factor in this story that Hawthorne's purpose cannot be fully understood if the reader is not familiar with the original work. The extended literary allusion is used to provide an essential ironic contrast. Like Bunyan, Hawthorne recounts a pilgrimage to the Celestial City, but unlike Bunyan's Christian, Hawthorne's narrator rides on a train; Apollyon is not his hated and fierce enemy but the railroad's chief engineer; his companions are not Faithful and Hopeful but Mister Smooth-it-away; their burdens are conveniently deposited in the baggage car; the wicket gate has been replaced by a spacious station house; the Hill Difficulty has a tunnel through it; the Slough of Despond, a bridge across it; the cave of the giants Pope and Pagan is occupied by the Giant Transcendentalist; and Vanity Fair accepts churches and ministers as fashionable conveniences. Hawthorne includes these important features of Christian's pilgrimage and more, each with appropriate changes (151:330; 244:164; 500:17). One extended analysis of *Pilgrim's Progress* as Hawthorne's source equates the narrator not with Christian but with Ignorance, Christian's erstwhile traveling companion, whose chief characteristic is his self-confident but obviously uninformed optimism (432:61–62). Bunyan's Ignorance believes in much the same doctrine that Hawthorne's "modern" thinkers espouse: Christ's atonement justified all men for all time, no sense of one's own depravity is necessary for salvation, and divine revelation is based on silly superstition.

That the first book given to Hawthorne, when he was four, was *Pilgrim's Progress* (244:156) and that his sister Elizabeth remembers him reading it when he was six (458.1) attest to Hawthorne's long-standing familiarity with his model. It was a familiarity, however, that he shared not only with the readers of his day, who would immediately recognize the allusions, but also with the writers who had written earlier adaptations of Bunyan's masterpiece to satirize nineteenth-century "progress." Hawthorne's is neither the first nor the most extensive of the American "Pilgrim's Progresses"; it is less tedious than its predecessors, but its targets are the same (432:60–62).

Because religious liberalism is one of these targets, today's reader will also better understand "The Celestial Rail-road" if he knows the history of the changes that occurred in New England between the Puritanism of the seventeenth century and the Unitarianism of Hawthorne's time. A notebook entry made on August 28, 1837, six years before Hawthorne wrote his satirical allegory, refers to a theological student who later became a prominent Unitarian minister. In a description of an excursion aboard a steamboat to Thompson's Island near Boston, Hawthorne includes "Mr. Waterston, talking poetry and philosophy" (*CE, VIII, 70.19*). Waterston with his kind of reformed religion is confirmed as Hawthorne's target in a letter the author wrote to Sophia on April 14, 1844. Having met Waterston again, Hawthorne writes: ". . . he merely spoke a few words, and then left me. This is so unlike his deportment in times past, that I suspect the Celestial Railroad must have given him a pique; and if so, I shall feel as if Providence had sufficiently rewarded me for that pious labor" (151:332; *CE, VIII, 581*). Waterston may well have been Mr. Smooth-it-away's prototype, and the 1837 steamboat excursion the inspiration for the steam ferryboat on which Hawthorne's pilgrims complete their journey.

Hawthorne had expressed the idea that pilgrimages in America would probably be taken in stagecoaches or railroad cars in 1836, in an essay on "Ancient Pilgrims" for the *American Magazine of Useful and Entertaining Knowledge*. The same article included the comment, which clearly prefigures "The Celestial Rail-road," that such a pilgrim would have "earthly cares" instead of "heavenly meditations" on his mind (481:105). Hawthorne may have incorporated some of the features of the Eastern Railroad from Salem to Boston, which opened in 1838, into his "celestial" version; the track through the coastal marshes, like that over the Slough of Despond, was laid on causeways and fills, and at the end of the line passengers took a ferry across the harbor to Boston—advertised, as in Hawthorne's story (*205.21*), as taking only three minutes (117:322). Hawthorne exploits the possibilities offered by the railroad metaphor to good advantage, perhaps even deriving the stylistic suggestions of a promotion scheme from the railroad companies' prospectuses. The optimistic manner and glib phrasing of such travel guidebooks as *Appleton's Railroad and Steamboat Companion* also seem to be part of Mr. Smooth-it-away's sale pitch in which the conveniences of railroad travel are touted and the dangers minimized (117:323–24).

One of Hawthorne's neighbors during the Old Manse years also questioned the advantages of these modern accoutrements. In their walks together, Thoreau may have influenced Hawthorne in his condemnation of progress measured in materialistic terms. Both men had serious misgivings about much of what was becoming the American way of life (133:538–39). A different kind of parallel has been noted between Hawthorne's criticism of Transcendentalism and Unitarianism and Samuel Johnson's objection to the Deism of Shaftsbury in the eighteenth century; both men rejected optimistic benevolence, but theirs is a matter of shared conservatism rather than direct influence (183:182–85).

## Relationship with Other Hawthorne Works

While "The Celestial Rail-road" is the one of all Hawthorne's works that is most completely dependent on *Pilgrim's Progress,* Bunyan's influence has been detected in other pieces as well. One reader finds three Bunyanesque images—the disingenuous pilgrim, pathways and byways in a labyrinthine wilderness, and the unsuccessful search for the Celestial City—at work together in *Fanshawe, The Scarlet Letter,* and *The Blithedale Romance.* He also sees the narrator in "The Celestial Rail-road" as the prototype for the self-deluded visionaries of the American romances—Dimmesdale in *The Scarlet Letter,* Clifford in *The House of Seven Gables,* and Coverdale in *The Blithedale Romance* (432:61–62). Another reader has found allusions to *Pilgrim's Progress* in each of these novels in episodes that deal with casting off "the evils of the past" (443).

This story has most often been linked with "Earth's Holocaust" as satirical allegories that explicitly criticize Hawthorne's contemporaries and attack reformers (188:86; 500:16). *The Blithedale Romance* does this too and is especially like "The Celestial Rail-road" in its depiction of the liberalized intellectuals who play at the hardships of a life of toil at Blithedale, a farming commune fashioned after Brook Farm where Hawthorne spent a frustrating half-year in 1841. The weakness in their philosophy of intellectual uplift is like that which characterizes the "wonderful improvements" in ethics and religion for those who hold common stock in the societies of Vanity Fair; in both cases, it is all "a bubble" (304:76). "Earth's Holocaust" and "The Celestial Rail-road" are also part of what has been called the "Day of Doom" phase of Hawthorne's development because of the recurrent image of ultimate destruction that marks them and several other pieces that he wrote during the Old Manse period (432:59). All of the sketchlike pieces in *Mosses* are similar in their portrayal of a person who asserts himself as a successful man of letters (43:100–02).

The only other works in which the railroad plays a significant role are *The House of Seven Gables,* in the chapter "The Flight of Two Owls" (117:325; 175), and "The Old Apple Dealer" (175), where the train is also emblematic of man's efforts to circumvent time (189:76).

## Interpretations and Criticism

The most surprising approval bestowed on "The Celestial Rail-road" comes from Emerson, Concord's own "Giant Transcendentalist," who, in spite of being one of the targets of the piece's satire, praised it. It was one of the few works by Hawthorne that Emerson enjoyed. He credited it with "a serene strength which we cannot afford not to praise in this low life" (151:332). Emerson was, in this instance, agreeing with the majority. The widespread popularity of this story can be gauged by the numerous pirated reprints it generated. Hawthorne, in championing a conservative point of view, found an approving mid-nineteenth-century public (432:62).

Twentieth-century reaction, however, is mixed and, on the whole, not as enthusiastic as that of Hawthorne's contemporaneous audience. One reader calls it "a clever, consistent, and well-sustained allegory" (151:332); another, "one of the finest things of its kind ever written" (500:17); but in both cases, the implication is that the author's accomplishments are qualified and limited by the genre he chose. Genre emerges as a dominant concern in almost all the reactions to the story; it is, as the two admirers just quoted assume, allegory, or it is a parody of allegory (304:75), or it is a satire (490:129), or it is both parody and satire (150; 280:54; 420:195). In one instance, it is deemed such an extreme parody of allegory that it is no longer allegorical at all (188:87–89); in another, it should be read as a dream-tale because the internal irony makes it self-defeating as allegory (364); while two others find enough strongly defined allegorical characteristics to recommend its use as a pedagogical aid in teaching the figurative in fiction (222) and *Pilgrim's Progress* (529).

The story's ending—"I awoke. Thank Heaven, it was a Dream,"—has been variously interpreted. It has most often been accepted simply as a part of the structure borrowed from *Pilgrim's Progress* (244:164), but one reader makes the point that unlike Bunyan's "Now I saw in a dream," which transforms Christian's adventures into a vision, Hawthorne simply awakes to avert a catastrophic demise (315:199). For this reader, "the feebleness of a dream ending" detracts from the story's otherwise sustained irony. For another, the dream ending transforms an ambivalent satire into an effective dream-tale with internally consistent irony; the banal last words are central to the ironic portrayal of a narrator who deliberately and repeatedly evades self-knowledge and on whom the relevance of Bunyan is lost (364).

Most readers agree that "modernism," both in the liberalizing of theological precepts and in the increasingly materialistic concerns with progress, is being attacked in "The Celestial Rail-road," and that Bunyan's fundamentalist allegory is used to provide a satiric contrast to the misguided and deluded modernists. A few, however, believe that Hawthorne's parody satirizes Bunyan as well and that the story reveals a "two-faced skepticism" (280:54), as much a rejection of Calvinism as of Unitarianism (420:195). To some readers, and this will include the growing number of environmentally conscious proponents of back-to-basics individualism, the most relevant aspect is the condemnation of the machine age (175). Hawthorne anticipates other mechanical shortcuts besides the puffing and snorting steam train and ferry; machines for "the wholesale manufacture of individual morality" are among the wonders at Vanity Fair, and the "ingenious methods" through which "any man may acquire an omnigenous erudition, without the trouble of even learning to read" (*198*) sound very much like the latest in mass-communication techniques (304:75).

Melville marked the passage in his copy of *Mosses* that describes the "societies for all manner of virtuous purposes, with which a man has merely to connect himself, throwing, as it were, his quota of virtue into the common stock, and the president and directors will take care that the aggregate amount be well applied" (304:75). An examination of Melville's novel *The Confidence-Man* (1857) reveals the title character's involvement in a similar scheme. While at London's World Fair where he is displaying a "Protean easy chair" designed to ease the torments of both body and conscience, he proposes a plan for the society called "World's Charity" whose one object would be "the methodisation of the world's benevolence" under the direction of its officers. One scholar suggests closer ties between the two fictional worlds, including Melville's transmutation of Hawthorne's steam ferryboat at the end of the Celestial Railroad line into the steamer, *Fidele* (429:364–73). That Melville plumbed Hawthorne for reinforcement of his own concerns is now an accepted premise of American Renaissance studies, but the areas where the two minds meet continue to provide surprisingly contemporary insights. "The Celestial Rail-road" is one example; in spite of its outmoded allegorical structure and its nineteenth-century targets, it still has something to say. Some readers, unlike Melville who knew Bunyan well, may have to familiarize themselves with Christian's adventures first, but once they recognize the allusions, their trip on Hawthorne's railroad becomes curiously relevant.

# VIII

# The Christmas Banquet

*(Centenary Edition, Volume X, Mosses from an Old Manse, 284–305.)*

## Publication History

This story was first published in January 1844 in *United States Magazine and Democratic Review* (XIV, 78–87) under Hawthorne's own name (*CE, X, 578*). Five other pieces by Hawthorne appeared in the *Democratic Review* during 1844, and another in 1845, but the only known payment from John L. O'Sullivan, its editor, for these contributions is $100 on October 1, 1845. If Hawthorne received no other remuneration from O'Sullivan between the $100 paid in December 1843 (for the six new pieces published in the magazine in 1843) and the $100 paid in 1845, the average per-page rate for the 1844 and 1845 material would be $1.41; "The Christmas Banquet" would have netted a little over $14, instead of the $50 that the standard magazine rate would have commanded. In spite of O'Sullivan's friendship with Hawthorne, payment from O'Sullivan was repeatedly late and below standard. (See publication history of "The New Adam and Eve.") Hawthorne continued to submit contributions to the *Democratic Review*, however, because the magazine market was limited and Hawthorne evidently had faith in his friend's efforts to get funds from the publishers. So acute was Hawthorne's plight in October 1845 that, according to his letter to Horatio Bridge, O'Sullivan's payment saved him from having to leave Concord in financial disgrace. In the face of such urgent need, Hawthorne was in no position to dispute the amount that O'Sullivan was finally able to procure for him (*CE, X, 505–15*). "The Christmas Banquet" was included in *Mosses from an Old Manse* in 1846.

## Circumstances of Composition, Sources, and Influences

According to Hawthorne's wife, he finished this story on December 12, 1843, read the manuscript to her, and sent it to O'Sullivan. It may have been almost entirely written on December 10 and 11 because Sophia describes her husband as writing until late in the afternoon of both days, whereas he ordinarily wrote only in the morning (323:28).

Seven years earlier an unusually well-developed germ for the story appears in an undated segment of the notebooks (between October 25, 1836 and 1837):

> A Thanksgiving dinner. All the miserable on earth are to be invited, —as the drunkard, the bereaved parent, the ruined merchant, the broken-hearted lover, the poor widow, the old man and woman who have outlived their generation, the disappointed author, the wounded, sick, and broken soldier, the diseased person, the infidel, the man with an evil conscience, little orphan children, or children of neglectful parents, shall be admitted to the table, and many others. The giver of the feast goes out to deliver his invitations. Some of the guests he meets in the streets, some he knocks for at the doors of their houses. The description must be rapid. But who must be the giver of the feast, and what his claims to preside? A man who has never found out what he is fit for, who has unsettled aims or objects in life, and whose mind gnaws him, making him the sufferer of many kinds of misery. He should meet some pious, old, sorrowful person, with more outward calamities than any other, and invite him with a reflection that piety would make all miserable company truly thankful. (*CE, VIII, 20.21–21.8*)

Four later entries scattered between 1837 and 1843 are somewhat more loosely related: "A company of men, none of whom have anything worth hoping for on earth, yet who do not look forward to anything beyond earth!" (*167.3–5*); "To have ice in one's blood" (*184*); "A person with an ice-cold hand—his right hand; which people ever afterwards remember, when once they have grasped it" (*235.12–14*); and, "The human Heart to be allegorized as a cavern. . . ." (*237.17*).

A letter written to Sophia on October 4, 1840 expresses a concept closely linked to Gervayse Hastings' alienation from life:

> Indeed, we are but shadows—we are not endowed with real life, and all that seems most real about us is but the thinnest substance of a dream—till the heart is touched. That touch creates us—then we begin to be—thereby we are beings of reality, and inheritors of eternity. (*455:lxx*)

Hastings explains his claim to misery in similar terms: "It is a chilliness— a want of earnestness—a feeling as if what should be my heart were a thing of vapor—a haunting perception of unreality!" (*304.28–31*). Hastings appears to represent the "moral monster" (*305.27*) that Hawthorne himself might have become. In a letter to Longfellow, written before Sophia had a place in his life, Hawthorne confesses: "By some witchcraft or other, . . . I have secluded myself from society . . . and now I cannot find the key to let myself out . . . there is no fate in this world so horrible as to have no share in its joys or sorrows" (455:xiii). Roderick Elliston reveals another autobiographical inference when he represents himself as the supposed author of "The Christmas Banquet" (27:135; 188:105–06). In the frame, Roderick's criticism of Hastings' portrayal parallels Hawthorne's explanation of the same kind of difficulties he had in describing the old apple dealer in the story of that name, who, like Hastings, seems "to be on the outside of everything" (*305.30*). That sketch, published early in 1843, opens with the following apology: "The lover of the moral picturesque may sometimes find what he seeks in a character, which is, nevertheless, of too negative a description to be seized upon, and represented to the imaginative vision by word-painting" (*CE, X, 439.1–5*). Similarly, Elliston's failure to express Hastings' character fully is termed "unavoidable because the characteristics are all negative" (*305.23–24*).

Two literary sources have been cited for "The Christmas Banquet": chapter XIX of Voltaire's *Candide* for the banquet for the most miserable people (134) and Samuel Johnson's *Rambler*, numbers 82 and 105, for the structural pattern (132).

## Relationship with Other Hawthorne Works

This story is most closely related to "Egotism; or, The Bosom-Serpent" because the three central characters in "Egotism" reappear in the frame of "The Christmas Banquet"—Roderick as narrator and Rosina and the sculptor as his audience. Both stories are subtitled "From the Unpublished 'Allegories of the Heart,'" a reference to a collection that never materialized. Adkins considers the possibility that several other pieces written during Hawthorne's stay at the Old Manse could have been intended for the series. "The Birthmark," "Rappaccini's Daughter," and "Earth's Holocaust," for example, all explore "the gloomy mysteries of the human heart" (*284.6–7*), as Roderick starts out to do. According to the notebooks, "Ethan Brand" was also conceived during those years at Concord; although it was not written until considerably later, its symbolism and theme are closely related to the "heart" allegories (11:146–47).

The idea of isolation is such a pervasive one in Hawthorne's works that Gervayse Hastings is, in that respect, related to all of Hawthorne's many troubled isolatoes (455:lxxi). Axelsson devotes an entire book to an analysis of the isolation and interdependence of Hawthorne's characters; he classifies Hastings as a victim of his own nature, lacking an essential ingredient in his psychic makeup necessary to effect communion with humanity. His closest parallel is Seymour-Colcord-Pearson in the unfinished *Doctor Grimshawe's Secret* (32:120–22). Unreality coupled with isolation is also especially notable in the early autobiographical "The Devil in Manuscript," in such stories as "Wakefield" and "Feathertop," and in several sketches written during the Old Manse years. Both "The Procession of Life" and "The Intelligence Office" describe mortals who "have lost or never found their proper place in the world," in some ways like "The Old Apple Dealer" discussed above. Hastings' kind of inner torment is closest, however, to that of "Young Goodman Brown" because both men's spiritual desolation is masked by the accoutrements of what appears to be a fulfilled life. "Fancy's Show Box" is a variation of this appearance–reality paradox. All three incorporate another typical Hawthornesque device—a contrived situation where a variety of sins can be explored and exploited.

Its frame qualifies "The Christmas Banquet" as one of Hawthorne's artist stories (38; 47:177; 385:48–49). Like "The Prophetic Pictures," "The Artist of the Beautiful," "Drowne's Wooden Image," and "The Snow-Image," it deals with the dilemma of the artist and the illusory nature of art. However, unlike the ambivalent accomplishments of most of Hawthorne's artists, Roderick's creative act confirms his redemption (255:165).

Gervayse Hastings' name is reminiscent of the rejected suitor, Jervase Helwyse, in "Lady Eleanore's Mantle." Both have been traced to a Gervais Helwyse in Hawthorne's own genealogy (293:95). However, the Gervayse in "The Christmas Banquet" is more like Lady Eleanore than like her suitor. Kaul uses the two stories, and "Young Goodman Brown," to illustrate how the "sense of community" can begin to break down in individual consciousness (255:170–71).

## Interpretations and Criticism

Whether "The Christmas Banquet" is a short story or not is a fundamental critical issue. Doubleday classifies it as one of eight satirical sketches in *Mosses from an Old Manse* (151); Walsh calls it "an illustrated idea," essentially an essay in which the dramatic situation is subordinated (510). Waggoner sums up the genre question succinctly: "No sharp separation can be made between the allegorical 'processions,' the sketches with some narrative ingredients, and the tales proper" (500:249). This story fits best in Waggoner's middle category; it has many of the characteristics of the sketch, but it also has a fully developed narrative thread, the requirement that qualifies it for inclusion in this study. Waggoner, too, includes it as a tale in his *Selected Tales and Sketches* (502).

The story's subtitle clearly identifies it as an allegory, a classification that subjects it to abuse from the antiallegorists. Poe and James are two of the most outspoken. In 1847, Poe writes: "In defense of allegory (however, or for whatever object, employed,) there is scarcely one respectable word to be said. . . . He [Hawthorne] is infinitely too fond of allegory, and can never hope for popularity so long as he persists in it" (378:24–26). In 1879, James concurs: "It has never seemed to me to be, as it were, a first-rate literary form . . . it is apt to spoil two good things—a story and a moral, a meaning and a form" (241:50). Neither mentions "The Christmas Banquet" specifically, but its absence in their commentaries, and in the major critical books devoted to Hawthorne's works, attests to this story's weaknesses. One source study in 1926 commends it as a "very powerful story" (385:48), but little else has been said in its favor. Even a reader who deplores "that curious but not infrequent assumption that all allegory is relatively unimportant" admits that its theme is "not powerfully embodied" (151:326–28). It could well have been one of the "blasted allegories" that Hawthorne himself belittles. (See "Egotism.") It, nevertheless, continues to be included in collections, probably because its faults are in many ways representative of Hawthorne's shortcomings. It illustrates his allegorical method (309:24–25) as well as his obsession with the limits of his talent. It is also his most explicit display of his most ubiquitous concern—the perils of alienation.

# IX

# David Swan; A Fantasy

*(Centenary Edition, Volume IX, Twice-told Tales,* 183–90).

## Publication History

This story was first published in the fall of 1836 in *The Token and Atlantic Souvenir* for 1837 (pp. 147–55), with no attribution. The editor, Samuel Goodrich, also inserted seven other pieces by Hawthorne without using his name. A September 25, 1836 letter from Horatio Bridge registers a significant reaction to Hawthorne's practice of writing anonymously:

> The "Token" is out, and I suppose you are getting your book ready for publication. . . . I hope to God that you will put your name upon the title-page, and come before the world at once and on your own responsibility. You could not fail to make a noise and an honorable name, and something besides.
>
> I've been thinking how singularly you stand among the writers of the day; known by name to very few, and yet your writings admired more than any others with which they are ushered forth. . . . Your articles in the last "Token" alone are enough to give you a respectable name, if you were known as their author. (233:I, 138–39)

For these "articles in the last 'Token,'" Hawthorne was eventually paid $108, making the net earnings from "David Swan" an approximate $8 (*CE, IX, 497*).

Shortly after Bridge's letter, Hawthorne followed his friend's advice and began selecting pieces for his first collection under his own name. In March 1837, *Twice-told Tales* was published, and "David Swan" was one of five works taken from the 1837 *Token* to appear in it.

## Circumstances of Composition, Sources, and Influences

The composition date for "David Swan" is an inexact one because of the possibility that it was originally written as a part of the aborted *Story Teller* series. One of the other stories published in the same *Token* issue, "The Great Carbuncle," has been established as a *Story Teller* segment, and "David Swan" may have been one of the other pieces in Goodrich's possession since early 1835 when serial publication of the project was dropped (11:141–42). The roadside setting, the fantasy-based premise, and the philosophical moral make it an appropriate selection for the wandering storyteller's repertoire. If so, "David Swan" was written in the fall and winter of 1832–33 or 1833–34. The fact that no letters asking for *Token* contributions have been found for this period suggests that Goodrich supplied himself from the *Story Teller* stock on hand. Hawthorne's other commitments to Goodrich in 1836 included editing *The American Magazine of Useful and Entertaining Knowledge* and writing *Peter Parley's Universal History* which left little time for independent endeavors. "David Swan," however, is short enough to have been written in the midst of his other duties; one early study places its composition date as fall 1835 or winter 1836 (84:58). A letter from Hawthorne to his sister Louisa dated February 15, 1836, and now in the Essex Institute collection, provides an insight into Hawthorne's feelings toward Goodrich at this time. Hawthorne complains about Goodrich's delay in paying him for some earlier contributions and declares: "I have now broke off all intercourse with him, and never think of going near him. . . . " (*CE, IX, 498*). It seems unlikely he would have voluntarily written new pieces for Goodrich at this time.

A notebook entry related to "David Swan" appears between August 22 and October 7, 1837, a year after the story was published. Hawthorne must have felt his earlier story had not exhausted the possibilities of its central idea because he wrote a variation on the theme as a story germ, although he never developed it further. The major change is in the portrayal of the young man; David Swan's innocent unawareness becomes deliberate distrust and final revelation:

> Distrust to be thus exemplified:—Various good and desirable things to be presented to a young man, and offered to his acceptance,—as a friend, a wife, a fortune; but he to refuse them all, suspecting that it is merely a delusion. Yet all to be real, and he to be told so, when too late. (*CE, VIII, 153*)

The eighteenth-century Eastern tale as written by Addison, Goldsmith, and Samuel Johnson has been suggested as an analogue for "David Swan" (149:67). While the fantasy and the moral of that genre are present, David's roadside nap on his way to Boston falls short of Rasselas's worldwide philosophical quest.

## Relationship with Other Hawthorne Works

The nameless heroine in "David Swan" has been called an early example of the wholesome New England girl whose type Hawthorne was to use repeatedly in his tales and develop into Phoebe of *The House of Seven Gables.* (See Susan in "The Village Uncle.")

A certain surface similarity exists between David Swan and Robin of "My Kinsman, Major Molineux." Each is a young man on his way to Boston to seek a kinsman's help in making a new life for himself, but David's story ends, without his acquiring any insights, where Robin's begins.

Thematically "David Swan" is the sunny side of the possibility/reality coin tossed in "Fancy's Show Box." The two stories "demonstrate the immense complexity inherent in what are apparently the most simple facts of experience" (188:22). David's reality remains a series of unrealized possibilities while Mr. Smith's possibilities become a guilt-ridden reality. Both are examples of "dream" stories in which what happens to a character in his sleep is related to what happens after he awakes. Hawthorne uses a similar device, but much more skillfully and meaningfully, in such stories as "Young Goodman Brown," "Rappaccini's Daughter," and "The Birthmark."

## Interpretations and Criticism

Because David Swan does not adventure upon the road but only sleeps in a shady spot along its way, this story has been called "characteristic" of its author's personal inclinations. Hawthorne returned to his mother's home after graduation from college and lived there for twelve years. "David Swan" was written during those years. A biographical interpretation is encouraged by Hawthorne's reminiscences about this period in his life. Retrospectively, he wrote: "I sat down by the wayside of life, like a man under enchantment, and a shrubbery sprung up around me" (*CE, XI, 5*). Hawthorne also called his last home "The Wayside" (280:48–49).

One critic uses "David Swan" as an example of a different Hawthorne characteristic—the projection of a Platonic universe in which some kind of analogical relationship exists between ultimate reality and the everyday world. David's two worlds, his experiences asleep and awake, have been interpreted as different phases of the same duality (188:22–24).

As a rule, this story, when mentioned at all, is used to demonstrate Hawthorne at his least effective. For example, Male, in an overall assessment of Hawthorne's strengths and weaknesses, points to "the problem of moral growth" as Hawthorne's most fruitful subject; he goes on to say that when Hawthorne's moral imagination was not engaged, he wrote things such as "Little Daffydowndilly" and "David Swan" (304:6).

Male's comment is typical. Perhaps the best use that "David Swan" can serve is to identify, by its shortcomings, what makes the better· stories as good as they are.

# X

# The Devil in Manuscript

(*Centenary Edition, Volume XI, The Snow-Image,* 170–78.)

## Publication History

"The Devil in Manuscript" was first published in the *New-England Magazine* in November 1835 (IX, 340–45) under the pseudonym Ashley A. Royce (*CE, XI, 430*). Hawthorne intended it to be part of the group called *The Story Teller*. Early in 1834, he submitted the two-volume manuscript to Samuel Goodrich, a Boston editor and publisher, who attempted to find a publisher for the book and then helped to arrange serial publication in the *New-England Magazine*. The first two installments appeared in the November and December 1834 issues, but a change in the editorial staff resulted in the dropping of the framework of the projected book and the separation of the collection into individual stories and essays. Fifteen of these, including "The Devil," appeared in the *New-England Magazine* during the next year, 1835 (11). Many years later in a letter dated August 13, 1857, to his sister-in-law Elizabeth Peabody, Hawthorne blamed Park Benjamin of the *New-England Magazine* for cutting up *The Story Teller* (*CE, IX, 494*).

At $1 per page, the standard rate paid by the *New-England Magazine* in 1834 (*CE, IX, 499, n.31*), "The Devil" should have brought Hawthorne $6, but his statement, reported by Elizabeth Peabody, that "he got little or nothing as pay" raises some doubt about his having been paid at all. Elizabeth Peabody also remembered Hawthorne as saying "he cared little for the stories afterwards, which had in their original place in *The Story Teller* a great degree of significance" (106:32).

The history of "The Devil" confirms Hawthorne's lack of interest in it. He ignored it when he collected pieces for his two editions of *Twice-told Tales* and for *Mosses from an Old Manse*, and it was included in *The Snow-Image* of 1852 only because James T. Fields, Hawthorne's editor and friend, had found it when he "got together" several early works in magazines and annuals at Hawthorne's request (*CE, XI, 389*).

## Circumstances of Composition, Sources, and Influences

As one of the segments of *The Story Teller*, "The Devil" was probably written in the fall and winter of 1832–33 or 1833–34. A letter to Franklin Pierce on June 28, 1832 reveals Hawthorne's plan to use his anticipated summer trip to Canada as the basis for "a book by which I intend to acquire an (undoubtedly) immense literary reputation" (*CE, IX, 493*). The first-person narrator of "The Devil" appears to be the same persona that appears in "The Story Teller No. I," later to be collected in *Mosses from an Old Manse* as "Passages from a Relinquished Work." Both are travelers who offer accounts of their experiences and encounters. Both are also would-be novelists; the storyteller prides himself on having "hit upon a method of uniting" the "novelist" and the "actor" in his new vocation (*CE, X, 408*), and the narrator in "The Devil" admits to "a desire to turn novelist" (*171.26–27*). In all probability, "Fragments from the Journal of a Solitary Man," one of the uncollected tales, is the conclusion of *The Story Teller*, revised to be published by itself. Oberon, the narrator's friend in "The Devil," is again the subject of the tale, but in "Fragments" Oberon has assumed the history, background, and traits of the narrator-storyteller. Through his journal, which he bequeathed to the narrator on his deathbed, Oberon concludes his adventures (and presumably the *Story Teller* sequence) with a description of his ignominious return home. Although the order in which Hawthorne actually wrote the series is not known, the narrative pattern suggests that "The Devil" belongs somewhere near the finale, which would make early 1834 the likeliest composition date.

The Oberon in "The Devil," who sets fire to his unpublished works, resembles his creator in that respect. Hawthorne recalls his early experiences as an aspiring author in a letter that he wrote from his mother's home in Salem: "Here I have written many tales,—many that have been burned to ashes" (458:36). Elsewhere, he again remembers having burned "whole quires of manuscript stories" (*CE, IX, 486*). The 1851 preface to *Twice-told Tales* also describes the fate of some of Hawthorne's unpublished earlier works in much the same terms as those used for Oberon's holocaust (*CE, IX, 4*). Two early biographers detail the circumstances leading to the conflagration, both confirming Hawthorne's Oberon-like exasperation with publishers (272:135; 63:68).

Hawthorne used the signature "Oberon" in corresponding with Horatio Bridge during their college days at Bowdoin (63:49). In "The Devil" the narrator acknowledges Oberon as a pseudonym; he refers to "my friend, whom I shall call Oberon" with an explanation reminiscent of the Bridge–Hawthorne college relationship:"—it was a name of fancy and friendship between him and me" (*171.7–8*).

But the identification of Hawthorne with Oberon may go beyond these surface parallels. In a letter to Longfellow from Salem on June 4, 1837, Hawthorne's attitude toward his twelve years as an aspiring writer since their graduation from Bowdoin is very similar to Oberon's analysis of how his years of writing have isolated him (455:lxviii). One biographer traces the roots of Hawthorne's periodic escapes into an inner, imaginary world of darkness to the three years he spent as a semi-invalid after an injury to his foot when he was nine. The schoolyard accident in 1818 is called "the birth of Oberon," the Oberon of medieval folklore and of Shakespeare's *Midsummer Night's Dream*, the magician-king who reigns supreme over the fairyland of the night (355:8–15). Another scholar cautions against equating Oberon, the persona, with Hawthorne, the man (149:11), but however much Hawthorne may have romantically exaggerated his feeling of frustration and alienation in his fiction, the basis for "The Devil" remains firmly rooted in the actual experiences of Hawthorne in the early years of his writing career.

## Relationship with Other Hawthorne Works

This story is most closely related to the other parts of *The Story Teller* that deal directly with Oberon, primarily the "Passages" and "Fragments" segments discussed above. In all of these, the Oberon character carries a stigma similar to the one of the narrator in "The Custom-House" when he imagines the shocked disapproval of his Puritan ancestors at having one of their progeny turn out to be a writer of storybooks (51:58–59; 127:57). This self-deprecatory attitude toward artists of all kinds as degenerate idlers is in some way reflected in all of the artist figures in Hawthorne's fiction, as is the corollary risk of isolation brought about by their inveterate fascination with observing others. Oberon's closest parallels are the anonymous painter in "The Prophetic Pictures" and the narrator-persona of many of the sketches—"Monsieur du Miroir," for example. In the novels, the detached observers include Kenyon in *The Marble Faun* and Holgrave in *The House of Seven Gables*, both of whom grow out of their spectator roles, and Coverdale in *The Blithedale Romance*, who never does (32:133–49). Bewley conceives of Oberon as burning his manuscript in a kind of act of expiation for his antisocial behavior, a sacrifice he finds comparable to Ethan Brand's self-destruction in the lime kiln (51:61). Another reader also links "The Devil" with "Ethan Brand," and with the many other works that embody a pact with the devil, as variations of the Faust myth (447:57–58).

## Interpretations and Criticism

The critical attention paid to this story has been limited in quantity and scope. Biographers have found it useful in providing insights into the first ten years of Hawthorne's experiences as an aspiring writer (63:68; 231:114–17; 272:135; 355:25–78). Some readers use it as an early statement on Hawthorne's view of the artist's position in an essentially hostile society (51:58–59; 32:134–36). One reader employs this story in the course of a book-length analysis that examines Hawthorne's career as a progression toward intimacy with his readers. According to Dauber, Hawthorne seeks intimacy in "The Devil," but he ends up resisting exposure. The story is a conversation with himself: Oberon, a projection of his artistic side, attempts to communicate with the narrator, who is the part of him that seeks social acceptability and also represents the audience for whom the story is intended. At the conclusion, however, the narrator-as-audience has moved away from the "possessed" artist, and the desired communion breaks down (127:56–60). Another reader assesses it as fundamentally comic but with an underlying serious theme: when Oberon says he has been embodying in his creations "the character of a fiend, as represented in our traditions and the written records of witchcraft" (*171.13–15*), he may be admitting to his role as a devil's disciple (189:9). For one other reader who also emphasizes the satanic images in the story, the "singular and inestimable value" of "The Devil" rests in the mythic associations with the devil that it establishes at the core of Hawthorne's artistic imagination (447:57–58). For the majority, however, it is merely a minor work with some revealing biographical overtones.

# XI

# Dr. Heidegger's Experiment

*(Centenary Edition, Volume IX, Twice-told Tales, 227–38.)*

## Publication History

This story was first published in the *Knickerbocker or New York Monthly Magazine* in January 1837 (IX, 27–33) as "The Fountain of Youth," with no attribution. The editor, Lewis G. Clark, who solicited it, wrote to Hawthorne after its publication thanking him with laudatory comments: "I have rarely read anything which delighted me more. The style is excellent and the *keeping* of the whole excellent." Clark invited him to submit more pieces and reminded him that his payment would be forthcoming promptly (223:I, 133). The *Knickerbocker* published "A Bell's Biography" the following March and "Edward Fane's Rosebud" in September, but no record of the amount of payment for any of the *Knickerbocker* contributions has been found. "The Fountain of Youth" was collected the same year in the first edition of *Twice-told Tales* with its title changed to "Dr. Heidegger's Experiment" and "The Fountain of Nature" as a running head *(CE, IX, 571, 496)*.

The author's note, refuting a charge that he had plagiarized the idea for the story from Alexandre Dumas, first appeared in the 1865 Ticknor and Fields edition. Hawthorne had written to his editor, James T. Fields, on September 23, 1860, asking him to append the note, which refers only to "an English review not long since." The review has been identified and reveals the following inconsequential linkage of Hawthorne to Dumas:

> In "Dr. Heidegger's Experiment" (which we fancy may have been suggested by a scene in Dumas' *Memoires d'un Medecin*), we are taught that, if we could renew our youth by some Medean draft, we should, unless altered in other respects, commit the same follies as we have now to look back to. (*Univeral Review*, III, 742–71, cited in 201)

It hardly seems to warrant Hawthorne's vituperative reaction, especially since the dates clearly establish his story as having preceded Dumas's novel, which, incidentally, in no way deals with Hawthorne's main theme spelled out in the review. Gibbens, who ferreted out the alleged charge, seems justified in viewing the incident as a demonstration that "once again . . . even the great are human and fallible" (201).

## Circumstances of Composition, Sources, and Influences

Since Hawthorne was occupied with his editorial duties for the *American Magazine of Useful and Entertaining Knowledge* from January through July of 1836 and had also completed *Peter Parley's Universal History* by September, "Dr. Heidegger's Experiment" was probably written in the fall of 1836 (*CE, IX, 496–99*).

One of the most influential sources for the "elixir of life" theme for Hawthorne must have been William Godwin's *St. Leon*, a novel he read and wrote enthusiastically about to his sister in 1820 (455:lxxxii). His notebooks reflect an early interest in the possibilities of prolonging life. One entry made between October 25, 1835 and August 31, 1836 suggests the fantasy of a man taking his life by installments, ten years of life alternating with ten years of suspended animation (*CE, VIII, 16.6–9*), while two more entries, appearing in the same sequence after August 31, 1836, consider how time devastates a man's accomplishments (*CE, VIII, 22.4–10*) and, conversely, how disastrous the abolition of death would be (*CE, VIII, 23.27–29*). None of these, however, directly parallels the action of "Dr. Heidegger's Experiment." The only entry incorporated in the story occurs a year earlier, between October 17 and 25, 1835: "An old volume in a large library,—every one to be afraid to unclasp and open it, because it was said to be a book of magic" (*CE, VIII, 14.22–24*). It becomes "the greatest curiosity" in Dr. Heidegger's study, "a ponderous folio volume . . . well known to be a book of magic" (*229.9–14*).

This ominous book, the skeleton in the closet, the enchanted liquor, the magic mirror, the moving portrait, and the talking statue are all easily recognizable as the conventional trappings of the Gothic novel (298: 100–01; 152). Faustian elements, often used in conjunction with Gothic devices, are also evident, with Faust's enchanted mirror and the supernaturally prolonged existence of the title character in Charles Robert Maturin's *Melmoth the Wanderer* as notable influences (447:82–83). The ambiguity with which Hawthorne handles the rejuvenation of Dr. Heidegger's four friends can also be traced to Gothic-related sources. Sir Walter Scott's use of "suggestion without affirmation" in *The Bride of Lammermoor* and William Austin's technique of discrediting his witnesses after convincingly conveying an alleged event from their perspective in "Peter Rugg, the Missing Man" have both been cited as models (149:47–52, 251).

Two other suggested sources prove less convincing. Cooke's proposal that Hawthorne is indebted to Swift's portrayal of the Struldbrugs encountered on the third voyage of *Gulliver's Travels* overlooks not only Hawthorne's stated disapproval of Swift as a satirist but a crucial difference between the two narratives. The Struldbrugs succeed only in postponing death, not in eliminating the horrors of old age; what the doctor's four friends seek is eternal youth, not prolonged senility (109:143–45). The other questionable source is an anonymous sketch entitled "The First and Last Dinner" used as a model for descriptive writing in *A Practical System of Rhetoric; or the Principles and Rules of Style* (Portland, 1829) by Samuel Phillips Newman, who was a professor at Bowdoin College when Hawthorne was a student there (221). Hastings suggests the possibility that Hawthorne might have written the piece himself, but the allegation has since been effectively disputed (437).

## Relationship with Other Hawthorne Works

In spite of the fact that Stewart rates the theme of earthly immortality and an elixir of life as one of Hawthorne's four major themes (455:lxxxii), "Dr. Heidegger's Experiment" is the only completed work published by Hawthorne based on that central concept. His determination to deal with the idea of eternal youth is nevertheless clearly evident in his repeated attempts to incorporate aspects of it in other short works, in his preoccupation with it in a host of notebook entries, and in his frustrating efforts to deal with it in two of his last unfinished romances.

"The Wedding Knell" is one example of a corollary that predates "Dr. Heidegger's Experiment"; it offers a prototype for the Widow Wycherly in the vain and foolish Mrs. Dabney who refuses to acknowledge her old age and dresses for her belated wedding as if she were a young bride. The groom's grim celebration of his senility and impending death is also a forerunner of Dr. Heidegger's acceptance of life's inevitable end, although the stories differ considerably in tone. "The Lily's Quest" is another corollary written several years later but based on a notebook entry made at about the time Hawthorne wrote "Dr. Heidegger's Experiment." It again counsels the acceptance of death but transforms resignation into glorification and illustrates one of the extremes Hawthorne could use to resolve the question.

Notebook entries after the publication of "Dr. Heidegger's Experiment" (*CE, VIII, 168.10–12* later in 1837 and *186.1–3* in 1840) indicate Hawthorne had not considered the theme exhausted. The elixir of life reappears in a minor role in "A Virtuoso's Collection" and in "The Birthmark" with Dr. Heidegger's condemnation and rejection repeated in both. Two notes presumably made after the painter Washington Allston died on July 9, 1843 (*CE, VIII, 241.1–5* and *242.12–14*) reverse this outlook and consider the advantages of a prolonged life in cases where great accomplishments might be fulfilled. Still another entry, this one in 1845 (*CE, VIII, 271.25–30*), contemplates the development of the Wandering Jew legend so as to reveal "some great truth."

A memorandum written on the back of a letter from Fields indicates Hawthorne was still debating the issue in July 1863, but the most prolonged and labored argumentation can be found in the sixteen drafts (eight apiece) that Hawthorne wrote of *Septimus Felton* and *The Dolliver Romance* before he died in 1864 (455:lxxxiii–xcvi). Of these two unfinished romances, *Septimus Felton* is most like "Dr. Heidegger's Experiment" in its disapproval of the search for an *elixir vitae*, while *The Dolliver Romance* entertains the possibility that the old apothecary's unselfish motive, his concern for "little Pansie," may have justified his attempts to prolong his life (176). One reader sees another similarity between the story and *Septimus Felton* in the ironic undertone, admittedly not worked out completely in the romance, but nevertheless suggesting the possibility that the whole affair is a delusory cheat (188:112).

Another reader aligns "Dr. Heidegger's Experiment" with "The Prophetic Pictures" as two variations on the concept of character as destiny, based on the four friends' repetition of their youthful follies. He also links the story to "The Birthmark" and "Ethan Brand" on the basis of central characters who are scientists in the Gothic tradition (149:180–91); but he does not include Rappaccini of "Rappaccini's Daughter," who is more similar to Heidegger than either Aylmer or Brand, although the tone of all three stories differs sharply from "Dr Heidegger's Experiment."

## Interpretations and Criticism

Twentieth-century criticism of "Dr. Heidegger's Experiment" ranges from adulation to condemnation. Doubleday calls the story "a little masterpiece, without fault of taste or failure in tone" and commends the author's controlled tension "between the comic surface and the somber implications of the tale" (149:181–82). At the other extreme is Folsom, who finds himself appalled at its superficiality (188:113). The motivation ascribed to the Gothic devices furnishes one key to the disparate responses. If the Gothic phenomena are taken at face value as the author's attempt to convert magic paraphernalia into moral symbols, Maxwell's charge that "the slight narrative sinks under this weightily manipulated symbolism" appears valid (316:90–91). If, on the other hand, the Gothic devices are interpreted as part of Hawthorne's ironic design, the story takes on a skillful subtlety. Such exaggerated heaping-on of Gothic conventions as found in the paragraph describing Dr. Heidegger's study (*228–29*) is more closely related to Jane Austen's parody of the Gothic in *Northanger Abbey* than to the terror-inducing stratagems of the genre itself.

Scanlon's reading enlarges Hawthorne's ironic intent to encompass every phase of the story, from the use of the word *venerable* to describe the doctor's obviously unvenerable friends in the first sentence to his identification of Dr. Heidegger, the inept experimenter and recreator of times past, as a self-caricature of the author's illusory experiments with fiction. Scanlon supports his interpretation of the story as a spoof with detailed documentation of the historical import of the characters' names; Killigrew and Wycherly, for example, are figures related to comedy and amusement, which reinforces the doctor's role as a master of the revels at a masquerade entertainment (409). Another reader who examines "Dr. Heidegger's Experiment" in a search for German romantic irony in Hawthorne's tales, also emphasizes the self-mockery and light tone (305:289–90).

Reservations about serious import notwithstanding (490:90–91), Poe set a precedence of acceptance and approval in 1842 when he called this story "exceedingly well imagined and executed with surpassing ability" (378:17). Since then, such critical luminaries as James in 1879 (241:51) and Matthiessen in 1941 (315:274) have expressed their general approval of it. One of the favorable commentaries generated by "Dr. Heidegger's Experiment" serves as an apt example of the extreme ingenuity resorted to by some Hawthorne enthusiasts in vying for innovative approaches to his works. Schubert envisages the first half of the story and the concluding seventeen lines as a massive, elaborate, rococo frame provided by the artist to enhance "the actual picture (which is the experiment)" and then likens the structure of the experiment episode to the incremental pattern of Ravel's "Bolero." His admission that "criticism of this kind is impressionistic" is appropriately self-incriminating (416:32–34).

# XII

# Drowne's Wooden Image

(*Centenary Edition, Volume X, Mosses from an Old Manse,* 306–20.)

## Publication History

This story was first published in July 1844 in *Godey's Magazine and Lady's Book* (XXXIX, 13–17) under Hawthorne's own name (*CE, X, 578*). On March 11, 1844 he submitted it to the magazine's editor, John Frost, with a letter that set his price for the story at $25 and asked that it be forwarded to John L. O'Sullivan, editor of *The Democratic Review,* if either the price or the story was not satisfactory. Although Hawthorne explains that he complied with Frost's request for a contribution because he considered it good policy for a writer to extend and vary his audience as much as possible, the letter clearly reveals a reluctance to become permanently associated with the popular Philadelphia magazine, which regularly featured the sentimental fiction of Catherine Sedgewick and Mrs. Sarah Hale. "Drowne's Wooden Image" remains Hawthorne's only work to be published in *Godey's (CE, X, 508).* The author included it in *Mosses from an Old Manse* in 1846.

## Circumstances of Composition, Sources, and Influences

Because no external evidence has been found to establish the composition date of this story, when and where Hawthorne wrote it remain conjectural. McDonald, who includes it in the Old Manse-period canon, sets the most likely time between February 16 and March 11, 1844 (323:30). Doubleday, on the other hand, finds it difficult to attribute a tale of unconsummated love to the Old Manse period. He believes its conception and composition came earlier in Hawthorne's career; therefore, he classifies it, with "Roger Malvin's Burial" and "Young Goodman Brown," as one of the early tales Hawthorne added to *Mosses* because he did not have enough current material for the collection (149:186–87). Bell contradicts Doubleday's theory by pointing out that the theme of the dependence of genius on the power of love is most appropriate to Hawthorne's honeymoon period at the Old Manse (47:127). Hawthorne's acute financial stress during the early years of his marriage is another factor to be taken into account. Since he needed to publish as much work as possible, it is not likely that he would have withheld the story had he completed it sooner. The early spring of 1844 remains the most probable time of composition.

The story itself acknowledges its primary source, the Pygmalion myth, when Hawthorne has Copley declare, "Who would have looked for a modern Pygmalion in the person of a Yankee mechanic!" (*312.6–8*). Ovid's *Metamorphoses,* Book X, which Hawthorne would have read in Latin during his school days, undoubtedly introduced him to the legend. He follows Ovid's narrative except for the ending, but converts it to an American setting with an American cast. The sculptor in marble becomes a wood-carver of ship figureheads. One critic credits Ovid's original for what the story says about art as well; Copley's exclamation, "Here is the divine, the life-giving touch!" echoes Ovid's description of the statue which was perfect enough to look like the work of nature (149:190–91).

Washington Irving and William Austin, two contemporaneous writers who successfully Americanized old world legends, could well have provided models for Hawthorne's adaptation. Austin's popular story, "Peter Rugg, the Missing Man" (1824), may have also encouraged Hawthorne's ambivalent style in which the preternatural is suggested but not affirmed; in any case, the Flying Dutchman's transformation into Boston's Peter Rugg follows a pattern that Hawthorne found remarkably congenial to his own talents (149:49–52, 187–89).

Deacon Shem Drowne (1684–1774) and John Singleton Copley (who left Boston to live in England in 1774) supply the historically identifiable names that Hawthorne gives to two of his key characters. The historical Drowne was a coppersmith and prominent citizen of Boston, best known for his famous grasshopper weather vane on Faneuil Hall. Hawthorne probably used his name because his first readers would have recognized the man as a relatively untutored artisan, put the fictional Drowne may also be based on Joseph True, who was a wood-carver in Salem during Hawthorne's time. Hawthorne's readers would also have recognized Copley's name because he was a well-known and established painter; as such, he portrays a celebrity whose comments add authority to the story as a statement on art (149:187–88).

## Relationship with Other Hawthorne Works

The story with which "Drowne's Wooden Image" is most often coupled is "The Artist of the Beautiful"; both are versions of the Pygmalion legend (304; 391), and both explore the relationship between the artist and his art. Because Hawthorne's habitual concern with the artist's relationship to society plays no part in "Drowne's Wooden Image" but is crucially important in "The Artist of the Beautiful," the latter has received much more attention as a statement of the author's view of the artist. Doubleday, for example, dismisses "Drowne's Wooden Image" as a vehicle for Hawthorne's aesthetic theories and recommends "The Artist of the Beautiful" as a different, and more valid, expression of Hawthorne's ideas on the subject (149:191). Bell concurs, but for her the significant difference between the two stories lies in Drowne's brief encounter with art as opposed to Owen Warland's lifetime commitment (47:134). A vigorous minority objects to these comparisons in which "Drowne's Wooden Image" is usually allotted second place. Bewley believes that "The Artist of the Beautiful" is less successful because of the irrelevant democratic distractions with which Hawthorne distorts the significance of artistic creation; he prefers "Drowne's Wooden Image" precisely because "Hawthorne does not trouble himself about Drowne's relationship to the community" (52:135–38). In direct opposition to Bell's assessment, Baym believes that Drowne represents the kind of total dedication to art against which Hawthorne measures Owen—and finds him wanting (43:112).

Other works that follow a transformation motif and also make aesthetic implications are "The Snow-Image," "The Prophetic Pictures," "Feather-top," and *The Marble Faun* (304; 391). Like "Drowne's Wooden Image," "The Snow-Image" portrays a statue that comes alive through love; the children, like Drowne, cannot rationally account for the lifelike qualities of their creation or the ease with which she took shape. In contrast, "The Prophetic Pictures" demonstrates how art without human compassion can alienate the artist and change love and hope to fear and despair (47:81–85, 126–27).

Drowne's figurehead, the snow maiden, and the prophetic pictures are all related to one of the conventions of the Gothic genre, the work of art with unusual powers. Similar phenomena can be found in "Edward Randolph's Portrait," "Sylph Etherege," *The House of Seven Gables*, and *The Marble Faun* (47:78–81).

In an unusual combination, "Drowne's Wooden Image" joins "The Great Stone Face" to serve as a demonstration of how Hawthorne's moral and aesthetic views shade into each other. Both Ernest's wisdom and Drowne's figurehead are the results of imitating an ideal, but the ideal in each remains a mystery knowable only in its earthly expression (188:34–35).

## Interpretations and Criticism

Critical response to "Drowne's Wooden Image" has centered primarily on Hawthorne's portrayal of the artist. Doubleday's protest that "the tale is not a treatise in aesthetic theory" has gone unheeded, even by Doubleday himself; he applies Drowne's statement, that it is the artist's business to find the hidden form within his materials, to Hawthorne's own historical fiction, an artistic process that allows "the hidden shape" of history to reveal itself (149:191). Similar positive interpretations of Hawthorne's romantic portrayal of the creative process abound. To McElderry, it is "unequivocally transcendental," embracing an inspirational theory not only for art but for all human experience (324:319–20); to Bewley, it is one of Hawthorne's "most appealing" stories, "a splendid statement on the selflessness of the artist and the impersonality of art" (52:136–38); and to Baym, it "points the way to a vision of art as a fully serious, absorbing enterprise." She calls it "an augur of the future," to the time when Hawthorne would, by following Drowne's example of total submission to artistic inspiration, produce his own masterpiece, *The Scarlet Letter* (43:111–12).

In a different vein, Stein emphasizes the brevity of Drowne's genius and the spiritual lethargy that precedes and follows his short-lived burst of creativity. Stein does not belittle the story; he admires the "marvelous skill" with which Hawthorne symbolizes the carver's defeat to the devil of negation, but he arbitrarily reverses the traditional Faust compact to fit his overall thesis (447:96–97).

Cowie's analysis does not concern itself with the portrayal of the artist figure. He uses the story to illustrate Hawthorne's method—what he calls "a deliberate flight from reality." The realistic details with which Hawthorne opens the story, "a craftsman, a client, and an oak log," become lost as he develops his fantasy, primarily with the conscious aim of demonstrating a moral truth (110:351–52).

Primarily, however, it is as an artist story that "Drowne's Wooden Image" is most significant. In many ways, it is the clearest statement in all of Hawthorne's fiction of how the creative artist creates. It merits more attention than it has been given; the questions it raises and the answers it suggests are as exciting as any proposed in the more widely read stories. "Drowne's Wooden Image" may be one of Hawthorne's as yet "undiscovered" masterpieces.

# XIII
# Edward Fane's Rosebud

(*Centenary Edition, Volume IX, Twice-told Tales,* 463–71.)

## Publication History

This story was first published in the *Knickerbocker, or New York Monthly Magazine* in September 1837 (X, 195–99) with no attribution in spite of the publication of *Twice-told Tales* in Hawthorne's name in the preceding March. A letter from Lewis G. Clark, the magazine's editor, implies that Hawthorne was paid promptly for his *Knickerbocker* contributions ("Dr. Heidegger's Experiment" and "A Bell's Biography" appeared earlier in the same year), but the amount is unknown. The author included this story in the second volume of the second edition of *Twice-told Tales* in 1842 (*CE, IX, 496–99, 514, 573*).

## Circumstances of Composition, Sources, and Influences

This story was probably written in the winter or spring of 1837 (84:22). Its germ is clearly stated in an undated notebook entry made between September 7 and October 17, 1835:

> A change from a gay young girl to an old woman; the melancholy events, the effects of which have clustered around her character, and gradually imbued it with their influences, till she becomes a lover of sick-chambers, taking pleasure in receiving dying breaths and in laying out the dead; also having her mind full of funeral reminiscences, and possessing more acquaintances beneath the burial turf than above it. (*CE, VIII, 10.17–23*)

At this point in his career with his first collection in his own name either in press or just out, Hawthorne was especially sensitive to his audience's expectations. "Edward Fane's Rosebud" appears to be one of his performances designed to give his readers what he thought they wanted—in this instance, pathos with a moral (43:53–93).

## Relationship with Other Hawthorne Works

Unfulfilled love and death dominate "Edward Fane's Rosebud" as they do a group of *Twice-told Tales* with a similar theme—"The Wedding Knell," "The White Old Maid," and "The Shaker Burial" (280:58). Widow Toothaker, formerly Rosebud, presents an early, negative counterpart to Hester Prynne of *The Scarlet Letter*. She is like Hester in that she marries a man much older than herself and spends most of her life caring for the sick, but Rosebud is more conventionally moralistic, pathetic rather than heroic. She comes to love her aged, infirm husband and spends her widowhood with the dying, while Hester finds fulfillment in her young lover and their child and becomes renowned for effecting cures.

## Interpretations and Criticism

In the May 1841 issue of his magazine, *Arcturus*, Evert A. Duyckinck presented an excerpt from "Edward Fane's Rosebud" to prepare the way for the 1842 edition of *Twice-told Tales*. He concluded his encomium of Hawthorne with a statement that sums up this story's essential effects: "The distinctive mark of Hawthorne's writings, is a fanciful pathos delighting in sepulchral images" (98:7). What Duyckinck regarded as praiseworthy, twentieth-century readers are more apt to dismiss as "anemic" (315:231) or a failure (490:90). One critic defends the story, and nine other pieces that he classifies as "illustrated ideas," on a generic basis, maintaining that Hawthorne's intent was to write an essay, not a short story. As such, he finds the Widow Toothaker serving the author's purpose effectively, her dramatic situation appropriately subordinated to the idea being presented (510:32).

This story remains most useful, however, as a foil for Hawthorne's most fully developed female character, Hester in *The Scarlet Letter*. Rosebud provides an illuminating contrast to Hester by equating stereotyped piety with stasis and death, thereby highlighting the positive aspects of Hawthorne's most attractive sinner.

# XIV
# Edward Randolph's Portrait

*(Centenary Edition, Volume IX, Twice-told Tales, 256–70.)*

## Publication History

This story was first published in July 1838 in *United States Magazine and Democratic Review* (II, 360–69) as No. II of "Tales of the Province-House" and attributed to the author of *Twice-told Tales*. All available evidence indicates that Hawthorne was paid approximately $2 per page for his contributions to John L. O'Sullivan's *Democratic Review*. (See publication history of "Howe's Masquerade," the first of the Province-House stories.) At this rate, the pay for "Edward Randolph's Portrait" would have been $20. In 1842, the story was included in the second volume of the second edition of *Twice-told Tales* with its subtitle changed to "Legends of the Province-House II" (*CE, IX, 571*).

## Circumstances of Composition, Sources, and Influences

"Edward Randolph's Portrait" was probably completed in early June 1838 (84:26). In a letter dated June 1, 1838, Sophia Peabody tells her sister, Elizabeth, of Hawthorne's visit the day before; she writes: "I never saw him look so brilliantly *rayonnant*. He said to me, '*Your story* will be finished soon, Sophia—tomorrow or next day'" (273:17–18). Julian Hawthorne quotes an extract from the same series of letters that helps to identify the story as "Edward Randolph's Portrait": "Mr. Hawthorne . . . said he had imagined a story of which the principal incident is my cleaning that picture of Fernandez. To be the means, in any way, of calling forth one of his divine creations is no small happiness" (223:I, 185). In some ways, Sophia may have served as a model for Alice Vane (84:26; 231:150), but Hawthorne's fascination with old portraits, especially those of historical figures, pre-dates his newly established friendship with Sophia in 1838. Sometime between August 22 and October 7 the year before, he had recorded his reactions to a visit to the Essex Historical Society in Salem: "In the cabinet . . . old portraits.—Governor Leverett; a dark moustachioed face . . . altogether very striking. . . . Nothing gives a stronger idea of old worm-eaten aristocracy . . . than these black, dusty, faded, antique-dressed portraits" (*CE, VIII, 154.14–155.20*). Sophia may also have influenced Hawthorne's writing of "Edward Randolph's Portrait" in another way. Her Cuban journal, kept during her 1834 extended visit at one of the island's great estates, could have suggested a contemporaneous application for the lessons of American colonial history; Hutchinson's predicament may have been intended as a forecast of the fate of the wealthy Cuban colonials who faced similar problems (47:83; 78:233–56).

But whatever nineteenth-century target Hawthorne may have intended, the source for the eighteenth-century incident central to the story is much closer to home—Thomas Hutchinson's own account, told from the perspective of an historian, of his decision in 1770 to carry out King George's order to garrison Castle William in Boston harbor with royal troops. Hutchinson's "antiquarian researches" (*261.25–26*) and devotion to "historic truth" (*262.19*) are noted in the story itself. In his book, *The History of the Colony and Province of Massachusetts Bay*, Hutchinson calls his dismissal of the provincial troops from Castle Williams "one of the most difficult affairs to manage, that happened during the lieutenant-governor's administration" (III, 222). One reader suggests that Hawthorne refrained from a more sympathetic depiction of Hutchinson's dilemma because he was writing his story for publication in the *Democratic Review*, a magazine notable for its strong nationalistic philosophy (149:125–26). The tale's second historical center involves an earlier troubled relationship between a representative of the Crown and New England, that is, the colonists' hatred of Edward Randolph whose career between 1676 and 1703 was dominated by his efforts to collect the king's customs and to get Parliament to annul Massachusetts' charter. Randolph's "continual watch upon the colony" is also documented in Hutchinson's *History* (I, 278–79). In the course of the "divers times" that Randolph sailed back to England with complaints and returned with "fresh orders and powers," two of Hawthorne's ancestors, Major William Hathorne and his son, Colonel John Hathorne, were among those singled out for special rebuke (293:86, 105). A passage in "The Gray Champion," published three years before "Edward Randolph's Portrait," reveals Hawthorne's prior acquaintance with Randolph's reputation; in fact, part of the description of the officials of Sir Edmund Andros' administration in 1689 may be the germ for this story (149:126). It identifies Randolph as "our arch-enemy, that 'blasted wretch,' as Cotton Mather calls him, who achieved the downfall of our ancient government, and was followed with a sensible curse, through life and to his grave" (*IX, 13.1–4*).

One detail in the nineteenth-century frame that closes "Edward Randolph's Portrait" can be traced to Hawthorne's experience in Boston itself. The narrator's plunge into a "drifting snow-storm" may be an echo of a visit Hawthorne paid to another Boston retreat where he had likewise warmed himself in front of a fire and indulged in reminiscences of the past. James T. Fields records having found him, "in the early period of our acquaintance," in the old Boston Exchange Coffee-House in Devonshire Street "shut up there before a blazing coal-fire, in the 'tumultuous privacy' of a great snowstorm, reading with apparent intereset an obsolete copy of the 'Old Farmer's Almanac,' which he had picked up about the house" (182:54).

The strongest literary influence on "Edward Randolph's Portrait" is unquestionably the Gothic novel (149:123–28; 298:103–04). A portrait with supernatural powers is a stock device traceable as far back as the first work in the genre, Walpole's *Castle of Otranto*. A later example of the convention is to be found in Scott's *The Bride of Lammermoor* (47:81), but the Gothic writer whose influence is most pervasive in this story is Ann Radcliffe. Hawthorne follows her technique of the "explained supernatural" when he suggests that Alice Vane's skill at restoring paintings is responsible for the portrait's temporary illumination. And the black silk veil that covers the portrait and is snatched away to reveal a horrifying sight is an exact parallel to an incident, in *The Mysteries of Udolpho*, made infamous by Jane Austen's ridicule of it in her Gothic parody, *Northanger Abbey*. A curse from the past and blood are two final Gothic touches incorporated into Hutchinson's death scene when he feels himself choking on the blood of the Boston Massacre.

## Relationship with Other Hawthorne Works

"Edward Randolph's Portrait" is most closely associated with the other three "Tales of the Province-House"—"Howe's Masquerade" that precedes it and "Lady Eleanore's Mantle" and "Old Esther Dudley" that follow. The three paragraphs that open the story and the one that closes it are a part of the continuing framework that holds the series together. The Province-House stories as an integrated unit have received considerable critical attention; these commentaries are reviewed under "Relationship with Other Hawthorne Works" for the first legend, "Howe's Masquerade," and for the last, "Old Esther Dudley."

"Edward Randolph's Portrait" shares a few specific similarities with "Old Esther Dudley." In each, the female protagonist has been interpreted as an artist-magician figure, comparable to Hawthorne himself (189:43) and in some ways to the painter in "The Prophetic Pictures" (47:81–83). The two legends also demonstrate Gothic devices that Hawthorne later used in *The House of Seven Gables* (149:134–37).

The Gothic features in "Edward Randolph's Portrait" that reappear in the novel include a magical portrait, blood, a curse from the past, a castlelike house, and superstitious belief in demonic powers. A letter to Fields, the publisher, reveals that Hawthorne knew what he was about in using such a stock array; a romance writer, the author explains, "is always, or always ought to be, careering on the utmost verge of a precipitous absurdity, and the skill lies in coming as close as possible, without actually tumbling over" (182:56). In "Edward Randolph's Portrait" and in *The House of Seven Gables*, Hawthorne takes the risk. Another aspect of the novel related to this story is the characterization of Alice Pyncheon and Priscilla. Both are versions of one of Hawthorne's recurrent types representatively embodied in Alice Vane. She is "a pale, ethereal creature, who ... seemed ... almost a being from another world" (*259.13–16*), a description that links her to the earlier prototypes in "Sylph Etherege" and "The Lily's Quest" (455:lviii).

## Interpretations and Criticism

The most negative assessment of "Edward Randolph's Portrait" comes from Doubleday. He believes Hawthorne fails to capitalize on the tragic possibilities of Hutchinson's dilemma by ignoring the governor's difficult position as a native Bostonian whose devotion to his fellow countrymen is at odds with his allegiance to the king. Doubleday also objects to the ineptness with which Hawthorne uses the Gothic conventions, labeling his extravagance "contemptuous" and interpreting it as an "ironic recognition" of how worn the devices had become (149:123–28).

While this story has not netted itself any voluminous acclaim to literary excellence, others who have commented on it have chosen to emphasize its merits, limited as they may be. Stein admires the "ineffable ingenuity" with which Hawthorne deepens the significance of a historic moment in New England history by equating Hutchinson's signature on the king's order with the signing away of one's soul to the devil (477:76–77). Schubert acclaims the story's dramatic color contrasts, explicitly the use of Alice, "clad entirely in white" (*259.13*), as a foil for the "void blackness" (*258.30*) of the picture (416:104–05). Bell praises the way Puritan dogma imbues the narrative with an atmosphere of seventeenth-century moral judgments; when Hawthorne has Hutchinson dismiss Randolph's alliance with the devil as one of Dr. Cotton Mather's "old women's tales" (*262.20–24*), the author invokes Puritan prejudices to suggest Puritan faith. Bell also credits the magic portrait with contributing to Hawthorne's theme of the power of art (47:81–83).

A related interpretation describes the "legend-tinged portrait" as an "analogue of Hawthorne's art, working on the imagination of its viewers as Hawthorne would have his tale work on his readers"; Alice is Hawthorne's counterpart, transmitting the lessons of history by revealing an image of the past. In this reading, Fossum suggests that Hawthorne is asking whether the evil that art revivifies might not better be left hidden and, ultimately, whether guiltless choices are ever possible (189:38–40, 42). Another reader focuses on this same issue of difficult choices but applies it to Hawthorne's attitude toward the American Revolution. Smith reads Hawthorne's portrayal of Hutchinson as essentially "fair"; the governor is an honorable man faced with the threat of mob rebellion. Here, as in the other Province-House stories, a basic ambivalence about the colonists' rebellion is subtly but unmistakably demonstrated (435:34–36).

The most ingenious interpretation of "Edward Randolph's Portrait" is a psychoanalytical one by Dauber, who sees "the dirty picture that hangs on the wall" as "an objectification outside the body of the magical powers of excremental manipulation." Accordingly, the story becomes a study in anality, a diagnosis confirmed by Hutchinson's display of aggressiveness which fits the behavior pattern Freud identifies with the anal state. The governor's aggressiveness is evident, covertly, in his writing of history (one way of becoming his own father) and, overtly, in his signing the order to mobilize the army. Randolph is Hutchinson's second self, a projection of a suppressed devil of the unconscious, and the portrait is "the dead self excreted" or, in Norman O. Brown's words, the "constipating past." The blood that chokes Hutchinson at the end points to the oral stage to be explored in the next Province-House story, "Lady Eleanore's Mantle"; the pattern from anality to orality helps to establish Dauber's thesis that the "Legends" as a series recapitulate a progressively regressive psychohistorical development (127:72–75).

For the average reader the value of "Edward Randolph's Portrait" probably will not rest on such an esoteric reading. As an example of Hawthorne's conflation of the Gothic and American history, the story offers a challenging array of questions that touch on some fundamental issues in Hawthorne studies. How effective is his adaptation of Gothic devices to the facts of the past? Why does he choose to portray verifiable events in deliberately nonverifiable terms? What is his attitude toward history? Toward the past? Toward the American Revolution? Toward art? This story offers relatively unexploited territory that invites further scrutiny. It may hold insights into its author's concerns and techniques that the more overworked historical pieces (such as "My Kinsman, Major Molineux") have not provided. It is not likely, however, that the status of "Edward Randolph's Portrait" will change very much. Its consummate artistry will remain debatable, but its array of Hawthorne idiosyncrasies offers an inviting challenge to the reader looking for a part of the Hawthorne canon on which he can still test his critical perceptions without being hopelessly engulfed by a host of predecessors.

# XV

# Egotism; or, The Bosom-Serpent

*(Centenary Edition, Volume X, Mosses from an Old Manse, 268–83).*

## Publication History

This story was first published in March 1843 in the *United States Magazine and Democratic Review* (XII, 255–61) under Hawthorne's own name. No exact record of how much Hawthorne was paid for it has been found; if the $100 received from the magazine's editor, John L. O'Sullivan, in December was the total payment for the six pieces published in the *Democratic Review* in 1843, "Egotism" would have netted $17.50, or approximately half of the standard magazine rate of $5 per page. (See publication history of "The Christmas Banquet" for Hawthorne's financial plight during the Old Manse years.) "Egotism" was included in *Mosses from an Old Manse* in 1846 (*CE, X, 577, 504–06*).

## Circumstances of Composition, Sources, and Influences

"Egotism" was probably written during the first two weeks of February 1843, begun after Hawthorne's completion of "The Birthmark" on February 1 and finished in time for the copy to reach the *Democratic Review* for its March issue (323:25). The fact that Sophia Peabody had become Hawthorne's wife only seven months earlier is undoubtedly reflected in the highly idealized portrayal of Elliston's wife. Her love "saves" the protagonist, a development easily attributable to Hawthorne's own newly found marital happiness (430:112–13).

Two notebook entries are directly related to this story. The first was written between October 25, 1836 and the end of the first 1837 notebook: "A snake, taken into a man's stomach and nourished there from fifteen years to thirty-five, tormenting him most horribly. A type of envy or some other evil passion" (*CE, VIII, 22.1–3*). The second appears over five years later, between January 23 and June 1, 1842: "A man to swallow a small snake—and it to be a symbol of a cherished sin" (*CE, VIII, 228.6–7*). However, Hawthorne's allusion to a bosom serpent predates the first notebook germ by four years; in "Roger Malvin's Burial," published in 1832, the protagonist's secret guilt is likened to "a serpent, gnawing into his heart" (*CE, X, 350.9–10*) (401).

The author himself provides a source for "Egotism" in his introductory footnote: "The physical fact, to which it is here attempted to give a moral signification, has been known to occur in more than one instance." No fewer than fourteen source studies have subsequently attempted to supplement Hawthorne's explanation; one 1975 review alone supplies twenty-three new citations in English literature that could have inspired Hawthorne's serpent (59). A multiplicity of influences undoubtedly helped to shape this symbol. Among the most significant are the first book of Spenser's *Faerie Queene*, the writings of Puritan theologians, and folklore accounts, encompassing medical, journalistic, and oral versions. Spenser's description of envy is generally accepted as the most likely origin for Hawthorne's image: "And in his bosome secretly there lay/ An hatefull snake, the which his taile uptyes/ In many folds, and mortall sting implyes" (*Faerie Queene*, I, iv, 31, quoted in 456:198). Parallels in plot, details, characters, and metaphorical themes strengthen the case that Spenser's legend of the Red Crosse Knight is a model for Elliston's tale (427). Several prominent Puritan theologians also use instances of serpent-infested breasts—Increase Mather in *Remarkable Providences* (482:545–50), Cotton Mather in his introduction to *Magnalia Christi Americana* (401), Thomas Shepard in *The Sincere Convert* (517), and Thomas Hooker, whose imagery specifically equates the serpent's activity with the pangs of conscience (74). Hawthorne's own footnote attests to some sort of nonliterary basis. Several seventeenth-century medical reports and at least five contemporaneous newspaper and magazine accounts have been cited, all of which detail cases where snakes, eels, and other assorted vipers were ingested and remained alive in a human's digestive system (218; 340; 74). A folklorist who compares three newspaper versions with collected oral variants comes to the conclusion that none is completely factual and that Hawthorne's immediate source may have been oral rather than published (37). Barnes also analyzes how Hawthorne adapts and transcends the folkloristic data (the empirical modes of entry, the physical characteristics of the snake, the remedies to expel it) to begin the literary tradition of the folk legend (35). Others emphasize Hawthorne's debt to his predecessors, not his originality; they simply define Hawthorne's place within a long-standing continuum, one that includes such disparate contributors as Aesop and Virgil (59), the medieval emblem tradition (338), Shakespeare and Milton (59), and Sir Walter Scott (149.46–47). A story called "Possessed of a Devil," which appeared in the December 1835 issue of *New-England Magazine*, has also been cited as an influence. Its plot, minus the celebrated serpent, is much like

Hawthorne's, and it may have served as an example of what the reading public expected in the popular magazines where his stories were being published (314).

## Relationship with Other Hawthorne Works

"Egotism" and "The Christmas Banquet" are the two stories that are subtitled "From the Unpublished 'Allegories of the Heart.' " The reference is apparently to a collection that never materialized, although heart imagery emerges throughout Hawthorne's fiction as an important symbolic device (430). Roderick, from "Egotism," is the narrator of "The Christmas Banquet," with Rosina and the sculptor as his audience, but the story that he tells is different from his own. The protagonist of "The Christmas Banquet" does not emerge from suffering into joy; he lives and dies with a "cold heart" that knows neither suffering nor joy.

Roderick is more closely related to those of Hawthorne's characters who are emblematic of secret sin such as Reuben of "Roger Malvin's Burial," Hooper of "The Minister's Black Veil," and Dimmesdale of *The Scarlet Letter*. When Dimmesdale develops the habit of holding his hand over his heart, his gesture is akin to Roderick's more violent clutching of his breast (455:xlvii–xlviii). Roderick is also like Hooper in his preoccupation with the evil in others, an obsession shared by "Young Goodman Brown" and "The Man of Adamant" as well. Roderick is unique among Hawthorne's sinners in that he accepts Rosina's help, overcomes his egotism, and emerges from his isolation. Other parallel figures who do not are "Ethan Brand," Aylmer of "The Birthmark," Rappaccini of "Rappaccini's Daughter," and Chillingworth of *The Scarlet Letter* (32:53; 43:109; 245; 333:212–13).

Hawthorne's use of the serpent to symbolize egotism is characteristic of his other attempts to find physical equivalents for spiritual phenomena. Examples include the butterfly in "The Artist of the Beautiful," the veil in "The Minister's Black Veil," the mantle in "Lady Eleanore's Mantle," the marble heart in "Ethan Brand," the petrified "Man of Adamant," and the melted "Snow-Image."

## Interpretations and Criticism

In 1850, this story helped introduce Melville to Hawthorne when, four years after its publication, Melville read *Mosses from an Old Manse* for the first time. Melville's enthusiastically favorable review singles out "The Bosom-Serpent" (and its allegorical companion, "The Christmas

Banquet") as "fine subjects" with which to explore the dark side of Hawthorne's soul—"the other side . . . shrouded in a blackness, ten times black." Melville points to Hawthorne's "mystical blackness" as a means of "wondrous effects" in "lights and shades" as well as a source of "great power" stemming from the "Calvinistic sense of Innate Depravity and Original Sin." His praise is extravagant; he sees a kinship between Hawthorne's "power of darkness" and Shakespeare's, defending such a comparison by avowing that "the difference between the two men is by no means immeasurable" (332, collected in 98:32–35).

All do not join Melville in his unqualified acclamation. Hawthorne, himself, when he was proofreading *Mosses* for a new edition in 1854, expresses some dismay over his "blasted allegories." (See "Rappaccini's Daughter.") Other readers have more often shared the author's misgivings than Melville's euphoric acceptance. James, for example, finds "something stiff and mechanical, slightly incongruous" in "Egotism," "as if the kernel had not assimilated its envelope" (241:51); Doubleday calls it "one of Hawthorne's least happy allegories" (149:46); and Von Abele diagnoses its ethnically based symbolism as a symptom of Hawthorne's artistic disintegration, an early sign of the disorder and chaotic symbolism that mar his unfinished novels (497). A few have found it admirable, or at least noteworthy. Mathews believes that "the bizarre central idea is handled with taste and restraint, the story has sound psychological insight and dramatic intensity" and that Hawthorne successfully converts popular motifs into "unique and lasting art" (314:160). Fogle admires the contrast created between the dark fantasy of the serpent and the light of Rosina's love (186:4). But more often than not, the story's virtues are offset by corresponding faults. What one reader hails as "meritorious" (427), another perceives as a defect (156). For Shroeder, the story is "an unqualified expression of Christian optimism" not to be matched elsewhere in Hawthorne's writings (427); for Durr, it is a failure because there is no ironic counterpoise to balance the dead seriousness and exaggerated effects (156).

Two interpretations challenge Durr's charge in an unusual way. They suggest specific and deliberate satiric targets—Poe in one case (306), Jones Very in the other (25). The internal evidence supporting "Egotism" as a personal satire on Poe is startling. Parallels exist between it and the names, characterizations, and devices in Poe's stories, many of which have long been established as autobiographical. For example, a debilitated and anguished protagonist named Roderick is found in "The Fall of the House of Usher" and a writhing "Conqueror Worm" in "Ligeia" (306). The other example on which Roderick Elliston may be modeled is the Salem poet and mystic, Jones Very. Very's spiritual pride and isolation are pointed out explicitly by Hawthorne in another piece, "The Hall of Fantasy," and many incidents in Very's life, such as a brief stay as a patient in an insane asylum, are the same as Roderick's (25). Both interpretations are more fascinating than conclusive.

For many American-literature buffs of today, the possibility that Roderick Elliston is intended to satirize Poe may be a single redeeming aspect. Without such a novel twist, most readers find "Egotism" as difficult to accept as James did. Yet in his short story, "The Jolly Corner," James echoes "Egotism" both in the protagonist's alienation and secret fears and in the use of a woman's love as a redeeming force in its conclusion (478). Like James, the modern reader feels the need to improve on Hawthorne's story, to liberate the kernel somehow from its unassimilated envelope and find a more compatible vehicle for it. One reader uses "Egotism" to illustrate how Hawthorne combines two apparently disparate worlds— everyday reality and Platonic truth (188:80–82). But the average reader is more apt to respond to the absurdity of Hawthorne's symbolic reality, not to its "paradoxical truth."

# XVI

# Endicott and the Red Cross

*(Centenary Edition, Volume IX, Twice-told Tales, 433–41.)*

## Publication History

This story was first published in the fall of 1837 in *The Token and Atlantic Souvenir* (pp. 69–78) dated 1838 with no attribution. Hawthorne's pay for this and four other pieces in the same edition is uncertain; the editor, Samuel Goodrich, may never have paid him at all. (See publication history of "Peter Goldthwaite's Treasure.") "Endicott and the Red Cross" was collected in the second volume of the second edition of *Twice-told Tales* in 1842 (*CE, IX, 574*).

## Circumstances of Composition, Sources, and Influences

This story was probably written in the early fall of 1837 (149:101). The central incident, the rending of the red cross from the flag of England by the Puritan leader of the colonial militia company in Salem, is based on a verifiable event in the history of the Massachusetts Bay Colony and the career of John Endecott (circa 1589–1665: Hawthorne uses Endicott spelling). On or about November 5, 1634, Endicott defaced the king's colors because he objected to serving under a flag with a cross on it. To the Puritans, such a symbol was idolatry and a part of the popery they had left England to escape. Hawthorne combines Endicott's display of religious scruples with another historical event recorded in Governor Winthrop's journal on September 18, 1634. Winthrop had on that day received a copy of a commission from King Charles I that would impose the discipline of the Church of England, a new governor, and tyrannical regulatory powers on the colonists (195).

Hawthorne could have read about the two occurrences in Governor Winthrop's *Journal*, Thomas Hutchinson's *History of Massachusetts*, or Joseph B. Felt's *Annals of Salem*, but Felt's *Annals* seems the likeliest source because it gives an account (1st ed., p. 73) of a meeting of the court in Salem, about two weeks after the flag episode, in which both matters were discussed (149:102). Felt's book also provides many of the details for the Puritan punishments described in the story as well as the reference to the wolf's head nailed to the porch of the meetinghouse as a means of claiming the bounty (149:103; 358). The sources are equally significant for what Hawthorne does not use because his manipulation of history is flagrantly evident here. Endicott's act was censured, not praised, by a special committee assigned to consider the incident; they "adjudged him worthy of admonition, and to be disabled for one year from bearing any public office; declining any heavier sentence, because they were persuaded he did it out of tenderness of conscience, and not of any evil intent" (Winthrop's *Journal*, ed. James Savage, 1853, I, 149–50). Another historical inaccuracy is the depiction of Roger Williams as elderly and moderate because, in fact, in 1634 Williams was only thirty-one and, according to Hutchinson and Cotton Mather, it was Williams' heated oratory that incited Endicott to deface the flag (195). Williams did, however, stand for tolerance. As "the first rebel against the divine church order established in the wilderness" (in Cotton Mather's words), he was forced to leave the following year, whereupon he took refuge with the Indians and founded Rhode Island in accordance with his liberal principles (275:45). Hawthorne was surely aware of all the facts; he followed them closely enough in *Grandfather's Chair* (46:57; 149:104). His purpose has been variously interpreted, but all agree that he changed the historical material deliberately to conform to his intent.

The historical accounts by Felt and Winthrop touch on Hawthorne's ancestral connections with Endicott. One ancestor, William Hathorne, served under Endicott for thirteen years as an assistant magistrate for Essex County, and William Hathorne's sister, Elizabeth, was married to Richard Davenport who was the ensign-bearer for the Salem company of militia and was initially charged with defacing the flag before Endicott assumed responsibility almost immediately (149:93, 102). In a notebook entry made sometime between August 22 and October 7, 1837, Hawthorne describes the "striking" old portraits on display in the Essex Historical Society, including one of Endicott (*CE, VIII, 154.24, 590*; Endicott's picture is still in the collection held by the Essex Institute in Salem).

Hawthorne's reliance on Puritan typology to present Puritan-American history seems particularly appropriate. Endicott's breastplate is such a "type," its prefiguration traceable to the "breastplate of judgment" that Moses had made for his brother Aaron (Exod. 28:21, 25:8; Lev. 8:8–15). Endicott's breastplate embodies the fusion of the roles of high priest and governor, taking its fundamental meaning from its association with the Israelite theocracy (49). A more startling analogue for the breastplate is the one used by the devil in John Bunyan's *Holy War*. Bercovitch establishes some clear correspondence between Hawthorne's

Endicott and Bunyan's Diabolus (48), while another reader detects unmistakable resemblances to Milton's Satan (189:34). According to Bell,
Endicott's portrayal may also have been influenced by the figure of the
stern but noble founding father which was a dominant conventional
character of the historical romance of New England in Hawthorne's day.
Endicott's courageous independence interwined with a self-righteous
intolerance follows the noble but narrow mold of the fictional predecessors (46:56–60, 109). Another possible analogue has been found in
Book V of Spenser's *Faerie Queene* (527).

## Relationship with Other Hawthorne Works

*The Scarlet Letter* is the work most often associated with "Endicott
and the Red Cross" because among the sinners being punished in the
story is "a young woman, with no mean share of beauty, whose doom it
was to wear the letter A on the breast of her gown, in the eyes of all the
world and her own children" (*435.22–24*). In addition to this clear early
prototype for Hester and the symbolic *A*, Endicott's story, written thirteen years before the novel, also prefigures two other symbols, the pillory
and the breastplate. The latter is used in chapter seven where it hangs
on the wall in Governor Bellingham's mansion and acts as a reflecting
device, as in the story, except that it also distorts and exaggerates Hester's
*A* (149:108). Leavis notes another parallel between the "few stately
savages, in all the pomp and dignity of the primeval Indian" who "stood
gazing at the spectacle" (*436.9–10*) and the party of Indians who watch
the governor's inauguration in chapter twenty-one of *The Scarlet Letter*.
More important, Leavis believes that the short story is the "kernel" of
the romance and that the author's concerns in both are primarily sociological and not moral. Hester's experiences, like the "sinners" undergoing
grotesque punishments in the story, become a "measure of the inhumanity" of Puritan society (275:43–45).

Readers with a historical bent will appreciate Leavis's chronological
accounting of some of Hawthorne's best-known works that deal with
America's past:

> *Endicott* comes in historical time after *The Maypole* (which
> begins with the first settlers) and is contemporary with *The Scarlet
> Letter*. They are both supposed to occur in the reign of Charles I,
> the age when the colonists felt menaced by the threatened
> Romanization of England by Laud and the royal family. *Endicott*

is followed by *The Gray Champion* which ends with the overthrow
of James II and that in turn is followed by *Major Molineux,* the
prophecy of the Revolution. (275:43)

She also emphasizes "Endicott" as a sequel to "The May-Pole of Merry
Mount" with the armored Puritans who were victorious at Merry Mount
in control and with Roger Williams serving a function similar to Blackstone's in spite of their obvious differences (275:43–44). The twentieth-
century poet Robert Lowell apparently saw the same parallels and
sequences because in his trilogy of verse dramas, *The Old Glory*, he
called his first play "Endecott and the Red Cross," citing both Hawthorne's story of the same name and "The May-Pole of Merry Mount"
as his sources, and he called the second "My Kinsman, Major Molineux"
(297).

The last paragraph of "The Gray Champion" sounds the same nationalistic note as the last paragraph of "Endicott." Both stories equate the
Puritans' strength of purpose with the successful pursuit of America's
independence. Baym points out that without resorting to the "supernatural business" of "The Gray Champion," Hawthorne uses "Endicott"
to vindicate "the Puritan character by showing that it is the root of American resistance to tyranny" (43:78–79). Doubleday believes that Hawthorne was influenced in both instances by the nationalistic critical
prescription that dominated the cultural scene in his day. The four
Province-House stories also conform in varying degrees to that prescription, but in all of them, and in "My Kinsman, Major Molineux," too,
Hawthorne's skeptical irony creates a tension between what is admirable
and what is reprehensible in the Puritans (156; 149:104–07). Fossum
groups the stories dealing with America's national past under the rubric,
"the burden of revolt" (189:23–44), a fitting sociological extension of
Hawthorne's personal attitude toward his forefathers.

That attitude is best represented by Hawthorne's characterization of
John Endicott, a portrayal that spans at least a half-dozen works and a
seventeen-year period, from "The Gentle Boy" in 1832 to "Main Street"
in 1849. In the former, Endicott is held chiefly responsible for the extreme
persecution of the Quakers. In "Mrs. Hutchinson" he is described as one
"who would stand with his drawn sword at the gate of heaven, and resist
to the death all pilgrims thither except they travelled his own path." In
both "The May-Pole of Merry Mount" and "Endicott" he is a paradoxical
combination of tyrant, bigot, hero, and saint. In "Main Street" a positive
note is sounded when his visage is described as "resolute, grave and
thoughtful, yet apt to kindle with that glow of cheerful spirit by which
men of strong character are enabled to go joyfully on their proper tasks"
(*CE, XI, 55.31–33*). More characteristic, however, and as much a defini-

tive evaluation of Endicott as of the Puritans in general, is another "Main Street" pronouncement: "Let us thank God for having given us such ancestors: and let each successive generation thank him, not less fervently, for being one step further from them in the march of ages" (*68.11–14*).

## Interpretations and Criticism

Several kinds of duality mark this story, and these dualities are the basis for several widely diverse interpretations. The historical situation itself involves both a political and a religious controversy, but the major discrepancies surround the depiction of Endicott. The concluding paragraph may herald "one of the boldest exploits which our history records" and call for the name of Endicott to be "for ever honored," but before that final fanfare, he has been indelibly associated with the whipping post and the pillory, with cropped ears and branded cheeks, with slit nostrils and cleft tongues—in short, with the cruel and extreme punishments that Puritans inflicted on those who rebelled in any way against their authority. Endicott's strength and purposefulness are countermanded by his harshness and intolerance. The diverse interpretations depend on which of these dual aspects is given more credence.

Leavis, whose reading emphasizes Hawthorne's sympathy with the victims of the tyrannical theocratic society, finds it "difficult to see how the last paragraph of the little drama can be anything but ironically intended" (275:45). Other readers deem the entire situation ironic (156). Fossum defines the circumstances as "a complex struggle involving two tyrants and two rebels," with Endicott a rebel in his relation with the tyranny of England but a tyrant himself in his relation with the Wanton Gospeller and the tolerant Roger Williams. The "Christ-like" Williams is seen as "the real opponent of Tyranny" and as a deliberate foil for Endicott's shortcomings (189:34–35). Doubleday detects a tension in the structure of the tale between what Hawthorne thought he was supposed to say and what his own natural skepticism made him say (149:104). Halligan takes the ironic skepticism one crucial step further and sees a serious criticism of the American democratic process in Hawthorne's portrayal of Endicott's demagogic and bigoted appeal to the multitude (217).

These, and most other readings, contrast the open praise of the last paragraph with the subtle derision in the rest of the story (48; 308:14; 420:207). Baym, however, rejects the theory that Hawthorne was concealing his hostility; she believes he was capitalizing on the "image of the intolerant and repressive Puritan" that his readers expected and recognized. (See Bell's discussion of influences, above.) Baym points out that "Endicott's aggressive response rather than Williams' conciliatory one is the right answer to British authority" and that Hawthorne's approach is secular and democratic, not religious or ethical (43:78–81).

The story's inherent ambiguity has been developed further in the verse-drama adaptation of it by Robert Lowell. Lowell uses three of Hawthorne's stories for the first two parts of his trilogy and Melville's *Benito Cereno* for the third. (See relationship with other Hawthorne works, above.) Although *The Old Glory* (1968) emerges finally as more Lowell than Hawthorne or Melville, the kind of response that Hawthorne's "Endicott" evokes from a twentieth-century poet is indicative of the appeal that Hawthorne's concerns have almost a century and a half later (295; 414; 515). The concerns in this story are typical of Hawthorne. The style is, too. Pearce calls Hawthorne "the symbolist as historian" (370:222); in "Endicott and the Red Cross" Hawthorne is the symbolist-historian as mythmaker.

# XVII

# Ethan Brand

(*Centenary Edition, Volume XI, The Snow-Image*, 83–102)

## Publication History

This story first appeared in print on January 5, 1850 in the *Boston Weekly Museum* (II, 234–35) entitled "The Unpardonable Sin. From an Unpublished Work" under Hawthorne's own name, but without his consent or approval. The newspaper had procured a copy from Charles W. Webber, to whom Hawthorne had submitted the story on December 14, 1848 for a projected magazine. *The American Review*, as it was to be called, reached printed form but was never distributed. The sheets were stored in a New York warehouse from which, apparently, Webber took the story about a year later to pass it on to the Boston newspaper. There is no record that Webber ever paid for the story, and Hawthorne's objections to its publication in the *Boston Museum* are recorded in a letter to Webber dated December 18, 1849:

> An acquaintance of mine told me, to day, that I am announced as having written a story for "The Museum," and that it is to appear on the 5th of January. Now, when we spoke together about the "Unpardonable Sin," I understood that it was to be published, not as a story written for this newspaper—The Museum—but as a specimen of a forth-coming book; and that the time of its appearance was to be all but co-incident with the publication of the book. On any other understanding, I should not have given my consent to your proposal. . . . I shall not have the book ready so soon as I expected and I do not wish the appearance of this article to precede that of the book so long as it must, if the announcement of the Editor of the Museum be carried into effect. Neither (to tell you the truth) does it quite suit me to be blazoned abroad as a contributor to this weekly Museum; which may be the very best publication in the universe, but of which I know nothing whatever. So that I wish, in the first place, that you would enjoin it on the Editor to "hold on," until I give him notice to "go ahead;" and, secondly, that, if not published merely as a specimen from the proof-sheets of my forth-coming book, it shall at least be stated that the article was originally contributed to your magazine, and that it is transferred to the Museum by an arrangement with the editor of that magazine, and not with the author of the article. (*CE, XI, 384*)

The story, nevertheless, appeared as announced under the misleading caption "For the Boston Weekly Museum." The only concession to Hawthorne's requests seems to have been the addition of the subhead "From an Unpublished Work," since that phrase is not part of the title in *The American Review*. The work Hawthorne refers to is the volume he planned to call "Old-Time Legends; together with SKETCHES, EXPERIMENTAL AND IDEAL" in which the still unfinished *Scarlet Letter* was to be the central tale. However, the editor, James T. Fields, decided to publish a shorter book consisting of "The Custom-House" and "The Scarlet Letter" alone; it appeared in March 1850 (*CE, XI 381–85; 417–19; 428–29*).

More than a year after the publication of *The Scarlet Letter,* "Ethan Brand" made its second printed appearance in May 1851 in the *Dollar Magazine* (VII, 193–201)—again under Hawthorne's name, but this time with his approval. Evert A. Duyckinck, who had recently acquired the magazine, procured the sheets of the story and an illustrative woodcut from Webber (*CE, XI, 383, n.9*). Hawthorne agreed to Duyckinck's suggestion that the title be changed to "Ethan Brand; or, The Unpardonable Sin" (*CE, VIII, 617*). The story was collected in *The Snow-Image and Other Tales* in December 1851, with the final form of the title as "Ethan Brand; A Chapter from an Abortive Romance" (*CE, XI, 428–29*).

## Circumstances of Composition, Sources, and Influences

When Hawthorne sent a copy of this story to Charles Webber on December 14, 1848, he wrote an accompanying letter giving this account of its composition:

> At last, by main strength, I have wrenched and torn an idea out of my miserable brain; or rather, the fragment of an idea, like a tooth ill-drawn, and leaving the roots to torture me. . . . When shall you want another article? Now that the spell is broken, I hope to get into a regular train of scribbling. (*CE, XI, 383*)

"The spell" he refers to here is his two-year abstinence from writing which started when he assumed his duties as surveyor in the Salem custom house in April 1846.

Letters written during this period confirm the fact that Hawthorne had stopped writing almost completely. On September 10, 1847 Sophia wrote to her mother: "He has now lived in the nursery a year without a chance for one hour's uninterrupted musing and without his desk being once opened" (223:I, 313). The nursery at this point held two Hawthorne children: Una, who had been born in Concord on March 3, 1844, and Julian, who was born July 14, 1846. On November 7, 1847, Hawthorne wrote to Longfellow about his writing difficulties:

> I am trying to resume my pen, but the influences of my situation and customary associates are so antiliterary, that I know not whether I shall succeed. Whenever I sit alone, or walk alone, I find myself dreaming about stories, as of old; but these forenoons in the Custom House undo all that the afternoons and evenings have done. I should be happier if I could write.... (*CE, XI, 380*)

By early December 1848 Hawthorne had completed "The Unpardonable Sin." He agreed to have Sophia send a copy to her sister, Elizabeth Peabody, for her book *Aesthetic Papers*. Sophia's description, in the letter she wrote to her mother accompanying it, identifies it unmistakably: "It is a tremendous truth, written, as he often writes truth, with characters of fire, upon an infinite gloom,—softened so as not wholly to terrify, by divine touches of beauty,—revealing pictures of nature, and also the tender spirit of a child" (*CE, XI, 381*). Miss Peabody did not assemble her anthology immediately; a few days after sending her the initial copy, Hawthorne responded to Webber's request with another copy and the letter quoted above.

Because of its final subtitle and because of the internal references to earlier episodes, such as Brand's relationship with the German diorama man and with old Humphrey's daughter, "the Esther of our tale" (*94.6*), some readers have theorized that Hawthorne may have begun writing this story as part of a longer work much earlier (43:117; 304:88). However, Hawthorne's own comment in his letter to Webber refers to what sounds like a freshly vivid experience in the immediate past, and the painful difficulties he describes are appropriate for a writer who is struggling to emerge from an hiatus of several years. One of Hawthorne's biographers finds it "difficult to believe" that the story, as presented to Webber, was not "the end product of several versions, and perhaps the product of the condensation of several hundreds of pages" (355:136). Another assesses it as "a final chapter" with those chapters which should have led up to it aborted as the subtitle suggests (280:62). Adkins also thinks that "Ethan Brand" is the "last and crowning chapter of a novel" but that Hawthorne found it impossible to finish what he had started (11). Still others see the story as a completed whole with a ring of finality of its own (186:43; 309:99; 489). But the question of whether Hawthorne intended what is now the text of "Ethan Brand" to be a part of a larger work is only one of several factors to be considered in determining when it was written. Given the corroborative details and Hawthorne's habit of resuming his literary efforts in the fall, the composition of "Ethan Brand" can most probably be dated in the autumn of 1848.

The notebook entries on which "Ethan Brand" is based appear much earlier, however, the earliest dating back to the fall of 1835: "The story of a man, cold and hard-hearted, and acknowledging no brotherhood with mankind. At his death . . . the body will petrify" (*CE, VIII, 13.1–8*). Many of these details are incorporated in the early story, "The Man of Adamant," but Brand's marble heart is clearly prefigured here as well. In 1836 another entry reveals an early interest in the devil-alliance theme: "A man to flatter himself with the idea that he would not be guilty of some certain wickedness,—as, for instance, to yield to the personal temptations of the devil,—yet to find, ultimately, that he was at that very time committing that same wickedness" (*CE, VIII, 25.26–30*). The same segment of entries contains one that mentions a diorama as a literary device (*30.14*).

But the notebook entries which provide the setting, all of the characters except Brand, many of the episodes, and a host of other details for this story are those that Hawthorne recorded during his stay at North Adams, Massachusetts, from July 26 to September 11, 1838 (*CE, VIII, 86.4–151*). Waggoner has noted that "Ethan Brand" is the "chief exception" to the general rule that Hawthorne could not do his best creative work when writing directly of his actual, present experience of things and external events (500:44). At that, the eighty-four pages he filled with detailed observations during his stay in the Berkshires were not utilized in his fiction until ten years after the fact. Several readers have closely examined the North Adams journal entries and compared them with the corresponding descriptions in the story (252; 373; 392). In spite of the almost verbatim transcriptions of some of the passages, most readers agree that Hawthorne transforms the random and disparate material of the notebook into an integral part of the artistic unity of his tale. Notable exceptions are Marx, who sees places where "passages from the notebooks have been imperfectly joined" (310:276), and Van Doren, who thinks that "the persons . . . out of the note-book . . . do not particularly belong where they are placed" (490:139).

In an essay originally published in the *Atlantic* in 1893, Perry retraces Hawthorne's trip into and about North Adams, noting that the intervening half-century had drastically changed what was in Hawthorne's day a picturesque approach by stage to the New England factory town (373). Perry catalogues the elements in the notebook that Hawthorne incorporates into his story. Joseph repeats the process, with slight modifications, in 1960 (252). The debauched village trio—the stage agent, the crippled exlawyer, and the brandy-possessed doctor—all have real-life counterparts who display some of the same characteristics, but with significant modifications. For example, the description of the lawyer-turned-soap-maker covers over four pages in the original notebook (*CE, VIII, 90–93*); in the story he is allotted a half-paragraph (*91.17–92.7*), but his essential qualities are skillfully evoked. The "underwitted old man" who asks Hawthorne to relay a message to his children becomes Humphrey; the old man's granddaughter, who had been taken away to be brought up in her parents' circus, is transformed into Humphrey's daughter, Esther, who "had gone off with a company of circus performers" (*93.26–27*). The old Dutchman traveling with a diorama on his back also appears in the notebook; his physical appearance, the dilapidated state of his show-box, his habit of calling everybody "Captain," and even his "gigantic, brown, hairy hand," identified as "the Hand of Destiny," are all in the journal. The description of the limekiln on Mount Graylock in the moonlight is also taken from the notebook, including the detail of an opening "large enough to admit a man in a stooping posture" (*CE, VIII, 144.14; CE, XI, 84.16–17*). The lime burner that Hawthorne meets, "a dark, black-bearded figure in shirt sleeves," is materialistically oriented like Bartram; when asked whether he would run across the top of the intensely burning kiln barefooted for a thousand dollars, he replies he would do it for ten (*145.14–16*). A young boy named Joe is also described (*97.11*). The mountainside's radiant appearance the morning after Brand's death parallels almost word for word Hawthorne's record of Graylock as he saw it one summer morning (*CE, VIII, 107; CE, XI, 101*).

The incident of the dog chasing his tail also comes from the notebook; it has been analyzed phrase by phrase by one reader who concludes that the modifications that Hawthorne makes amplify and dramatize the theme (392). To heighten the parallel to Brand, Hawthorne "humanizes" the dog; he emphasizes the absurdity of the quest by making the tail "an object that could not possibly be attained," whereas originally the dog had actually caught hold of his tail. Finally, he draws attention to the unnaturalness of a being divided against itself when he describes the dog as growling and snarling "as if one end of the ridiculous brute's body was at deadly and *most unforgiveable* enmity with the other" (*96.27–28*; my italics). The phrase "most unforgiveable" is added to stress the similarity to Ethan Brand, whose intellect had devoured his heart in an equally unpardonable enmity between two parts of himself.

All of these characters and episodes in the story—the drunken exlawyer and doctor, the old man looking for his daughter who ran away with the circus, the old Dutchman with the diorama, the young boy Joe, Bartram the lime burner, the kiln ablaze by moonlight, the sunrise over Mount

Graylock—are clearly derived from the journal entries made a decade earlier.

In 1842 two notebook entries appear that are related to the idea of the moral enslavement of one person by another: "Some man of powerful character to command a person, morally subjected to him, to perform some act" (*CE, VIII, 226.30–31*), and "A moral philosopher to buy a slave, or otherwise get possession of a human being, and to use him for the sake of experiment, by trying the operation of a certain vice on him" (*237.7–9*). But the central idea of "Ethan Brand" is found in two 1844 entries: "The search of an investigator for the Unpardonable Sin;—he at last finds it in his own heart and practice" (*251.8–9*) and

> The Unpardonable Sin might consist in a want of love and reverence for the Human Soul; in consequence of which, the investigator pried into its dark depths, not with a hope or purpose of making it better, but from a cold philosophical curiosity,—content that it should be wicked in what ever kind or degree, and only desiring to study it out. Would not this, in other words, be the separation of the intellect from the heart? (*251.12–19*)

The latter is found in expanded form in the story itself (*90.10–18* and *99.1–24*).

Several readers have proposed some 1849 journal entries which describe Hawthorne's son, Julian, as a source for this story. One sees aspects of little Joe in the "tenderness, love and sensibility" attributed to Julian, who was three when his father recorded the observation on July 29, 1849 (*CE, VIII, 824.32*; 442:207). Another associates Julian's statement "I love all people," recorded by Hawthorne on September 6, 1849 (*CE, VIII, 435.10–11*), with the young Ethan Brand, who contemplated all mankind with "tenderness . . . love and sympathy" (*98.24–25*; 252.253–54). However, since the story was completed by December 1848, the 1849 entries appear to be an echo of the story instead of the reverse.

The extent to which "Ethan Brand" is a self-portrait has been variously estimated. Some believe there is a strong projection of Hawthorne's own Brand-like diabolic intelligence in his protagonist (355:193; 385; 460:134); others merely acknowledge an identification with the tendency to observe detachedly, for artistic purposes, the behavior of other humans (255:163, n.13; 455:lxii–lxiii; 500:4). The conversation that Hawthorne records in his North Adams journal with the one-armed soapmaker, "Black-Hawk" Haynes, strongly suggests that Hawthorne himself was aware of the undue fascination that the plight of others held for him. After describing Haynes as a derelict who nevertheless had "something of the gentleman and man of intellect" about him, the notebook continues:

" 'My study is man,' said he. And looking at me, 'I do not know your name,' said he, 'but there is something of the hawk-eye about you too' " (*CE, VIII, 92.5–7*). Perry believes that Hawthorne concurs with "Black-Hawk" and that the moral problem in "Ethan Brand" is Hawthorne's own problem in the summer of 1838 (373:134). If so, Hawthorne recaptures the trauma from the perspective of a decade later, a span of time that saw him change from a lone bachelor to a devoted husband and father of two.

The Bible has been cited as the source for several elements in this story. Matthew 12:31–32 provides a definition for the unpardonable sin: "Wherefore I say unto you, All manner of sin and blasphemy shall be forgiven unto men but the blasphemy against the Holy Ghost shall not be forgiven unto men." One reader argues that since the human heart is the traditional dwelling place of the Holy Ghost, Brand has willfully succeeded in hardening his heart so that this dwelling place is destroyed. His sin is, therefore, the same sin that Matthew says cannot be forgiven—the deliberate destruction of the Spirit of God in Man (158). Other readers, while acknowledging Hawthorne's familiarity with Matthew's definition, believe that Hawthorne's portrayal is more directly dependent on Thomas Stackhouse's commentary in *A New History of the Holy Bible* (London, 1752), which Hawthorne is known to have seen:

> ... the sin against the Holy Ghost is unpardonable not because there is not a Sufficiency of Merit in *Christ* to atone for it, or of *Mercy* in God the Father to forgive it, but because those, who commit it, are of such refractory and incorrigible Spirit, that they resist the last utmost Means of the Conviction, and, consequently, neither will, nor can repent. (II, 1340, as cited in 61:125–26)

Brand's declaration, "Freely, were it to do again, would I incur the guilt" (*90.16–17*), appears to be totally in keeping with Stackhouse's interpretation (61; 176; 180.5; 321.5).

Stock proposes a wider biblical context for "Ethan Brand," the most significant aspect of which is the story of Cain in Genesis 4 (460). The relationship between Matthew's definition of the unpardonable sin and the murder of Abel by Cain is established by the practice, common in the annotated Bibles of Hawthorne's day, of making marginal references to Genesis 4 at Matthew 12:32 as an illustration of the first unpardonable sin. Because Hawthorne's story emphasizes Brand's sin as a violation of "the sense of brotherhood" (*90.13–14*) and because of several analogies between the stories of Cain and of Ethan Brand, Stock believes that Hawthorne modeled some aspects of Brand on the biblical figure of Cain. Brand as a wanderer follows the fate assigned to Cain in Genesis 4:13.

Ethan's surname appears to be closely related to the mark set upon Cain in Genesis 4:15, a mark conventionally interpreted as a "brand" on the forehead. Furthermore, the "indescribable something" in Brand's wild appearance evokes the vague legendary associations which had developed on the subject of the mark of Cain. Another legend involving Cain's conversation with the devil before the murder of Abel is recorded in Stackhouse's biblical commentary (p. 75), quoted above; Hawthorne's story alludes to a similar legendary account: "stories . . . had grown traditionary in reference to this strange man. . . . Ethan Brand, it was said, had conversed with Satan himself" (*88–89*).

Two other biblical derivations from Ethan Brand's name have been suggested, both with ironic implication. Ethan the Ezrahite in I Kings 4:29–31, who is also the author of Psalm 89, could have provided a "superbly ironic" prototype in his role as a psalmist (460:116–20). The expression, "a brand plucked out of the burning," which is also derived from the Bible, is another possible source for the name of a protagonist who willfully thrusts himself into the burning (325). A biblical origin has also been cited for the eighteen years assigned to Brand's quest; two Bible stories, one in Luke 13 and the other in Judges 10, involve similar eighteen-year intervals (524).

The biblical analogues linking the figure of Cain to the devil and to the unpardonable sin are echoed and reinforced in what one reader calls a more important source—Byron's verse drama, *Cain: A Mystery* (1821) (460:125–33). Byron's and Hawthorne's protagonists are also similar in that each is a Hamlet-like characterization of the nineteenth-century intellectual. Byron's Lucifer, who acts as a spokesman for post-Renaissance scientific thought, is reflected in Brand's portrayal as well.

The Cain archetype has traditional associations with another myth that Hawthorne draws upon in this story, the legend of the Wandering Jew. Because of the Lord's injunction that no one could slay Cain, many of the Cain myths have been drawn into the stories surrounding the "Jew of Nuremberg" for whom death was similarly forbidden (460:123–24). The German showman in "Ethan Brand" has been repeatedly identified as a Wandering Jew figure (21; 152; 280:62; 439; 460:123–24), one who reflects Brand's tragic situation (439). The Wandering Jew is a stock Gothic convention that reached its apex in Charles Robert Maturin's *Melmoth the Wanderer* (1820). Maturin describes the Wanderer as the "Cain of the moral world" bearing a "brand" (460:124). Ethan Brand is much like Melmoth in his tormented mental state, in his reputed alliance with Satan, and in his desperate final act of self-destruction. Hawthorne might have been influenced by Maturin's Gothic villain, but he adapts the type, and the pattern of his Wandering Jew, to his own purposes in "Ethan Brand" (152). He also incorporates the monstrous and terrifying effects of the Gothic mode by projecting the idea of the despair of a lost soul against mountain imagery that is evocative of the religious sublime (282:398–99).

That Ethan Brand, like any character who makes a pact with the devil, owes his genesis in part to the Faust myth is uncontestable (126; 200; 228; 299; 447:98–100). His prototypes, in Marlowe's *Doctor Faustus,* Goethe's *Faust, and* Byron's *Manfred,* are like him in their roles as conjurers, wanderers, violators of women (Brand's experiments with Esther), proud egotists, and monomaniacal pursuers of knowledge (228). Stein emphasizes Goethe's influence, pointing to Hawthorne's intimacy with Longfellow, Hillard, and the other Faust votaries of the Peabody circle, especially after his marriage to Sophia Peabody in 1842 (447:87). Another reader questions Hawthorne's direct knowledge of Goethe's work but establishes a strong likelihood that he knew *Blackwood's* review of *Faust* (126). A striking similarity has been demonstrated between Brand's experiences and the ideas proposed by Horace Bushnell, a mid-nineteenth-century philosopher. Although no evidence is available that Hawthorne knew Bushnell's writings, the "magnetic chain of humanity" that Brand rejects and the ordeal of evil that he undergoes do recapitulate the message Bushnell presents to his followers (447:99–100).

The allusion to *Pilgrim's Progress* in the story—"an opening at the bottom of the tower . . . resembled nothing so much as the private entrance to the infernal regions, which the shepherds of the Delectable Mountains were accustomed to show to pilgrims" (*84.15–22*)—suggests that Hawthorne had Bunyan's allegory in mind while writing "Ethan Brand" (280:63; 417:240; 442:338). It is significant that it is from the Delectable Mountains that Christian first sees the Celestial City, especially since Brand begins his quest with Christian-like good intentions directed toward a similar goal.

Hawthorne's depiction of the fire of the limekiln as an earthly counterpart of the fires of hell may have been influenced not only by Bunyan's side gate to hell but by Dante's vision in the *Inferno* as well (150). Like the lowest regions in Dante's hell, where Satan himself is embedded in ice, Hawthorne's sinner suffers intense emotional cold although surrounded by hellfire; Brand's heart is marble, paradoxically unmeltable. Doubleday sees a parallel between Brand and the heretics in the sixth circle of the *Inferno* who are eternally rebellious and victims of their own proud intellects (150:669–70), while another reader envisions Brand's soul as condemned to the seventh circle of Dante's hell with the violent and the suicidal (489:456). Other less direct parallels have been cited with *Gesta*

*Romanorum* (374) and with the romantic irony of Tieck's tales (311; 377).

The theory that the characterization of Ethan Brand is based on Melville, which was proposed by Mumford (348) and seconded by Arvin (27:169), has been thoroughly refuted (69; 455:xcv; 457). "Ethan Brand" was published seven months before Hawthorne met Melville, although Melville did not read it until it was reprinted in 1851. The concepts in the story are organic to Hawthorne's vision and are clearly related to other works that pre-date Hawthorne's friendship with Melville by years.

## Relationship with Other Hawthorne Works

Because this is the one story in which Hawthorne attempts a definition of the unpardonable sin, and because Hawthorne's best-wrought characters constantly verge on the brink of damnation, Ethan Brand's sin provides the most popular basis for relating this story to the rest of Hawthorne's canon. This sin is explicitly defined in the story as the separation of the intellect from the heart (*90.10–15*; *99.1–24*); consequently, those characters whose behavior is dominated by intellectual achievements and pursuits without regard for human sympathy or suffering are most often classified with Brand as unpardonable sinners. These invariably include Chillingworth of *The Scarlet Letter*, Aylmer of "The Birthmark," Rappaccini of "Rappaccini's Daughter," Hollingsworth and Westervelt of *The Blithedale Romance*, and sometimes Jeoffrey Pyncheon of *The House of Seven Gables* (32:56–75; 61; 442:339; 309:99; 490:139; etc.) In this group, Aylmer and Rappaccini are specifically like Brand in their involvement in scientific experiments that recklessly endanger others (455:lxxiv) and in the admirable intentions with which they begin the pursuits that somehow develop into monomaniacal obsessions (61; 186:99; 333). All three display Faust's lust for knowledge and an inordinate pride that attempts to transcend the limits of human nature (47:71; 31; 150:666; 447:87–103). Brand's psychological manipulation of Esther links him in a more demonic way with Chillingworth and Westervelt, as well as with Maule of *The House of Seven Gables*, all of whom violate the sanctity of another's soul (32:88–89; 61; 309:99–100; 321.5; 455:lxxvi). Brand and Chillingworth are also alike as examples of the reciprocal nature of this kind of moral enslavement in which the manipulator is destroyed as a result of the power he exercises over his victim. The concept, which is expressed in a notebook entry (*CE, VIII,* *253:5–10*), is most explicitly worked out in Chillingworth's deterioration after Dimmesdale's death but is also reflected in Brand's suicide (455: lxxiv).

From a theological perspective, Brand is most like Chillingworth and Digby, "The Man of Adamant." These three characters have been called the only "eternally damned" sinners in all of Hawthorne's canon (325.5). By one count, their unpardonable sin is their willful final impenitence (281; 321.5); by another, they are guilty of deliberately destroying man's faith in God (158). Another reader who minimizes Hawthorne's theological concerns groups Brand and Chillingworth with Aylmer on a different basis. Contrary to most interpretations, they are seen as sinners who are motivated not by intellect but by selfish passions unrelated to the quest for knowledge per se (41).

Insofar as Brand and Chillingworth are cold observers who remain detached from the human suffering they are witnessing, they bear an affinity to the anonymous painter in "The Prophetic Pictures," to Coverdale in *The Blithedale Romance*, to the "spiritualized Paul Pry" of "Sights from a Steeple," and possibly to Hawthorne himself whose notebooks are filled with objective observations unemotionally recorded (47:176; 189:92–93; 255:164; 385; 442:207; 500:4). Two other versions of artist-like showmen who, like the Dutchman with the diorama, put humanity on display for public perusal are found in "Main Street" and "Fancy's Show Box" (189:92–93). The itinerant showmen in "Ethan Brand" and "Fancy's Show Box" are also related to the legend of the Wandering Jew. (See sources, above.) This myth is most completely worked out in the characterization of the Virtuoso in "The Virtuoso's Collection" (47:71; 21; 304:88–89) and is also evident among the guests at "A Select Party" (21) and in the restlessness of *Septimus Felton* (41:71). The detachment that characterizes Hawthorne's wanderers and artist figures is associated in its extreme form with "Wakefield." Brand becomes the kind of "Outcast of the Universe" that is described in Wakefield's story (442:207), while Wakefield breaks "the magnetic chain of humanity" that is described in Brand's (500:76).

Structurally, "Ethan Brand" follows a motif found in many of Hawthorne's tales, that of the journey or quest. Some typical examples are "The Canterbury Pilgrims" (500:101) and "The Great Carbuncle" (417). More specifically, the pattern traces a night journey that begins at dusk and ends the next morning; in this respect, the time structure of "Ethan Brand" is exactly like that of "Young Goodman Brown" and "My Kinsman, Major Molineux" (393). The latter is also like "Ethan Brand" in employing laughter as an essential ingredient that provides a central focus for the plot and skillful revelation of character (157). Another of the journey-quest stories, "Roger Malvin's Burial," has been assessed as a companion piece to "Ethan Brand" because it presents an alternate conclusion to the same general situation. The two stories are alike in the eighteen-year cycle that intervenes between departure and return, a detail that may have been provided by the two Bible stories that incorporate a similar eighteen-year interval (524).

## Interpretations and Criticism

In spite of what appears to be a clear-cut definition of the unpardonable sin in Ethan Brand's own words, one of the interpretative issues on which readers disagree is the nature of Brand's sin and the grounds on which he is damned. While one reader maintains that he is not damned at all and that his suicide is a penitential act that insures his spiritual salvation (372), the majority on record accept his eternal condemnation, though they differ markedly in identifying his specific offense. From a theological perspective, Brand's transgressions are rooted in his monstrous pride, but again that pride is seen as manifesting itself in a variety of ways. It takes the form of blasphemy against the Holy Ghost by destroying the heart which is the dwelling place of the Spirit within man (158), or it makes Brand willfully impenitent and blinds him to the fact that impenitence itself, and not any other kind of sin, is responsible for his damnation (321.5; 281). Some see the unpardonable sin as the idea of knowledge as an end in itself (310:273). Or, as in the eyes of a preponderance of readers, the quest itself, by presuming to limit God's infinite mercy, is the ultimate sin of rebellion; it is an attempt to defeat God by overreaching him and, in effect, becoming God himself (126; 186:44; 200; 228; 299; 309:100; 447:98–100).

One reader blames Brand's isolation as a part of the cause of the unpardonable sin of pride; Brand cuts himself off from others when his intellectual development transgresses the bounds established for man. The phenomenon is interpreted as a break in the "Chain of Being," which is part of a Platonic concept embraced by Christianity that assigns a particular place in nature to every creature according to his capabilities (313). Such a reading raises the question of Hawthorne's attitude toward knowledge. Geist takes the position that "Ethan Brand" is an attack on a "dispassionate . . . worker in the cause of enlightenment." In a disparaging contrast to Goethe, whom he envisions as having been "born calling for more light," he characterizes Hawthorne as having been "born calling for more darkness" (200). Kaul disagrees. He calls Hawthorne's reputed antipathy to knowledge erroneous and points to Brand's original examination of man's moral nature as the most heroic aspect of Brand's character (255:161–63).

One explanation of what appears to be a severe anti-intellectual bias in the story is revealed in the interpretation offered by several readers who maintain that "Ethan Brand" is intended to be a criticism of Transcendentalism (419; 447:100; 489:456). Stein calls the attack "subtle" (447:100), but Schwartz sees Brand's development as the clear logical consequence of Emerson's notion of the deification of man and as a result of Emersonian self-reliance pursued to its ultimate implications (419). Vanderbilt concurs; Brand is conceived as Emerson's "common man," and Brand's kind of quest for final truths that transcend human relations is first a corroboration and then a refutation of Emersonian principles (489:456, n.4).

A reader who maintains that Hawthorne's speculations about evil and the human heart are basically atheological rejects all these speculations. Baym believes that Brand is motivated by selfish passion, that what Brand "really wants is not to *find* an unpardonable sin but to commit one," and that his search and his vision of himself are presented as self-delusions (41:41–46; 43:117). Another interpretation that uses a generic approach reaches a similar conclusion but in different terms. As the hero of a self-styled quest romance, Brand's crisis is one of identity; the chimerical and subjective nature of his goal and the intensity of his search turn his quest into self-pursuit. It becomes imperative for him to retain his "idea" because he identifies himself with it completely even though he is spasmodically aware of its absurdity and its illusoriness. This self-inflicted delusion explains Brand's "odd theatrical behavior, his reasons for returning . . . and the extravagant mode of his death" (417).

A few readers have appointed Brand as a representative figure for the artist, especially in the parallels set up between Brand and the German with the diorama (52:117–23; 115:156; 186:55; 255:165). Insofar as Brand incorporates the Cain myth, Cain, who is the progenitor of artists and craftsmen, confirms the association (460:134). Brand as the symbol of the artist is most extensively developed by Bewley who reads "Ethan Brand" as a politically slanted version of the problem of the artist in a democratic society. Having categorized Brand as "clearly no Jacksonian democrat," Bewley judges Hawthorne as feeling "called upon to press the claims of democracy against the individual and the artist." To this end, Hawthorne gives "the stupid and vulgar Bartram a practical and repulsive triumph over Ethan Brand" and "rejects the creatively gifted who cannot or will not be levelled down" (52:117–23).

Another reader traces similar egalitarian tendencies in the story and relates them to Hawthorne's political activities with the Young America wing of the Democratic party (413). Such sociopolitical approaches are objected to by Spencer; he rejects Bewley's "regal Republicanism" dogma and asserts the superiority of centrifugal—that is, formalistic—criticism over the centripetal, or historical, variety (441).

An equally "centripetal" reading that is culturally rather than politically oriented is proffered by Marx who examines the story for evidences of the "machine in the garden" or the invasion of technology on the pastoral ideal (310:265–77). Although the North Adams journal that Hawthorne uses as a source for "Ethan Brand" contains descriptions of "factories . . . in the midst of . . . wild scenery" (*CE, VIII, 88.9–10*), the factories do not appear in the story. Marx believes that Hawthorne reflects the industrialization in other ways—in the sense of loss, anxiety, and dislocation that characterizes the villagers; in the images, words, and phrases used to describe the kiln and its fire which link them to technology; and in Brand himself who is an agent and victim of scientific empiricism or "mechanism." According to Marx, Brand is destroyed by the fires of change associated with factories, a fact forcibly confirmed by the ironically sentimental pastoralism of the idyllic vision of nature that follows his death; the story conveys Hawthorne's "inchoate sense of doom awaiting the self-contained village culture."

The kind of "centrifugal" criticism advocated by Spencer has produced some of the most valuable readings of "Ethan Brand." Fogle's chapter, for example, provides enough insights into the story to insure most readers' apprehension of the work's aesthetic validity (186:41–58). Stallman and Vanderbilt provide similarly useful formalistic observations (442:338–39; 489). The unity in the story offers an ideal base for any New Critic who is primarily concerned with how the text presents, develops, and resolves itself on its own ground. In "Ethan Brand" the circular structure of the tale (it ends exactly as it began, with Bartram and Little Joe in front of the kiln) is reinforced by the circular pattern of the plot (Brand returns to his point of departure, both geographically and spiritually; the sin is in himself). The motif is echoed again in the circularity of the protagonist's logic (the quest itself is the sin, even if Brand doesn't fully realize it); in the circular imagery of the setting—"circling flames within a round, tower-like kiln on a mountain side which lies within a surrounding forest and surrounding mountains" (489:455)—and of the "two concentric circles of vision" established by the action in front of the kiln's firelight (186:50); and even in the episode of the dog who runs around in circles chasing his own tail.

The obvious paralled between Brand and the dog is one of several parallels that Hawthorne constructs. The itinerant showman with the diorama is a "twin" figure, a double for Brand's kind of evil and for his separation from humanity, whether he is interpreted as the Wandering Jew (388; 439; 442:338) or as an incarnation of the devil with whom Brand made his pact and with whom he identifies himself (126; 228; 299; 447:98–100). Esther's father as a bewildered wanderer-searcher also echoes Brand's predicament (388; 442:338).

The other villagers in the story are not as easily categorized, although they too serve symbolic functions designed to illumine the protagonist and the theme. Some readers believe that the stage agent, the lawyer, and the doctor are meant as antipodal figures to Brand's inhumanity; in spite of their apparent derelictions, they do not lose touch with their fellow men as he does (281:189–90; 309:102). Others see the trio as "microcosmic reflectors" of Brand's perversion rather than as contrasts. The three characters display Brand's kind of destructive curiosity in their callous reactions to his dilemma (138). Their physical deformities suggest less obvious spiritual shortcomings (138; 442:338). Yet, although they are profligates and failures, their sense of community provides a momentary but meaningful contrast with Brand that ironically demonstrates their superiority (163:100–11). The doctor who scoffs at Brand's quest may be grossly insensitive, but there is a sense in which his disclaimer for the unpardonable sin is true and makes clear Brand's deluded monomania (281). In the morality-play scheme that Fogle sets up for the story, the villagers are assigned a middle position above Brand—who is farthest from the ideal, but below little Joe—who displays the highest degree of spiritual perfection (186:43–46). The boy serves as a foil for the shortcomings of the villagers, including his father, and of Brand as well. Bartram's position is as debatable as the townsmen's. For one reader he is an obtuse materialist whose final comment raises the question of who is the most "selfish, smug, and hard" of them all (442:339). But another reader assesses Bartram's "homely reactions" less pejoratively; he is the "sensible man" used by Hawthorne to provide a necessary ironic "ballast" to the tale (156:493–94).

In addition to these parallels of contrast and comparison in the characterizations, Hawthorne uses several other devices to enhance the story's unity. The setting is used to provide a realistic reflection of Brand's tortured soul in the fiery kiln (163:106–07; 186:49, 53–54) as well as to prefigure his last desperate act. Foreshadowing also occurs when Brand is described as having "earlier thrown his dark thoughts" into the furnace (*84.7–8*), when Bartram half expects him "to plunge bodily into the flames to confer with the devil" (*89.33–34*), and when Brand tells his double, the Dutch diorama man, to "get thee into the furnace yonder" (*96.10–11*). One reader applauds the selection, rhythm, and contrast that Hawthorne displays in the "seven long waves of laughter that roll through 'Ethan Brand' " (416:118–19), while others note the laughter's dramatic effectiveness and the ironic counterpoise it contributes to the tale (156:493–94; 157:285–86; 186:47–48; 442:338).

While the ubiquitous circular motif remains the most recognized unifying element in "Ethan Brand," Male suggests another element that Hawthorne could have used to unite form and content further. Male theorizes that the allusions which suggest that the story is a fragment of an uncompleted work are part of the theme that is related to the incomplete and fragmentary nature of man's knowledge. The allusions serve to have the work itself acknowledge its author's necessarily partial achievements in contrast to the completeness that accompanies the fulfillment of Brand's quest (304:87–88).

Establishing the author's intent on such a subtly rendered thematic position is difficult, if not impossible, but four other explications of "Ethan Brand" proceed without reference to or concern for the author's milieu or purpose. They are so far removed from what can be ascertained as Hawthorne's concerns that they must be called exercises in reader reaction and association. One discussion sets up a series of similarities between Brand and a myth created by the English poet, William Blake (1757–1827); Brand emerges as an "Urizen character" who "falls to a satanic state, realizes his error, annihilates it, and in effect redeems his past sinful life" (372). Hawthorne would probably be as surprised to learn of Brand's reprieve as he would be to discover that Brand's pursuit of the unpardonable sin is an example of the "teleological suspension of the ethical" (91). The latter is a concept of Kierkegaard's that one reader applies to Brand. Kierkegaard uses it to describe Abraham's willingness to sacrifice his son Isaac in obedience to an esoteric supernatural voice in the face of a prevailing moral code that forbids murder. The reader credits Brand with executing a similar act of faith when he follows what he perceives to be the will of God. Such a conclusion ignores the text of the story which clearly states that "*Thus* Ethan Brand became a fiend" (*99.19*; my italics). A third reader discovers a parallel with the Greek myth of the overthrow of Uranus by Chromus at the instigation of his mother, Ge, or Earth (256). And a fourth considers "Ethan Brand" as an example of "heart-transplant fiction" for reasons that are not clear either medically or aesthetically (376).

Such a bizarre assortment of reactions attests as much to the story's wide circulation as to its mythic suggestibility. "Ethan Brand" is among Hawthorne's best-known stories. As such, it is fair game for a mixed collection of readers, most of whom admire it. The review that Whipple wrote in *Graham's Magazine* in April 1852 called this story "one of the most powerful of Hawthorne's works" (118:240). Readers have been calling it powerful ever since. Each of the formalistic analyses reviewed above is a tribute to the story's artistic achievements. Fogle admires its "dramatic and emotional intensity . . . profound depth, tragic seriousness" (186:53), and the accolades go on, seemingly ad infinitum.

A significant number of negative appraisals accompany the voluminous praise, partly due, no doubt, to the story's extensive exposure. Green, whose stated purpose is to "destroy the peace" of the American literary establishment, maintains that Hawthorne's reputation is based on a half-century of anti-Emersonianism. He charges Hawthorne with having handled the idea in "Ethan Brand" "ignorantly," his chief objection stemming from the author's use of capital letters for the "IDEA" (203:4, 71–75). To be taken more seriously is Geist's claim that in "Ethan Brand" Hawthorne is melodramatic, simpleminded, and "so old-fashioned that he can no longer be read without a smile" (200:202). Fiedler's assessment is not very different: in "Ethan Brand" "the intent is tragic, but the tone is false, and what begins in terror ends in mere rant" (181:425). Bewley calls the story "unsatisfactory" because it totters "on the brink of ultimate incoherence" (52:121). But beyond these desultory censures, what should disturb "Brand" admirers most is the doubt expressed by two exceptionally dedicated Hawthorne scholars, Doubleday and Baym. Doubleday considers the story disfigured by the "almost desperate authorial interpretation in which Hawthorne struggles to justify his theme" (149:181). Baym suggests that Hawthorne himself may have thought the story "too stiff and schematic in its presentation." She considers it an "anachronism" that does not fit into the shape that his career was taking at the time he wrote it (43:117). Significantly, however, she joins the host of readers alluded to above when she deems it "at once among the most *powerful* and least satisfactory of Hawthorne's stories" (41:41; my italics).

This small but vocal group of dissenters agree in principle on what is wrong with "Ethan Brand." The fact remains that the structural and symbolic merits outweigh the obtrusive authorial presence and the dated, stylized rhetoric. Equally important in any final evaluation of "Ethan Brand" is the archetypal pull it exercises as an authentically realized, American-based Faust legend.

# XVIII

# Fancy's Show Box: A Morality

(*Centenary Edition, Volume IX, Twice-told Tales, 220–26.*)

## Publication History

This story was first published in the fall of 1836 in *The Token and Atlantic Souvenir* (pp. 177–84) dated 1837, with no attribution. The editor, Samuel Goodrich, arranged to pay $108 for the eight pieces by Hawthorne in this issue, none of which carried the author's name. Based on an approximate per-page average, "Fancy's Show Box" would have earned $8. Hawthorne included it, along with four other 1837 *Token* pieces, in his first collection, *Twice-told Tales*, in 1837 (*CE, IV, 570, 497*).

## Circumstances of Composition, Sources, and Influences

While one of the stories published with "Fancy's Show Box," "The Great Carbuncle," is considered by many scholars to have been written originally as part of *The Story Teller*, the history of the seven other pieces appearing in the same issue is much more uncertain. (See circumstances of composition under "David Swan.") Of these, "Fancy's Show Box," the shortest of the group, best fits Crowley's category of the several "slight enough" for Hawthorne to have been able to write them simultaneously with his other commitments in the fall and winter of 1835–36 (*CE IX, 494–96*). This estimated date and the publication history rule out Julian Hawthorne's assumption that "Fancy's Show Box" was written to express his father's remorse over the part he played in his friend Cilley's death in a duel in 1838. Bridge presents a less exaggerated account of Hawthorne's sense of involvement; he does not believe that Cilley's decision to accept the challenge could have been based solely on Hawthorne's willingness to fight a duel under similar circumstances (233:I, 167–75; 84:20).

One notebook entry and part of another, both undated but appearing after October 25, 1836, are related in a very general way to the theme:

A man to flatter himself with the idea that he would not be guilty of some certain wickedness,—as, for instance, to yield to the personal temptations of the Devil,—yet to find, ultimately, that he was at that very time committing that same wickedness. (*CE, VIII,* *25.26–30*)

There is evil in every human heart, which may remain latent, perhaps, through the whole of life; but circumstances may rouse it to activity. To imagine such circumstances. . . . (*29.28–30*)

The following passage from Jeremy Taylor's *Doctor Dubitantium: or,* *The Rule of Conscience* (1660) has been cited as a source for the general theme: "The act of the will alone, although no external action or event do follow, is imputed to good or evil by God and men" (Rule III, Part II, Book IV, Chapter I, as cited in 153). The six steps outlined by Taylor in his discussion of this rule parallel the various phases in Mr. Smith's sinful volition. In the first example, the question of his seduction of a young girl, Memory finds "a record merely of sinful thought, which was never embodied in an act" (*223.2–3*), which closely parallels Taylor's second step, "the will stops and arrests itself upon the tempting object." The last example concerns Mr. Smith's part in a lawsuit against the orphaned heirs of a large estate, unpursued because of legal obstacles; this parallels Taylor's fourth step in which the sinful action is prevented by "something that lies cross in the way." Taylor concludes his explication of Rule III by pointing out that while "God for ends of His own providence does often hinder" the external act of sin, the sinner "is not at all excused." Hawthorne differs with Taylor here in expressing the hope that "all the dreadful consequences of sin will not be incurred, unless the act have set its seal upon the thought" (*226.20–22*), but in the final paragraph he almost returns to Taylor's position in his emphasis on the "flitting phantoms of iniquity" that pollute every man's heart. These echoes, coupled with Hawthorne's withdrawal of *Doctor Dubitantium* from the Salem Athenaeum in 1834, provide strong support for Doubleday's contention that Jeremy Taylor was an important influence on the writing of "Fancy's Show Box" (149:155–59). Folsom (188:24–25) suggests a more obvious, less esoteric source from Christ's Sermon on the Mount: "I say unto you, that whosoever looketh on a woman to lust after her hath committed adultery with her already in his heart" (Matthew 5:27–28).

Another parallel, this one encompassing narrative mode as well as thematic intent, has been found in the adventures of Little-faith in *Pilgrim's Progress* (244:159–60). In John Bunyan's book, Little-faith is confronted by Faint-heart, Mistrust, and Guilt, who together rob him of his riches (his grace) after Guilt, "with a great club that was in his hand, strook Little-faith in the head, and with that blow fell'd him flat to the ground." Hawthorne also uses three personifications—Fantasy, Memory, and Conscience—in his attack on Mr. Smith's soul. Conscience strikes a dagger to Mr. Smith's heart and leaves him injured, much like the fate of Bunyan's Little-faith.

The eighteenth-century Eastern tale as written by Addison, Goldsmith, and Johnson has also been suggested as an analogue (149:67).

## Relationship with Other Hawthorne Works

Insofar as form is concerned, "Fancy's Show Box" is among what Waggoner calls "the sketches with some narrative ingredients" (500:253). Like "The Christmas Banquet" or "A Select Party," it differs markedly from works such as "Ethan Brand" or "Young Goodman Brown" that meet the current expectations of short-story readers. Walsh classifies "Fancy's Show Box" as an "illustrated idea" (510). He identifies ten pieces in Hawthorne's canon that he believes are often erroneously judged as tales, and he groups "Fancy's Show Box" with "David Swan" and "Wakefield" as philosophically oriented sketches in which the narratives are secondary to the idea being examined. Doubleday also links "Fancy's Show Box" with "Wakefield" on a similar basis, both tales demonstrating Hawthorne's penchant for turning moral ideas about so as to display all their facets (149:151).

"Fancy's Show Box" is related to "The Celestial Rail-road" in its indebtedness to Bunyan's *Pilgrim's Progress* (244), but it is in its Puritan-like concept of universal sin that "Fancy's Show Box" is most significantly related to other works in Hawthorne's canon. It provides an important corollary to such esteemed short stories as "Young Goodman Brown," "The Minister's Black Veil," and "Roger Malvin's Burial." Its moral— "Man must not disclaim his brotherhood, even with the guiltiest, since, though his hand be clean, his heart has surely been polluted by the flitting phantoms of iniquity" (226.24–27)—provides an insight into the reasons for young Goodman Brown's desolate isolation. The torment inflicted on Mr. Smith as a result of his mere contemplation of sinful deeds helps to explain why Mr. Hooper is driven to wear the black veil and why Reuben Bourne feels compelled to make reparation for Roger Malvin's death even though he did not kill him. In other works, Hawthorne more explicitly links intent with commission. Miriam, in *The Marble Faun*, is morally guilty of murder simply by having suggested it to Donatello with a look. In "David Swan" the two rascals who were deterred from their plan to kill and rob David by a barking dog never "imagined that the recording angel had written down the crime of murder against their souls, in letters as durable as eternity" *(CE, IX, 189.13–16)*.

Waggoner uses the moral from "Fancy's Show Box" to illustrate Hawthorne's attitude toward his villains, an outlook that emphasizes the vulnerability they share with all mankind (500:51). Rappaccini, Wakefield, and Chillingworth are his examples, but almost all of Hawthorne's villains—Ethan Brand, Aylmer of "The Birthmark," Hollingsworth in *The Blithedale Romance*—fit into the category of fallible humans gone wrong.

Two critics have coupled "Fancy's Show Box" with another sketch, "The Haunted Mind" *(CE, IX 304–09)*, published two years earlier. Lewisohn sees them both as uninhibited and therapeutic outpourings of Hawthorne's painful preoccupation with sin (286:178–80). Baym perceptively recognizes the severely inhibiting form Hawthorne chose for these two uninhibited explorations of the mind so that his unconventional discoveries are filtered through highly conventional language, a series of literary stereotypes for "The Haunted Mind" and a deliberately quaint, "mechanical and awkward" allegory for "Fancy's Show Box" (43:64–67).

The form that Fancy's personification takes in "Fancy's Show Box," an itinerant showman with a box of pictures, is a figure found in several of Hawthorne's works. The showman whose wagon "The Seven Vagabonds" share is one version, and the old Dutchman traveling with a diorama on his back in "Ethan Brand" is another. The portrayal closest to Fancy's is in "Main Street" where the narrator-puppeteer is an artist figure faced with the problem of creating illusions of reality. Fancy succeeds much more effectively than the "Main Street" narrator; in the process, the author impugns authors in general with a measure of participatory guilt in the evil they imagine in their works.

## Interpretations and Criticism

Hawthorne's characteristic ambivalence is well demonstrated in "Fancy's Show Box," which has been used by various prestigious authorities to support everything from Hawthorne's strict adherence to puritanical doctrines, to a variety of moderate Christian positions, to his outright rejection of all theological considerations. Stewart believes that the closing paragraph of "Fancy's Show Box" states the doctrine of universal depravity with sufficient explicitness to satisfy the most rigorous theologian of the puritanical school (455:lxxii). Fairbanks disagrees: "It is not only not explicit," he argues, "it is not even implicit." For him, Hawthorne's answer to the opening question of "What is Guilt?" is "strictly in the

Christian tradition," a Christianity older than Calvinism and as modern as Kierkegaard and Niebuhr (177). Doubleday agrees with Fairbanks—this story "is in no way especially Calvinistic" (149:158)—and Waggoner concurs (500:12–16). According to Waggoner, when Hawthorne seems closest to the Puritans, he is also closest to classic Christianity. When Hawthorne writes that Penitence must kneel and divine Mercy forgive, he is in line with the Calvinists' denial of salvation by works and their emphasis on atonement and faith, but Waggoner notes that Hawthorne avoids the fatalism of predestination by qualifying his denial of free will with the phrase "settled and full" in the statement: "In truth, there is no such thing in man's nature, as a settled and full resolve, either for good or evil, except at the very moment of execution" (*226.17–19*). Baym, at the other end of the spectrum, insists that in spite of the theological aura of the questions Hawthorne poses, his interests are purely psychological and that theological issues have no place in his writing (43:68).

Ultimately, whether psychological or theological issues were uppermost in Hawthorne's mind when he wrote this story is of secondary concern. "Fancy's Show Box" illustrates both the psychological phenomenon of a guilt complex and the theological principle of universal innate depravity. The story remains an important piece in Hawthorne's canon because it offers a view of the pervasiveness of sin and guilt that explicitly illuminates many of his more important and more subtle stories. Mr. Smith, in spite of his puppetlike role in what is essentially a morality play, functions as an effective reflector for one of Hawthorne's most typical character types.

# XIX

# Feathertop: A Moralized Legend

*(Centenary Edition, Volume X, Mosses from an Old Manse, 223–46.)*

## Publication History

"Feathertop" was first published in the *International Monthly Magazine of Literature, Science, and Art* in two parts, on February 1 and March 1, 1852 (V, 182–86, 333–37), under Hawthorne's own name (*CE, X, 577*).

In contrast to the minimal pay he received for his earlier short stories, Hawthorne, as the author of the successful *Scarlet Letter* and *The House of Seven Gables*, could finally negotiate profitably with the magazine publishers. On December 15, 1851 he wrote to Rufus W. Griswold, the *International*'s editor, "I cannot afford it for less than $100, and would not write another for the same price." He had been offered $100 by Dr. Bailey for a contribution to the *National Era*, but Hawthorne thought "Feathertop" "somewhat grotesque in its character and therefore not quite adapted to the grave and sedate character of that Journal." On December 4, 1851 he had offered the story to John Sartain. When *Sartain's Union Magazine* would not or could not take it, Griswold accepted it at Hawthorne's asking price, ten times his average per-page pay for the pieces collected in *Twice-told Tales* and more than twice the average for those in the first edition of *Mosses from an Old Manse* in 1846 (*CE, X, 521–26*).

Three years later, during Hawthorne's appointment as United States consul in Liverpool, England, he was asked by W. D Ticknor to suggest uncollected works that might be added to a second edition of *Mosses* that Ticknor, Reed, and Fields were eager to publish. On June 7, 1854 Hawthorne replied, "You put me to my trumps by asking for additional matter for the "Mosses"; for I considered myself exhausted on that score, long ago. Nevertheless, there is "Feathertop"—which is about as good as any of them. Let that go in." "Feathertop" was added to the first volume of the 1854 edition (*CE, X, 523*).

The original manuscript for all but the final three paragraphs is now in the Morgan Library collection and served as the copy text for the Centenary Edition (*CE, X, 576–77*). An examination of the extant manuscript revealed no significant editorial revisions (213).

## Circumstances of Composition, Sources, and Influences

Hawthorne's letter to John Sartain, mentioned above, establishes the time and place of composition; Hawthorne wrote, "I happened to have a little time, just before leaving Lenox, which I could not fill up better than by writing this story" (*CE, X, 525*). The Hawthornes left the "Little Red House" in Lenox on November 21, 1851 (458:121), taking what was to be Hawthorne's last short story with them on their move to West Newton where Hawthorne, convinced that longer fiction was a more rewarding form both artistically and financially, soon began *The Blithedale Romance*.

The earliest source for the story is an 1840 notebook entry:

> To make a story out of a scarecrow, giving it odd attributes. From different points of view, it should appear to change,—now an old man, now an old woman,—a gunner, a farmer, or the Old Nick. (*CE, VIII, 185.8–11*)

Nine years later, sometime between March 16 and September 17, 1849, a second, more closely related entry appears:

> A modern magician to make the semblance of a human being, with two laths for legs, a pumpkin for a head &c—of the rudest and most meagre materials. Then a tailor helps him to finish his work, and transforms this scarecrow into quite a fashionable figure. N.B.–R.S.R. At the end of the story, after deceiving the world for a long time, the spell should be broken; and the gray dandy be discovered to be nothing but a suit of clothes, with these few sticks inside of it. All through his seeming existence as a human being, there shall be some characteristics, some tokens, that, to the man of close observation and insight, betray him to be a mere thing of laths and clothes, without heart, soul, or intellect. And so this wretched old thing shall become the symbol of a large class. (*CE, VIII, 286.14–27*)

The story retains only the fundamental idea of the first entry dated eleven years earlier. The modern magician has become a witch in Puritan times, the tailor has been replaced by an invisible servant, and the deception lasts only one day rather than "a long time." In fact, "Feathertop" serves as a typical example of Hawthorne's method of writing by a process of slow evolution, beginning with an idea and then considering a variety of fictional embodiments over an extended period of time until an appropriate one is developed (483; 455:xxii–xliii).

Another source, between 1840 and 1849, that fits in well with Hawthorne's developmental method has been proposed—Hawthorne's reading of an unidentified tale by Ludwig Tieck in April 1843 (*CE, VIII, 369–79*).

Hawthorne's interest in the scarecrow motif, revealed in the 1840 entry, could have led him to attempt to read Tieck's 365-page tale entitled "The Scarecrow," available only in German. The basic idea in Tieck's opening chapters is identical with the theme expressed in the second notebook entry (258). Although one authority dismisses the parallelism between the two tales as "little more than a peculiar *Geistesverwandtschaft* between the two authors" (377:386), most critics, beginning with several of Hawthorne's contemporaries, have more persuasively assessed the similarities as significant. Most notable is Edgar Allan Poe's accusation that Hawthorne imitated Tieck (378.1:143). In a comprehensive review of the Tieck, Poe, and Hawthorne issue, Matenko supports Tieck's "Die Vogelscheuche" as a palpable force on the shaping of "Feathertop" (311).

A personal satiric attack has also been established as part of the motivation behind this story. The "R.S.R." in the middle of the 1849 entry, originally transcribed as R.L.R. (455:126), is positively identified by Sophia Hawthorne in a letter to her mother as Richard Saltonstall Rogers, a Salem merchant who was among the group of Whigs Hawthorne held responsible for his removal from the Custom House post on June 8, 1849 (*CE, VIII, 627*). The position of the notebook entry between March and September 1849 supports the likelihood that it was written at a time when Hawthorne was reacting most bitterly to his dismissal. The identification of R.S.R. was first hypothesized by Kern (257), who believed the character of Feathertop had been drawn to satirize Hawthorne's former friend. One of Kern's colleagues agrees, extending the revenge motive to Hawthorne's use of Roger's name in Roger Chillingworth of *The Scarlet Letter* (434). Another does not, arguing that Hawthorne's intent mellowed in the two years between the entry and the story. Feathertop, whose portrayal is assessed as sympathetic rather than critical, becomes not the target of Hawthorne's satire, but a device that satirizes the gullibility of people in general (234).

Another personal basis has been suggested for another aspect of Feathertop's story. The possibility that Polly's love might have made him human has been traced to Hawthorne's conviction that Sophia Peabody's love had miraculously rescued him from a life of isolation and unreality (455:lxx). Feathertop, however, turns out to be less fortunate than his authorial predecessor.

Except for the much-debated German sources discussed above, the only other literary influence associated with this story comes from the eighteenth-century Gothic novel. Two elements in the story are clearly part of the supernatural apparatus of the genre: Mother Rigby, the witch capable of performing magic with the assistance of her invisible, devilish servant, and the mirror with the extraordinary power to expose fraud and reveal truth (298:110–11).

## Relationship with Other Hawthorne Works

Although several readers have included "Feathertop" with "Young Goodman Brown" and "The Hollow of the Three Hills" as one of Hawthorne's witch stories (232:155; 315:161–62; 359:63–67), it does not concern itself with delusory evil like the former or with the consequences of sin like the latter. In many ways, it is more like a children's story of the "Little Daffydowndilly" type.

Nevertheless, some readers have classified Feathertop as an "Outcast of the Universe" comparable to Wakefield, Brown, and Gervayse Hastings of "The Christmas Banquet" (5; 455:lxx). Others have linked it, through its transformation motif, to "Drowne's Wooden Image," "The Artist of the Beautiful," "The Birthmark," "The Snow-Image," and *The Marble Faun* (303; 391).

## Interpretations and Criticism

"Feathertop" has been interpreted as "an allegory of the creative process" with special attention directed at Hawthorne's description of Mother Rigby's act of creation. His inability to explain the process except by acknowledging her "singular power and dexterity" as a witch is taken to mean that "the actual production of a work of art is in its nature undiscoverable" (188:38–39).

Most readers interpret "Feathertop" as a satire intended to attack frivolous hypocrisy. Durr considers it ironically effective except for a sentimental flaw. He objects to the interjection of the theme of regeneration through love, which he sees as a distraction from the satiric intent of the story. Axelsson takes the one truly approbative stand. He commends the first part of the story for its simple and straightforward moral, much like the well known fairy tale by Hans Christian Andersen, *The Emperor's New Clothes*. He also approves of the second half, in which Feathertop develops into a human character capable of self-recognition. By satirically reversing the characteristics of the scarecrow and those of humanity, Feathertop exposes the emptiness and superficiality of much of the human world (32:153–54).

As the last short story Hawthorne ever wrote, "Feathertop" serves as an apt illustration of the validity of the author's retrospective self-appraisal.

In the preface to *The Snow-Image*, Hawthorne writes, "The ripened autumnal fruit tastes but little better than the early windfalls" (*CE, XI, 6*). In the case of "Feathertop" most readers agree. Far from being a culminating point for Hawthorne's short-story artistry, it is usually considered moralistically obvious and farfetched; it is seldom included in anthologies while such "early windfalls" as "My Kinsman, Major Molineux" and "Young Goodman Brown" invariably are.

# XX

# Fragments from the Journal of a
# Solitary Man

(*Centenary Edition, Volume XI, Uncollected Tales*, 312–28.)


## Publication History

This story was first published in the *American Monthly Magazine* in July 1837 (X, 45–56) with no attribution. One of its passages, "There . . . coolness" (*322.16–323.4*), was published earlier, in the December 1835 issue of the *New-England Magazine* (IX), as "An Afternoon Scene" under the heading "Sketches from Memory. No. II. By a Pedestrian" (*CE, XI, 432–33*).

"Fragments" is undoubtedly the conclusion of a projected book, *The Story Teller*, that Hawthorne originally gave to Samuel Goodrich in 1834 in an effort to find a publisher. Goodrich passed the manuscript on to Park Benjamin, who was owner and editor of the *New-England Magazine* when it was absorbed by the *American Monthly* at the end of 1835. Benjamin carried the fragments of *The Story Teller* with him to his new position as coeditor of the *American Monthly*. Hawthorne's friend, Horatio Bridge, tells of "a mass of manuscript . . . as yet unpublished" in the editor's possession, "scornfully bestowed" by the author (63:69). Apparently Hawthorne himself did not recall exactly where Benjamin had published the conclusion of *The Story Teller*, because in 1854 he refers his editor, James T. Fields, to the *New-England Magazine* under Benjamin's editorship for both its beginning and ending. Fields found "Story Teller No. I and II" for inclusion in the 1854 *Mosses from an Old Manse*, but he did not locate the conclusion in the *American Monthly* where Benjamin had published it as "Fragments" (*CE, XI, 395–96*). It was never collected by Hawthorne and is included under "Uncollected Tales" in the Centenary Edition with four other acknowledged but uncollected segments of *The Story Teller*, "My Visit to Niagara," "Graves and Goblins," "A Visit to the Clerk of the Weather," and "Sketches from Memory." The last is further divided into "The Inland Part," "Rochester," and "A Night Scene." A fourth part of the original "Sketches from Memory No. II," published in the December 1835 *New-England Magazine* as "The Canal Boat," was collected in the 1854 *Mosses* with the two parts of "Sketches from Memory No. I" ("The Notch of the White

Mountains" and "Our Evening Party Among the Mountains") under the heading "Sketches from Memory." This haphazard history links "Fragments" indisputably to the scattered segments of *The Story Teller*, as does the subject matter and narrative style.

The fact that one of the descriptive passages from Oberon's account of his return home was published as part of another piece suggests that revisions were made, although no record of their extent or of who made them has been found. One theory suggests that Park Benjamin may have written the passages in "Fragments" which are attributed to Oberon's literary executor and which bind the final journal entries together. The uncharacteristic style and factual inconsistencies of the executor's framing segments make such a possibility plausible, especially in the light of the way in which *The Story Teller* had been divided to supply as much magazine copy as possible (362).

## Circumstances of Composition, Sources, and Influences

Like the rest of *The Story Teller* pieces, "Fragments" was written in the fall and winter of 1832–33 or 1833–34 (11:131–46). This story serves as an excellent example of Hawthorne's debt to the Gothic tradition and the graveyard school in general. From the opening description of a death chamber and its corpse to the final passage from the twenty four-year-old's journal in which, just before his death, he looks forward to soon becoming "all spirit" (*27.23*), the characteristic devices of the genre are evident.

## Relationship with Other Hawthorne Works

As the conclusion of *The Story Teller*, "Fragments" is intimately related to all the pieces associated with that projected collection. The Oberon figure in "Fragments" is the same character found in "Passages from a Relinquished Work" and "The Devil in Manuscript." All three pieces could be read as a single narrative although the characterizations and chronology are not always consistent. (See publication history, above.) There is also much in Oberon's journal that sounds like the sketch, "The Haunted Mind" (*CE, IX, 304–09*).

## Interpretations and Criticism

Like the other Oberon stories, "Fragments" has continually been interpreted as autobiographical. As early as 1841, Evert A. Duyckinck called the final confession of Oberon in "Fragments" a revelation of "the sombre, half-disappointed spirit" of the author himself (98:7).

Readers interested in nineteenth-century American literature will find "Fragments" valuable as an illustration of Hawthorne at his most Poe-like. When Oberon yields himself to his habitual "morbid fancies" (317.24) and dreams of promenading down Broadway in his shroud, the Gothic grotesqueries of Hawthorne rival those of Poe at his most bizarre.

# XXI

# The Gentle Boy

(*Centenary Edition, Volume IX, Twice-told Tales*, 68–105.)

## Publication History

This story was first published in 1831 in the *Token* (pp. 193–240) dated 1832 with no attribution. Samuel Goodrich, the editor, offered Hawthorne $35 for it in January 1830 shortly after Hawthorne submitted it for his perusal as one of the *Provincial Tales*; however, whether Goodrich ever paid for the story when Hawthorne gave him permission to use it in *The Token* two years later is not certain. (See publication history for "The Wives of the Dead.") "The Gentle Boy" was included in the first edition of *Twice-told Tales* in 1837 after Hawthorne made extensive revisions, including several lengthy deletions. (See interpretations, below.) In 1839 the story was published separately, subtitled "A Thrice Told Tale," and dedicated to "Miss Sophia A. Peabody," who would become Mrs. Hawthorne in 1842. The booklet was illustrated with an engraving derived from a drawing by Sophia of Tobias Pearson's first meeting with Ilbrahim, and it included a preface praising her sketch of "The Puritan and the Gentle Boy" (*CE, IX, 491, 497, 520, 566–68*).

## Circumstances of Composition, Sources, and Influences

This story was probably written in the fall of 1829 when Hawthorne withdrew William Sewel's *History of the Quakers* from the Salem Athenaeum for a month, but he may have started working on it as early as January of 1828 when he first borrowed Sewel's account. Hawthorne cites "the historian of the sect" (*69.32*), meaning Sewel, in the background essay that opens the story, but Hawthorne's balanced presentation must have relied on Puritan annalists as well. Among the likeliest are Hutchinson, Hubbard, Neal, Baylies, and Cotton Mather himself. The factual basis for the story could have been derived from any or all of these; the condemnation of Endicott (*69.21–70.7*), who is not named but who was governor during the Quaker persecutions, comes directly from Sewel. The action of the story takes place between two verifiable events: the execution of two Quaker men on October 27, 1659 and the arrival of the letters from Charles II ordering the end of the executions on September 9, 1661—although Hawthorne postpones the letters' arrival somewhat to coincide with Ilbrahim's death on the night of a winter storm (149:159–63; 361).

Historical precedents exist for both Tobias Pearson and Catherine, Ilbrahim's mother. Sewel documents several conversions to Quakerism, like Pearson's, among Puritans repelled by the cruelties inflicted by their brethren on the minority sect. Catherine's life history is pieced from the careers of several famous Quakeresses. Like Catherine Evans, she "had pined in the cells of a Catholic Inquisition" (*88.1–2*). Like Mary Fisher, she had found temporary refuge in Turkey. Like Mary Prince, she "had assaulted the Governor with frightful language, as he passed by the window of her prison" (*83.16–17*). And like Mary Dyer, she was banished by the Puritans to the wilderness under punishment of death if she returned. Catherine's appearance at the meetinghouse in sackcloth and ashes and her extravagant and malignant tirade from the pulpit likewise have historical analogues, as do the minor characters of the Puritan minister, whose own persecution under Archbishop Laud does not temper his attack on other minority sects, and the Old Quaker, whose zeal drives him to abandon his family (149:159–63; 361).

"The Gentle Boy" has long been regarded as Hawthorne's "imaginative atonement" for the part his ancestor, William Hathorne, played in the Quaker persecution (511:360). According to Sewel, "Anne Coleman and four of her friends were whipped through Salem, Boston, and Dedham, by order of Willam Hawthorn, who before he was a magistrate had opposed compulsion for conscience" (149:160). This same ancestor had also presided over the court that ordered Deborah Wilson whipped at a cart's tail for appearing on the streets of Salem in the nude. Ironically, she was protesting against the community's practice of punishing women by stripping and whipping them publicly (293:62–63). Hawthorne's awareness of his ancestral involvement is confirmed in both "The Custom-House" and "Main Street," where he refers specifically to William Hathorne's persecution of a Quakeress.

These historical allusions, both overt and covert, are supplemented by a battery of biblical allusions that fall into a significant pattern. The language and spirit of the Old Testament (Isa. 65:5; Prov. 14:14) are reflected in the speech and actions of the Puritans, while the Quakers draw heavily, but erratically, from the New Testament (Rev. 8:13, 16:6; 2 Cor. 11:23–27; Matt. 5:3–11, 6:19–20, 10:30, 20:1). Perhaps the most immediately identifiable echo is from the well-known passage in St. Paul's epistle to the Corinthians that Hawthorne parallels in Catherine's response to Ilbrahim's impending death: "I have been wounded sore; I have suffered much; many things in the body, many in the mind;..." (*101–02*). Thompson points out that Hawthorne invests this and the other Biblical allusions with corrosive irony designed to expose the limitations of both sects—the irresponsible brotherhood of the Quakers and the harsh paternal order of the Puritans (473).

## Relationship with Other Hawthorne Works

As one of Hawthorne's Puritan stories, "The Gentle Boy" is probably closest to "The Man of Adamant" in its condemnation of Puritan intolerance (420; 500:108); however, some aspects of the narrowness, bigotry, and harshness that mark the Puritans in these two tales are evident in more subtle ways in the apparently laudatory "Gray Champion" and "Endicott and the Red Cross," in the clearly ambivalent "May-Pole of Merry Mount," "Main Street," and Province-House stories, and in the more perplexing "Minister's Black Veil" and "Young Goodman Brown."

Hawthorne's most famous Puritan narrative, *The Scarlet Letter*, has much in common with "The Gentle Boy." Both expose cruel and unusual punishments inflicted on women by the community in the name of religious righteousness, and both portray Puritan children as inhumanly cruel. The children are called "the most intolerant brood that ever lived" in the novel (chapter 6) and "a brood of baby-fiends" in the story (*92.17–18*). The perversion of the original Puritan spirit that this younger generation manifests is described in "Main Street":

> All was well, so long as their lamps were freshly kindled at the heavenly flame. After a while, however, whether in their time or their children's, these lamps began to burn more dimly, or with a less genuine lustre; and then it might be seen, how hard, cold and confined, was their system.... (*CE, XI, 58.23–28*)

One reader believes that this "children's declension" theme operates as a myth in Hawthorne's fiction (249), a theory that establishes Ilbrahim's and Pearl's peers as dramatic evidence of how far the Puritans' originally admirable spiritual and moral standards had declined. The perverse friendship that Ilbrahim establishes with the crippled Puritan boy, who turns on him, has been likened to Dimmesdale's relationship to Chillingworth, while Catherine's position by the end of the story is like Hester's at the end of the novel—both are ex-outcasts who are spiritually better than the Puritan community (115:68, 70). An unironic reading of the closing paragraph suggests that the community's feeling of responsibility for

Ilbrahim's death has had a beneficent effect; this phenomenon has been classified with other examples of the educative power of sin found not only in *The Scarlet Letter*, but in *The House of Seven Gables* and, most explicitly, in *The Marble Faun* (188:123–26).

"My Kinsman, Major Molineux" has been classified with "The Gentle Boy" on several counts. The two stories were part of the projected *Provincial Tales* collection and were originally published in the same issue of the *Token*. Pearce calls "The Gentle Boy," in its first version, "a full-blown variation on the Molineux theme." He defines the motif as "the imputation simultaneously of guilt and righteousness through history" (368:148). Male points out another theme found in both stories—the search for a home (304:45). And Crews identifies "a common substratum of attitude and a common logic of motivation" which is ultimately Oedipal and which takes the form of submission in one and revolt in the other (115:61–79).

Hawthorne's condemnatory portrayal of Catherine's monomaniacal zeal may be considered a "pre-study of the dominance of ambitious projects over human concerns." This antireform authorial stance is most evident in "Egotism," "Rappaccini's Daughter," and *The Blithedale Romance* (361:675–76).

## Interpretations and Criticism

The one consistent observation made by contemporary readers who have paid any attention to "The Gentle Boy" is that the story is not what it seems. It is, they say, a tale of great duplicity (115:72) and deceptive simplicity (147:159), a work easy to underestimate (304:45) whose quality goes beyond its surface pathos (149:170). The rationale appears to be an attempt to explain why most twentieth-century readers have dismissed the story as inferior, primarily because of its oversentimentality.

Hawthorne himself acknowledges an unaesthetic excess of emotional indulgence in the story in the preface that appears with the 1839 separate edition: "Nature here led ... deeper into the Universal heart, than Art has been able to follow" (*CE, IX, 567*). The reading public of his day recognized no such flaw. The "gentle" boy was "genteel" as well, and his story was the most popular of Hawthorne's tales during his lifetime. Longfellow called it "the finest thing he ever wrote" (98:10), and in an anonymous review of *Twice-told Tales*, Elizabeth Peabody singled it out as a masterpiece (480).

Doubleday classifies "The Gentle Boy" as one of three "masterpieces" in Hawthorne's first collection (149:159), but few others in today's reading audience would agree with his and Miss Peabody's assessment. In addition to the general charge of unrestrained emotionalism, the story has been faulted for excess, in and of itself, that is, an overabundance of material (315:218) or, as another reader put it, "the multiplicity of its ingredients" (490:72). James touches on its superfluousness when he describes it as "one of the longest, though by no means one of the most successful" of Hawthorne's tales (241:5). Hawthorne may have been aware of this problem, too, because he deleted several lengthy passages in the original story when he included it in *Twice-told Tales*. In an analysis of these revisions, Gross credits Hawthorne with conscious artistry aimed at thematic compactness and dramatic intensity (210). Apparently, some readers think Hawthorne's deletions did not go far enough.

Others, however, commend the story for its balanced presentation of the mutuality of guilt between the Quakers and the Puritans (147:159; 188:123–26; 210; 304:45–48; 309:71–72; 447:63–65; 473; 511:360). One of the longest of the deleted passages (*CE, IX, 614–15*) rationalizes the Puritans' harsh measures by detailing the extenuating circumstances of 1656. Obviously, its removal contributes to a more objective view of the shortcomings of both kinds of religious fanaticism. Matthiessen believes that Hawthorne's "sensitively accurate scale of wrongs and rights" is the most remarkable feature of the story (315:216). Hawthorne exposes the hypocrisy and dehumanization in both sects, condemning as equally reprehensible the Puritans' cold and loveless bigotry and the Quaker's all-consuming zeal that negates family responsibilities.

Tobias and Dorothy Pearson emerge as the *via media* between the two religous extremes (188:123), although their position can be considered "an entrapment" rather than a happy medium (115:65). Dorothy's capacity for love on the human level is in direct contrast to the abstractions worshipped by the others (309:72), but the Pearsons' position is complicated by their roles as victims. Tobias, especially, presents an interpretative dilemma. In following the dictates of essential Christianity, he precipitates a series of events that culminate in his rejecting what he had always considered "his" Christian faith. In this respect, Male's definition of the story's theme as the "agonizing difficulty of finding an integrated, fruitful religious experience in America" is right on target and applies to Tobias as well as to Ilbrahim. The search for a home is part of this motif (46:111–17; 304:45–48). Gross also considers Tobias and Ilbrahim as the tragic centers of the story (210), while Doubleday's analysis suggests that Tobias is important enough to have the four major episodes in the story structured around him and designed so as to mark the changes in his spiritual outlook (149:164). Dauner appraises Tobias as a minor figure who nevertheless illustrates a concern with the spiritual ambiguities of life rather than any specific definition of Christianity. Tobias becomes "a disillusioned, embittered, and defeated man" in spite of—or, perhaps, because of—his Christian ethic (128). To another reader, Tobias' Christian compassion is heavily laced with feelings of inadequacy and guilt; Crews judges him to be "a peculiarly neurotic Good Samaritan" who is as much a victim of psychological determinism as is Ilbrahim. As for the balance between opposing forces, the contest, in behavioral terms, is between the arch-sadism of the Puritans and the self-destructive masochism of the Quakers (115:61–72).

To these religious, philosophical, and psychological implications, Bell adds a specifically historical dimension: "The Gentle Boy" has for its theme, as does most of Hawthorne's historical fiction, the transformation of the English character in the American wilderness. Migration to the New World distorts the original mission of both Puritans and Quakers. The intolerant Puritan children represent the transplanted element that will survive, while Ilbrahim and the dead Pearson children are associated with Old World possibilities that become stunted and withered by the conditions in the New World (46:111–17).

The factor that contributes most to the belying appearance of this story is its irony. One reader calls the irony "heavy-handed" (149:166), but the majority admire it as a powerful rhetorical device that is skillfully integrated with character and plot development (128; 147:158–70; 156; 305:274; 473). Donahue details how Hawthorne sets up explicit and astringent ironic effects by incorporating his horror and rejection of man's depravity with his faltering acknowledgment of it. The last sentence in the story demonstrates how Hawthorne can dispassionately and urbanely damn "all lukewarm unloving humanity to hell with his faint praise" (147:167).

Allegory is practically nonexistent in this realistically oriented story. One touch of it is found in the climax of the meetinghouse scene when Dorothy and Catherine are described as forming "a practical allegory" of "rational piety and unbridled fanaticism" (85.29–30). In a reconsideration of Hawthorne's concept of allegory, Rees uses this example to show how Hawthorne occasionally succeeds in fusing the art of allegory with life, in spite of what Rees sees as Hawthorne's disdain of allegory (387). Waggoner inadvertently countermands Rees's implication that Hawthorne's best kind of allegory is to be found in "The Gentle Boy." In a discussion of Hawthorne's genre, Waggoner contrasts the allegorical "Young Goodman Brown" with the realistic "Gentle Boy" and acknowledges "the more allegorical one" as the "greater of the two" (500:253).

The same would readily apply to a contest between "The Gentle Boy" and "My Kinsman, Major Molineux." Crews, however, opts for "My Kinsman" on a different basis. He admits that the buried psychological aspects of "The Gentle Boy" hold an "appeal to the modern taste for intellectual tension, irony and depth," but he makes a strong aesthetic distinction between the surface-depth contradictions of "The Gentle Boy" and the more satisfying, total unity of effect achieved in "My Kinsman" (115:72). Yet, Hawthorne enthusiasts do not write off "The Gentle Boy" entirely. Several see it as an influence on Melville's *Moby Dick* (115:71; 192) and *Pierre* (128): Ilbrahim's homelessness parallels Ishmael's; Catherine's blasphemous closing speech and her inverted piety are like Ahab's; and Tobias Pearson is analogous to Pierre in his basic goodness and tragic denouement. Some of these close readers maintain that there is more to "The Gentle Boy" than the surfeit of surface pathos that greets the casual observer. They corroborate the judgment of Hawthorne's family, friends, and contemporaries, who always considered it one of his best stories.

# XXII

# The Gray Champion

(*Centenary Edition, Volume IX, Twice-told Tales, 9–18.*)

## Publication History

"The Gray Champion" was first published in January 1835 in the *New-England Magazine* (VIII, 20–26) as the work of the author of "The Gentle Boy" (*CE, IX, 564*). As one of the seventeen pieces by Hawthorne to appear in this magazine under Park Benjamin's editorship in 1834 and 1835, "The Gray Champion" was part of *The Story Teller*, a projected work for which its author "got little or nothing as pay." (See publication history for "The Devil in Manuscript.")

Many scholars believe this story was also intended originally to be a part of *Provincial Tales* (10; 11:127–30; 84:12–13; 514:83). When Hawthorne, in an effort to find a publisher for *Provincial Tales*, sent some of its stories to Samuel Goodrich on December 20, 1829, he mentioned "two or three others, not at present in a condition to be sent" (*CE, IX, 488*). One of these "two or three others" was probably "The Gray Champion." Hawthorne's search for a publisher proved to be in vain, and by the end of 1832, he had embarked on another collection, *The Story Teller*. It was never published in book form either; when it was broken up for the magazines and annuals, "The Gray Champion" was among its segments. Why Hawthorne waited four years before publishing this piece appears to be related to his determination to present his work to the public in book form instead of in magazines (*CE, IX, 491*). "The Gray Champion," which did not succeed in finding a publisher as a part of either *Provincial Tales* or *The Story Teller,* accordingly made its first appearance as an anonymous contribution in a Boston magazine. In 1837 Hawthorne chose it as the opening piece for *Twice-told Tales.* Since Hawthorne's selection for his first collection rested on the tastes of the reading public (120), his placing "The Gray Champion" in such a strategic position suggests that he thought it was the kind of story his audience would approve of and admire (43:72).

## Circumstances of Composition, Sources, and Influences

As a part of *Provincial Tales,* this story was probably written in 1828 or 1829. Although Hawthorne's notebooks and letters offer no insights into the genesis of "The Gray Champion," he is reported to have expressed a particular interest in the regicide judges in 1828, when he visited their alleged graves while on a trip through New Haven in October of that year (458:41).

Hawthorne's sources for this story appear to be two actual historical events—the first, the revolt against the government of Sir Edmund Andros in Boston in 1689, and the second, the participation of a regicide judge in an Indian skirmish at Hadley, Massachusetts, during King Phillip's War in 1675. Both of these are recorded in the first volume of Thomas Hutchinson's *History of Massachusetts* (1765), a book charged out to Hawthorne from the Salem Athenaeum in 1826 and again in 1829 (259). The first two paragraphs of Hawthorne's story provide the background for the confrontation between the colonists and the rulers imposed on them by James II. The rumor that Hawthorne refers to was the news that William of Orange had landed in England and had issued a declaration that magistrates unjustly removed from office should be reinstated. In spite of an attempt to suppress this information by jailing John Winslow, who had returned from England with a printed copy of the declaration, the colonists heard about it and were ready to return the former governor and his magistrates to power. The venerable governor Bradstreet's plea for caution in Hawthorne's story (*CE, IX, 12*) follows Hutchinson's description of the situation:

> The old magistrates and heads of the people silently wished, and secretly prayed, for success to the glorious undertaking, and determined quietly to wait the event. The body of the people were more impatient. The flame, which had been long smothered in their breasts, burst forth with violence, Thursday the 18th of April, when the governor and such of the council as had been most active, and other obnoxious persons, about fifty in the whole, were seized and confined, and the old magistrates were reinstated. (*The History of the Colony and Province of Massachusetts-Bay*, ed. Lawrence Shaw Mayo; Cambridge, Mass., 1936, I, 317)

Hutchinson's phrase, "and other obnoxious persons," was expanded by Hawthorne into a detailed description of Andros' group, "all magnificently clad, flushed with wine, proud of unjust authority" (*12–13*).

In the same volume, Hutchinson also related the escape to New England of three of the fifty-nine regicide judges who in 1649 had condemned Charles I (I, 183–87). At the end of a long footnote in which he reviewed the attitude of respect that the colonists held for the fugitives, he added the particulars of the "Angel of Hadley" story:

I am loath to omit an anecdote handed down through governor
Leveret's family. I find Goffe takes notice in his journal of Leveret's
being at Hadley. The town of Hadley was alarmed by the Indians
in 1675, in the time of publick worship, and the people were in
the utmost confusion. Suddenly, a grave elderly person appeared
in the midst of them. In his mien and dress he differed from the
rest of the people. He not only encouraged them to defend themselves; but he put himself at their head, rallied, instructed and led
them on to encounter the enemy, who by this means were repulsed.
As suddenly, the deliverer of Hadley disappeared. The people were
left in consternation, utterly unable to account for this strange
phenomenon. It is not probable, that they were ever able to explain
it. If Goffe had been then discovered, it must have come to the
knowledge of those persons, who declare by their letters that they
never knew what became of him. (Hutchinson, I, 187)

The first fictional use of this incident occurred in Sir Walter Scott's
*Peveril of the Peak* published in 1822. In fact, Hawthorne probably
first encountered the Hadley legend in chapter 14 of Scott's novel, where it
was presented as a part of the American reminiscences of Major Bridgenorth (356:261–63, 267; 149:87). Scott enjoyed tremendous esteem and
popularity in the early nineteenth century. The title of an 1833 oration
by Rufus Choate reveals the magnitude of Scott's following in America:
Choate called it "The Importance of Illustrating New-England History
by a Series of Romances like the Waverly Novels." Hawthorne, too,
was one of Scott's American admirers. In a letter to his sister in 1820,
he enthuiastically anticipates reading the one Scott novel he had not yet
read and wishes he "might have the pleasure of reading" the others again
(458:8). Both the title for Hawthorne's story and the symbolical ending are
undoubtedly indebted to Scott's version. In *Peveril*, the regicide is described as having august features "overshadowed by locks of grey hair,
which mingled with a long beard of the same color" and with a "grey eye
that retained all its lustre." Bridgenorth refers to him as "an inspired
champion" and concludes his account on a prophetic note similar to
Hawthorne's closing statement: Bridgenorth conjectures, "perhaps his
voice may be heard in the fields once more, should England need one of
her noblest hearts." Hawthorne's portrayal of the confrontation between
the two factions also displays a Scott trademark—a sharp eye for depicting
human tableaux (490:71).

At the same time, Hawthorne's story differs from Scott's account in
several ways. For one thing, Hawthorne mythologizes the figure of the
regicide rather than merely romanticizing him as Scott did. Hawthorne
leaves Goffe nameless, whereas Scott had identified him as Richard

Whalley, an error not only in mistaking one regicide for another, but in confusing Edward Whalley with his father, Richard (356:261).

Three American writers also preceded Hawthorne in adapting the legend—James McHenry in his novel *The Spectre of the Forest* in 1823, James Nelson Barker in his blank-verse tragedy *Superstition* in 1826, and James Fenimore Cooper in *The Wept of Wish-ton-Wish* in 1829. McHenry's novel might have suggested to Hawthorne the idea of assigning a significant role to a regicide after the Hadley incident (356:267), but all of these fictionalized accounts are like Hawthorne's in a very basic way. They equate the regicides not only with the spirit of the founding fathers, but with the principles of the American Revolution too (46:27-33). Bell's survey of the historical fiction of Hawthorne's contemporaries adds an 1824 anonymous work, *The Witch of New England,* to the pre-Hawthorne list of regicide stories (46:32).

While the association of the regicides with the Colonial spirit of independence may have been almost a literary convention in the American historical romance of the 1820s, Hawthorne's juxtaposition of the regicides' legend with the Boston revolt of 1689 was his original contribution to the tradition, a twist that makes "The Gray Champion" unique from its predecessors. Doubleday attributes this development, in part, to Hawthorne's tacit compliance with the prescriptions of a body of nationalistic literary theorists who were active in early nineteenth-century America (149:128-26). For example, William Tudor, in a Phi Beta Kappa address printed in 1815, suggests that American writers use such historical material as the "incident . . . of . . . one of the regicides suddenly emerging from his concealment"; John Gorham Palfrey and John Neal, in magazine articles during the 1820s, also propose the exiled judges as appropriate story material; and Rufus Choate, in orations in 1833 and 1834, makes the resistance to Andros the prime example of the kind of Colonial spirit that should be taught to succeeding generations. Another source for the view of the Revolution of 1689 as a precursor to the Spirit of 1776 is suggested by Bell, who emphasizes the influence of such romantic historians as George Bancroft (46:34-35, 49-51).

In addition to these analogues in specific subject matter, William Austin's story, "Peter Rugg, the Missing Man," has been suggested as an influence on Hawthorne's method and intent. The almost instantaneous fame Austin's story achieved when it was published in 1824 precludes Hawthorne's having known it in 1828. (In 1842, Hawthorne used Austin's title character as the doorkeeper of the museum in "The Virtuoso's Collection.") "The Gray Champion" is like Austin's tale in its attempt to establish a continuing legend of historical import and in its ambiguous handling of preternatural possibilities (149:49-52).

## Relationship with Other Hawthorne Works

Two other pieces in Hawthorne's canon deal with the Boston revolt against Andros—the children's book *Grandfather's Chair,* first published in 1841 and the biographical sketch "Dr. Bullivant" of 1831. Hawthorne does not take fictional liberties with his children's version; the regicide plays no part in Grandfather's account. Neither is he mentioned in the biographical sketch, which does place Bullivant at the confrontation. The little apothecary, who was censured by the Puritans for his bizarre sense of humor as well as for his political alliances, is described briefly as a member of Andros' party in "The Gray Champion" (*13.4–6*).

Among the *Provincial Tales,* "The Gray Champion" is most often compared to "The May-Pole of Merry Mount" because of the dramatic allegorical contrast between the dark Puritans and their brightly clad foes, the Andros party in one, the Merry Mounters in the other (84:13; 149:90–91). The standoff between opposing social systems in each of these tales has been identified by Becker as one of the typical structural patterns of allegory, the battle of configuration (45:174).

The historical aspects of "The Gray Champion," on which much of its claim to being a *Provincial Tale* is based, are also the grounds for its kinship with historically oriented works published after 1837. These include "Endicott and the Red Cross," the four "Legends of the Province-House" ("Howe's Masquerade," "Edward Randolph's Portrait," "Lady Eleanore's Mantle," and "Old Esther Dudley"), "Main Street," and *The Scarlet Letter.*

The four "Legends," in addition to continuing the exploration of America's past, are like "The Gray Champion" in style as well as substance. Tableauxlike presentations of crowds mark all five stories (20; 490:71), as does a deliberate ambiguity—a device used, according to Fogle, to dissolve the irrelevant actualities of the past in order to present a more idealized history (186:12). The allegorical technique of ornamentation is also used to achieve the same purpose in "The Gray Champion" and two of the "Legends." The basic disorder masked by the magnificent raiments of Andros' faction in "The Gray Champion" is paralleled in the ornate displays in "Howe's Masquerade" and "Lady Eleanore's Mantle," where the device effectively undercuts the social hierarchies it creates (45:175).

"The Gray Champion" is related to all of the above-mentioned historical works in its ambivalence toward Puritanism and the revolutionary spirit. Many readers would agree with Hoffman's assessment of "The Gray Champion," "Endicott and the Red Cross," and the four "Legends" as works that share a vision of the spirit of revolt as the divine right of an oppressed people (232:124); on the other hand, some interpret parts of the story as ironic. Hawthorne invariably includes enough ambivalence to allow each reader to find the kind of verification his perspective seeks. The narrator in "Main Street" demonstrates how difficult any clear-cut "for" or "against" decision is when he states, "Let us thank God for having given us such ancestors; and let each successive generation thank Him, not less fervently, for being one step further from them in the march of ages" (*CE, IX, 68*).

## Interpretations and Criticism

Two widely diverse interpretations will serve as representative extremes of the kind of reaction "The Gray Champion" has generated. Baym says, " 'The Gray Champion' is unambiguously patriotic and its attitude toward Puritanism entirely affirmative" (43:72). To Crews, on the other hand, it is an intentionally disdainful handling of a patriotic theme; the attitude of apparent approval expressed in the opening and closing statements is exposed as absurd by the "overpowering" irony of the intervening pages (115:39–41). Crews uses Hawthorne's description of the Puritans to support his view that theirs is only a pretense of standing for justice and freedom: among the assembled colonists, Hawthorne points out the "old soldiers of the Parliament . . . smiling grimly at the thought, that their aged arms might strike another blow against the house of Stuart"; "the veterans of King Phillip's war, who had burnt villages and slaughtered young and old, with pious fierceness, while the godly souls throughout the land were helping them with prayer"; and finally, the ministers who "assumed a more apostolic dignity, as well befitted a candidate for the highest honor of his profession, the crown of martyrdom" (*CE, IX, 11*). Crews maintains that these details and the action contradict the ostensible moral purpose; instead of showing "the deformity of any government that does not grow out of the nature of things and the character of the people" (*13.20–22*), the tale "really implies that authority can only be overmatched by greater authority" and graphically shows the colonists not meeting "tyranny with freedom," but setting up "a rival system of ancestor-worship" (115:40–41).

Baym's pro-Puritan reading finds support in a great many quarters (498:13; 84:13; 95; 233:210; 241:52; 420:206; 498:175). Crews's anti-Puritan interpretation finds fewer allies. Stein is one; he sees "The Gray Champion" as one of a series of works that re-create "the decline and disintegration of Puritan civilization" (447:32–33). Fossum is another; he accounts for the harsh details in the Puritans' description by recognizing them as revelations of their guilty fear of retaliation

(189:32–33). However, Fossum's conclusion, that the Champion is a conciliatory figure who mediates between submission and rebellion, is unlike anyone else's, including—on the basis of the literal action in the story—the author's. On the whole even those critics who acknowledge Hawthorne's ironic reservations do not share Crews's view that he is disparaging the Puritans (46:50–53; 149:92).

Bell's reading is very much like Crews's in its emphasis on the patriarchal and authoritative nature of the Champion, but unlike Crews, Bell interprets the story as "a sincere expression" of the "conservative ideal of the Revolution," an ideal that envisioned its greatest revolutionary hero as "the Father of our Country" (46:50–53). The fact that Crews's language and method can be put to use by someone such as Bell (and Baym, too, who discusses the story's dominant father-figure in her pro-Puritan reading) illustrates how pervasive and diversified the psychoanalytic approach to Hawthorne's works has become.

Another approach, the mythological, also lends itself comfortably to "The Gray Champion." Hoffman, who is a prominent myth and folklore scholar, attributes Hawthorne's tendency to mythologize actual history to his instinctive view of history as fabulous (233:209–10). "The Gray Champion" is perhaps the best example of Hawthorne's history-mythologizing process; the source studies clearly reveal how Hawthorne reworked the historical material to create his desired effect. Because he was familiar with the traditions of providence and wonders in Puritan writings (232:23–32), Hawthorne could recognize in the regicide story, which had been transmitted orally for generations before Hutchinson included it in his footnote, another example of the special Puritan-providence relationship. Hawthorne, however, transformed the regicide's heroic leadership into a spectral legend (148). Hoffman identifies the story as a local variant of the theme in world folklore of the ancient hero, originally a god, who returns at a time of crisis to deliver his people (233:466, n.11). When Hawthorne describes his Champion as "combining the leader and the saint" (*15:20*), he is reinforcing the dual aspects of the myth, that is, supernatural intervention and worship of a culture hero. Thompson, who lists this theme as Motif A580 in *Motif-Index of Folk Literature,* includes citations with references to legends of Holger, Balder, and King Arthur (233:466, n.11). While such associations are archetypally valid, a more specific indication of Hawthorne's mythological bent is his choice of sunset as the time for the Champion's appearance. By casting the action at the close of the day, Hawthorne evokes the primitive rituals associated with the setting of the sun and establishes the chiaroscuro of twilight when things are not always what they seem.

To historicists such as Pearce, such myth criticism is nothing more than pointless archetype-hunting. Pearce believes that Hawthorne "derives his symbols not from myth . . . but from the facts of history itself" (370:222). Therefore, even "The Gray Champion," which he admits "is a kind of folk-tale," must have its basis in verifiable fact. Although neither its author nor its readers can literally believe in the actual existence of the central figure, Pearce maintains that Hawthorne provides authentication for the phenomenon he describes; the old man was a kind of invention of the communal mind at a time when it desperately needed a symbol. Pearce's argument is that the Champion, as part of a concrete and specific sociocultural situation, is historically verifiable and therefore credible (370:230–35).

Dauber offers a psychostructural reading based on Hawthorne's efforts to form a relationship with his audience. "The Gray Champion" is considered a turning point in Hawthorne's narrative; it is an attempt to create a national and public myth, but because Hawthorne's art seeks a more personal intimacy with the reader, the story demythologizes "New England's hereditary spirit" (*18.10–11*) even as it purports to celebrate it (127:53–56).

Critics have also examined "The Gray Champion" from a variety of stylistic perspectives with the result that it has been used to document Hawthorne as a symbolist (370), an allegorist (45), a typologist (46), and an emblemist (72). While all agree that Puritan typology plays a role in Hawthorne's method, the degree and nature of that influence is a matter of controversy. To Becker, the typological mode of thought, with its respect for historical figures, merely opened the way for Hawthorne's creation of historical allegory (45:163–75). To Brumm, the Gray Champion is not a literary embodiment of an abstract idea; he is a concrete figure of a determined historical period and Hawthorne's "most explicit example of a 'type'" (72:118–23). Like Becker, but unlike more historically oriented critics such as Pearce and Bell, she minimizes the importance of the Puritan typological tradition. She sees it merely as the background that helped Hawthorne develop into an emblemist, one who sees real "things, persons, and scenes" as repositories for universally significant concepts.

"The Gray Champion" has been commended for its "adroit shifts of narrative technique" (149:90) and for its dramatically effective contrasts (20:43; 45:174; 84:13; 490:71), but for most of its readers its most noteworthy aspect remains its unabashed Americanism. Even Henry James, who prefaces his approval with the observation that Hawthorne is not enough of a realist, sounds a patriotic note (241:52); James is grateful to Hawthorne for recounting, in "The Gray Champion," one of the "traditions" of our national past.

# XXIII

## The Great Carbuncle:
## A Mystery of the White Mountains

*(Centenary Edition, Volume IX, Twice-told Tales, 149–65.)*

### Publication History

This story was first published in the fall of 1836 in the *Token and Atlantic Souvenir* (pp. 156–75) dated 1837 as the work of the author of "The Wedding Knell" (*CE, IX, 569*). Samuel Goodrich, the editor, published eleven of Hawthorne's tales and sketches in the two volumes of the *Token* following the failure of *The Story Teller* in 1834; this was most probably one of the tales originally intended for the projected collection (*CE, IX, 495*; 11:41–42). In one section of the framework of *The Story Teller*, called "Our Evening Party Among the Mountains," the storyteller briefly relates the legend of the carbuncle and remarks, "On this theme me-thinks I could frame a tale with a deep moral" (*CE, XI, 428*).

For the eight pieces published in the *Token* in 1836, Hawthorne was paid $108, an average of $1 per page, making his income from "The Great Carbuncle" an approximate $20 (*CE, IX, 497*). The author included the story in his first collection, *Twice-told Tales*, in 1837.

### Circumstances of Composition, Sources, and Influences

As a part of *The Story Teller*, and thus closely related to Hawthorne's visit to the White Mountains detailed in a letter to his mother dated September 16, 1832, this story was probably written in the winter of 1832–33. (See circumstances of composition for "The Ambitious Guest.") Its primary source remains the local Indian legend that the author heard as a guest at Ethan Crawford's house in Franconia Notch. In spite of his exclamation in the persona of the storyteller, "I do abhor an Indian story" (*CE, XI, 427*), Hawthorne acknowledges "the Indian tradition, on which this somewhat extravagant tale is founded" in his own footnote to the story, offering as corroborative evidence the admission by an early historian of the bordering state of Maine that "even then, the existence of the Great Carbuncle was not entirely discredited" (*149*).

With oral tradition as an accepted factor in this story's genesis

(184:218–19), one twentieth-century reader, who spent some time working as an attendant at the Mt. Agassiz Observatory in the White Mountains, offers his personal sighting of the "marvelous stone" to suggest the
possibility that perhaps Hawthorne saw it as he did: a sudden burst of
splendor "as if a huge diamond had been exposed by a landslide" (219).
Haskell followed up his accidental sighting with a timed repetition the
following day aided by a 60-diameter telescope. With the telescope
aimed at a ravine between Mt. Garfield and Mt. Lafayette five miles
away, Haskell was momentarily blinded by a flash of intense light. He
then discerned the natural phenomenon responsible for the great-carbuncle
myth—a bare precipice of white granite, quartz, and mica over which
fell a thin, foamy sheet of water, creating a perfect mirror for reflecting
the sun's rays. When he tried to repeat the experience twenty-four hours
later, however, the surface water from the preceding day's heavy rain-
fall had drained to the forest and streams below, leaving the precipice
dry and lusterless, and the "wondrous gem" was gone. Hawthorne's notebooks and letters record no such literal sighting; a decade later, in the
persona of the narrator, he does see "this mighty gem" in " A Virtuoso's
Collection" but admits only that its discovery was "one of the wild
projects" of his youth (CE, X, 488.28–31). More to the point, however,
would be an autobiographical identification with the narrator of "The
Great Carbuncle" who does confess in the concluding paragraph that,
like Hawthorne's reader a century later, he saw from a distance of many
miles away "a wondrous light" around the summits of the Crystal Hills.

A variety of literary influences have been credited with contributing
to the form of this story, from the "subjective history" of Irving, who
wrote as a "sensitive tourist" would, developing the historical associations
of picturesque scenes (46:197), to the allegory, name symbolism, and
pilgrimage theme of Bunyan (244). The Gothic tradition has been cited
as the source for the sorcererlike Seeker, the deformed scholar, and a
variant of the carbuncle itself, "the Carbuncle of Giamschid . . . promised
to the beautiful Nourouinihar if she forsakes her betrothed" in William
Beckford's Vathek (298:95–96). Another Gothic convention is evident
in the convergence of picturesque and sublime elements, in the manner
of Salvator Rosa's paintings and Ann Radcliffe's novels, that Hawthorne
included in his description of the terrain encountered during the pilgrims'
ascent (282:392–93). Biblical analogues for Hannah and Matthew have
also been proposed; the scriptural Hannah accompanies her husband on
an unselfish pilgrimage in 1 Samuel, while a passage in the Gospel according to St. Matthew (5:14–16) is paralleled by the light imagery in the
story (474). A possible but less direct influence may have been "Der
Runenberg," a tale by Tieck of a broken-down old man who returns

from a search for jewels in the mountains with a sackful of worthless pebbles which he regards as precious stones (311; 377:384).

## Relationship with Other Hawthorne Works

This story shares the setting of the White Mountains of New Hampshire with "The Ambitious Guest" and "The Great Stone Face." In "The Great Carbuncle" and in "The Ambitious Guest" the natural sublime is portrayed as a fear-inspiring force beyond man's comprehension, an attitude that is also clearly discernible in the sketch, "My Visit to Niagara" (*CE, XI, 281–88*) (282).

"The Great Carbuncle" belongs to what one critic has called a "Pilgrimage Group," characterized by a number of seekers in a gestalt-like configuration moving toward self-revealing goals. Among these are the characters of "The Celestial Rail-road," "The Christmas Banquet," and "The Canterbury Pilgrims" (342:157–58). Another thematic grouping links it with "The Birthmark" and "The Artist of the Beautiful" as explorations of the "pursuit of the ideal" and its consequences (395).

Bewley points out similarities between "The Great Carbuncle" and "The New Adam and Eve." The couples in both stories relate successfully to their "inner spheres of reality," which is the only significant reality for Hawthorne's characters. Since his most effective tales deal with individuals whose relationship with that inner sphere has been violated, the two stories are also alike in being considered as not among his best (52:127–29).

## Interpretations and Criticism

A crucial question in this story centers on the significance of Hannah's and Matthew's rejection of the carbuncle after having been the only pilgrims privileged to see it. To Levy, this suggests "that the power of faith [exemplified by the couple's simple virtues] is at odds with religious illumination" if it puts aside primary human considerations. The carbuncle's forbidding power, therefore, suggests not only the "awful splendor of the Hebraic deity," but the religious zeal and fanaticism of Puritanism as well (282:394). In a similar vein, Eisinger sees the carbuncle as the object of an abnormal monomania (162:32–33). Thompson, on the other hand, equates it with the concept of brotherhood; the couple's decision to reject the carbuncle indicates moral growth because they have learned not to desire what they cannot share with others (474:6–7). Morrow, by differentiating between "how man relates to the carbuncle" and "how the carbuncle relates to man," encompasses both negative and positive aspects of the carbuncle's meaning while also taking into account its two standard dictionary definitions. In the latter, as "a red stone of the garnet family," the jewel is associated with light and offers a "powerful and deep insight into the human condition." In the former, the carbuncle is a projection of each man's personal folly, like "a pus-bearing sore," an external manifestation of an inner sickness. Varieties of pride and greed mark the follies of the seeker, the scholar, the merchant, the poet, the aristocrat, and the cynic; Hannah and Matthew differ from the group only in that they are guilty of the least amount of folly. Morrow interprets their rejection of the carbuncle as a somewhat dubious blessing; he calls them "accomodationists" who "pay for peace of mind with a lack of insight and knowledge" (342:161). Clearly, each reader is free to choose between accepting Hannah and Matthew as conformists who settle for a mundane existence or as good Christians who reject delusory distractions. Hawthorne contributes further to the ambiguity by not allowing his narrator to make a clear-cut choice between humanistic piety and idealistic goals. He affirms the simple wisdom of the two mortals who "reject a jewel which would have dimmed all earthly things" (*165.18–19*), but he concludes their story with the confession that he is "the latest pilgrim of the GREAT CARBUNCLE," still searching for the vision his protagonists rejected.

Another aspect of the story that has received considerable attention is its landscape. One critic admires the way the scenic background undergoes "a persuasively gradual diminution of reality" as its symbolic function increases, without losing its solidly compacted realistic basis (316:179–80). Another interprets the "vast extent of wilderness" in which the pilgrims find themselves as a western landscape. In this story, he says, "ascent is the same as going West," and the "rise from the forest into a barren landscape" provides the same kind of shock for Hannah and Matthew as the rise from the Great Plains to the Rocky Mountains did for nineteenth-century Americans who expected the West to be a succession of green perspectives. The landscape is both enchanting and dangerous, and in this respect is typical of all of Hawthorne's symbols for the West (193:85–86). These same qualities also mark it as a manifestation of the natural sublime. The contrast between the awesome, stark heights and the tranquil, lush landscape in the lower regions of the mountains provides the basis, in another discussion, for Hawthorne's attitude toward the sublime (282:392–93).

In 1837, in a review of *Twice-told Tales*, Longfellow singled out "The Great Carbuncle" as his "especial favorite" (98:9). In 1879 Henry James also praised this story for "the ingenuity and felicity" of its "analogies and correspondences" (241:51). The subsequent century, however, has not followed their lead. One article devoted exclusively to an analysis of "The Great Carbuncle" opens with a two-paragraph demonstration of how it fails as a short story (342:157). Another seven-page explication of its theme and method concludes with an admission that "the transition from idea to event is too slight to permit the tale's being ranked with the author's very best" (474:10). It has also been called "tedious" and "insipid" (52:127, 29), a judgment most twentieth-century readers would probably echo. The strongest argument offered on its behalf is its usefulness as a source of seminal character types, ideas, and devices (342:164). "The Great Carbuncle" does, in Waggoner's words, represent Hawthorne at his most "perfectly traditional (and 'rationalistic')" (499: 189). Because its forte is its typicality, it continues to be read and to garner attention. Readers just beginning their explorations of Hawthorne's short stories should be alerted to what most Hawthorne enthusiasts readily admit: Hawthorne at his most traditional usually means Hawthorne at his least compelling.

# XXIV

## The Great Stone Face

(*Centenary Edition, Volume XI, The Snow-Image,* 26–48.)


### Publication History

This story was first published in *National Era,* a leading antislavery newspaper, on January 24, 1850 (IV, I) under Hawthorne's own name (*CE, XI, 428*). On February 22, 1850 he was paid $25 for it by John Greenleaf Whittier, the contributing editor, who also sent apologies for the inadequate and belated compensation (*CE, XI, 384, n.11*).

This story was probably one of the "half a dozen shorter ones" Hawthorne planned to include in a proposed but never-published book to be called "Old Time Legends" with "The Scarlet Letter" as the central tale (*CE, XI, 385*). Instead, "The Great Stone Face" was collected in *The Snow-Image* edition of 1851, immediately following the opening title story.


### Circumstances of Composition, Sources, and Influences

The exact date of composition is unknown, but scholars agree that Hawthorne wote "The Great Stone Face" during his years as the Custom House surveyor in Salem from 1846 to 1849 and most probably in the winter of 1848–49 when Sophia Hawthorne describes her husband, in a letter to her mother, as busily engaged in writing three separate works. Because, as Hawthorne admits in a letter to Longfellow on November 11, 1847 about his attempts to start writing again, "—also I should like to add something to my income, which, though tolerable, is a tight fit," the publication date of 1850 suggests he may not have completed it until later in 1849. It seems unlikely he would have delayed publishing a finished piece for an entire year (*CE, XI, 380–82*).

The germ appeared in Hawthorne's notebook at least ten years earlier. Sometime between January 4, 1839 and 1840, Hawthorne wrote:

> The semblance of a human face to be formed on the side of a mountain, or in the fracture of a small stone, by a *lusus naturae.* The face is an object of curiosity for years or for centuries, and by and by a boy is born whose features gradually assume the

> aspect of that portrait. At some critical juncture the resemblance
> is found to be correct. A prophecy might be connected. (*CE,
> VIII, 184.19–25*)

The entry gives no indication that Hawthorne had actually seen Profile
Mountain in the White Mountains of New Hampshire, and although
letters and sketches describe several early New Hampshire visits, no
record of his first view of it has been found. Several years after having
written the story, he is purported to have stayed at the Profile House and
to have studied the mountain's profile daily (84:39).

Ralph Waldo Emerson has traditionally been recognized as the prototype for Ernest in the story. Hawthorne's description of his Concord
neighbor in "The Old Manse," written at the beginning of the Custom
House period, closely parallels the "mild, sweet, thoughtful" (*48.3–4*),
and humble hero:

> It was good . . . to meet him in the wood-paths, or sometimes
> in our avenue, with that pure, intellectual gleam diffused about
> his presence, like the garment of a shining-one; and he so quiet,
> so simple, so without pretension, encountering each man alive as
> if expecting to receive more than he could impart . . . it was
> impossible to dwell in his vicinity, without inhaling, more or less,
> the mountain-atmosphere of his lofty thought. (*CE, X, 31*)

The story's moral has been called Emersonian as well—"the power of
an ideal to shape an individual life" (458:107).

Other prototypes have been proposed. One reader believes Ernest is
modeled on the character and way of life of Christ (282:395), while
another emphasizes Ernest's Wordsworthian aspects and divides the concepts traceable to Wordsworth's influence between Ernest and the poet
in the story (349). Wordsworth's poetry has also been cited as the
source for the themes Hawthorne ascribes to the nameless poet and for
the diction and phrasing he uses in describing him (375). Models for
two other story characters have been suggested: Daniel Webster for the
eloquent politician, "Old Stony Phiz," (223:I, 476) and Andrew Jackson
for "Old Blood and Thunder" (438:76).

Hawthorne's familiarity with and indebtedness to the theories of Washington Allston, a well-known landscape painter of his day, have been
documented as significant in Hawthorne's depiction of the sublime in
this story. Allston modified Edmund Burke's idea of the sublime by
seeking its sources in states of the human mind rather than in the wild
and limitless aspects of nature beyond the grasp of the mind; Hawthorne's
"moral sublime" incorporates such a humanized vision (282).

## Relationship with Other Hawthorne Works

"The Great Stone Face" has been called a "companion piece" to "Ethan Brand," a story also written during the Custom House period. Ernest's lifelong search for the great and noble person who will exactly resemble the Great Stone Face ends, like Brand's more compulsive life-long quest, with himself, but in every other way they are exact counterparts—Ernest's heart in opposition to Brand's intellect, his diffusion of good works in place of Brand's monomania, his humility a contrast to Brand's pride (333:225–26).

Another story written during this period, "The Snow-Image," has also been linked to "The Great Stone Face" as parallel in their "fastidious attitude toward actuality." The poet in "The Great Stone Face" is disqualified for the position of honor because he has lived "among poor and mean realities." Such a judgment has been called a swing backward for Hawthorne from the "profound connection between actuality and imagination" toward which his works had been moving (43:119).

In a more approbative comparison, "The Great Stone Face" is matched with "Drowne's Wooden Image" to show how Hawthorne's moral and aesthetic views shade into each other. Drowne's artistic masterpiece and Ernest's wisdom are embodiments of both truth and beauty, and both result from imitating the Ideal (188:34).

The White Mountains of New Hampshire provide the setting for two earlier stories, "The Ambitious Guest" in 1835 and "The Great Carbuncle" in 1836. In both these stories, the awesome power of nature is depicted as destructive and overwhelming, but "The Great Stone Face," written almost fifteen years later, projects a less Gothic, more Christian concept of the sublime (282).

## Interpretations and Criticism

Hawthorne's own assessment of "The Great Stone Face" has generally been echoed by his readers. He is reputed to have said he was "dissatisfied with it as a work of art" and "rather ashamed of the mechanical structure, the moral being so plain and manifest" (223:I, 354). Sophia Hawthorne was correct, however, when she added that "some persons would prefer it precisely on account of its evident design." One critic has commended its "balanced structure" (416:27–28); another, its allegorical "progressions" through the four ages of man in Ernest's development and the four chief preoccupations of men in the rich merchant, the general, the politician, and the poet who attempt to fulfill the legend's prophecy (300).

In spite of Hawthorne's admission that the story is patently moral, ironic intent has been detected by two readers. One sees it in the rhetoric used to describe Gathergold's mansion (156:487), and another in Ernest's self-deprecatory refusal to acknowledge himself in contrast to the people's readiness to accept each of the proposed candidates (305: 293–94).

In educators' journals as early as 1900, this story has been cited as a pedagogically effective device (438; 220). It has also been credited with helping to shape two American novels, William Dean Howells' *The Landlord at Lion's Head* in 1897 (329) and Ross Lockridge's *Raintree County* in 1948 (292). Howells, in his allusion to "The Great Stone Face" in the opening description of Lion's Head Mountain, prefigures his manipulation of point of view to convey the many-sided perspectives from which reality can be perceived. Hawthorne's tale holds a more central position in *Raintree County*, where the protagonist recalls it in detail in a flashback to an influential moment in his boyhood. Lockridge's central theme has been interpreted as an extension and elaboration of the mythical elements of Hawthorne's story, with the Shawmucky River, whose path traces the shape of the hero's initials on the map, a parallel to Hawthorne's "Great Stone Face" on the mountain.

"The Great Stone Face" is seldom reprinted in anthologies or collections today. Its greatest appeal may be to those tourists visiting New England who want to know the story that was inspired by Profile Mountain in New Hampshire's White Mountains.

# XXV

# The Hollow of the Three Hills

*(Centenary Edition, Volume IX, Twice-told Tales, 199–204.)*

## Publication History

This story was first published on November 12, 1830 in the *Salem Gazette* (XLIV, n.s., VII, 1) with no attribution. According to the Centenary Edition, "it is doubtful that Hawthorne received anything for the six tales and articles he gave to the *Salem Gazette*" (*CE, IX, 499*). The other five were two stories, "The Battle-Omen" on November 2 and "An Old Woman's Tale" on December 21, and three biographical sketches, "Sir William Phips" on November 23, "Mrs. Hutchinson" on December 7, and "Dr. Bullivant" on January 11, 1831, all of which remained uncollected during Hawthorne's lifetime (*CE, IX, 487*). "The Hollow of the Three Hills" was the only one of these early *Salem Gazette* pieces to be included in Hawthorne's first collection, the 1837 edition of *Twice-told Tales* (*CE, IX, 570*).

## Circumstances of Composition, Sources, and Influences

Most scholars believe this story to be part of Hawthorne's first projected collection, *Seven Tales of My Native Land,* most of which he burned after his attempts to find a publisher were unsuccessful. Hawthorne gives fictional accounts of this experience in "The Devil in Manuscript" and in "Alice Doane's Appeal." In the latter, he identifies "the story now to be introduced and another" as having escaped destruction because they "chanced to be in kinder custody at the time." Because Hawthorne's sister, Elizabeth, remembers the early stories as having to do with witchcraft, "The Hollow" has been proposed as a likely candidate for the other story that did not get destroyed (11:121; *CE, IX, 487*).

Its composition date remains conjectural nonetheless, because Elizabeth Hawthorne's recollection of when her brother showed her *Seven Tales* is not always consistent. Julian Hawthorne quotes her as saying that she saw it in "the summer of 1825"; this assigns its composition to Hawthorne's senior year at Bowdoin, possibly as early as 1824 (223:123–24; 298:92). But in her letters to James T. Fields in response to his request for help in writing Hawthorne's biography, Elizabeth distinctly says it was written "soon after Nathaniel left College." She adds "I read the Tales in Manuscript; some of them were very striking, particularly one or two Witch Stories" (458.1:323). This observation would appear to establish 1825 as the most probable date of composition.

A witchlike old hag and an ominously weird landscape uncontestably identify one of the influences reflected in this story—that of the Gothic novel (73; 149:57–58; 298:92–93; 309:50; 500:46). Although the witchcraft folklore of New England was available to provide a specifically American kind of Gothic, this story makes no use of native material. The lady identifies herself as a recent emigrant from Europe, a "stranger in this land" (200.20), but the setting remains unlocalized (43:23; 149:57).

Such an unspecified setting is associated with another kind of "marvelous" effect as well. Martin, while acknowledging the Gothic machinery, attributes part of the successful suspension of time and space to the opening sentence in which Hawthorne captures the aura of the fairy tale. By allowing "those strange old times" (199.1) to function as the setting for the story, Hawthorne adapts the method of the fairy tale and creates a "stylized drama" that relates a "domestic tragedy from a thoroughly nondomestic point of view" (309:50). Stylization of a decidedly different sort is proposed by another reader who sees in the "archaic diction" and "highly artificial" description of nature evidences of Hawthorne's imitation of the Augustan authors he admired, especially Samuel Johnson and James Thomson (315:207).

The Faust myth, which has also been credited with shaping this story, is more closely related to the supernatural elements of the Gothic and fairy-tale influences. The idea of a binding contract with the devil is only implicitly suggested, but the Faustian covenant is projected in several ways. The ritual invocation of evil demons who will intercede in obtaining otherwise unattainable information is accompanied by images of satanic worship. The lady's kneeling position and the baptismal-like rite when her garment dips into the pool reaffirm her consecration to the devil (447:55–57). The circular basin which forms the setting also echoes the demonic circle of black magic which Marlowe's Doctor Faustus draws around him to call forth the devil (363:180).

A biblical analogue has also been tendered in the story of Saul and the Witch of Endor from I Samuel 28. Like Saul, the lady appears to be compelled to resort to unholy means in an attempt to resolve guilt feelings; both find that their visions extract retribution for their sins. The auditory technique that Hawthorne employs may also have been prompted by the biblical commentaries that adduced that the Witch of Endor was really a ventriloquist because Saul never sees the shade of Samuel, but instead hears him. Another correspondence exists between the fictional setting and the locale where Saul sought the Witch (462).

## Relationship with Other Hawthorne Works

The most significant relationship is with *The Scarlet Letter* because this story foreshadows the novel's protagonist and several aspects of its theme. Like Hester Prynne, the lady is excluded from "normal" society as a result of infidelity (52:145). Both works focus on the consequences of sin, not on the sin itself (455:lxxii). Although the problem of sin, from a Christian perspective, is handled more superficially in "The Hollow" (129), the pervasive effect of sin is an important part of both tale and novel. In each, the sinner herself is psychologically affected, as are the lives of all who are associated with her (212). The lady embodies some aspects of the Cain myth as Hester does; she is described as "a wanderer . . . bearing dishonor along with her" (202.3–4), one who has "sinned against natural affection" (204.16–17; 462:33). The lady has also been classified with Hester and the other two "dark" heroines, Zenobia in *The Blithedale Romance* and Miriam in *The Marble Faun,* as individuals who are isolated as a result of "acute wrong-doing." Other women in the same category are the Widow Toothaker in "Edward Fane's Rosebud," Prudence in "John Inglefield's Thanksgiving," and the title character in "The White Old Maid" (32:76–91). In a fundamental way, the lady is related to every other isolated sinner in Hawthorne's canon from "Wakefield" to "Ethan Brand."

In its genesis and stature, "The Hollow" is most clearly related to "Alice Doane's Appeal" and "An Old Woman's Tale" (*CE, IX, 487;* 43:26–27). While the latter is not always included because it was never acknowledged by Hawthorne himself, all three early stories may be remnants of the otherwise destroyed *Seven Tales of My Native Land.* All three are witchcraft stories in which visions and actual events are portrayed as equally real (43:27). These early tales are generally considered "apprentice work" (149:58), but one reader credits "The Hollow" with comparatively better control (115:44, n.1).

This story has been likened to "Roger Malvin's Burial" on two counts. The first has to do with time—with the terrible burden of remembered guilt and the destructive consequences of disrupting temporal continuity that mark both stories (189:12–13). The second relates the decaying oak stump in the hollow to the oak-tree image in "Roger Malvin's Burial" (363).

The fairy-tale opening of "The Hollow" is repeated in several other stories—"The Great Carbuncle" and "The Lily's Quest"—and in the sketch "Earth's Holocaust" (309:51). The witch's evil eye finds a psychological equivalent in the mesmerism that Hawthorne depicts with such reprehension in *The Blithedale Romance* and *The House of Seven Gables* (315:205–06).

## Interpretations and Criticism

In the May 1842 issue of *Graham's Magazine*, Edgar Allan Poe devotes a paragraph to praising this story in his review of the second edition of *Twice-told Tales*. He begins his review by defining his subject, the short story, as "a short prose narrative requiring from a half-hour to one or two hours in its perusal" and by establishing his major criteria, that is, the conception and execution of a "single effect" or the "totality" and unity of the piece. He then applies his principles to this story:

> "The Hollow of the Three Hills" we would quote in full, had we space;—not as evincing higher talent than any of the other pieces, but as affording an excellent example of the author's peculiar ability. The subject is commonplace. A witch subjects the Distant and the Past to the view of a mourner. It has been the fashion to describe, in such cases, a mirror in which the images of the absent appear; or a cloud of smoke is made to arise, and thence the figures are gradually unfolded. Mr. Hawthorne has wonderfully heightened his effect by making the ear, in place of the eye, the medium by which the fantasy is conveyed. The head of the mourner is enveloped in the cloak of the witch, and within its magic folds there arise sounds which have an all-sufficient intelligence. Throughout this article also, the artist is conspicuous —not more in positive than in negative merits. Not only is all done that should be done, but (what perhaps is an end with more difficulty attained) there is nothing done which should not be. Every word *tells*, aud there is not a word which does *not* tell. (378:92)

The concluding line has been quoted by innumerable formalists who have adopted Poe's critical creed and who continue to apply it to the genre that has burgeoned beyond the wildest expectations of even the enthusiastic Poe.

Ironically, the story which prompted Poe's comment is not held in especially high esteem by many of those who follow Poe's critical precepts. "The Hollow" is not considered one of Hawthorne's best stories. Doubleday characterizes it as one of his unpromising first efforts (149:57). Von Abele discerns the reasons for Hawthorne's artistic disintegration in it (497). Dauber faults it for its "deliberate indefiniteness" and lack of narrative continuity (127:48–51). Fogle ignores it entirely (186).

Those who do pay attention to it invariably explain that they do so because it offers an inventory of representative concerns that Hawthorne will develop and improve upon in subsequent works. Among the most characteristic concepts are his preoccupation with sin and guilt (73), the central role assigned to death (500:230), a fictional world free from "the insistence on actualities" (309:49), and the use of physical phenomena to reflect spiritual conditions. In this story, the spiritual decay of both the lady and the witch is reflected in the dying grass, moldering trees, and putrid water (363:179), while the sense of sin is conceived in much simpler terms than in the later writings (73:295). Bewley sums up the key position assigned to this story when he says that Hawthorne's "later and better work . . . carries no radical quantity, either of meaning or technique, that is not clearly indicated in this little work" (52:142).

Although "this little work" is considered by Bewley to be "intolerable claptrap" as fiction, he believes it is saved by its imagery, which functions as it would in a poem (52:143). The story-as-poem aspect of "The Hollow" has been admired by several readers (73:295, 318), one of whom believes it may have influenced Emily Dickinson's "I Felt a Funeral in My Brain" (318). Bewley especially admires the sense of emotional unity imparted by the symbolic significance of the three hills; they correspond to the three human ties depicted in the story (child to parent, wife to husband, mother to child), while the hollow represents the lady's heart, which is described in terms of desiccation and death that effectively suggest the lady's spiritual death and foreshadow the end of the story. He also points out that by reserving the death of the child to the last, Hawthorne evokes the death of hope itself (52:142–46). Another reader also applauds the tripartite design, a device reinforced by the rhythmic motif of having the three hills mentioned six times (416:23–24).

Bewley uses "The Hollow" to support his contention that Hawthorne is a symbolist rather than an allegorist (53). Because Hawthorne is at his most symbolic and least allegorical in this story, Bewley's example supports his claim, but his conclusion is a partial one. Waggoner gives a more complete view when he reflects the variety and scope of Hawthorne's stories by setting up a scale with "The Hollow" at one end and the explicitly allegorical "Man of Adamant" at the other (500:111). The fact that "The Hollow" offers only an implicit moral rather than the laboriously spelled-out "lessons" of some of his other tales compounds its unallegorical qualifications (309:51).

As much as twentieth-century readers prefer symbolism to allegory, it is surprising that "The Hollow" has not been given more attention. While its claim to greatness should not be exaggerated, it deserves more recognition than it has received. It is rich with suggestions and implications. Its psychological and archetypal possibilities have not been explored in print, although in an unpublished manuscript both Freudian and Jungian theories have been applied to it with worthwhile results. Especially provocative is the "terrible mother" archetype it embodies. Hawthorne does suggest much in this story, but he specifies little—in the final analysis, too little. The story is too diffused (127:48), too introspectively conceived and executed (497), and too abstract for effective fiction. It functions best, as the majority of readers have asserted, as an embryonic viewfinder for Hawthorne's persistent preoccupations and techniques. It provides an ideal prospect from which to enjoy *The Scarlet Letter*. The contrast between the amorphous lady and the fully realized Hester affords an instantaneous insight into the latter's effective characterization. Equally dramatic and visible is the development from the simplistic absolutes of right and wrong in the story to the complex and ambiguous questions of sin as an inevitable and possibly redemptive part of human experience in the novel. "The Hollow," not in spite of but because of its limitations, may be the foil that every Hawthorne novice needs to appreciate fully *The Scarlet Letter* as Hawthorne's masterpiece.

# XXVI

# Howe's Masquerade

(*Centenary Edition, Volume IX, Twice-told Tales*, 239–55.)

## Publication History

This story was first published in May 1838 in *United States Magazine and Democratic Review* (II, 129–40) as No. I of "Tales of the Province-House" and attributed to the author of *Twice-told Tales* (*CE, IX, 571*). After hearing about Hawthorne's work from Jonathan Cilley, who was a classmate of Hawthorne's at Bowdoin College, the magazine editor, John L. O'Sullivan, wrote to Hawthorne, asking him to contribute to the new politically oriented literary journal published in Washington, D. C. His letter, dated April 19, 1837, proposes "to give five dollars per page, depending on the kind and merit of the writing" (223:I, 159). The only available account of what Hawthorne was actually paid is in a letter to O'Sullivan dated May 19, 1839 in which Hawthorne writes: "I find that you really do not owe me anything. You have paid me . . . $150 in all . . . this sum may surely be considered a fair compensation" (*CE, IX, 518, n.74*). Since Hawthorne had written a total of seventy-five pages for the *Democratic Review* by then (nine pieces, including an esay on Cilley, four sketches, and the four "Tales of the Province-House"), his pay for "Howe's Masquerade" would have been approximately $24, or $2 per page. The story was reprinted under his own name, but without the series title, in the 1841 *Boston Book* published by Hawthorne's friend, George Hillard (*CE, IX, 519, n.75*). In the spring of 1841 when Hawthorne was putting together the second edition of *Twice-told Tales*, he had to buy *The Boston Book* to get a copy of "Howe's Masquerade" for his new collection (*CE, IX, 540*). The story appeared in the second volume of the 1842 edition with its subtitle changed to "Legends of the Province-House I" (*CE, IX, 571, 239*).

## Circumstances of Composition, Sources, and Influences

"Howe's Masquerade" was probably written during the winter of 1837–38 (84:60). Doubleday toys with the possibility that its composition, and that of the three other Province-House tales that followed, was prompted by O'Sullivan's request; he sees the publisher's influence in the O'Sullivan kind of militant nationalism that the stories express (149:118–20). His hypothesis is undermined, however, by those who read Hawthorne's attitude in the "Legends" as ambivalent or anti-Revolutionary (435; 508). Regardless of the degree of direct influence that O'Sullivan's outspokenly democratic patriotism may have had on the stories themselves, Hawthorne's willingness to accept the offer is totally in keeping with his own inclinations and aims. He had unsuccessfully attempted to get a coherent series of stories published three times before: *Seven Tales of My Native Land*, *Provincial Tales*, and *The Story Teller* (11; 386:105). He had also been using American historical material since his earliest writing. The Province-House stories followed the same nineteenth-century prescriptions for literary nationalism that helped to shape *Provincial Tales*, written almost a decade before (149:13–32, 120).

A notebook entry made after December 6, 1837 provides a partial germ for "Howe's Masquerade" and the other Province-House stories: "A partially insane man to believe himself the Provincial Governor or other great official of Massachusetts. The scene might be the "Province House" (*CE, VIII, 169.23–25*). In the opening paragraph of this story, which introduces the entire series, Hawthorne identifies the inn that had formerly been "the mansion of the old royal governors of Massachusetts" as the "Old Province-House, kept by Thomas Waite," and he locates it in Boston, on Washington Street "nearly opposite the Old South Church." James T. Fields, Hawthorne's friend and editor, recalls Hawthorne's delight in visiting the actual Province-House when Thomas Waite was its proprietor (182:54). Waite operated it as an inn from 1835 to 1851; in 1864, it was gutted by fire (189:36, n.15); and by 1879, James speaks of it as having "disappeared some years ago" (241:53). Fields's reminiscences confirm not so much its identity, which is factually verifiable, but the similarities between the persona and the author, which is a more elusive matter.

Another notebook entry is more explicitly related to the action of the inner story of "Howe's Masquerade": "A phantom of the old royal governors, or some such shadowy pageant, on the night of the evacuation of Boston by the British" (*CE, VIII, 186.11–13*). The dating of the story as "during the latter part of the siege of Boston" (*243.14*) and the ghostly procession that dominates the plot attest to the relevancy of this entry, although it appears as part of the 1840 notebook. Sophia Hawthorne is known to have altered some of the notebook material, and the two-year discrepancy may be due to a shift in her original editing (24:234, n.2).

The Mischianza ball, a pompous and fantastic affair held on May 18,

1778 to celebrate Howe's departure from Philadelphia, may have provided Hawthorne with a situation that he could transfer to the seige of
Boston and transform into a more ominous and preternatural spectacle.
An account of the extravaganza appears in the August 1778 issue of
*Gentlemen's Magazine*, a volume Hawthorne withdrew from the Salem
Athenaeum in 1830 (24:231–32). The caricature of Washington
(*244.11–13*) may have been suggested by a farce called *The Blockade of
Boston* presented at Faneuil Hall in January 1776. Howe reportedly
enjoyed the portrayal of the American general as a ridiculous-looking
figure carrying a rusty sword (24:234, n.3).

The Gothic novel and Spenser's *Faerie Queene* have been cited as
literary influences. The "explained supernatural," one of the Gothic conventions perfected by Ann Radcliffe, is most notable; Hawthorne offers
the rational explanation that Colonel Joliffe and the Boston Whig party
could have arranged the macabre pageant deliberately to discomfit Howe,
but unlike Radcliffe, Hawthorne leaves the true nature of the spectacle
unresolved (149:122; 298:101–03). A less obvious indebtedness is
the similarity of the elaborate charade to the procession of Deadly Sins
in *The Faerie Queene*, a parallel that conjoins the "dead carcases" that
fill Spenser's House of Pride with the "dead corpse" of British colonial
rule in the Province-House (247:112).

Another source theory, while highly conjectural, offers a provocative
explanation of Poe's notorious suggestion in his 1842 review of *Twicetold Tales* that Hawthorne might have plagiarized Howe's confrontation
with his muffled phantom from a similar scene at the conclusion of Poe's
"William Wilson." "An Unwritten Drama of Lord Byron" by Washington Irving, which appeared in the *Knickerbocker* for August 1835
and in the 1836 *Gift*, has been proposed as a common inspiration for
both Hawthorne and Poe. (Poe's suspicions were mistaken; he did not
know that Hawthorne's story had originally been published before "William Wilson.") In Hawthorne's case, Irving's influence is less clear and,
in any event, related only to the final episode in which Howe drops his
drawn sword when his double reveals his face (327; 475).

## Relationship with Other Hawthorne Works

As the first of the four "Legends of the Province-House," "Howe's
Masquerade" is conceptually related to the other tales in the series—
"Edward Randolph's Portrait," "Lady Eleanore's Mantle," and "Old
Esther Dudley." The opening pages of "Howe's Masquerade" serve as an
introductory device for the entire group, while its closing paragraph,

and the corresponding beginnings and endings of each legend, complete the nineteenth-century frame in which the eighteenth-century incidents are recounted. These frame segments provide continuity and coherency to the series both stylistically and thematically. In them, Hawthorne uses a screening narrator whose point of view colors the telling of all four tales. One reader accepts the "I"-narrator as a full-fledged character, one whose "drama of attraction and repulsion to the house and 'history'" illuminates the struggle between past and present that emerges as a concept holding the series together (386). The final paragraph of "Howe's Masquerade" is often quoted to illustrate the frustration Hawthorne experienced in his attempts to capture the past while surrounded by the ubiquitous present. Through his persona, he concludes:

> In truth, it is desperately hard work when we attempt to throw the spell of hoar antiquity over localities with which the living world, and the day that is passing over us, have aught to do. (*CE, IX,* 255.21–24)

Another reader identifies an ironic dimension in the asseverations the persona makes about the historical objectivity of his narrators (the aging Mr. Bela Tiffany for the first three and an unnamed old loyalist for the last); in purporting to defend the reliability of his sources, he actually undermines them (305:278–80). Because the frame segments point up the distortions of memory and the imprecision of our knowledge of the past, they have been interpreted elsewhere as evidence that the artist is the best historian because he is not limited to facts alone (16). Baym, on the other hand, observes the same interaction of fancy and fact in the telling of the tales, but she concludes that the "I"-narrator, who begins by courting historical legends, ends up renouncing them: he awakens to the parallels between the false perceptions of the protagonists in the four "Legends" and his own anachronistic Gothicism, and he rejects the quest for the past both as a writer and as an American (43:75–78). Other readers who have analyzed the frame and the persona-narrator's role have reacted differently. Some read the series not as a rejection of historical material, but as a working example of how history can be transformed into legend (16; 159; 233:212). One such critique traces the author's transformation of historical perspective until it is elongated into an archaic tradition (159). A more historically based observer sees the framework as another effort to exploit the legendary associations of a historical object, in the same way that "The Custom-House" accounts for the making of a legend out of *The Scarlet Letter* (46:198–202). Another interpretation that emerges more clearly when the four stories are read as a group in a framing device is the portrayal of the American Revolution in highly ambivalent and sometimes critical terms; in the frame, and within each of the stories, the pride of the loyalists is often offset by the equally objectionable traits of the colonial democrats (435).

Here, and in several other contexts, the Province-House itself acts as a cohesive agent. It provides the setting for crucial scenes in each of the legends and for the tavern in which they are all heard. Its present tawdry condition, which is a result of the Revolution, indicates, according to Hoffman, one of "the unfortunate leveling effects of democracy" (233:212). Like the Custom House in the essay that introduces *The Scarlet Letter*, the Province-House becomes a realistic link with the past that communicates a sense of contemporary decay (45:172). *The House of Seven Gables* has a similar aura, with the title building in the novel, as in the series, participating directly in the action that develops. The Province-House also functions as a symbol for the mind, haunted by figures from the past, and as a means of retreat from the actual world (16:435, n.7). A psychoanalytical reading expands the house-mind analogy further; the Province-House becomes "a locus for a collective unconscious," that is, a place where Hawthorne's unconscious and his public's unconscious can merge. Through the historical reminiscences that Hawthorne hears and transcribes there, private and public experiences become one, and past and present exist simultaneously; in effect, the house by substituting association for chronological sequence, transforms history into psychology (127:65–67).

The first three "Legends" are alike in several ways. The title character in each is an aristocrat whose illusions of superiority are shattered by American democratic forces (43:76). All three are variants of the Faust myth and utilize some aspect of the symbolic pact with the devil to magnify political tyranny in the American colonies (447:76). A significant change in attitude toward history and toward the American Revolution has been detected in the last legend. This shift from the apparently anti-British sentiment of the first three legends affects the tenor of the earlier tales and raises the question of the extent of Hawthorne's commitment to orthodox patriotism. (See "Relationship with Other Hawthorne Works" under "Old Esther Dudley.")

All four "Legends" are related to Hawthorne's tales and sketches in which the American national past is the central subject. The most notable similarities are with the Revolutionary ambivalence of "My Kinsman, Major Molineux" and the mythic heroism of "The Gray Champion" and "Endicott and the Red Cross." The latter two are also like the "Legends" in affirming Hawthorne's approval of one aspect of Puritanism—its contribution to the early struggle for political liberty in America

(420:205). The Province-House stories, however, are the only ones that deal with the Revolution itself. They reveal Hawthorne's increasingly subjective approach to history, an attitude that was to become more apparent in *The House of Seven Gables* and the fragments of the unfinished English romance (46:198–203).

"Howe's Masquerade" has a unique formalistic relationship to the "Legends." The pageant portrayed at the ball has been proposed as a paradigm for the series itself; each tale is an emblematic tableau of the historical past presented in the context of the fictional present, with Colonel Joliffe's role as guide and commentator corresponding to Hawthorne's (189:37).

## Interpretations and Criticism

James applauds the "definite images" with which "Howe's Masquerade" beguiles its readers into believing Hawthorne's "shadowy" visions of the past; the "Legends" as a whole reveal a "historic consciousness" that manifests itself not in broad and general strokes but on a "minute" scale (241:53). Such diminutives characterize the reception given this story. In one instance, it is called "a flimsy bit of writing that just barely demonstrates Hawthorne's power to evoke an eerie scene" (420:206); in another, on a more positive note, it is a "compact little tale," its mystery and suspense achieved economically to make it "technically a success" (149:122–23).

Becker, who analyzes the allegorical techniques, is equally approbative. He sees Hawthorne adapting traditional devices to fit his own kind of history-oriented allegory, thereby effectively incorporating personification (Howe and Joliffe as representative of historical forces), the convention of the guide (the Colonel as interpreter of the pageant), and decorative imagery (the sword and Bible that identify Endicott, and Sir Henry Vane's blood-stained ruff). Hawthorne is also credited with combining two typical structural patterns, ritual progress and battle. The primary allegory, the "battle" between Howe and Joliffe, is worked out dramatically through the opposed reactions to the secondary allegory, the "rituals" of the masquerade and the procession. At both levels, the causal principle is a metaphysical type of "over-riding historical determinism" that is associated with allegory (45:43–49).

Becker chalks up the victory as a resounding one for Joliffe and the colonists, interpreting Hawthorne's basic indictment of royalist British rule as resting on their "failure of nerve before reality" (45:47). Baym's reading suggests a more tolerant attitude; she sees Howe as another of

Hawthorne's deluded isolationists (43:76). But the majority of readers agree that the author's sympathy in this first Province-House story rests primarily with the democratic colonists and their Puritan forebears (149:120; 189:37; 233:212; 420:206). The minority, who find a significant ambivalence amidst the nationalistic rhetoric, capitalize on Hawthorne's depiction of Howe as an honorable man who happens to be the last defender of a no-longer-viable system of government (354; 435).

A psychohistorical reading identifies the crisis in "Howe's Masquerade" as a national-genital conflict that ushers in the Oedipal edge of childhood but then retreats from it. The malevolent father, Howe, is confronted not with the potent Washington but with the sterile Joliffe and his "fair grand-daughter," who together form a "genital-less anti-couple." The imagery of the closing paragraph castrates oppressor and rebels alike and delineates psychological regress to an earlier sexual state (127:70–72).

Whatever insights into Hawthorne's development such an analysis may offer, most readers opt for a more straightforward interpretation. Poe enthusiasts should welcome the theory that Poe's "The Masque of the Red Death" is a subtle critical parody of the Gothic effects in "Howe's Masquerade" (389). Whether Hawthorne's story "inspired" Poe or not, "Howe's Masquerade" does not emerge in any review of Hawthorne's canon as one of his best or more important stories. It does, however, offer a representative sampling of Hawthorne trademarks. The scowling Puritan, the vanquished father figure, and the Gothic trappings that transform American history into myth are all here to provide a useful introduction to Hawthorne's fictional world.

# XXVII

# John Inglefield's Thanksgiving

(*Centenary Edition, Volume IX, The Snow-Image*, 179–85.)

## Publication History

"John Inglefield's Thanksgiving" was first published in March 1840 in the *United States Magazine and Democratic Review* (VII, 209–12) under the pseudonym, Rev. A. A. Royce (*CS, XI, 430*). When the editor, John L. O'Sullivan, wrote to Hawthorne in 1837 to solicit contributions, he established the rate of pay at between $3 and $5 a page (223:I, 159). In the case of this story, however, the likelihood is that Hawthorne gave it, without expecting payment, to O'Sullivan, who was fast becoming a close friend. In May 1839, when Hawthorne heard of the *Democratic Review*'s financial difficulties, he wrote to O'Sullivan to reassure him that he considered himself reimbursed in full for his past contributions; furthermore, he suggested "fresh contributions" from him might be in order to make up for a possible overpayment. The only new piece by Hawthorne to appear in the *Democratic Review* until 1843 was "John Inglefield's Thanksgiving." In 1840 Hawthorne's authorial self-esteem was suffering as a result of his inability to write while working as a measurer of salt and coal at the Boston Custom House. He had declared himself "no longer a literary man" and did, in fact, write nothing else for the magazines between 1839 and 1841 except this story. He thought so little of it that he used a pseudonym with the apparent purpose of assuring its divorce from the author of *Twcie-told Tales*, which had been published in 1837 (*CE, IX, 518*; *CE, X, 502*). Under these circumstances, and with no evidence to the contrary, "John Inglefield's Thanksgiving" can be assessed as having brought Hawthorne no financial remuneration. It was not included in a collection until 1851 when the editorial firm of Ticknor & Co. retrieved a copy of it through the help of *Literary World* for *The Snow-Image* (*CE, XI, 413*).

## Circumstances of Composition, Sources, and Influences

As established above, this story was written in 1839 or very early 1840 in Boston, during the period when Hawthorne was devoting most of his writing energies to the love letters he was sending Sophia Peabody (87).

Some of the details of the story can be traced to an early notebook entry, undated but appearing between October 25, 1836, and the summer of 1837:

> To picture a virtuous family, the different members examples of virtuous dispositions in their way; then introduce a vicious person, and trace out the relations that arise between him and them, and the manner in which all are affected. (*CE, VIII, 251.22–25*)

As Chandler notes, the "vicious person" in the story is an erring daughter, and the emphasis is placed on the effect the visit to her virtuous family has on her (84:28–29). Another story germ in the same series of entries suggests a Thanksgiving-dinner setting (*CE, VIII, 20.21–22*); it then outlines the narrative device ("All the miserable on earth to be invited") which Hawthorne developed into "The Christmas Banquet" in 1843. Hawthorne reiterates his regard for the traditional celebration of Thanksgiving in a subsequent entry dated Thursday, November 24, 1842, in which he describes how he and his wife kept the holiday "with our hearts, and besides have made good cheer upon our turkey, and pudding, and pies, and custards" (*CE, VIII, 365.1–8*). Later still, in a letter from Liverpool to Ticknor dated December 18, 1854, he observes: "We kept the New England Thanksgiving as descendants of the old Puritans should" (*CE, VIII, 644*).

Other source studies have been minimal. Stein finds a close parallel between Prudence Inglefield's attempt at repentance and Doctor Faustus' unsuccessful struggle to resist the devil in the Faust chapbook and in Christopher Marlowe's *Faustus* (447:79–80). Baym implies a Gothic origin (43:57). But no one has commented on the influence of the many sermons and religious tracts that Hawthorne read between 1825 and 1839 (269). Their outlook is manifested in Prudence's abject failure to fight off "the fiend" without God's help.

## Relationship with Other Hawthorne Works

Since the alienating effect of sin and guilt dominates Hawthorne's entire canon, Prudence's final estrangement from her family links "John Inglefield's Thanksgiving" to almost all of his stories. Another typically Hawthornian aspect is the vague description given of Prudence's sins. She is "among the painted beauties at the theatre of a neighboring city" (*194.27–*

28), but as in the case of Hester in *The Scarlet Letter*, Zenobia in *The Blithedale Romance*, and Miriam in *The Marble Faun*, the details of past transgressions are less important than how the resultant guilt affects the sinner and her relationship to others. When, in the final paragraph, Hawthorne calls the Thanksgiving visit a "waking dream," he also aligns this story with another of his recurrent preoccupations, the exploration of the power of fantasy to reveal the unconscious and to activate conscience, as in such tales as "The Hollow of the Three Hills," "Young Goodman Brown," and "Fancy's Show Box."

## Interpretations and Criticism

As perhaps the least known of Hawthorne's short stories, "John Inglefield's Thanksgiving" has received even less critical attention than his other minor pieces. Hawthorne's disdain for the tale, reflected in its publication history, has not been challenged. Van Doren calls it "moral melodrama without moral meaning" (490:108). Its only possible value to Hawthorne's readers today is as a display of its author's most obsessive concerns.

# XXVIII
# Lady Eleanore's Mantle

(*Centenary Edition, Volume IX, Twice-told Tales*, 271–89.)

## Publication History

This story was first published in December 1838 in *United States Magazine and Democratic Review* (III, 321–32) as No. III of "Tales of the Province-House" under Hawthorne's own name. All available evidence indicates that Hawthorne received approximately $2 per page for his contributions to John L. O'Sullivan's *Democratic Review* before 1840. (See publication history of "Howe's Masquerade," the first of the Province-House stories.) This would have made his pay for "Lady Eleanore's Mantle" $24. In 1842, it was included in the second volume of the second edition of *Twice-told Tales* with its subtitle changed to "Legends of the Province-House III" (*CE, IX, 571–72*).

## Circumstances of Composition, Sources, and Influences

"Lady Eleanore's Mantle" was probably written in November 1838, shortly after Hawthorne had expressed his intention "to throw off an article or two . . . within a week or ten days" in a letter to O'Sullivan, the *Democratic Review*'s editor (*CE, IX, 518*).

While the notebooks do not contain any one precise germ for this story, several entries hold hints that are loosely related. Sometime between October 25, 1836 and July 5, 1837, Hawthorne wrote: "Diseases of the mind and soul,—even more common than bodily disease" (*CE, VIII, 30.23–24*). In an undated segment spanning the period from December 6, 1837 to June 15, 1838, the following were entered: "An ornament to be worn about the person of a lady,—as a jeweled heart. After many years, it happens to be broken or unscrewed, and a poisonous odor comes out" (*167.14–16*); "To poison a person or a party of persons with the sacramental wine" (*168.21–22*); and "The scene might be the Province-House" (*169.24–25*). It is also possible that the character of Lady Eleanore is based on the stories Hawthorne heard about Lady Knox when he was on his way home from Maine in the summer of 1837. The August 12 entry gives some of the details. General Knox's wife is described as "a haughty English lady...a woman of violent passions, fond of gallants, and so proud an aristocrat, that, as long as she lived, she would never enter any house...except her own" (*67.11–17*). Later the same month, Hawthorne also heard about the excessive pride of one of his own ancestors. Eben Hathorne, whose great hobby was "the pride of ancestry," told him about Susy Ingersoll, whose mother or grandmother was a Hawthorne and who was remembered for being "proud of being proud" (*CE, VIII, 75.17–18*).

The suggestion for the disease-laden garment has been traced to two articles that appeared in the *American Magazine of Useful and Entertaining Knowledge* in 1836 while Hawthorne was its editor. They were entitled "The Plague" and "Infection" and dealt with the transmission of a pestilence through the personal effects of its victims (85). A passage in "Edward Fane's Rosebud," which Hawthorne wrote the year after his association with the *American Magazine*, adds the connotation of luxury to the infection-carrier; it refers to "strange maladies that have broken out, as if spontaneously, but were found to have been imported from foreign lands, with rich silks and other merchandise, the costliest portion of the cargo" (*CE, IX, 469.28–31*). Another analogue appears earlier in the same paragraph; one line describes smallpox as having "hoisted a red-banner on almost every house along the street."

Two histories that Hawthorne is known to have consulted also report information that is incorporated into the story. Caleb Snow's *History of Boston* (p. 218) rests the blame for bringing smallpox to Boston on the Sal Tortugas fleet in April 1721 (149:128), and Thomas Hutchinson's *History of Massachusetts* (II, 205–06) sets 1722 as the year in which nearly six thousand people in Massachusetts Bay were struck by the "dread disease" (208:549). Hawthorne adapts these facts to his fictional purpose. He dates the story "not long after Colonel Shute had assumed the government of Massachusetts Bay" (*273.16–17*), thereby establishing the turbulent and troubled years of Governor Shute's administration (1716–28) as the historical base for his allegorical tale (149:128; 208:549).

The name of Jervase Helwyse comes from Hawthorne's own genealogy; a Gervais Helwyse is listed in Major William Hathorne's will (293:95). One source study states, "It is also a fact that a Hathorne brought the smallpox to Salem," but no documentation is given (84:27). Such a "fact" would further illuminate Hawthorne's preoccupation with inherited guilt, and ancestral atonement might help to explain the severe retribution heaped on Lady Eleanore.

Spenser's *Faerie Queene* and the Gothic novel are the two literary influences explicitly discernible in this story. Lady Eleanore is a "British colonial Lucifera" living in an eighteenth-century "House of Pride," the Province-House in its heyday (247:112); and the bewitched mantle as well as the reported ghost are variations of the Gothic conventions of magic objects and supernatural phenomena (298:104–05).

## Relationship with Other Hawthorne Works

"Lady Eleanore's Mantle," as the third Province-House story, is most closely related to the other legends, "Howe's Masquerade" and "Edward Randolph's Portrait," which precede it, and "Old Esther Dudley," which follows. The interrelationships among the four tales, the significance of the framing segments that introduce and close each story, and the meanings revealed when the "Legends" are read as one unit are explored and documented under the "Relationship with Other Hawthorne Works" section for the first Province-House story, "Howe's Masquerade," and for the last, "Old Esther Dudley." In this connection, "Lady Eleanore's Mantle" has been singled out as a "metaphorical key" to the central theme of the entire series; the figure of the mantle embodies the underlying reason for the British defeat in Boston, which is the central action that dominates each of the legends (90).

Pride, therefore, links "Lady Eleanore's Mantle" to all the other Province-House tales, but as an aspect of the Faust myth, Lady Eleanore's pride is closest to Edward Randolph's (447:76–78). It is also like that of Hawthorne's best-known Faust figures, "Ethan Brand" and "Young Goodman Brown." Because pride is Hawthorne's favorite target and isolation its most constant companion, Lady Eleanore also finds herself kin to such unlikely companions as "The Man of Adamant," Hooper in "The Minister's Black Veil," Aylmer in "The Birthmark," "Wakefield," Hollingsworth in *The Blithedale Romance*, and Chillingworth in *The Scarlet Letter*. More specifically, as a character who willfully withdraws from her fellow men because of egotistical pride heightened by aristocratic pretensions, she is most closely allied to the Pyncheons, especially Alice Pyncheon, in *The House of Seven Gables* (32:31–32).

Notebook entries made in 1841 and 1842 (*CE, VIII, 222.13–15; 229.23; 235.18*) show Hawthorne's continued interest in using physical manifestations to indicate spiritual conditions. This device groups "Lady Eleanore's Mantle" with another story of extreme pride, "Egotism; or, the Bosom-Serpent." Variations of this technique are used in Beatrice's characterization in "Rappaccini's Daughter" and Dimmesdale's in *The Scarlet Letter*.

Kaul classifies "Lady Eleanore's Mantle" with "The Christmas Banquet" and "Young Goodman Brown" on the basis that each shows how "all men are bound together by their common weakness"—sorrow in "The Christmas Banquet," sin in "Young Goodman Brown," and disease in "Lady Eleanore's Mantle." Lady Eleanore becomes another of Hawthorne's characters who denies the sense of community precisely where it needs to be established, in the "deepest consciousness of the individual" (255:170–71).

## Interpretations and Criticism

"Labored and strident" is what Doubleday calls this story. Few readers disagree. Warren thinks its moral is expressed in "inartistically explicit" terms (511:363), while other leading Hawthorne specialists, almost as if embarrassed by its excesses, simyly leave it alone. Doubleday attributes the story's failure to Hawthorne's attempt to portray pride as a matter of class to be overcome by democratic forces; the experiment does not work because Hawthorne himself cannot fully accept this political application of his moral conviction (149:130).

The author's ambivalence has been noted, in other contexts, by several readers. Approaching the story from a historical perspective, Gross sees "an unmistakable counterstatement, in the form of the crazed Jervase Helwyse and the populace in general," that keeps the story from being an "unmodified tribute to pre-Revolutionary America." Helwyse's desire to abase himself to aristocratic pride and the crowd's "acclamation" of his self-debasement (276.11–14) become as much a shortcoming as Lady Eleanore's egotism (208:549, 553). Smith proposes a historically causal relationship for the two seemingly proroyalist factions; both contributed to the Revolution, the loyal colonists by continuing to pay tribute to British traditions and the English authorities by responding with disdain (435). One reader calls Helwyse a symbol for the "stupified abjection of common man" (45:49); another sees "a singular lack of charity" in his coming to taunt Lady Eleanore on her deathbed as in her stepping on his prostrate body upon her arrival in Boston (188:83–84). Helwyse's name as a possible pun on "Hell-wise" has also been explored, but his ambiguous portrayal has resulted in interpretations that place him both with and against the Devil (447:78; 188:83). Another character whose apparently sympathetic portrayal has been questioned is Dr. Clarke. He is described as a "famous champion of the popular party" (275.11), and a few readers accept his egalitarian rhetoric as an expression of Hawthorne's avowal of the principles of the Young America wing of the Democratic party (413; 162:44–47). O'Sullivan, who was a leader in the movement and the editor of the *Democratic Review*, probably did. But some reservations in Hawthorne's seemingly approbative attitude do emerge. One reader concludes that Clarke is the villain of the piece; the "good" doctor, driven by revolutionary enthusiasm, poisons the wine that Helwyse offers Lady Eleanore (287).

One aspect of this story that has received critical attention is its allegorical form. Waggoner sees it as "one of Hawthorne's most traditionally allegorical tales" (500:262). Becker concurs, offering a ten-page analysis of the conventions that it follows, most notably in characterization, causality, and imagery (45:49–59). Eleanore and Helwyse are such pure allegorical symbols that Hawthorne has to make them mad to fit the realistic demands of his story, and Dr. Clarke is a fully developed example of the allegorical guide. Magic, which is the causality principle proper to allegory, is used to link the plague with punishment for pride. It becomes an apt illustration of how the Puritan anthropomorphic conception of providence is reduced to superstitious magic. Equally paradoxical is the hierarchal imagery that Hawthorne uses to undercut social strata rather than to support them. Becker's thesis is that Hawthorne adapts the techniques of allegory in such a way as to attack the basic imaginative requirements on which allegory is based. While agreement on the traditionally allegorical nature of "Lady Eleanore's Mantle" is general, all do not agree that the allegory is effective. Folsom calls "the allegorical frame of reference . . meaningless" (188:83). Doubleday thinks the story "turns out to be more successful as a tale of terror than as an allegory" (149:130). Both its terror and its allegory have been cited as evidence that it may have influenced Poe in writing "The Masque of the Red Death." The two stories share a devastating pestilence, references to blood and spots of red, a fantastically ornate ball, and the horrors of death (327:263; 389).

The allegorization in "Lady Eleanore's Mantle" has been validated from a new perspective in the psychoanalytical reading that seeks to integrate the national and the psychic. The analysis locates this story, within the child-development pattern recapitulated in the Province-House series, in the second oral or "oral-sadistic" phase. Oral aggressiveness characterizes the oyster supper in the frame and the verbal satire that punctuates all of the story. Lady Eleanore, as a "queenly maiden," is an "unyielding" kind of Virgin Mother who denies Helwyse sustenance of any kind. He, in turn, evolves from being her footstool to offering her nourishment in the form of sacramental wine to finally being the one she calls to for water when she is dying. Refraining from any literary assessment, the conclusion sees Eleanore's death dissipating Helwyse's madness and preparing the Province-House for a new era of Eros (127:68, 75–78).

Praise has been extended to this story in one quarter; Miller admires the way Hawthorne uses physical isolation to symbolize spiritual withdrawal from humanity. In the ball scene, Eleanore stands "apart from the mob of guests"; as the scene progresses, her circle grows smaller; at the end of the story, she is totally alone. He calls the scene in which Eleanore uses Helwyse as a footstool "one of the finest of Hawthorne's sharply drawn vignettes." Notwithstanding the already overexplained moral symbolism, he points out that the sacred wine spilling on the mantle signifies "compassion . . . wasted on pride" (333:216–19).

Waggoner provides an insight into Hawthorne's style that helps to explain some of the objections to this story. For example, one of its most outspoken detractors, Doubleday, charges that the plot is melodramatic, the morals are gratuitous, and the irony turns to "preachment" (149:129). Waggoner theorizes that when Hawthorne deals with subjects that have strong theological implications, he treats them ambiguously, mythically, and subjectively, while he renders subjects not involving ultimate religious beliefs, such as Eleanore's aristocratic pride, with clarity and conviction and in an allegorical mode (500:190–91). Waggoner and Doubleday disagree on the merits of this story, but they would find themselves in agreement with Warren's statement that its "subject, manner of treatment, and moral are characteristic of Hawthorne" (511:363). "Lady Eleanore's Mantle" is unquestionably a typical Hawthorne story; its place in Hawthorne's canon is debatable because it is as representative of his shortcomings as of his strengths.

# XXIX

# The Lily's Quest: An Apologue

*(Centenary Edition, Volume IX, Twice-told Tales, 442–50.)*

## Publication History

"The Lily's Quest" was first published in the Charleston, South Carolina *Southern Rose* on January 19, 1839 (VII, 161–64) under Hawthorne's own name (*CE, IX, 575*). He sent the manuscript to Caroline Gilman, the magazine's editor, on December 27, 1838 in appreciation of her favorable notice of the 1837 *Twice-told Tales* (*CE, IX, 514, n.65*; 251). In 1842 he included the story in the second volume of the second edition of *Twice-told Tales*. The original manuscript, now in the William E. Stockhausen collection, served as the copy text for the Centenary Edition (*CE, IX, 546*).

## Circumstances of Composition, Sources, and Influences

An undated entry in Hawthorne's notebook between October 25, 1836 and July 5, 1837 provides a germ for the story:

> Two lovers to plan the building of a pleasure-house on a certain spot of ground, but various seeming accidents prevent it. Once they find a group of miserable children there; once it is the scene where crime is plotted; at last the dead body of one of the lovers or of a dear friend is found there; and instead of a pleasure-house, they build a marble tomb. The moral,—that there is no place on earth fit for the site of a pleasure-house, because there is no spot that may not have been saddened by human grief, stained by crime, or hallowed by death. It might be three friends who plan it, instead of two lovers; and the dearest one dies. (*CE, VIII, 25.1–11*)

Hawthorne followed several of the details of the entry almost exactly; he omitted some—the miserable children, the plotting of a crime; and he added others—the mysterious, dark relative with the stock characteristics of the Gothic villain. He also brightened the moral with an exclamation of joy at the end: Adam buries his beloved Lilias with the cry, "Joy! Joy!

...On a Grave be the site of our Temple; and now our happiness is for Eternity" (*CE, IX, 450*).

"The Lily's Quest" was written sometime between the notebook entry and Hawthorne's letter to the editor of the *Southern Rose* on December 27, 1838. Since Hawthorne had met Sophia Peabody by the fall of 1838, his characterization of the frail, delicate Lilias may have been influenced by his growing devotion to the semi-invalid he was to become engaged to in 1839 (84:27–28). A parallelism between the flight imagery in some of his love letters to Sophia in 1839 and in his description of Adam Forrester with his arms raised heavenward is also notable (285:341). After she was married, Sophia wrote to her sister, "I fast ceased to represent Lilias Fay, under the influence of happiness, peace, and rest" (278:52). However, sylphlike and ethereal maidens can also be found in Hawthorne's fiction before he met Sophia. Edith in "The White Old Maid" in 1835, Mary Goffe in "The Man of Adamant" in 1836, and the title character in "Sylph Etherege" in 1837 are all fragile, sensitive heroines who may well have predisposed Hawthorne to his almost instantaneous attraction to Sophia and certainly helped to shape the personality and destiny of Lilias Fay.

A diversity of literary echoes have been explicated for "The Lily's Quest." Hawthorne's depiction of Lilias can be traced in part to the influence of Dante's idealization of Beatrice, another maiden who died young and was a spiritual force for good (285:341). The moral tone and "once upon a time" setting may have been modeled on the eighteenth-century Eastern tale in the style of Goldsmith and Johnson (149:70). Hawthorne's protagonist, like Rasselas in Johnson's fable, searches for earthly happiness; both finally realize the vanity of human wishes, Rasselas while standing in the "Mansions of the dead," Adam at his mistress's tomb (183:194–95). The pursuit of death also has romantic affiliations, and Keats and Shelley have been cited as influences in the shaping of Adam's final declaration of victory in defeat (285:342). But perhaps most obvious is the allegorical use, in the John Bunyan tradition, of names as labels. Hawthorne uses the names both to classify and to characterize: "Adam" recalls man's Edenic origins while "Forrester" suggests "the pastoral ideal of natural simplicity"; "Lilias Fay" recalls Lilith, Adam's first wife, and evokes fairy and flower images, specifically the lily, associated with death and rebirth (244:58).

## Relationship with Other Hawthorne Works

"Graves and Goblins" (*CE, XI, 289–97*) and "Chippings with a

Chisel" (*CE, IX, 407–18*), originally published in 1835 and 1838 respectively, are sketches that have been associated with "The Lily's Quest" (285:341, 490:90). Both predate it, and both deal with graveyard trappings. The first includes a description of the ghost of a young maiden, a "pure, ethereal spirit" (*296*); the second, the death of "a young girl, a pale, slender, feeble creature . . . fading away" (*417*). The lesson learned by the narrator of "Chippings," that the sorrows and regrets of life may hold as much comfort as life's joys, is very like Adam Forrester's joyful acceptance of Lilias' death.

"The Man of Adamant" shares the same subtitle, "An Apologue," and although "David Swan," "Fancy's Show Box," and "The Threefold Destiny" are not called apologues, they too are allegorical fables. All five are more concerned with moral purpose than narrative skill and have consistently been relegated, probably justifiably, to serving as examples of Hawthorne's less effective efforts (149:67; 490:90).

Lilias Fay and her early counterparts, discussed above, are part of one of Hawthorne's recurring character types, "the frail, sylph-like creature," aspects of whom can also be identified in Alice Vane of "Edward Randolph's Portrait," in Alice Pyncheon of *The House of Seven Gables,* and, in a more individualized form, in Priscilla of *The Blithedale Romance* (455:lviii–lix).

## Interpretations and Criticism

Most critics have dismissed "The Lily's Quest" as "anemic" (315:231) or as "complacent allegory" (490:90). The only extensive analysis (285) has been called more ingenious than convincing (55:123). In it, Levy views Adam and Lilias as Man-and-Death; the conventional Christian reading of Adam's joy in anticipation of their reunion in heaven is extended to a more humanistic acceptance of man's limitations and the interdependence of life and death.

# XXX

# The Man of Adamant: An Apologue

*(Centenary Edition, Volume XI, The Snow-Image, 161–69.)*

## Publication History

This story was first published in the fall of 1836 in the *Token and Atlantic Souvenir* (pp. 119–28) dated 1837 as the work of the author of "The Gentle Boy" (*CE, XI, 430*). The editor, Samuel Goodrich, paid $108 for the eight anonymous pieces Hawthorne contributed to this issue, making the pay for "The Man of Adamant" about $9 (*CE, IX, 497*). The story was not published as Hawthorne's work until *The Snow-Image* of 1851, after it had been located by James T. Fields, Hawthorne's editor, in a search through the *Token* for uncollected pieces to include in Hawthorne's last collection (*CE, XI, 389–90*).

## Circumstances of Composition, Sources, and Influences

This story was probably written during the fall of 1835 or the winter of 1836. Two related notebook entries were entered between September 7 and October 17, 1835:

> The story of a man, cold and hard-hearted, and acknowledging no brotherhood with mankind. At his death they might try to dig him a grave, but, at a little space beneath the ground, strike upon a rock, as if the earth refused to receive the unnatural son into her bosom. Then they would put him into an old sepulchre, where the coffins and corpses were all turned to dust, and so he would be alone. Then the body would petrify; and he having died in some characteristic act and expression, he would seem, through endless ages of death, to repel society as in life, and no one would be buried in that tomb forever. (*CE, VIII, 13.1–11*)

> It might be stated, as the closing circumstance of a tale, that the body of one of the characters had been petrified, and still existed in that state. (*CE, VIII, 13.20–22*)

A convincing and well-documented source study attributes the differences between these story germs and the shape that the story finally assumed to the influence of the "Legend of Holinesse' from Book One of Edmund Spenser's *The Faerie Queene* (428). The main source is located specifically in the first half of the first canto of Book One, the episode of the Wandering Wood and Error's Den, with the crucial difference that Digby does not fight a three-day battle with the monster in the cave, but makes the den his retreat, in a sense becoming Error himself for the three days before Mary Goffe's appearance. Like Una, Mary represents Truth and True Religion. Other Spenserian parallels abound, but the verbal similarities are the most striking. For example, Spenser's "Errour's den" and "darksome hole" become Hawthorne's "darksome den." Although Hawthorne rejects Spenser's Christian optimism when he denies Digby the salvation that the Knight found, he does accept Spenser's mode of double allegory— simultaneously spiritual and historical —as a model for handling the American historical material in his fiction. One addendum to this seminal study cites echoes of the Red Crosse Knight's encounter with Despair (248:38–39); another proposes merging Malbecco from Book Three with Fadubio and the Knight for Digby's prototype (199).

Another analogue shares enough verbal, imagistic, and thematic parallels with "The Man of Adamant" to warrant Hawthorne's story's being called "a rather obvious reworking of the episode at the cave of John Balfour of Burley in Chapter 43 of Sir Walter Scott's *Old Mortality*" (248). Both accounts deal with Calvinist extremists who retreat to the harsh isolation of a cave to practice demonic "soul exercises." The same kind of cave dweller can be found in two other works by contemporaneous and popular Romantic writers, James Fenimore Cooper's *The Spy* (1821) and William Ware's *Zenobia* (1838).

Nineteenth-century aesthetic theory undoubtedly affected Hawthorne's portrayal of the landscape in "The Man of Adamant" (248). In several philosophy-of-art books that Hawthorne read in the summer of 1827 and in the writings of Thomas C. Upham, his philosophy professor at Bowdoin College, the picturesque is recognized as a viable mode, distinct from the sublime. Hawthorne's story follows the "associational" and "emotional" concepts of the picturesque that these men described; the natural setting is subordinated so that the human figures and the moral issues that they embody can dominate the scene.

Some of the biblical allusions in this story are directly stated: "Elijah's cave at Horeb, ... Abraham's sepulchral cave, at Machpelah" (*162.30–33*). Others are more subtly integrated in the images and situations. Mary Goffe, for example, whose feet have been "wounded by thorns," is repeatedly described in terms of Christ. Her similarity to Dante's Beatrice has also been noted (149:219–20). While one Spenserian scholar dismisses the biblical references as the author's "conscious deceptions" (428:

754–55), others have proposed St. Matthew's description of the un-pardonable sin (12:31–32) as the key factor in Hawthorne's portrayal of Digby (61; 158). The parallels in the tale to the situation from which the unpardonable sin stems support this reading. Digby, like the Pharisees who imputed Christ's power over evil spirits to his complicity with the devil, accuses Mary Goffe of being an agent for the devil, a sinful, "accursed woman," out to tempt him. A biblical commentary that Hawthorne read in 1832 may also have been an influence (61). Thomas Stackhouse's *A New History of the Bible* (London, 1752) ex-plicates the passage from St. Matthew about "blasphemy against the Holy Ghost" and provides all the essentials of Hawthorne's treatment, including Digby's "refractory and incorrigible Spirit" that "neither will, nor can repent" (II, 1339–40, cited in 61).

A likely source for the name of the central character has been located in Sir Kenelm Digby (1603–65), who published a famous account of a petrified city (196).

## Relationship with Other Hawthorne Works

The subtitle "An Apologue," shared by "The Man of Adamant" and "The Lily's Quest," links the two stories to "Fancy's Show Box" and "David Swan" as pieces that follow the conventions of the eighteenth-century moralistic "oriental tale" as written by Addison, Goldsmith, and Johnson (149:67). "Egotism; or, The Bosom-Serpent" bears an even closer source-related kinship to "The Man of Adamant," because both are "thoroughgoing" Spenserian paraphrases whose final forms are directly attributable to *The Faerie Queene* as a model (427). The symbolism of Spenser's Wandering Wood is as evident in "Young Good-man Brown" (290) and in *The Scarlet Letter* (456) as it is in Digby's wilderness (428).

The story most closely related to "The Man of Adamant" is "Ethan Brand." As a rule, "The Man of Adamant" is considered the inferior of the two (149:218), although one reader thinks it equally powerful (420:197). Both stories portray a man's allegorical "stoniness of the heart" (*CE, XI, 164*), and both end with physical petrification and spiritual damnation. While the unpardonable sin is not specifically named in "The Man of Adamant," one comprehensive reexamination of this concept in Hawthorne's works concludes that Digby is one of three unpardonable sinners in the Hawthorne canon (321.5). According to a set of criteria based not on the seriousness of the sin but on its unpardon-able nature, Chillingworth of *The Scarlet Letter* and Brand are the only other two who qualify because they are willful impenitents who, by definite textual statements, are excluded from salvation. Because the dwelling place of the Holy Ghost is traditionally the heart, the heart-destruction imagery used in the portrayal of these three characters reinforces their status as unpardonable sinners, guilty of violating the Holy Ghost (158).

Others who have been grouped with Digby because of the nature of their sins include such perfection-seeking and overly self-reliant individualists as Aylmer of "The Birthmark" (43:259; 61:129; 149:222; 381; 500:108) and Rappaccini of "Rappaccini's Daughter" (149:222); such misguided religious extremists as Mr. Hooper of "The Minister's Black Veil" (32:41–42; 115:262; 255:156–57; 260) and the Quaker, Catherine, of "The Gentle Boy" (32:41; 150:666; 186:214); and such proud egotists as Eleanore of "Lady Eleanores Mantle" (32:40; 381; 420:198) and Roderick of "Egotism" (43:259; 255:156–57). Digby's isolation and withdrawal also align him with another "Outcast of the Universe," "Wakefield," and with the many other alienated characters Hawthorne depicts (32:54–55; 255:156–57; 381).

As a condemnation of the rigidity and bigotry of Puritanism, "The Man of Adamant" is like "Young Goodman Brown," "The Gentle Boy," "Main Street," and *The Scarlet Letter* (420:205), and parts of "The May-Pole of Merry Mount" (500:106). "The Man of Adamant" and "The Minister's Black Veil" criticize the Puritans for seeing nothing but sin in the world (46:65–68).

"The Prophetic Pictures" has been discussed with "The Man of Adamant" because of a more subtle connection related to the apologue's aesthetic mode (248:34–35). The two stories were originally published in the same *Token*, and the problems of the artist of the prophetic pictures parallel some of the problems Hawthorne was confronting as a writer. In "The Man of Adamant," Hawthorne uses the very technique that he attributes to the artist, that is, de-emphasizing the natural scenery and using it only "as a framework for the delineations of the human form and face." By incorporating picturesque elements into Digby's story, Hawthorne follows the same antisublime principles that the artist practices when he refuses to attempt to paint such overpoweringly sublime scenes as Mount Washington and Niagara Falls. In the sketch, "My Visit to Niagara" (*CE, XI, 281-88*), which is based on Hawthorne's actual visit there, the narrator comes to a similar conclusion. (See "The Great Carbuncle" and "The Great Stone Face" for other works that reveal Hawthorne's attitude toward the sublime and the picturesque in landscapes.) By calling himself a "lover of the moral picturesque" in "The Old Apple Dealer" (*CE, X, 439-46*), Hawthorne coins a phrase that describes the method he uses in "The Man of Adamant" and, at the same time, identifies that method as a revision of the acknowledged "moral sublime."

## Interpretations and Criticism

The earliest available critique for "The Man of Adamant" predates the story's appearance under Hawthorne's name by ten years. It was made by Hawthorne himself. In a letter to Sophia Peabody dated September 16, 1841, he wrote:

> Sweetest, thou dost please me much by criticizing thy husband's stories, and finding fault with them. . . . I recollect that the Man of Adamant seemed a fine idea to me, when I looked at it prophetically; but I failed in giving shape and substance to the vision which I saw. I don't think it can be very good. (*CE*, *IX, 521*)

Readers since then have generally agreed with the author's assessment. One decides that the subtitle must be an apology for writing an allegory without substantiation (149:221). Another calls the story "a static and thinly disguised theological tract" (61:129). A few have praised it. They have found some positive elements: it "improves with deep acquaintance" (428:745), its irony is well handled (156:495), and in one instance it even qualifies as "a work of art" (500:106).

The standard reading for this story is that Digby stands for American Puritanism and that Hawthorne totally rejects its bigotry (500:110). In Digby, Hawthorne incorporates many clearly identifiable aspects of the experience of his Puritan ancestors—the journey from England across the sea into the wilderness, the reliance on private biblical reading, the intolerance toward all other creeds, and the conviction that they were the elect and that those who were not were totally depraved. While this interpretation finds a wide consensus, theories as to how, why, and if it works are less unanimous. What is "pure allegory" to one (500:106) is "exaggeration" to another (490:89), "satire" to others (149:220; 420:197), and a parody of John Bunyan's Christian to still another (244:162).

A philosophy totally opposed to Puritanism has been suggested as another target. Digby may also represent the Transcendental ideal of self-sufficiency, a school of thought that was very much a part of the New England of Hawthorne's own day (255:158–59; 149:221). This story might be a prophetic vision of the kind of disastrous end that awaited

the man who relied completely on the "infinitude of the self" and therefore rejected fellow humanity and, ultimately, God.

But neither Transcendentalism nor Puritanism is pertinent to an understanding of "The Man of Adamant" according to a Freudian reading
(115:114–15, 262). In the face of Digby's Calvinistic traits and Mary
Goffe's religious symbolism, this critique asserts that " 'true religion'
is not involved" because the "genital obsession" that underlies their
relationship overpowers any spiritual contest they may represent. Digby,
who is the "most grotesque and openly pathological of all Hawthorne's
escapists," is running away from Mary Goffe who threatens him with
the prospect of normal married love. His asceticism has a subreligious
motive; his aggressive saintliness is really a flight from sexuality. Read
from a Freudian perspective, the effect of the description of his retreat
is, indeed, "virtually pornographic' (115:123). It is a dark cave with
"so dense a veil of tangled foliage about it that none but a sworn lover
of gloomy recesses would have discovered the low arch of its entrance,
or have dared to step within its vaulted chamber" (162–63). Much is
made of the final two paragraphs, in which the petrified corpse is discovered a century after Digby's death, but is quickly reinterred and subsequently avoided by all. The author's admonition that Friendship, Love,
and Piety should keep aloof from the cave is interpreted as Hawthorne's
counsel to his readers to cover up the psychic terrors that Digby has
become an image of, that is, to bury them behind a heap of stones. This
psychoanalytic critique attributes some of Hawthorne's subsequent artistic
failures to his having followed his own advice in this story and having
become more and more ingeniously hypocritical and aesthetically confused.

An examination of one central passage in this story reveals a remarkable number of elements directly associated with Christ's burial and
resurrection: "a sepulchral cave," "three days," a "tomb," "awaking to
the solitude of death," a figure who "stood before the mouth of the
cave, and . . . seemed to possess a radiance of its own" (164.12–33). This
Christian symbolism emphasizes Digby's anti-Christian traits and effectively presents his subsequent eternal entombment as an exact reversal
of Christ's resurrection (189:65–68).

A significant question that "The Man of Adamant" raises is: should
the salvation of one's own soul be the uppermost concern of each individual, or is the welfare of one's fellow man more important? In
Hawthorne's story—and this may be its crucial weakness—Digby is obviously wrong. The answer is too easy.

# XXXI

## The May-Pole of Merry Mount

(*Centenary Edition, Volume IX, Twice-told Tales,* 54–67.)

### Publication History

This story was first published in the fall of 1835 in *The Token and Atlantic Souvenir* (pp. 283–97) dated 1836 as the work of the author of "The Gentle Boy." It may have been one of the *Provincial Tales* that Hawthorne tried to get published with the help of the *Token*'s editor, Samuel Goodrich, between 1829 and 1831. Four of the stories submitted for Goodrich's perusal were published in the 1832 *Token*, and "The May-Pole of Merry Mount" may have been one of the "two or three others" intended originally for that projected collection (10; 11:130–31; *CE, IX, 488;* 84:12–13). It may have been incorporated as a part of the subsequent collection, *The Story Teller,* which Hawthorne attempted to get published—also unsuccessfully—in 1834 (204). A manuscript fragment at the Essex Institute establishes Hawthorne's pay for his 1836 *Token* contributions at $1 per page, a total of $15 for "The May-Pole." The story was included in *Twice-told Tales* in 1837 (*CE, IX, 497, 565*).

### Circumstances of Composition, Sources, and Influences

If this story was a part of the *Provincial Tales* project, it was probably written during or before 1829. Doubleday notes that Salem celebrated the two-hundredth anniversary of Endicott s landing in 1828 and that Hawthorne may have been working on "The May-Pole" at that time (149:94). However, since the story is never mentioned specifically in the correspondence between Goodrich and Hawthorne, it is equally probable that Hawthorne wrote it, or revised and completed it, as late as the early fall of 1835. In the headnote, he cites "Strutt's Book of English Sports and Pastimes" as his source; he withdrew this volume from the Salem Anthenaeum in 1827 and again in January of 1835, which could mean that an early version may have been rewritten for publication in the 1836 *Token* (259).

Hawthorne also cites "the grave pages of our New England annalists" in his headnote, but two of the primary accounts that deal directly with the tale's material, William Bradford's *History of Plymouth Plantation* and Thomas Morton's *New English Canaan,* were not available to Hawthorne prior to the story's publication. Morton's book was not available in America until 1838, and Bradford's *History* was not published until 1865. However, several of the historians whose work Hawthorne is known to have seen did have access to Bradford's manuscript and included redactions of it in their annals. Among these are *New England Memorial* by Nathaniel Morton, who was Governor Bradford's nephew, *Memoir of New Plymouth* by Baylies, *Annals of Salem* by Felt, Cotton Mather's *Magnalia Christi,* and Hubbard's account, which was part of the *Massachusetts Historical Collections.* All of them refer to the central situation essentially as Bradford does, including the description of Merry Mount as a symbol of merriment and licentiousness (149:96–100; 357).

John Endicott, who was acting governor of the Massachusetts Bay Colony in Salem, led the Maypole destruction raid on Merry Mount in 1628. (Originally named Mount Wollaston, the settlement was located at what is now Quincy, Massachusetts.) Earlier that year, Captain Miles Standish of Plymouth had arrested Thomas Morton, who was the leader at Merry Mount and was then sent back to England. Although Hawthorne makes no mention of the Standish–Morton incident, he appears to have borrowed from it the idea of terminating the story with an arrest (357). What is more significant is his omission of any reference to the Merry Mounters' practice of furnishing guns to the Indians, which was the Puritan community's chief complaint against them. The military implications of the Merry Mount affair are deliberately ignored by Hawthorne, whose concern is obviously more thematic and artistic than historic.

Hawthorne questions the historical accuracy of another feature of his story in the footnote he appends to Endicott's identification of Blackstone as the priest at Merry Mount (63). Hawthorne's choice of Blackstone has prompted both questions and theories. Orians identifies him as the Anglican clergyman, William Blackstone, sometimes spelled Blaxton (357:163). Martin notes that when the story was first published in the *Token,* the priest was named Claxton. The Reverend Laurence Claxton was an Anabaptist who tolerated Maypoles and was known as a ranter, but had never been in the colonies. Martin theorizes that the change was intended to lessen the criticism against Merry Mount, to emphasize Endicott's tendency toward exaggeration when he calls the minister "priest of Baal," and to contribute to the balance between the opposing forces in the story (309:87). Bell thinks Hawthorne made the change to intensify the identification of the sensual life of the revelers with the English religious forms rejected by the Puritans (46:123, n.9). It is true that Maypoles were associated with a number of traditional activities that the Anglican church fostered. Not only did the English church approve of the traditional Sunday pastimes that were holdovers from pagan rites, such as the May festivities, but Archbishop Laud's mandate that every English clergyman encourage the hereditary Sunday practices was one of the issues that prompted some of the clergy to come to New England (149:99). Another hypothesis for the Blackstone identification is that Hawthorne deliberately chose him to represent the un-Puritan virtue of tolerance (275:32). The statement attributed to him by several of the sources Hawthorne used establishes Blackstone's reputation as a man who guarded his religious independence. Upon leaving Boston in 1635 he is reported to have said: "I came from England because I did not like the LORD-BISHOPS; but I cannot join with you because I would not be under the LORD BRETHREN" (149:97; 275:32; 357:163–64). Another reader believes that Hawthorne knowingly goes beyond his Puritan sources to incorporate this element of religious freedom as a significant part of the real conflict between the Puritans and the revelers; therefore, although Blackstone had no historical connection with Merry Mount, his presence renders the confrontation more profoundly historical than if Hawthorne had adhered to the facts provided him by the anna- lists whose perspective was limited (525).

A perusal of the text and illustrations in the source cited in Hawthorne's headnote, Joseph Strutt's *The Sports and Pastimes of the People of England* (London, 1801), confirms the authenticity of many of the de- tails used to describe the festivities at Merry Mount (149:97–99). Another book by the editor of Strutt's account, William Hone's *Every Day Book* (London, 1826), has also been suggested as a source, one that presents a less pejorative account of the British traditions. However, Hawthorne did not borrow the *Every Day Book* until September of 1835 and some question remains as to whether "The May-Pole" may not have been on its way to the publisher by then (232:134–39; 149:94, n.16). Herrick's seventeenth-century poem, "Corinna's Going a-Maying," which is included in Hone's May Day section but which Hawthorne could have read elsewhere as well, may have been an influence on Hawthorne's de- piction of the confrontation between pagan and Christian values in a May-festival setting (141).

The literary echo most often recognized in "The May-Pole" is found in the final sentence of the story. Edgar's and Edith's expulsion from Merry Mount by Endicott is strongly reminiscent of Milton's description in *Paradise Lost* (XII, especially 648–49) of how Adam and Eve were driven from the Garden of Eden by Michael (46:125; 149:100; 232:132;

275:34; 280:53). Hawthorne alludes to Comus in describing the cos-
tumed revelers at Merry Mount (56.20–23) and their priest (57.8), and
he may also have structured some of the imagery and action on Milton's
masque entitled *Comus* (232:133; 275:34; 533:60; 115:20–21).

## Relationship with Other Hawthorne Works

"The May-Pole" is more closely related to "Endicott and the Red
Cross" than to any other work in Hawthorne's canon because of the
dominant role that John Endicott, "the Puritan of Puritans" (63.7), is
assigned in each. Although the latter is essentially political and nationalistic while the former is religious and ethical, both stories use the
dramatic pageantry of allegory to contrast the Puritans with their avowed
enemies. Bell makes the point that "The May-Pole" is simply a more
abstract rendering of the same repudiation of England and establishment
of American identity and independence that marks Endicott's mutilation
of the British flag (46:119–26). The thematic relationship to Robin's
new-found independence in "My Kinsman, Major  Molineux" is clear,
as are the parallels between Robin's equivocal laugh and the balanced
contradictory attitudes in the two Endicott stories (127:53). These three
historical tales are used by the poet Robert Lowell as a basis for the
first two verse dramas of his trilogy *The Old Glory* (297; 295; 414; 515).
He capitalizes on Hawthorne's image of Puritanism in these stories; this
is the same kind of ironically ambiguous portrayal evident in "The Gray
Champion," the four Province-House stories, "Main Street," and *The
Scarlet Letter*. Most of these, and "Young Goodman Brown" as well,
illustrate how Hawthorne adapts traditional allegorical techniques to
create a unique, multilevel historical allegory of his own (45). Puritan
intolerance is also evident in "The Gentle Boy," another historically based
story that reflects Hawthorne's ambivalence toward Puritanism (469:335).
"The Minister's Black Veil," which was first published in the same issue
of *The Token* as "The May-Pole," projects an equally dark and gloomy
vision of Puritanism in action.

The same conjunction of duty and vanity personified by the Puritans
and the Merry Mounters appears in a piece that was published two years
earlier and called "Passages from a Relinquished Work." The narrator,
who temporarily joins a traveling show, says:

> I seemed to see the Puritanic figure of my guardian standing,
> among the fripperies of the theatre, and pointing to the players

> ...with solemn ridicule, and eyeing me with stern rebuke. His image was a type of the austere duty, and they of the vanities of life. (*CE, X, 421.2–8*)

"The Custom-House" and "The Artist of the Beautiful" echo the ancestral rebuke that maintains that art is an escape from "real" life (232:146–48). The critic in "Main Street" makes a similar objection when he accuses the narrator of manipulating historical reality, something that the Maypole revelers are attempting to do by practicing pagan rites of the past and that Hawthorne himself admittedly does in his fiction (189:62). The "iron" imagery used to describe the Puritans in the two Endicott stories and in *The Scarlet Letter* is given a more graphic rendering in "Main Street": "how hard, cold and confined was their system,—how like an iron cage was that which they called Liberty" (*CE, XI, 58.28–30*).

The major romances, and many of the other stories, confront the shattering "truth" that Hawthorne has Edith realize: "From the moment that they truly loved, they had subjected themselves to earth's doom of care, and sorrow, and troubled joy, and had no more a home at Merry Mount" (*58.26–29*). This kind of transition to maturity—or lack of it—marks all of Hawthorne's most memorable characters, from Hooper in "The Minister's Black Veil" to Giovanni in "Rappaccini's Daughter." The pattern is related to the Edenic myth of Original Sin, to the mutual love between man and woman as its basis, and to the achievement of humanistic values (29; 304:8). The one whose fall and subsequent moral growth bears the closest affinity to the Merry Mount revelers is Donatello in *The Marble Faun*, in which the animal-human imagery of the mummers is repeated and expanded (193:117–19). Other echoes of the fertility rites in "The May-Pole" can be found in the carnival episode of *The Marble Faun*, in the Election Day procession in *The Scarlet Letter*, and in the masquerade in *The Blithedale Romance* (304:42; 533).

## Interpretations and Criticism

The third sentence of this story straightforwardly identifies the theme and the forces in conflict: "Jollity and gloom were contending for an empire" (*54.5–6*). Unanimity among readers begins and ends here. All agree that Merry Mount personifies jollity and the Puritans gloom, but how the conflict is resolved and what "empire" is under contention are matters open to controversy and subject to a wide spectrum of interpretations.

The "empire" or realm has been defined as religious myth (phallic cults versus Christianity), as cultural anthropology (primitive fertility rites versus humanism in a communal context), as psychological allegory (the narcissistic fantasies of childhood versus the realities of maturity), and as political history (England's way of life versus America's survival in the wilderness). Each definition has garnered notable spokesmen. Vickery uses Frazer's *The Golden Bough* to enrich the implications of several significant incidents in the story—the Maypole festivities as ecstatic rites to Dionysus, Edgar's and Edith's change of clothes and Edgar's haircut as purificatory and initiatory rituals, and Endicott's final gesture of throwing the wreath from the Maypole over the couple's heads as a recapitulation of the traditional Christian technique of assimilating pagan rites (494). Hoffman promotes a folkloric rather than a mythic reading; he minimizes the importance of ritual origins, observing that although the forms persist, their functions change in response to cultural pressures. The vestigial pagan ceremonial forms incorporated into the story reflect the humanization of phallic cults and the development of the concept of love on the level of individual fulfillment; the story becomes "a perfect objectification for the soul's progress from innocence and delight through recognition of mutability and responsibility to submission to law in order to live in the human community" (232:140–46).

Those who approach the story from a psychological perspective come to similar conclusions but couch them in different terms. Crews finds a "crisis of maturity," but it is defined by "insistent suggestions of impotence and castration." The "empire" is not the sociocultural world of behavioral patterns but "the general mind of man." This mind has been "fractured into two imperfect tyrannies of indulgence and conscience, neither of which can entirely suppress the other." Edith and Edgar exchange "the overt gratification of hedonism [the Maypole] for the more furtive gratification of an ascetic sadism [the whipping post]," but their love matures and survives because they can reconcile the unchecked fantasy and decadence of Merry Mount with a measure of Puritan restraint (115:17–26). Askew's final assessment is similar: the couple progress from a narcissistic, infantile Eden through the "psychological pattern of Love, Acceptance-responsibility-maturity, and Life." Their "fall" is not theological or social but a psychological one into mature humanity (29).

Three historically oriented readers see essentially the same theme of conflict between a juvenile kind of carefree life-style and the adult responsibilities of maturity. One rejects any "nationalistic" ramifications (149:99); the other two accept the allegory as historical as well as psychological (45:25; 46:120). Bell, one of the latter, finds the forces of jollity and gloom consistently associated with the opposed life-styles of Old World and New World. The "empire" for him is the literal one of America, and the struggle is between the continuation of British tradition and the development of a new, independent value system (46:119–26). Other history-minded readers ignore the psychological parallels and define an exclusively political and cultural arena. Leavis distinguishes between the Puritans who, as New Englanders, become representative of America and the non-Puritans who were, to Hawthorne, merely the English in America. The old way is depicted as an imported artifice that does not face up to the realities of life in the New World (275:29–35). Another critic sees not rejection but synthesis embodied in the fabric of the story; it conveys the typical American conception of the western frontier as a reconciliation of opposites. Edgar and Edith are comparable to two of the age's representative heroes, Leatherstocking and Henry Thoreau, both of whom understand the virtues of white civilization and the Indian way of life (193:114–19). "Prototypical Americans" is what a third historicist calls the Lord and Lady of May. He sees them as "poised on the brink of a new world," having rejected both Merry Mount's attempt to escape history and the Puritans' prideful sense of historical infallibility (189:59–64).

The question of whether the ending is a happy one has as many answers as the question of who and what is at stake. The story's own ambiguity is the culprit. Its structure has been divided by one reader into a series of mutually incompatible positions: plot and allegory, pro-Puritan; imagery and sound, pro-Merry Mount; characterization, diction, symbolism, and theme, alternatingly for and against both of the factions (179). For example, the Puritans are "most dismal wretches" (*60.30–31*), but the Merry Mounters are "sworn triflers of a lifetime" (*60.2*). It is little wonder that readers can follow their own persuasions, or their own concepts of Hawthorne's persuasion, to find whatever they seek. Consequently, the revels at Merry Mount are to one reader "a picture of the harmony between man and beast and nature" (275:31); to another, they reveal "a regressive drive toward the inhuman and the irresponsible" (45:27). While most admit that history mandates a Puritan victory, a minority claim Hawthorne's story celebrates the Christian triumph wholeheartedly (289; 141:283). The majority agree that he accepts a reconciliatory middle ground. However, like the proverbial half-glass of water which optimists call half full and pessimists call half empty, Hawthorne's middle position has been seen as a rejection of both positions (45:23–24; 232:131), as a tempered acceptance of the best in both (115:25; 149:101; 186:64–65; 189:64; 193:117; 229; 280:53–54; 468:76–77; 500:156–57), and as a smoke screen to obscure the fact that the party of gloom unfortunately wins (46:125).

One element in the story, Hawthorne's shifting of May Day festivities to Midsummer Eve, has received some specific attention and several explanations. Hawthorne's sources verify a year-long veneration of the Maypole, and setting the celebration at the height of the summer makes it possible to introduce garden flowers and blossoms realistically (357:165). The sources also establish Midsummer Eve as a time associated with love's fulfillment in folklore and poetry and, therefore, an appropriate date for Edgar's and Edith's ceremony of love (232:142). As the beginning of the end of the summer season, the time also indicates the oncoming winter and the death of the vegetative deity; more covertly, the death of the fertility cult itself at the hands of the Puritans is foreshadowed (494:212-13). Finally, by extending the celebration of May into midsummer, Hawthorne emphasizes Merry Mount's organized and frantic attempt to stop the passage of time (115:22).

James includes "The May-Pole" among "the most successful specimens" of Hawthorne's "admirable . . . little tales of New England history" (241:45). The story is almost always included in American-literature anthologies and also appears in a great many short-story collections. The content and style make it representative Hawthorne. Its allegorical properties are analyzed in detail by Becker. He includes a discussion of the dialectical, nonsequential narrative technique, the unrealistic characterizations that are "incarnations" of abstractions, the historical essay that stops the action in the middle of the story, and the extensive ornamental imagery that is presented in contemplative terms. Becker concludes that Hawthorne persuades his readers to accept his allegorical vision even in a twentieth-century society that is not comfortable with allegory (45:21-29). Fogle, who also analyzes the allegorical artistry, accounts for the story's effectiveness in another way. He suggests that "The May-Pole" uses the texture of symbol to go beyond the limitations of allegory (186:66-69).

Several articles published since 1965 point to another explanation for the persistent reappearances of this story—its content and theme as a relevant social issue. Hawthorne's Merry Mounters and Puritans have been considered forerunners of the hippies and the squares (229), of the flower children and the police (464), and of the displaced Americans of the counterculture and the establishment (302). West Africans have responded to the story's sociohistorical symbols and transferred them to their experiences in emerging democracies (425). Hawthorne's story has also been credited with originating an American-based asceticism-voluptuousness theme that has produced echoes and variations in the fiction of Thomas Wolfe, James Baldwin, and Sherwood Anderson (464) and in the dramatic poetry of Richard L. Stokes and Robert Lowell (453; 414; 295; 515). In spite of an unpopular allegorical mode, the archetypal confrontation the story presents between two seventeenth-century life-styles continues to attract editors and social commentators, and, along with them, readers. The Endicott-Merry Mount controversy remains as provocative and fraught with relevance a century and a half after Hawthorne retold it as it was for him two hundred years after the fact.

# XXXII

# The Minister's Black Veil

(*Centenary Edition, Volume IX, Twice-told Tales, 37–53.*)


## Publication History

This story was first published in the fall of 1835 in the *Token and Atlantic Souvenir* (pp. 302–20) dated 1836 as the work of the author of "Sights from a Steeple." It may have been a part of two projected works, neither of which Hawthorne ever succeeded in getting published as collections: *Provincial Tales* (11:130; *CE, IX, 491*) and *The Story Teller* (11:144; *CE, IX, 495*; 204). *Token* editor Samuel Goodrich paid Hawthorne $46 for the three pieces he contributed to the 1836 issue, making the pay for this story about $17 (*CE, IX, 497, n.28*). "The Minister's Black Veil" was included in the first edition of *Twice-told Tales* in 1837 (*CE, IX, 565*).


## Circumstances of Composition, Sources, and Influences

This story may have been written as early as 1829 or as late as 1835. The date of composition remains conjectural because the story is never mentioned by name in the extant correspondence, but it could well have been one of the "two or three others" in the *Provincial Tales* project that Hawthorne refers to in his letter to Goodrich on December 20, 1829. They were not, he writes, "in a condition to be sent," to which he adds, "If I ever finish them, I suppose they will be about on a par with the rest" (11:127). The story could, therefore, have been completed anytime between 1829 and just before its *Token* publication date (149:170).

In a footnote to the story, Hawthorne identifies another clergyman in New England who made himself remarkable with the same eccentricity as did the Reverend Mr. Hooper. The author explains that in the case of Mr. Joseph Moody of York, Maine, however, "the symbol had a different import. In early life he had accidentally killed a beloved friend; and from that day till the hour of his own death, he hid his face from men." Another version of the story of Moody (1700–53) is told by Dr. William Sprague in *Annals of the American Pulpit* (I, 248–49, as cited in 511:364). The face-covering was a handkerchief, and the cause was the death of his wife. When in the pulpit, he would turn his back to the people, turn up his handkerchief, and read a printed sermon; but when he prayed, he would turn down his handkerchief and face the congregation. Hawthorne could have heard about Moody through oral tradition; in any case, he does not attempt to follow Moody's history in the details of Hooper's life.

Another clergyman, a Mr. Ruggles of Guilford, Connecticut, has also been suggested as a possible model for Hooper (19). Trumbull's *History of Connecticut* (1818), a book Hawthorne is supposed to have read, describes Ruggles as a scholar of unimpeachable morals who was "a dull and unanimating preacher" with "a great talent in hiding his real sentiments" (II, 134, as cited in 19). Hawthorne describes Hooper in much the same terms: Hooper had "the reputation of a good preacher but not an energetic one; he strove to win his people heavenward by mild persuasive influences rather than to drive them thither by the thunder of the Word" (*39.31–34*).

Altschuler's identification of Ruggles is part of his demonstration that Hooper is a man affected by the tumult of the Great Awakening (19). Several readers (149:171; 46:68) establish the time of the story as between 1730 and 1741, the dates of Governor Belcher's administration, because Hooper preaches one of Belcher's election sermons (*49.21–22*). Altschuler proposes that Hooper's transformation into a spellbinding preacher occurs after his conversion, which takes place just before the story opens. Hawthorne's description of the congregation appears to indicate that Awakening is needed: "spruce bachelors looked sidelong at the pretty maidens" (*37.7–8*), certainly a far cry from the piety due the Lord on his day by Puritan standards. The congregation's terrified response to Hooper's sermon can be viewed as Hawthorne's critique of the Great Awakening, while Hooper's alienation from the community is a part of the separatism that Trumbull's *History* refers to: "Instead of loving and cleaving to the ministers, who had been their spiritual fathers . . . they were strangely alienated from them" (p. 170, cited in 19). Hooper's devotion to his religious beliefs and his stifling of the familial impulse (ironically noted in his acquired appellation of "Father") are in the tradition of the "New Light" itinerants described by Trumbull. Even his question to Elizabeth, after she finally "awakens" with "trembling" to the "terror" of the veil, is couched in emotional terms: "And do you feel it then, at last?" (*47.10*).

Four distinct biblical echoes have been detected in "The Minister's Black Veil." The first equates Hooper's seemingly capricious conduct with the ancient Hebrew prophets' practice of using striking symbolic acts to shock heedless sinners into repentence. Analogues are Jeremiah's wearing a yoke around his neck as a sign of the captivity of sin, Ezekiel's shaving his head as a symbol of approaching death, and Hosea's marrying a prostitute to typify unfaithfulness (495). A second Old Testament source has been suggested by Turner, who cites Exodus, Leviticus, and Isaiah as places where the veil is used to symbolize that which divides men from the kind of knowledge which will come to them in the next world (484).

The other two proposed biblical analogues are in the New Testament. The most controversial suggestion comes from Stein, who asserts that Hawthorne depicts Hooper so as to pervert deliberately the teachings in Paul's second epistle to the Corinthians (2:7–17). Hawthorne contrives a series of events—the sermon on secret sin, the funeral, the wedding, Hooper's rejection of Elizabeth—in which Hooper's behavior contradicts the Pauline principles of love as the basis for the relationship between a minister and his followers. Instead of "speaking the word of God in the sight of God," Hooper faces his congregation wearing a veil that throws "its obscurity between him and the holy page" and lays "heavily on his uplifted countenance." At that point in the story, the authorial voice confirms the biblical reversal by asking rhetorically, "Did he seek to hide it from the dread Being whom he was addressing?" (*39.22–26*). The fourth analogue follows a similar perversion pattern; the theological mysteries as outlined in Mark 4:10–12 are debased by Hooper's veil into his own finite, earthbound mystery which is, in effect, a sacrilege (339).

The use of the veil as a symbol, but in different contexts, has been noted in Ann Radcliffe's *Mysteries of Udolpho* and in stories by Charles Dickens (14). For example, under the heading of "The Black Veil," Dickens was concurrently telling a grimly realistic story about a mad widow and her criminal son as part of *Sketches by Boz* that was, except for the allusion in the title, totally different from Hawthorne's "black veil" story (280:42).

## Relationship with Other Hawthorne Works

Young Goodman Brown and Richard Digby, the man of adamant—and the two stories that bear their names—come closest to embodying the concepts exemplified by Mr. Hooper in "The Minister's Black Veil." In their obsession with sin and guilt all three characters parallel the outlook expressed in "Fancy's Show Box," that is, that every human heart "has surely been polluted by the flitting phantoms of iniquity" (*CE, IX, 226.25–26*). This pervasive iniquity takes the form of another symbol in "The Birthmark." There the mark echoes the veil as an emblem of mortality or human imperfection, and the folly of inacceptance is again dramatized (309:83; 92:344).

Aylmer of "The Birthmark," Hooper, Brown, and Digby belong to a group defined by Crews as Hawthorne's sexual escapists; the category also includes other unrealistic idealists such as Giovanni of "Rappaccini's Daughter" and Dimmesdale of *The Scarlet Letter* (115; 43:110). Askew describes this Hawthorne type as men incapable of accepting mature responsibility who either destroy or reject the women who love them (29). Beatrice of "Rappaccini's Daughter" and Georgiana of "The Birthmark" are, like Elizabeth, spiritual guides whose help is rejected; Rosina of "Egotism" also represents the saving grace of love, but her case offers a contrast because Roderick, unlike the other egotists, is able to end his isolation by forgetting himself in his love for Rosina (189:58; 448:392). Hooper, Brown, and Giovanni are especially notable for their subjective view of individual morality and their lack of faith (445), while Gervayse Hastings of "The Christmas Banquet" has a related "defect of heart" that excludes him from human reality, too (52:134). Wakefield is another narcissistic character who is isolated by his ego-tistical individualism (255:158). He is among the Hawthorne characters, Hooper included, that Axelsson classifies under the rubric of "Voluntary Isolation" (32:54–55).

Hooper is more closely related to those who withdraw actively as a result of misguided religious zeal. Among these religious extremists are Digby, Catherine of "The Gentle Boy," and Father Ephraim of "The Shaker Bridal" (32:39–44; 260). Goodman Brown has been called a secular parallel to Hooper (448:391) with both of their outlooks founded on dark and foreboding theological principles. Many readers equate Hooper's veil with Brown's dream because both experiences change the characters; each lives out his life in misanthropic darkness, pessimistically ignoring what is good, overemphasizing evil, and cutting himself off from human love and companionship. One reader assesses their melancholy obsession with sin as part of the pattern of conservatism expressed by Samuel Johnson in *Rasselas* (183:190–91), while another distinguishes Hooper from Brown as a "more subtle protagonist" in his parallel con-frontation with the doctrine of "visible sanctity." Each is profoundly shaken, and both find themselves separated from the community and spiritually apart from their fellow men (19). Arvin says that the "un-healthy preoccupation with guilt" in these two stories "assumes the form of a misanthropy that far out-Puritans the Puritans" (27:61). A certain brand of mentality that Hawthorne associates with second- and third-generation Puritans characterizes Hooper and Brown, and Digby and Leonard Doane of "Alice Doane's Appeal" as well (46:60–81). Hawthorne describes these descendants of the founding fathers in "Main Street" as "a race of lower and narrower souls than their progenitors had been" (*CE, XI, 68.1–3*).

This attitude is also discernible in Hawthorne's portrayal of another young minister, Dimmesdale (46:134–36), which is only one of the ways in which *The Scarlet Letter* has been likened to "The Minister's Black Veil." Doubleday applauds the technique that Hawthorne uses in both works to explore successfully every nuance of one basic idea, and he notes the parallel between Hester's *A* and Hooper's veil as symbols which are worn publicly to connote sin—Hester's, as an acknowledgement of a specific sin enforced by the community, and Hooper's, as an emblem for concealed sin voluntarily assumed (149:173; 455:xlviii). Dimmesdale has attributes nearly identical with some of Mr. Hooper's; both are effective clergymen who, in spite of their being set apart from their parishioners, are able to reach sinners and eloquently preach on the depravity of mankind (149:177–78; 32:43). In his relentless probing for sin, Hooper is like Dimmesdale's nemesis, Chillingworth, and another of Hawthorne's monomaniacs, Ethan Brand (459). Dimmesdale's actual secret sin appears to be the kind associated with Hooper's obsession (455:xlviii), but some readers reject the possibility of any specific wrongdoing on Hooper's part. (See interpretations below.)

A similar controversy, but on a larger scale, has developed over Hooper's alleged similarity to Goodman Brown. Cochran, for example, maintains that the two characters represent opposite extremes of reaction to the fact of man's sinful nature with Brown's life ending in "darkness, disillusionment, and despair" and Hooper's in "a firm belief in a traditional afterlife" (92; see also 467). This position has been explicitly rebutted (102) in addition to the implicit counterarguments in the readings discussed above. One of the readers who rejects Brown as a parallel figure for Hooper proposes Owen Warland of "The Artist of the Beautiful" instead; like Owen, who is a mask for Hawthorne the artist in pursuit of beauty, Hooper functions as the artist figure dedicated to truth (467).

The veil image, which is central to Hooper's story, is used again in *The House of Seven Gables* (116) and in *The Blithedale Romance* (116; 80). Carnochan sees in the depiction of Hooper's veil the inception of the difficulties Hawthorne was to have with symbols in his later works. He believes that Zenobia's legend of the veiled lady in *The Blithedale Romance* and the conclusion of *The Marble Faun* are subsequent points in a downward curve leading to the symbolic confusion of the final, unfinished romances (80).

One reader finds it significant that the story immediately preceding

"The Minister's Black Veil" in *Twice-told Tales* is "The Wedding Knell," a tale in which the bridegroom wears a shroud, the wedding bells sound like a funeral knell, and the aged bride is invited to ride a hearse (116:213–14).

## Interpretations and Criticism

Of the thirteen "moralized fictions" that Hawthorne wrote between 1834 and 1840, this story is one of the two that is admired by twentieth-century readers. Baym attributes its popularity to the fact that while it does celebrate "the common highway of life" like the others, it cannot be easily reduced to the moral that "he who is not like his fellows is not normal"; Hooper seems "too good a man for the severe judgment that the structure of the story make on him" (43:56). Essentially the interpretative difficulties reflected in this story's critical history can be reduced to that simple dilemma, but it is a problem that has captured the imagination of a host of readers. Is Hooper a sinner who deserves his life of isolation, or is he a dedicated, saintlike hero who sacrifices his personal happiness to carry out his ministry?

One of the earliest interpretations on record is Poe's, and he unhesitatingly opts for the former viewpoint:

> "The Minister's Black Veil" is a masterly composition of which the sole defect is that to the rabble its exquisite skill will be *cavaire*. The *obvious* meaning of this article will be found to smother its insinuated one. The *moral* put into the mouth of the dying minister will be supposed to convey the *true* import of the narrative: and that a crime of dark dye, (having reference to the "young lady") has been committed, is a point which only minds congenial with that of the author will perceive. (378:92)

Since 1842 when these comments appeared as part of Poe's review of *Twice-told Tales,* a number of readers have agreed that Hawthorne suggests the possibility of some actual and serious crime in Hooper's past (186:36; 447:81; 47:23; 416:165). A few have concurred with Poe that Hooper's veil is somehow related to the girl whose funeral takes place on the Sunday he first wears it. Lang takes into account Hooper's over-tender conscience and propensity for excessive penance to conclude that Hooper's "secret sin" is having loved the girl in secret, without telling her or anyone, while engaged to Elizabeth (270:93). Wycherly, on the other hand, defines what Poe calls "a crime of dark dye" as murder: Hooper assumes the veil because he was the agent of the girl's death (531).

Others have judged Hooper guilty but of a different kind of sin: excessive pride. Stibitz offers the most convincing defense of this position. Admitting the validity of the veil as a symbol for man's hidden guilt or hypocrisy, Stibitz shows how Hawthorne uses Hooper's veil ironically to comment on the hidden nature of the sin that arises when Hooper self-righteously exalts his idea until it becomes a form of spiritual egotism. Hooper's self-deceptive insistence on wearing the veil is an ironic dramatization of his own inability to see his sin of pride even as he seeks to reveal the hidden sin in others. Stibitz reviews the minister's egotistic assumptions and actions in five successive narrative divisions in the story to show how Hawthorne juxtaposes the two levels, the sin of concealment that Hooper preaches and the sin of pride that he inadvertently conceals, so that one level ironically reinforces the other. Good intentions notwithstanding, Hooper dies as he lived, "an unbalanced and unredeemed sinner" (459).

With varying degrees of certainty and from differing perspectives, Hooper's eventual damnation has been projected by other readers as well. Citing the description of the veil as something that will "shade him from the sunshine of eternity" (50.27), one reader sees Hawthorne "hinting" rather than proclaiming that Hooper is mistaken in his assumption that a heavenly reward awaits him. In this reading, Altschuler calls Hooper "the most sympathetic Puritan" Hawthorne was able to devise but one whose pathetic situation nevertheless serves to highlight the dangers of the deluded theology he follows (19:27). Another reader interprets Hooper's smile, which is consistently linked with light in opposition to the veil's darkness, as a key to the sadistic and masochistic nature of Hooper's obsession; he concludes that in the minister's misguided attempt to save others, he seriously endangers their salvation and his own (507). Bell's assessment is similar: "by assuming the veil Hooper himself has become a sinner, perhaps the greatest sinner of them all" (46:67).

The harshest indictment is pronounced by Stein, who does not wait until Hooper's death to impose a sentence of damnation on him. Stein unveils Hooper as an agent of the devil while he lives. As an Antichrist he so terrifies his followers with an all-encompassing, dark vision of evil that he denies the light of Christian redemptive love. When Hawthorne describes Hooper as inciting his parishioners, even to "the most innocent girl," into sinful introspection, the ministerial duties become a profanation of divine office. Various symbolic actions, such as Hooper's spilling of the wine at the wedding, also suggest blasphemy and sacrilege (448).

In direct contrast to these inauspicious judges are the Hooper admirers who applaud his determination to fulfill his calling and who assess his ministry as successful. To one, he is a "godly preacher" who uses a striking symbolic act to reach sinners who otherwise would not have heeded the word of God (495). To another, he is a man of "great stead-fastness" and "quiet, hopeful patience" who has arrived at "the outer limits of earthly wisdom" without becoming self-righteous or contemptuous of others (92). A third reader sees Hooper's lonely existence as "a lifelong sacrifice in the service of truth." The minister does not recoil in horror from an iniquitous world; it recoils from him when he pursues his mission to convey his deepest vision of reality to others (467). Doubleday makes the point that the central concern of the tale is not the minister but the effect of the black veil on the town; in this respect, he too, affirms Hooper's achievements, because he believes the people of Milford do get the veil's message (149:175–76).

Several readers acknowledge Hooper's sincerity of purpose but have mixed reactions about his success. The deathbed scene can be used as evidence of the entrenched blindness of the congregation and of Hooper's failure to communicate with them (309:85). Or, taking the whole character into account, Hooper can be considered as a man whose ministry may be a partial success but who "fails at life" (29:342). Turner, who interprets the veil as a symbol for the mortal ignorance man must accept while in this world, believes that Hooper dons it to acknowledge that it is humanly impossible to comprehend fully the nature and extent of sin. Because to a minister the question of sin is a crucial one, such an admission reflects cognizance of inadequacy or humility, but certainly not pride (484).

The most illuminating statement of these more or less neutral positions is Fogle's. He refuses to reconcile the "dubiety" in the tale. The veil is as much a symbol for secret sin (and Hooper for Everyman) as it is a symbol for perverse pride (and Hooper for the ostracized sinner). Fogle attributes the former to the ancestral Hawthorne who instinctively shares Hooper's dark vision and the latter to the nineteenth-century Hawthorne who sides with Elizabeth's steady view of life. As a result, the reader leaves the story with "a sense of depths unplumbed" and the realization that any single meaning is ultimately inadequate (186:33–40).

These "unplumbed depths" have invited exploration of a psychological sort from some readers. The earliest appears to be Von Abele, who points to Hooper's veil as a protective device behind which its wearer can hide from the sexual demands of a normal life (497:29, 104). Others have pursued similar Freudian investigations into the minister's psyche. One discovers a basic dependence upon yet fear of women (116); another notes a faint but suggestive undercurrent of "tidy womanliness" in Hooper's behaviorisms (115:108); others stress the indirection and equivocation of the literary structure of the story as a key to the minister's ineffectuality (382). The most startling of the conclusions broached is the one that claims that all the characters except Hooper are as totally repressed at the end of the story as they were at the beginning. For Hooper, and for the readers who are sensitive to the story's ironic intent, Hawthorne projects the disheartening realization that "the best approximation to happiness rests in an ignorant, busy involvement with a society of unconscious hypocrites" (115:106–11).

An existential reading is equally critical of the townspeople: they are "the dead in life" because they deny the concept of nonbeing that the veil represents. When Hooper wears the veil, which stands for nothingness, he shows himself as one who accepts death in the center of being (475). One cannot help wondering how Hooper, the devout Puritan, and Hawthorne, the avowed theist, would react to such an interpretation.

Two notebook entries offer some insight into the author's own interpretation of this story. The first, written at least a year after the story was originally published, contains an apparent afterthought on veils: "A veil may be needful, but never a mask" (*CE, VII, 23.11–16*). This admission, in the middle of a germ for "an essay on the misery of being always under a mask," appears to validate Hooper's action. The other entry is an account of a discussion prompted by the story itself. Mr. Shaeffer, the French teacher who lived with Horatio Bridge and Hawthorne in Augusta, Maine, during the summer of 1837, mentioned "The Minister's Black Veil" as having been translated into French as an exercise by a Miss Appleton of Boston. This prompted Shaeffer to express his willingness, in spite of its being "a very foolish thing," to expose his whole heart—his whole inner man—to the view of the world," not because there was no evil there, but because he "was conscious of being in a state of mental and moral improvement" (*CE, VIII, 49.22–32*). Hawthorne does not comment directly on Shaeffer's response to his story, but he does, elsewhere in the Augusta journal, commend "the little Frenchman" as one who impresses him very strongly (*33.27*). Neither does he, however, record any objections to the moral that Shaeffer derives from the story and applies to himself.

Notwithstanding this implicit confirmation of the moral import of the story on the author's part, one twentieth-century reader dismisses moral assessments as irrelevant to the story's major concern. He defines that concern as "questions about the notion of a symbol," and he analyzes the veil, which both conceals and is a symbol of concealment, as a symbol for language, which gives meaning to experience but also prevents direct perception of it (80). Another reader sees a similar parable, that is, the effects on audience and artist of symbolism, as an auxiliary theme (189:58, n.7).

What may be the highest praise bestowed on "The Minister's Black Veil" is in the form of a three-page analysis by the structuralist Paul Goodman. Because he draws on such world masterpieces as Sophocles' *Oedipus Rex*, Shakespeare's *Hamlet*, Flaubert's *L'Education sentimentale*, and Kafka's *The Castle* to illustrate his method, Goodman's inclusion of "The Minister's Black Veil" is commendation in itself. He analyzes the story as an example of a work that, formally, is excellently unified and yet makes the reader feel something beyond what is "presented":

> The over-all structure is a continuum of the ordinary, the plausible, the odd, the wonderful, and the preternatural, with the dual effect of making the meaning of the veil actual, that is, continuous with the actual persons and scene, and yet inexplicable. ...The climax of mystery and sublimity in this story occurs in the very passage which is handled as if it were to be the explanation, 'Why do you tremble at me alone?' ... And this remarkable scene gains enormously in magnitude from the fact that the universality of the symbol, whose career could be traced from the beginning, becomes the nonsymbolic mystery that only compounds the mystery; there *is* a fact, but it is mysterious. This uncanny paragraph cannot be read without dread and awe. (202.5:256–57)

Precisely because Goodman is not an Americanist and because his scope is comparative literature, his approbation carries added significance. Doubleday assigns the story the same kind of international stature when he likens its technique to Tolstoy's *The Death of Ivan Ilych* and Camus' *The Fall* (149:171).

What Goodman identifies as "sublime or symbolical effect" and Stibitz terms "effective tightly knit ironic unity" (459), others have less laudably referred to as "irresolution" (490:87) and "a blurred lack of clarity" (52:130–34). One reader complains that nothing much happens in the story and that the protagonist is primarily a preacher who preaches on behalf of the author (280:42). For most, however, it is, in Fogle's words, a "thoroughly successful story" (186:33). It is almost invariably included in any representative collection of Hawthorne's works—and justly so, because it portrays his most pervasive concern, how man accepts the presence of sin in himself and in his world. It also uses his most characteristic device—a remarkably appropriate color-coded symbol—to communicate vividly a dilemma for which, also typically, he refuses to provide any easy answers. In Coleridge's terms, he combines the specific (a historically verifiable religious sect, a geographically identifiable setting, a uniquely individualistic set of circumstances) with the general (the universality of sin that transcends time and space) to create the unity and the reconciliation of opposites that mark the greatest works of literature.

# XXXIII

# Mr. Higginbotham's Catastrophe

*(Centenary Edition, Volume IX, Twice-told Tales, 106–20.)*


## Publication History

"Mr. Higginbotham's Catastrophe" was first published in the *New-England Magazine* in December 1834 (VII, 450–58) as a part of "The Story Teller No. II" (449–59) with no attribution (*CE, IX, 568*). The discouragement and paltry remuneration connected with Hawthorne's projected but never-published book, *The Story Teller*, of which this was a part, is detailed under the publication history of "The Devil in Manuscript."

In 1837 Hawthorne included "Mr. Higginbotham's Catastrophe" in *Twice-told Tales* to provide the bright comic touch he felt his first collection needed to appeal to a range of tastes. He included "Little Annie's Ramble" on the same principle. In his determined effort to become a "popular" writer, he also extracted "Mr. Higginbotham's Catastrophe" from "The Village Theatre" segment of *The Story Teller* frame, because he did not want to offend the current prudish standards of taste with an episode the reading public might find prurient. In the deleted frame (collected subsequently as "Passages from a Relinquished Work," *CE, X, 419.8–19*), the narrator is puzzled by the appearance of "a young person of doubtful sex." After drinking "a glass of wine and water," he decides the person is "bewitching . . . in either case" and asks for a dance. In 1837, Hawthorne was not willing to publish under his name what had been published earlier anonymously; when he included "Mr. Higginbotham's Catastrophe" in the first edition of *Twice-told Tales*, he dropped the framework apparatus entirely (120; *CE, IX, 503–04*).


## Circumstances of Composition, Sources, and Influences

As a part of "The Village Theatre," one of the opening sections of *The Story Teller*, "Mr. Higginbotham's Castastrophe" was probably written in the fall and winter of 1832. Like the frame that originally encompassed it, it owes many of its details to the summer trips throughout New England Hawthorne took between 1825 and 1832. Also like *The Story Teller*, whose structure bears a close resemblance to Washington Irving's successful *Sketch Book* of 1819–20, this story shares the comic intent, the native American setting, and the folk material of two of the best-known stories in Irving's collection, "Rip Van Winkle" and "The Legend of Sleepy Hollow." Dominicus Pike, Hawthorne's peddler, is as unlikely a "knight-errant" as Ichabod Crane, Irving's schoolteacher. Both entertain the possibility of ghosts, and both are likened, in Hawthorne's words, "to the heroes of old romances" (*120.2*), a simile whose satire is heightened by Ichabod's passion for the plenty of his beloved's pantry and estate and by Pike's happy ending in a profitable marriage to Higginbotham's niece.

Hoffman has traced Pike's personality, "his provincialism, inquisitiveness, resourcefulness, and insouciance," to the Sam Slick version of the Yankee bumpkin tradition (232:107). Pike's speech, too, is of the vernacular variety, effectively capturing the colloquial twang and rhythm and testifying to Hawthorne's ability to reproduce the popular idiom of his day when he chose to (70; 331). Less convincing is one critic's conclusion that Hawthorne himself is a prototype for Pike because the peddler is also a storyteller of sorts (367).

## Relationship with Other Hawthorne Works

The openly comic mode being a rare one with Hawthorne, "Mr. Higginbotham's Catastrophe" has most often been linked, usually to its advantage, with his one other farcical story, "Mrs. Bullfrog" (331). One critic calls both tales "under praised" and interprets them as comic treatments of the serious theme of initiation into the meaning of truth. He also sees a similar seriocomic reversal on the theme of foreknowledge as a mode of perception in "Mr. Higginbotham's Catastrophe" and "The Prophetic Pictures" (188:27–28). In its relationship to *The Story Teller*, "Mr. Higginbotham's Catastrophe" has been heralded as the one instance in the projected work where the story fits the dramatic framework (11:144).

## Interpretations and Criticism

In a review dated May 1842, Edgar Allan Poe called "Mr. Higginbotham's Catastrophe" "vividly original and managed most dexterously" (378:92). The earlier reviews of the 1837 edition of *Twice-told Tales* had also spoken approvingly of it, expressing a preference for such "sunny" offerings and confirming Hawthorne's acuity in providing a variety of selections (*CE, IX, 506–08*). Since then, however, the story has received little critical attention precisely because it is so atypical, with none of Hawthorne's characteristic allegory, irony, or celebrated "blackness." Most of the criticism that has been generated is, with some variety in emphasis, a restatement of the unusual nature of the genre for a writer of Hawthorne's temperament (70:331). The story is at the same time acclaimed a success. Adkins calls it a "merry, rollicking" tale (11:144). Hoffman deems it "an early and masterful representation" of a folk motif (232:107). A philosophic note is sounded by one critic who interprets the basic conflict in the story as a question of primacy between two orders of truth, Pike's version of Mr. Higginbotham's robbery and hanging and that of the witnesses who attest to his well-being (188:27–29). The fact that both are, in part, right serves to illustrate the complexity of the most basic facts of experience, a demonstration that culminates comically in Pike's plea: "Mr. Higginbotham . . . you're an honest man, and I'll take your word for it. Have you been hanged or not?" (*119.26–28*)

As an antidote to a full dosage of Hawthorne's more somber tales, "Mr. Higginbotham's Catastrophe" presents a refreshing change of pace, but its uniqueness makes it misleading for the uninitiated Hawthorne reader. It is best read as an entertaining exception once the controlling rules of the Hawthorne canon have been established.

# XXXIV

# Mrs. Bullfrog

(*Centenary Edition, Volume X, Mosses from an Old Manse,* 129–37.)

## Publication History

"Mrs. Bullfrog" was first published in the fall of 1836 in the *Token and Atlantic Souvenir* (pp. 66–75) dated 1837 as the work of the author of "Wives of the Dead" (*CE, X, 574*). The editor, Samuel Goodrich, paid $108 for the eight pieces Hawthorne contributed to this issue, making Hawthorne's pay for "Mrs. Bullfrog," at the average rate of $1 per page, an approximate $10 (*CE, IX, 497*). Ten years later, Hawthorne included this story, and "Monsieur du Miroir" from the same *Token,* in *Mosses from an Old Manse* in order to add humor and variety to the collection (*CE, X, 518*; 149:185; 43:112).

## Circumstances of Composition, Sources, and Influences

Hawthorne probably wrote this story during the fall and winter of 1835–36 (84:59). The following undated notebook entry, made between September 7 and October 17, 1835 is loosely related:

> To represent the process by which sober truth gradually strips off all the beautiful draperies with which imagination has enveloped a beloved object, till from an angel she turns out to be a merely ordinary woman. This to be done without caricature, perhaps with a quiet humor interfused, but the prevailing impression to be a sad one. (*CE, VIII, 11.24–29*)

Two other entries, made after the story was written, reveal that one of the ideas in "Mrs. Bullfrog" was still on Hawthorne's mind in the fall of 1836 and that his attitude toward marriage was still cynical in the summer of 1838. The first of these reads: "Those who are very difficult in choosing wives seem as if they would take none of Nature's ready-made works, but want a woman manufactured particularly to their order" (*CE, VIII, 20.13–15*). The second describes the "Paradisaical mood" of a young bride and bridegroom who were riding in a stage with him. His long, detailed account of their displays of affection concludes with the matter-of-fact comment, "It would be pleasant to meet them again next summer, and note the change" (*CE, VIII, 86.27–28*).

The entry written before the story's composition differs markedly from the form Hawthorne's concepts take in "Mrs. Bullfrog." The "ideal" Mrs. Bullfrog is only partially a product of her husband's imagination; her wig, false teeth, and affected gentility are artifices she contrives to ensnare Mr. Bullfrog into marriage. Mr. and Mrs. Bullfrog are caricatures of the broadest sort; grotesque comedy replaces quiet humor; and the "prevailing impression" is farcical, not sad. Hawthorne obviously changed his mind about both theme and style. His own remarks about "Mrs. Bullfrog" help to account for the difference between the germ in the notebook and its uncharacteristic development in the story. He explains that it "was written as a mere experiment" and "did not come from any depth within me" (*CE, X, 518*).

One critic suggests that Hawthorne's choice of a humorous, satirical treatment may have been influenced by Samuel Johnson's handling of similar themes in *The Rambler* (96). Another source study cites chapter III of Le Sage's "The Devil Upon Two Sticks" as a possible model (4). Two other critiques credit the folktale as a contributing factor, one attributing the "fraud begets fraud" ending to the tradition of the jesting demon (444:71), the other tracing Hawthorne's reversal of the Frog-Prince transformation motif to the folktale of wonder, possibly the German *Märchen* (440).

## Relationship with Other Hawthorne Works

"Mrs. Bullfrog" and "Mr. Higginbotham's Catastrophe" share the distinction of being Hawthorne's only stories in an openly comic vein. Folklore material and motifs play a role in each, and both tales end with the male protagonist having negotiated a financially profitable marriage for himself. Folsom, who sees them as comic treatments of the theme of initiation, calls them both "underpraised" (88:29), but as a rule, "Mrs. Bullfrog" is considered the inferior of the two.

Similarities also exist with "Monsieur du Miroir" and "Peter Goldthwaite's Treasure." Mr. Bullfrog's whimsical comment that he had almost been "driven to perpetrate matrimony with my own image in the looking-glass" (*130.11–13*) reveals the same narcissistic strain central to "Monsieur du Miroir" (113:9–10), while the follies of Peter in "Peter Goldthwaite's Treasure" echo the duplicities of Mrs. Bullfrog (447:71).

According to Baym, all the fiction that Hawthorne wrote between 1834 and 1840 celebrates the normative, therefore, Mr. Bullfrog's disillusionment fits the pattern because he tried to fulfill his fantasy instead of conforming to the realistic norm (43:57). A more surprising relationship with a story written during the Old Manse period has been suggested by Solensten (440). He calls "The New Adam and Eve" an "act of penance" for "Mrs. Bullrog." While that may be putting it strongly, a causal relationship can be established through first, the satirical reference to "Adam and Eve in Paradise" (*131.9–10*) in "Mrs. Bullfrog," written before Hawthorne met Sophia; second, Hawthorne's willingness to disavow the story when Sophia criticized it adversely during their engagement (*CE, IX, 521*); and finally, the idyllic bliss portrayed in "The New Adam and Eve," written during the first year of their marriage.

## Interpretations and Criticism

Considering that Hawthorne's comic pieces are invariably classified as uncharacteristic and therefore, by implication, not important, "Mrs. Bullfrog" has received an unexpected variety of interpretations. It has been discussed as a satire on marriage (96); as an ironic attack on the commercial values in American society that contaminate even the most personal relationships (255:73–74); and as a revelation of primal sexual motifs (440). The last of these identifies the wedding journey as a rite of passage to sexual knowledge for the priggish Mr. Bullfrog and as a victory celebration for Mrs. Bullfrog, who seduces her Adam as successfully as D. H. Lawrence claims Hester seduces Dimmesdale in *The Scarlet Letter*.

Hawthorne's most devoted admirer, his wife, disliked "Mrs. Bullfrog"; Hawthorne agreed with her judgment and dismissed the story as "a mere experiment" in which neither his "heart nor mind had anything to do" (*CE, IX, 52*). Some critics have joined the Hawthornes in their disparagement, calling it "a mediocre story . . . a failure" (96:386) and "an embarrassment to anyone with a respect for Hawthorne's work (149:184). Surprisingly enough, *Blackwood's Magazine* (LXII, 587–92) concluded its favorable review of *Mosses from an Old Manse* in November 1847 with an extract illustrating the successful humor of "Mrs. Bullfrog." To this day, a substantial number of Hawthorne readers find this story to be the refreshing change of pace that Hawthorne intended when, in spite of his reservations about it, he decided to include it in his *Mosses* collection.

# XXXV

# My Kinsman, Major Molineux

*(Centenary Edition, Volume XI, The Snow-Image, 208–31.)*

## Publication History

This story was first published in 1831 in the *Token* (pp. 89–116) dated 1832 and attributed to the author of "Sights from a Steeple." It was one of several stories intended for the projected collection *Provincial Tales* that Hawthorne sent to Samuel Goodrich, the editor, in December 1829 in hopes of finding a publisher. On January 19, 1830, Goodrich wrote to Hawthorne, promising to use his influence to help and mentioning "My Uncle Molineaux" [sic] as one of the stories that he "liked particularly." When, by the spring of 1831, no publisher had materialized, Goodrich convinced Hawthorne to let this story and three others be published in the *Token* for 1832. Estimates of how much Hawthorne was paid for these contributions range from 75¢ a page (207) to nothing (250:106), although no exact record of payment has been found. Twenty years later "Major Molineux" was collected in *The Snow-Image* (1851), but not without some complications because Hawthorne, who was in Liverpool, England then, did not have a copy available. His publisher managed to procure the text through the editors of *Literary World*, but apparently it was imperfect. On November 3, 1851, Hawthorne offered to rewrite what was missing if a perfect copy could not be found. However, on November 5, George Ticknor located an 1832 *Token* which he arranged to have copied for the printer (*CE, IX, 487–91; CE, XI, 413–14, 431*).

## Circumstances of Composition, Sources, and Influences

As one of the *Provincial Tales*, this story was probably written in 1828 or 1829 (10; 84:12). The opening paragraph cites the annals of Massachusetts Bay in general and Hutchinson's account in particular as a source for the remarks that preface the story. They allude to the problems experienced by the "six governors in the space of about forty years from the surrender of the old charter under James II." According to Thomas Hutchinson's *History of Massachusetts*, this surrender occurred in 1684, and the four decades in question began with the governorship of Sir Edmund Andros in 1686 and ended with that of William Burnet in 1729 (149:229; 404).

The adventures in the story are assigned to "a summer night, not far from a hundred years ago," but the "temporary inflammation of the popular mind" that the story depicts parallels the events of 1765 rather than the political tenor of the 1720s and 1730s. The Stamp Act was to go into effect on November 1, 1765, but before that date the Sons of Liberty had resorted to violence often enough to force all the stamp agents in the colonies to resign. Hutchinson records the hanging in effigy of his son-in-law, who was the newly appointed distributor of stamps for Massachusetts, and on the night of August 16, 1765, Hutchinson himself, who was lieutenant governor at the time, had his house attacked by a mob led by two men in disguise. The action was condemned the next day by the citizens at a public meeting in Faneuil Hall, but, as Hutchinson's account observes, many who had participated in the violence supported the unanimous vote, and even those who were opposed to the rioting were helpless to stop it and afraid to oppose it. Tarring and feathering was another form of violence that the Sons of Liberty pursued that summer. In short, much of the action of the story parallels the historic activity of sixty-five years earlier and not the hundred or so specified in the story. Doubleday attributes this confusion to the author's "calculated vagueness," a part of the distancing that Hawthorne felt was necessary when dealing with events of the comparatively recent past (149:228–30).

Equally confusing is the identification of a historical counterpart for Major Molineux. A William Molineux is mentioned twice in Hutchinson's *History* (149:229) and three times in Caleb Snow's *History of Boston*, another source Hawthorne is known to have had access to before and during the probable composition dates for this story (368:139). The problem is that the historic William Molineux (1717–74) was not one of "the inferior members of the court party," as the preface indicates the fictional Molineux is; in fact, William Molineux was no Tory at all but a radical leader of anti-Loyalist mobs, a Whig rabble-rouser, and a member of the Boston Revolutionary Committee of Correspondence reputed to have been at the Boston Tea Party (368:137; 149:229, n.14; 424:563; 433:120). Two readers infer that Hawthorne deliberately assigned the name of a notorious rebel to a persecuted Tory for thematic purposes. Pearce believes that "the two in artistic fact are one," united in the figure of Robin, who is a Molineux like his kinsman and who, when he also becomes one of the rebellious mob, helps destroy and drive away part of himself (368:140–41). Shaw emphasizes the reversal of roles involved when Hawthorne chastises the excesses of the real Molineux by humiliating the fictional one; he sees the reversed role as one of several in a pattern of doubleness and displacement that dominates the tale (424: 563–64). Another reader goes further afield to find an analogue for Molineux in Jonathan Swift's *Drapier's Letters*. According to Abernathy, the mention of Molineux in the American historical account re-evoked the two Molineuxes described by Swift, especially the ironic account of the execution in effigy of one of the Molineuxes' brother-in-law. Molineux himself as a participant in the mob, the scope, and the ironic tone of Swift's piece are credited with having provided a grounding for Hawthorne's story (7). The prototype for the "double-faced fellow" has been identified as Joyce Jr., the celebrated Boston mob leader who is described in Hezekiah Niles's *Principles and Acts of the Revolution* (Baltimore, 1822) as having worn a parti-colored face for such occasions (368:143). "Joyce Jr." is an assumed name that refers to one of the executioners of King Charles and that carries with it the associations of regicide as the ultimate crime against the king (424:564).

But Hawthorne's description of these two major figures in the tarring and feathering procession, and of the crowd in general, evokes associations that go beyond the political agitations of the American Revolutionary movement recorded in the histories that he consulted. When Hawthorne describes the "counterfeited pomp," "senseless uproar," and "frenzied merriment" of the mob, which he likens to "fiends that throng in mockery round some dead potentate, mighty no more" (*230.15–18*), he makes Major Molineux and the mob's leader embodiments of a scapegoat king and a lord of misrule. The source for these concepts is Joseph Strutt's *Sports and Pastimes of the People of England*, a book on British antiquities that surveys folk traditions. Hawthorne withdrew it from the Salem Athenaeum in 1827, a time when he could have been formulating, consciously or otherwise, the concepts that he uses in depicting Molineux's overthrow (259). Strutt's book describes the sacrifice of a scapegoat king as a part of the Roman Saturnalia, a precursor to the English May festivals. The celebration features the ritual overthrow of authority by a licentious crowd with leaders in disguise. All manner of disruptions of order and reversal are involved with servants assuming mock titles and being waited on by their masters (424:567). The parallels between Strutt's Saturnalian revels and the mob scene in the story are obvious. Hoffman assumes that Hawthorne intuited these anthropological theories, later developed by Frazer in *The Golden Bough*, but he credits the American folk tradition of the naif for Hawthorne's characterization of Robin. A series of antecedent bumpkins from the country precede Robin in popular tradition. These include Jack Downing, Sam Slick, and Brother Jonathan, but Robin's self-proclaimed "shrewdness" makes him the

"Great American Boob" whose Yankee self-reliance backfires (232: 119–21).

Another folkloric allusion, again attributed to Strutt, has been discovered in the name of the young protagonist, Robin. Strutt's survey reveals that the mock king of the May celebration often was played by Robin Hood, a legendary figure long associated with rebellion to authority (424:569). Robin's more generally accepted allusive referent is Shakespeare's Robin Goodfellow, better known as Puck, in *A Midsummer Night's Dream*. Shakespeare's comedy may have also suggested the possibility of moving the May Day observances to the middle of summer as Hawthorne appears to do in "My Kinsman" and as he more openly does in another story written about the same time, "The May-Pole of Merry Mount." The headnote to "The May-Pole" (*CE, IX, 54*) confirms Hawthorne's familiarity with Strutt's book.

Echoes from *A Midsummer Night's Dream* are not limited to these similarities, however; verbal and thematic parallels abound (130; 149: 231–32; 227; 424). Hawthorne makes a direct reference to the play in the description of the watchman who "like the Moonshine of Pyramus and Thisbe, carried a lantern, needlessly aiding his sister luminary in the heavens" (*218.12–13*). Pyramus and Thisbe are characters in Shakespeare's farcical play within a play in which workingmen assume aristocratic roles. The moonlight, which is heralded for its magical powers in both works, casts the same kind of confusing spell on the events of a midsummer night in Boston as it does on another midsummer night in Oberon's and Titania's fairy kingdom in Shakespeare's play. The themes of disguise, mistaken identity, resistance to authority, lost ways, and dreamlike occurrences punctuate each piece. When Hawthorne introduces his protagonist as "The youth, one of whose names was Robin" (*209.30*), and then refers to him as "shrewd" eight times in the course of the story, he appears to have had these lines in mind:

> Either I mistake your shape and making quite,
> Or else you are that shrewd and knavish sprite
> Call'd Robin Goodfellow. . . . (II, i, 32–34)

Robin's comment "Strange things we travellers see!" (*220.28*) also is reminiscent of Puck's famous "What fools these mortals be" (III, ii, 115), and Robin's climactic burst of laughter has been interpreted as a reflection of Puck's laughing mockery at human folly (227).

In spite of the fact that the reference to Shakespeare's Pyramus and Thisbe is the only direct literary allusion in this story, an extraordinary number of influences have been detected. The subtlety with which the many proposed analogues have been absorbed into the fabric of this most eclectic of Hawthorne's stories, however, makes even the most convincing explication ultimately conjectural. In "My Kinsman" Hawthorne seems to be following the advice he once gave his sister Elizabeth: "You should not make quotations; but put other people's thoughts into your own words and amalgamate the whole into a mass" (66:172; 7:5; 224).

Difficulties notwithstanding, undaunted readers of all persuasions have claimed Robin's archetypal journey of initiation as their own. When Robin arrives in an unfamiliar and frightening place by being ferried over a river, he is following the adventures of Odysseus, Heracles, Aeneas, and Dante, all of whom were ferried over the River Styx into Hades. Like Odysseus, Robin carries the epithet "shrewd," and like Heracles, Robin uses a crude wooden club as a weapon. However, by adopting an ironic, elevated style, Hawthorne makes Robin a mock version of his epic-hero counterparts (17). Robin's cudgel can also be seen as a kind of Cumaean bough like the one Aeneas carries for protection on his descent to the underworld in the sixth book of Virgil's *Aeneid*. Although both Robin and Aeneas are searching for older kinsmen and are associated with emerging national purposes, these similarities merely serve to establish how banal Robin is by setting off his shortcomings against Aeneas' heroic accomplishments (266).

Some of the heroes who have been nominated as models for Robin come from Christian allegories—Spenser's *Faerie Queene*, Bunyan's *Pilgrim's Progress*, and Dante's *Divine Comedy*. Each of these works also offers a parallel for the city that Robin enters.

Robin resembles Spenser's Redcrosse Knight in his initial overconfidence in himself and in his subsequent rude awakening to the evils of the world; the city dwellers that he meets form "a thinly veiled, if not always fully developed" allegory comparable to Spenser's pageant of the Seven Deadly Sins (66:175). Spenser's archvillain Archimago has been proposed as the model for the kindly-appearing stranger who, based on this analogue, masks his malicious intentions with a venerable and misleading demeanor (66:181).

Robin resembles Bunyan's Christian in the wallet that he carries on his back; his encounters in the city are reminiscent of Christian's trials and temptations in the town of Vanity. However, Robin's is a pilgrim's progress in reverse with his destination, like that of the passengers on "The Celestial Railroad," ironically changed from heaven to hell (66:177).

Robin resembles Dante's pilgrim as well, and Boston, as traversed during the night by Robin, reveals an hierarchy of sins similar to that outlined in the geography of the *Inferno*. One readers sees Robin himself as marked for a place among the traitors in the final circle of hell (17).

The disagreement at the beginning of the story between Robin and the ferryman recalls a similar episode between Virgil, Dante's guide, and Charon, the boatman on the River Styx in the third canto of the *Inferno*. Charon does not want to admit Dante into hell because he is not dead; the ferryman's reluctance in the story serves a similar allegorical function showing that Robin is still morally alive while the city is peopled with the spiritually dead (66:174). A parallel not previously noted is in the dramatic effect achieved when the procession stops directly in front of Robin and he faces the cart holding his kinsman. A similar halt is called in the procession described in cantos 29 and 30 of *Purgatorio* when, as part of a formal masque, a line of devout mummers in allegorical guises marches before Dante. The procession stops directly in front of him, symbolizing the church's one-to-one relationship with every soul. He faces a chariot holding Beatrice, who because of her identification with Christ has the same scapegoat connotations as does the Major. Hawthorne's procession is infernal rather than heavenly, but both climactic recognition scenes allegorize the relationship between institutions—the church for Dante, democracy for Hawthorne—and individuals.

Robin has also been identified with two American youths and their initiatory adventures in the city—Benjamin Franklin (433; 165) and Arthur Mervyn, the title character of Charles Brockden Brown's novel (488). Some of the details of Robin's arrival parallel Franklin's account of his first encounters in Philadelphia recorded in his *Autobiography*. Robin pays the ferryman, gets hungry but only has a "parchment three-penny" left, looks with "scrutiny into people's faces," and falls asleep on the steps of a church; Franklin pays the boatman, gets hungry and buys "three penny worth" of bread, looks "in the Faces of People," and falls asleep in a Quaker meetinghouse. Again, the similarities appear to have been established to emphasize the differences. One reader convincingly demonstrates that Robin's experiences serve implicitly to criticize Franklin's vision of reality, one that is based on the efficacy of the will. Unlike Franklin's pragmatic rationalism, Robin's alleged "shrewdness" does not resolve the "ambiguous discontinuity" of his experiences (165). The other young American whose footsteps Robin may be following is fictional. In the opening chapters of Brown's novel *Arthur Mervyn*, the title character is a naive country boy who travels to the city to seek help, becomes confused and overwhelmed by what happens there, and has to choose between returning home or staying in the city to rise in the world (488). Insofar as Robin is involved in political events that he does not understand, he is also like the young heroes in the novels of Sir Walter Scott, a British writer whose historical fiction provides models for several of Hawthorne's American variations (149:235, n.23).

Other literary echoes include Aristotle's "pity and terror," with which Robin initially views his kinsman (476); Coleridge's alliance of moonlight and imagination which permeates all the story's action (130; 186:112), and Milton's Michael in *Paradise Lost* and the Attendant Spirit in *Comus*, upon whom, according to one reader, the kindly stranger is based (262).

## Relationship with Other Hawthorne Works

Several sketches and two pieces for children are useful in establishing a clear historical and thematic perspective on this story. "Old News" (*CE, XI, 132–60*) provides the factual background for "My Kinsman" (189:26, n.3). The final section contains an authorial comment that suggests a condemnatory view: "A revolution, or anything, that interrupts social order, may afford opportunities for the individual display of eminent virtue; but, its effects are pernicious to general morality" (*159.29–32*). In *Grandfather's Chair*, a historical book for children, Hawthorne describes one of the violent acts of the same pre-Revolutionary period; he retells Hutchinson's account of a mob attack on his house, calling it "a most unjustifiable act" (149:230). Another of his children's books, *Tanglewood Tales*, includes a myth he titles "The Minotaur." It can be used to enrich "My Kinsman" by identifying the parallels between Hawthorne's version of the Theseus legend and Robin's adventures, especially the labyrinthine setting, the monster figures, and the ordeal he undergoes (399). "Night Sketches" (*CE, IX, 426–32*) is suggested by another reader as a key to the significance of the moonlit Bible in the church in "My Kinsman." The man with the lantern in "Night Sketches" who will find his way by the "lamp of Faith" reinforces what the appearance of the helpful stranger and the vision of the moonlit Bible mean, that is, Robin's need to salvage the faith of his childhood (502:34–35).

The story that most readers compare "My Kinsman" to is "Young Goodman Brown." The obvious similarity is thematic; both tell of a young man's initiation into an unfamiliar world of evil (393; 476). Each story follows the quest motif (81; 186:105–06), projects an ambiguous mixture of good and the evil of the world (500:56–64; 51:80–81), and leaves its protagonist ontologically insecure in an existential world he cannot comprehend (68). The two stories are also alike stylistically. Their detachment in tone creates a tension between manner and subject matter that produces an effect of weird mockery in both (187). Their basic structure is the ritual progress of allegory, achieved by a series of discontinuous encounters between the hero and representatives of the society into which he is entering. The traditional allegorical figure of the guide appears in each—the friendly stranger in "My Kinsman" and Satan in "Young Goodman Brown" (45:174–76). Most pronounced, however, is the interaction between dream and reality that makes it difficult to distinguish between the actual and the imaginary in both Robin's and Brown's worlds (45:7–13; 227).

"The May-Pole of Merry Mount" also creates a kind of dream world. Like "My Kinsman" it depicts Saturnalian revels at midsummer (227; 424:569; 533) and translates a moral question into an ambiguous psychological and ritual drama (424). It also shares a historical setting and a maturation theme with "My Kinsman" and the other *Provincial Tales*, which probably included "Young Goodman Brown," "The Gentle Boy," "The Gray Champion," and "Roger Malvin's Burial" (10). Of these, "The Gray Champion" is most like "My Kinsman" in dealing directly with the concept of the American Revolutionary movement. As in "Endicott and the Red Cross" and the Province-House legends, especially "Old Esther Dudley," the admiration has ironic overtones and is tempered with reservations. This ambivalence is reflected in a dramatic version of "My Kinsman" written by the twentieth-century poet, Robert Lowell. He groups the story with two of the other historically based tales, "The May-Pole" and "Endicott and the Red Cross," as his source material for the first two parts of his verse drama, *The Old Glory* (297).

A moral understanding of history permeates most of these stories as it does *The Scarlet Letter* and *The House of Seven Gables* (263; 368). "Roger Malvin's Burial" is especially notable for its representation of the past (Malvin) that is sacrificed for the present (Bourne) in the same kind of father-figure and son relationship as in "My Kinsman" (189:27–29; 115). Like "The Gentle Boy," "Alice Doane's Appeal," and "The Wives of the Dead," "Roger Malvin's Burial" and "My Kinsman" do not concentrate on actual historical personages. By creating fictional protagonists, Hawthorne succeeds in disengaging the main focus from history while utilizing all the aspects of the past that he needs (43:30–33).

"Ethan Brand" is a later story that follows the night-journey motif of "My Kinsman" (393) as well as its pattern of fiendish laughter (157).

## Interpretations and Criticism

The number and the extravagance of the readings generated by this story lead one Hawthorne admirer to consider whether such a diversity is possible simply because the author did not have full control of the tale (149:228). Another, who is more representative of the majority, attributes the multitude of meanings to a positive richness of imagination and not to artistic confusion (442:331). Confusion, however, is what the uninitiated reader experiences when confronted with the sophisticated and persuasive rationales used to support diametrically opposed conclusions about what happens in the story. For example, the crucial question of why Robin laughs has been answered in a bewildering variety of ways. As part of a historical allegory, his laughter signifies young America's determination to break free from the political and economic domination of England (275:38–42; 304:52). But to one reader, it signifies the ineptness, insecurity, and unfitness of the colonists for self-government (398:33). From a psychological perspective, the laughter is a release from the rebellious and hostile feelings Robin unconsciously harbors toward his kinsman as a father figure (277:212–24). As part of the re-enactment of the Dionysian revels that accompany initiation rites and the ritual sacrifice of a scapegoat king, Robin's laugh is one of abandonment in keeping with the archetypal motif of regeneration (232:113–25). But it is also an inarticulate kind of self-condemnation (209), a reaction to his disillusioned quest for a worldly inheritance (304:52), an expression of a new awareness (309:107), and an act of self-preservation (246). The moral ramifications of these views have been pursued and augmented until Robin's laugh has become, for some, a sure sign of his damnation. Consequently, the reader faces a bewildering array of assessments that cover the gamut from Robin as a mature adult ready to assume responsibility to Robin as a reprobate who has betrayed his principles—with a goodly number of "undecided" pronouncements from those who declare the story to be open-ended and Robin's future unsettled.

The twenty or so sources and influences that are reviewed above contribute to this disparity because each suggests a corresponding interpretation—some historical, some mythic, some psychological, and each with a different moral slant. Historicists have the least difficulty claiming this story as their province. (Here, and elsewhere in this study, the term *historicism* is used to pertain to the general theory that all cultural phenomena are historically determined.) The opening paragraph, for all its convoluted ambiguity, is clearly political. Leavis is generally credited with first equating the Major with British rule and Robin with the colonies; she suggests "America Comes of Age" as an appropriate subtitle for the story (275:38). Pearce extends Robin's identification with young America to all Americans, past and present. He believes Hawthorne wants to teach his readers the lessons of the past by imputing to them the communal righteousness and the guilt that is experienced by Robin (368). Another history-based, allegorical interpretation assigns Robin to the Tory side of the conflict; for this reader, Robin is a composite figure embodying the six governors of the Massachusetts Bay Colony that Hawthorne refers to in the opening paragraph. Like them, Robin is overconfident, obstinate, obtuse, and naive, and his six encounters parallel the unhappy fates of the six governors (404).

For Robin to be hailed as a hero and also to qualify as one of the enemy, the distinction between the warring factions must be blurred. In fact, Hawthorne's ambivalence toward the American Revolution is unmistakable in this story. Although many readers conclude that Hawthorne ultimately applauds Robin's—and young America's—decision to rise in the world without the help of his kinsman, the rebel cause is not glorified, nor are the Tories portrayed unfavorably. Both factions are charged with the pursuit and abuse of power; the Major is described as a "steady soul" whose head had "grown grey in honor" (228–29); and the red-and-black-visaged leader and his wild, grotesque followers are cast in satanic roles (433; 424:565; 476:60). According to Adkins, the Americans are presented in such "a cruel and ignominious mood" that Hawthorne feared his patriotic nineteenth-century readers would be revolted, which could account for his long delay in acknowledging the story (13).

Another historical phenomenon that is equally complex, and that Robin also becomes emblematic of, is the growth from rural dependency to urban independency. Robin's boyhood in the country has been viewed as a modified version of the agrarian ideal, the perfect American life in Jeffersonian terms. Yet here, too, simplistic labels of "good" or "bad" are impossible (465).

The archetypal fabric of the tale is one factor that colors these sociopolitical themes and contributes further to the ambiguity. Mythic overtones are created by the initiation, night-journey, quest, and scapegoat motifs that are as much a basis for Hawthorne's story as the situation outlined in the historical preface. The mythic source studies, detailed above, define these motifs in terms of the analogues that each considers most influential; consequently, the relationship perceived between the role models and Hawthorne's story shapes the reader's appraisal of "My Kinsman." For example, Hoffman finds a "qualified, half-skeptical hope" that when the town wakes from its collective nightmare of scapegoat sacrifice and Saturnalian revelries, order will again be established under the new reign of freedom. Robin's personal fate can only be inferred, but in his role as the Yankee naif, no undue confidence is allowable (232:123–25). Gross, on the other hand, sees Robin as completing his initiation and fulfilling his quest for moral reality; his adventures are "a journey from dark innocence to painfully illuminated knowledge," an experience that prepares him for a new life (209). Broes's conclusions are more grim. He believes that, unlike the quests of Robin's prototypes in the allegories of Dante, Spenser, and Bunyan, Robin's quest ends not in illumination but in the "moral darkness of hell" (66).

Other readers have advocated each of the three positions taken by Hoffman, Gross, and Broes: uncertainty as to Robin's achievements and future (189:31; 309:107; 476); approval of his decision to accept moral reality and face the future on his own (8; 32:124–25; 186:104; 572:42; 504); and condemnation of his behavior as treacherous, cowardly, and depraved (142; 82; 291; 105; 81; 149:235–38; 246).

One of the issues taken into account in arriving at these conclusions is Robin's alleged shrewdness. Most readers perceive an ironic tinge in Hawthorne's emphasis on it because in the eight times in the story that it is mentioned, it is usually followed by an erroneous judgment on Robin's part. This qualifies him as the Yankee bumpkin (232:119–21), but he can also be seen as a young folk hero, the younger brother who, not in line to inherit the family farm, sets out to seek his fortune. As such, Robin is not entirely a bumbler; Fogle calls him "essentially sound," his shrewdness and goodness "genuine" (186:109). One reader establishes the extent of Robin's shrewdness by analyzing the narrator's point of view. In the course of the story, when the narrator calls Robin "shrewd," he is reflecting Robin's self-image, which is patently inflated, but by the last sentence of the tale, when the stranger addresses him as "shrewd," Robin's new-found wisdom is objectively corroborated (504). The most pejorative appraisal of Robin's shrewdness classifies it as part of his survival tactics; it enables him calculatedly to choose what is expedient and self-serving (246).

The communal aspects of the story have also been used to support the various positions, many of them focusing on the nature of Robin's encounters during the night. Robin's experiences are a condensation of a lifetime journey with each incident reflective of society's institutions and the human abstractions they encompass. The barbershop, tavern, brothel, mansion, and church where Robin stops are symbols of vanity, intemperance, promiscuity, aristocratic pride, and religion (149:235–38; 442:331–32; 449). The people that Robin meets are the townfolk, and their behavior imposes a "societal initiation" on Robin that he appears to complete successfully (8). In acquiescing to the town's will and not defying the mob on his kinsman's behalf, Robin becomes a bona fide member of the community, for good or evil. Doubleday attributes Robin's behavior to his need to avoid society's rejection, and he likens the events of the night to an accelerated version of the slow, insidious process in which, without full consciousness of depravity, a man compromises himself (149:235–38). The prevailing consensus is that Robin's joining the community is part of his maturing process, but a growing number condemn his actions as a capitulation to social conformity and corruption (81; 142; 291; 476).

Among those who see the essential issue as moral rather than social, the analogies made by Cervo illustrate the extreme positions possible. He classifies the story as a Christian satire in which Molineux represents "the sublime courtesy of Christ" and Robin, "the unutterable vileness of Satan." Because Robin is a traitor to "prescribed loyalty, to family, and to courtesy," he becomes a "Gargouille anti-hero," the butt of the joke that exposes him for the opportunist he is (82).

These moral judgments are expressed in different terms by the psychologically oriented readers, but the pattern is the same. For them, it is Robin's "adjustment" that is deemed successful (115; 304; 277; 353), a failure (365; 398), or uncertain (424; 68).

Lesser's analysis of "My Kinsman" has led the way in establishing the Oedipal nature of Robin's search for his kinsman. Unconsciously, Robin does not want to find the Major, who is a father substitute and therefore a symbol of restraint and unwelcome authority; the boy seeks freedom, especially sexual freedom about which he feels constrained, as the episode with the "lady of the scarlet petticoat" (216–18) reveals (277:212–24). Crews emphasizes Robin's merger with "a jealous, jostling democracy of father-haters" as an experience that cathartically rids him of "both filial dependence and filial resentment" (115:78–79). Paul, however, is less optimistic about Robin's psychological balance; he views Robin's adjustment as neurotic rather than healthy because at the end Robin merely replaces one father figure, the Major, with another, the benevolent friend (365; 398:39).

The dream structure of the story serves as a firm basis for these psychoanalytical interpretations (304:48–53; 353; 398). Robin's search follows a typical dream pattern of isolation and rejection. Each incident becomes symbolic of his inner conflict and an objectification of his psychological state. His subconscious hostility toward his father is revealed in the recurrent encounters with older men in authority who rebuke him and turn him away. He finds himself laughed at, and then lost again, after he asks for help from three such figures—the old man with the cane, the innkeeper, and the watchman. When he dreams of his actual father, the rejection is confirmed by the latch that keeps him from entering his old home and joining his family. The "double-faced fellow" is a distorted father image that fuses misrepresentations of both his actual father and his actual uncle, and the kindly stranger is, for some readers, an embodiment of the perfect father image (304:51–52; 398:39). The malleability of Hawthorne's presentation must be held responsible for the fact that Robin's assumed decision to follow the stranger's advice can be judged as evidence both of his psychological independence (304:52) and of the abandonment of his quest for identity (398:39).

In addition to anticipating Freud's Oedipal theory in Robin's personal conflicts, this story is credited with linking the scapegoat ritual and coming of age in a way that foreshadows Freud's concepts in *Totem and Taboo*. Freud's analysis of mass hysteria in *Group Psychology and the Analysis of the Ego* is also anticipated in Hawthorne's depiction of the crowd leader's paternal aspects and the power he wields over the submissive mob, Robin included (424:572–74). R. D. Laing's existential psychology has also been proposed as relevant to a better understanding of this story. Laing's concept of "disorientation" offers an explanation of why Robin reacts as he does; his "ontological" security is shattered when, despite his repeated attempts to find rational explanations, he cannot make sense out of the townspeople's behavior. Hawthorne renders the town "absurd" in the general existentialist sense, giving Robin a right to the "ambiguity and weariness" he feels (68).

Whatever reservations some traditional readers may have had about the psychological approach to this story (369), few readers today can ignore the insights it offers. "My Kinsman" is Hawthorne at his most eclectic; to experience the story fully, readers must be equally eclectic in using all the methods available to illuminate its complexities. Shaw's reading is a case in point. Entitled "Fathers, Sons, and the Ambiguity of Revolution," his explication traces the motif of doubleness and reversal, especially the polarity between obedience and revolt, on all levels. In the process, he uses resources from a myriad of disciplines including such secondary materials as Samuel Adams' arguments about America's right to come of age, studies of Puritanism as a revolutionary ideology, the history of the regicides in New England, newspaper accounts of how disturbances among English weavers spurred the Stamp Act riots, socio-logical surveys of crowds and power, research into the roles of Robin Hood and Maid Marian in English May Day festivities, the use of Masonic passwords among the colonial rebels, and Theodor Reik's psy-choanalytic theories about ritual (424).

A legitimate question arises in the face of such a formidable effort: Is "My Kinsman" worth it? Quite simply, yes. Superlatives are applied routinely to this story. Bewley calls it "one of the greatest masterpieces in American literature" (51:81). Waggoner says it achieves a "perfec-tion of embodiment" (500:61). Even its detractors qualify their criticism with positive connotations; it is, says one who finds the complexities too complex, a "fascinating kind of failure" (149:238).

Hawthorne must have had "My Kinsman" in mind when, in the preface to the collection in which he finally acknowledges it as his, he writes:

"The ripened autumnal fruit tastes but little better than the early wind-falls." Readers agree that this story does indeed come "up to the standard of the best" that he can achieve (*CE, XI, 6.9–11*)—witness the countless times it has been reprinted, collected and anthologized since then. In fact, because of its diversified appeal, it may be the most widely read of Hawthorne's stories. It can be put to good use in history classes, in urban studies, in ethics seminars, in myth surveys, in adolescent-psychology sessions and mob-behavior clinics. Above all, it belongs in all manner of literature courses, from those as general as an introductory survey to those as specialized as a course on the Odyssey theme in the American short story. It is here, in the realm of literature per se, that Hawthorne's art is most viable. It is in the dreamlike aura of Robin's night journey that every reader ultimately recognizes himself and his human dilemma.

# XXXVI

## The New Adam and Eve

(*Centenary Edition, Volume X, Mosses from an Old Manse, 247–67.*)

### Publication History

"The New Adam and Eve" was first published in the *United States Magazine and Democratic Review* in February 1843 (XII, 146–55) under Hawthorne's own name (*CE, X, 577*). How much Hawthorne was paid for the story, or when, remains unclear. John L. O'Sullivan, the magazine's editor and a close personal friend of Hawthorne's, was a guest at the Old Manse from January 10 through 13 and was expected to leave some money for Hawthorne with Sophia's mother on his return to Boston. Presumably the payment was for "The New Adam and Eve" which was to appear in the next month's issue. O'Sullivan's visit to the Peabodys is confirmed in a letter from Sophia's sister Mary, but no reference is made to O'Sullivan's leaving any money (323:23, 35, nn. 23, 24). Hawthorne's correspondence suggests he was not paid then, or for quite some time. A March 16, 1843 letter to Sophia reads: "Nobody pays us. It was very strange—at least inconsiderate—in Mr. O'Sullivan not to send some money, my request being so urgent." A March 25 letter to his friend Horatio Bridge complains of his "having been disappointed in money that I had expected from three or four sources." And a notebook entry dated March 31 repeats the allegation: "Meantime, the Magazine people do not pay their debts." According to Sophia's journal, O'Sullivan's payment did not come until December. If the $100 recorded by Sophia is all that Hawthorne received for the six new pieces published in the *Democratic Review* in 1843, his pay for "The New Adam and Eve" came to approximately $22.50, less than half the standard magazine rate of $5 per page (*CE, X, 504–06*). Hawthorne included "The New Adam and Eve," and the other five 1843 *Democratic Review* contributions, in the 1846 edition of *Mosses from an Old Manse*.

### Circumstances of Composition, Sources, and Influences

"The New Adam and Eve" was probably written between December 18, 1842 and January 12, 1843. These dates, while admittedly conjectural,

are substantiated by the publication data discussed above and by Hawthorne's practice of writing his stories sequentially rather than working
on several concurrently (323:15–17, 23). Fall 1842 has also been proposed as the composition date, based largely on internal evidence and
and the wish "to believe that the first tale written in the Old Manse
after the heat of summer was 'The New Adam and Eve'" (84:31).

Hawthorne's own statements have contributed to the development of
this myth. In a letter to Sophia during their engagement, he wrote:

> How happy were Adam and Eve! We love one another as
> well as they; but there is no silent and lovely garden of Eden
> for us. . . . Do you not think that God has reserved one for us,
> ever since the beginning of the world? (233:I, 215)

In a letter to his sister Louisa from the Old Manse the day after his
wedding, he proclaimed: "We . . . came straight to Paradise" (84:32).
Almost two months later, in a letter to Margaret Fuller on August 28,
1842, he again parallels his and Sophia's life at the Old Manse with
Adam's and Eve's in Paradise (228:I, 253). The notebook entries for
this period sound the paradisaical theme as well. The evidence overwhelm-
ingly establishes the newlyweds' idyllic happiness at the Old Manse in
1842 as an influence in the shaping of Hawthorne's re-created primordial
couple (113; 56.5). But the original idea dates back to a journal entry
made between October 25, 1836 and July 5, 1837:

> The race of mankind to be swept away, leaving all their cities
> and works. Then another human pair to be placed in the world,
> with native intelligence like Adam and Eve, but knowing nothing
> of their predecessors or of their own nature and destiny. They, per-
> haps, to be described as working out this knowledge by their
> sympathy with what they saw, and by their own feelings. (CE,
> VIII, 21)

An earlier entry, under September 1836, has been proposed as the
initial germ for the concept before Hawthorne developed it into a usable
form (483:305): "To picture the predicament of worldly people, if
admitted to paradise" (CE, VIII, 18). The story, written at least five
years after the detailed entry, is developed exactly according to the proposed outline.

The Bible, Milton, Shakespeare, and Swift have all been credited with
contributing to Hawthorne's final version. The account given in Genesis
is obviously basic to Hawthorne's concept, but the Miltonic adaptation in
Paradise Lost is also reflected (482:561; 131.5:16–17). Specifically,

the following passage condemning man's perversion of nature is cited as influencing Hawthorne's presentation of unspoiled natural beings exploring an environment perverted by mankind:

> . . . Dishonest shame
> Of Nature's works, honor dishonourable,
> Sin-bred, how have ye troubled all mankind
> With shews instead, mere shews of seeming pure,
> And banished from man's life his happiest life,
> Simplicity and spotless innocence!
> (*Paradise Lost*, IV, 313–18, quoted in 131.5:17)

Another Miltonic essential emphasized by Hawthorne is free will. His new Adam "has at least the freedom—no worthless one—to make errors for himself" (*265–66*). In letters to her friend Mrs. Caleb Foote during the first year of her marriage, Sophia describes the winter evenings she and Hawthorne spent reading the "old English writers." She mentions Shakespeare as well as Milton, and a possible echo from *King Lear* has also been detected in this story written during the same winter (131.5:14–18). Hawthorne alludes to the "rich garment" that hides "the plague spot" of sin in those who relegate their less sumptuously concealed counterparts to prisons (*254.28–29*). King Lear's attack on the hypocrites of his day is strikingly similar:

> Thou rascal beadle, hold thy bloody hand!
> Why dost thou lash that whore? Strip thine own back;
> Thou hotly lust'st to use her in that kind
> For which thou whip'st her. The usurer hangs the cozener.
> Through tatter'd clothes small vices do appear;
> Robes and furr'd gowns hide all. Plate sin with gold,
> And the strong lance of justice hurtless breaks;
> Arm it in rags, a pigmy's straw doth pierce it.
> (IV, vi, 165–72, quoted in 131.5:18)

A less distinguished artistic influence of a more contemporaneous nature may be found in the American "school of catastrophe," a popular though now largely forgotten group of early-nineteenth-century writers and painters (122). The only Hawthorne story connected with these "connoisseurs of holocausts" has been "The Ambitious Guest," but the premise of "The New Adam and Eve"—the worldwide destruction of the whole race of men—links it to this group and to a possible attempt on Hawthorne's part to cater to popular taste.

## Relationship with Other Hawthorne Works

The other seven allegorical and satiric sketches written during the Old Manse period have been associated with "The New Adam and Eve" in both method and theme (151; 27:125–31). Of these pieces, "Earth's Holocaust" bears the closest, and most significant, relationship. It, too, is predicated on renewal through destruction, but in it the chances for success are much dimmer. As Satan points out at the close of the story, unless the reformers who have set fire to all they consider evil in the world find "some method of purifying that foul cavern," the human heart, "all the shapes of wrongs and misery" will simply reappear (*CE, X, 381–404*). In creating a new Adam and Eve who are without original sin, Hawthorne supplies the purified heart without which any reform is meaningless. In this respect, the more hopeful Doomsday story is "complementary" to the darker and more sinister one (151:328). Both stories introduce the question of whether earthly schemes for utopian societies can succeed, an issue Hawthorne would also explore in two of his novels, *The Scarlet Letter* and *The Blithedale Romance* (255:171–213).

*The Scarlet Letter* has also been associated with "The New Adam and Eve" because the earlier story attacks society's moral shortcomings in much the same way the novel does. In the passage describing "the dark lazar-house into which Adam and Eve have wandered" (*255.1*), the prison is a symbol for blind and loveless bigotry as is the "wooden edifice" in front of which Hawthorne introduces his readers to Hester Prynne. A metaphor in the passage (*254.18–28*) is remarkably appropriate as a simile for Hester's punishment; her imposed isolation from the Puritan community is like "the banishment of a leper from a leper colony" (255:179).

Another story written at the Old Manse that is also a study in how man perverts nature is "Rappaccini's Daughter." Both stories draw on Hawthorne's knowledge of the Bible and of Milton (131.5:18–21), but while Eve has been included in the list of Hawthorne heroines who fit "the wholesome New England girl" type (such as Susan in "The Village Uncle"), Beatrice is another kind of Eve, in some interpretations qualifying as a seductress.

## Interpretations and Criticism

As an example of Hawthorne's satirical allegory, "The New Adam and Eve" demonstrates an inherent weakness of the genre while it effectively illustrates Hawthorne's penchant for creating characters who symbolize ideas or conditions rather than individuals or specific types (151:325–26).

As Newton Arvin put it, the "embodiment in personality" necessary for powerful social satire is missing (27:131). The new Adam is no Gulliver, and while the story deals with some typical Hawthornesque concerns, it remains significant primarily from a biographical and developmental perspective.

# XXXVII

# Old Esther Dudley

(*Centenary Edition, Volume IX, Twice-told Tales*, 290–303.)

## Publication History

This story was first published in January 1839 in *United States Magazine and Democratic Review* (V, 51–59) as No. IV of "Tales of the Province-House" and attributed to Nathaniel Hawthorne. All available evidence indicates that Hawthorne received approximately $2 per page for his contributions to John L. O'Sullivan's *Democratic Review*. (See publication history of "Howe's Masquerade," the first of the Province-House stories.) This would have made his pay for "Old Esther Dudley" $18. In 1842, the story was included in the second volume of the second edition of *Twice-told Tales* with the subtitle changed to "Legends of the Province-House IV" (*CE, IX, 572*).

## Circumstances of Composition, Sources, and Influences

"Old Esther Dudley" was probably written late in 1838. In a letter dated November 5, 1838, to O'Sullivan, Hawthorne appears to be explaining his delay in continuing the Province-House series, the first two stories of which had appeared in the *Democratic Review* the previous May and July. Hawthorne wrote: "Whenever my poor brains get into working order, the first use I make of them shall be to throw off an article or two. I hope to do so within a week or ten days." The "article or two" were probably "Lady Eleanore's Mantle," which appeared in the December 1838 issue, and "Old Esther Dudley," which completed the series (*CE, IX, 518*).

Hints for this story appear in two notebook entries in close proximity to each other, both found within the segment entered between December 16, 1837 and June 15, 1838: "An old looking-glass. Somebody finds out the secret of making all the images that have been reflected in it pass back again across its surface" (*CE, VIII, 169.1–3*) and "A partially insane man to believe himself the Provincial Governor or other great official of Massachusetts. The scene might be the Province House" (*169.23–25*). Equally revealing, although in a more general way, are other 1837–38 entries dealing with the decline of aristocratic families. These include Hawthorne's account of his visit to General Knox's old estate in Maine (65–68), comments on his own ancestors (74–75), and his reaction to the portraits in the Essex Historical Society in Salem (154–55). Of the paintings, he wrote: "Nothing gives a stronger idea of old worm-eaten aristocracy—of a family being crazy with age, and of its being time that it was extinct" (155.17–19); and he described Eben Hathorne as a "truly forlorn . . . old bachelor" whose great hobby was "the pride of ancestry" (74.5–7). Both Esther and the old loyalist who tells her story reflect aspects of these appraisals, as does the title character in "Peter Goldthwaite's Treasure," who is in many ways a prototype for Esther (455:lxxviii).

Spenser's Lucifera in Book I of *The Faerie Queene* has also been cited as an analogue for Esther; like Lucifera, Esther is "the Lady of that Pallace bright," and she shares similar delusions (247:112). The most apparent literary tradition in "Old Esther Dudley" is, however, the Gothic (149:134–35; 298:105–07). The magic mirror and the ghostly grave-yard revels come straight from the Gothic novel without the attempted explanations that accompany similar Gothic devices in the preceding Province-House stories. One reader interprets this as a part of the author's disenchantment with the genre and his realization, at the series' end, that "tales of the supernatural are unsuitable for the American pragmatic and rational character" (43:78). Others have argued that the blatant Gothic elements support a legendary approach to the past (16) and a basic antihistoricism (354).

In the same way that the motives for following the Gothic conventions can be used to support a variety of readings, the sources for Hancock's final speech can determine whether it is meant to be read literally or ironically. Doubleday says that Hancock "sounds like" the writings of O'Sullivan, specifically like a passage from his introduction to the *Democratic Review*. The similarity extends to the use of such key words as *forward, our race,* and *onward.* At the same time, Doubleday points out that these ideas are not in keeping with Hawthorne's usual outlook (149:130–33). Walsh notes the same discrepancies between Hawthorne's more habitual disdain of the idea of progress and Hancock's avowal of manifest destiny, but for Walsh the inconsistencies become the basis for a satirical reading. He rests his case primarily on Hawthorne's use of the word *projecting,* tracing its pejorative use to Swift and citing the objects and methods of Swiftian satire as an identifiable influence on Hancock's oration (508).

## Relationship with Other Hawthorne Works

As the last of the four "Legends of the Province-House," this story is most closely related to the other tales in the series—"Howe's Masquerade," "Edward Randolph's Portrait," and "Lady Eleanore's Mantle." The framework that binds the four stories together as a unit culminates in the last paragraph of "Old Esther Dudley." When the stories are read as a series, "Old Esther Dudley" becomes the climax and the conclusion. Those readers who have analyzed the four tales as a group see this story as crucially different from the three that precede it; as a result thematic interpretations of the Province-House group invariably focus on "Old Esther Dudley" as a key to Hawthorne's overall intent (16; 43:75–78; 127:65–81; 159; 189:36–44; 305:278–80; 354; 386; 435). (Also see relationship with other Hawthorne works of "Howe's Masquerade" for additional details.)

The time element, for example, becomes a significant factor when the reader realizes that the fourth legend begins with the event prophesied in the first legend, Howe's final departure from the Province-House "in defeat and humiliation" (*291.21*). Equally notable is the dating of the individual stories; each of the first three is set successively deeper in the past (1775, 1770, and 1716), but "Old Esther Dudley" returns to the time period of the first, where it then moves in the direction of the frame's fictive present. What this means has been variously interpreted. Assuming the perspective of an historicist, Fossum takes this as Hawthorne's affirmation of the value to be derived from heeding the lessons of the past (189:42–44). Dauber, in an effort to integrate the psychic and the historic, outlines a deep structure of regression that moves back toward a childhood of American man. Recasting each of the American events presented as an element of psychic regression at a national level, he sees the stories moving from the genital fixation of "Howe's Masquerade" to the anality of "Edward Randolph's Portrait" and finally to the oral gratification of "Lady Eleanore's Mantle." In "Old Esther Dudley," the alienated adulthood disposed of in the first story is again confronted, only to be ultimately rejected (127:65–81). Rejection also plays an important part in one archetypal reading except that it is chronological time itself that is being rejected, along with the progressivism and historicism that it embodies. Because of the hostility projected in varying but significant degrees toward all of the historically conscious characters in the series, and because the democrat John Hancock, who succeeds Howe in the Province-House, is not much different—or better than—his British predecessors, the "Legends" become a reflection of Hawthorne's search for a cyclic concept of time in which national fluctuations are irrelevant (354).

Another development in "Old Esther Dudley" that retrospectively colors each of the Province-House tales is the persona's decision, at the very end of the series, "not to show my face in the Province-House for a good while hence—if ever" (303.9–10). This apparent change in attitude toward the past has been taken into account by all the readers who have examined the "Legends" as a unit. The closest examination of the persona's ambivalence toward history and its effect on the telling of the "Legends" has been undertaken by Reed. He concludes that the "frames and the carefully ordered tales which they link clearly work together to focus a life view in the American present" (386.111). Two other readers agree with Reed, and essentially with each other, although Fossum's emphasis is on the lessons of the past (189:42–44) and Baym's is on the need to break away from it (43:75–76). When Fossum sees Esther as a caricature of Hawthorne, he supports Baym's contention that the writer's hasty exit from the Province-House is prompted by his fear that he may become, like Esther, "antiquated, eccentric, and absurd." A large faction of readers do not interpret the persona's peremptory departure as a confirmation of Hancock's advice to "press onward, onward!" (301.32); they attribute the abrupt change to the author's disappointment with his attempts to use the factual data of history as a basis for his art (16; 149:133; 159; 233:212; 305:279–80; 354). The psychohistorical analysis of the "Legends" (127, discussed above) finds it difficult to account for Hawthorne's "violent escape" from the Province-House because "Old Esther Dudley" is in many ways the completion of the therapeutically regressive pattern toward which the first three stories have been moving. The Freudian-based conclusion does not differ markedly from the others, however; in spite of the reader intimacy establshed in "Old Esther Dudley" (the loyalist narrator is accommodated; Esther is the "good mother" who maintains the house as "a labor of love"), Hawthorne's extreme alienation drives him to doubt his achievement and to fear that his efforts to engage his readers may have failed (127:78–81).

Along with a shift in attitude toward the past, "Old Esther Dudley" also embodies a turnaround from a pro-Revolutionary stance. Esther's story is told by a sympathetically involved narrator, not by the neutral Mr. Tiffany who recounts the first three stories. The old loyalist, who is introduced in the frame of "Lady Eleanore's Mantle" as a "venerable personage" (272.16), is emotionally shaken as he describes Esther's staunch devotion to the royalist cause. The persona admits to having revised the old man's story in keeping with his own views as "a thorough-going democrat" (291.16), but several readers believe that the transformation is minimal and that the final effect is equally critical of the democratic forces and of the British (45:40; 354; 435). (See interpretations below.)

Esther and Hancock represent not only the contrast between monarchy and democracy but also the more seminal opposition between "misty past" and "harsh present." The concept emerges again in the differences between Maule and Pyncheon in *The House of Seven Gables* and between England and America in the unfinished English romances (46:203–08). Echoes of Hancock's impassioned rejection of the past can be found in Holgrave's attitude and in the moral projected for the uncompleted *Ancestral Footstep* (149:133). The past intrudes into the present by means of Esther Dudley's magic mirror, and the looking glass in the Pyncheon house, described in the novel's first chapter, creates the same effect (149:134–35).

The story that offers the most convincing argument for a satirical reading of "Old Esther Dudley" is "Earth's Holocaust"; it leaves no doubt that Hawthorne is skeptical of the idea of progress (149:132), and it demonstrates his use of *reductio ad absurdum* to satirize the one-tracked fanaticism of reformers not unlike Hancock (508:32). "A Book of Autographs," in which Hawthorne describes Hancock as a "man without a head or heart," casts further doubt on Hancock's qualifications as the author's spokesman (508:33).

## Interpretations and Criticism

The most debated question about "Old Esther Dudley" is precisely the issue of who speaks for Hawthorne and how much irony, if any, is present. Baym accepts Hancock's final statement as a blunt and unironic affirmation of the superiority of the present over the past and of American democracy over British royalty (43:76–78). Several readers see it differently: Smith perceives Hancock as being as proud and pompous as the British governor he replaces (435); Walsh finds him obtuse, callous, and without compassion (508:39); and Doubleday interprets his claim to represent "a new race of men" as inherently ironic (149:132). These readers do not believe that Hancock's views are Hawthorne's, or that Hawthorne ever meant to imply that the past could be obliterated, as Hancock would have it. These disparate readings are countered by two equally disparate compromise solutions. One contends that both Esther and Hancock express Hawthorne's view (189:42–44); the other, that neither does (354). The first believes that, like Esther, Hawthorne wants to incorporate the past into the present, but that, like Hancock, he senses the dangers of becoming obsessed by it. The second believes that Esther and Hancock follow equally undesirable views of history as irreversible—she cannot accept the American victory; he cannot allow any return to British tradition; both are locked into linear time. Hawthorne, in his search for a cyclical time structure, rejects both of them.

Few readers have appraised "Old Esther Dudley," and few editors have republished it. Doubleday calls it, with minor reservations, "a fine tale" (149:130), but Waggoner does not include it in his collection (502), and the readers who discuss it do so because of the pivotal role it plays in the Province-House series. It is in this capacity that "Old Esther Dudley" deserves attention. Like its title character, it cannot stand alone, but supported by the three tales that it follows, it provides the illumination by which the Province-House legends can profitably be read. Together, the four Province-House stories become a barometer of the fluctuations in mood and method that characterize Hawthorne at his best—and at his worst.

# XXXVIII

# Passages from a Relinquished Work

*(Centenary Edition, Volume X, Mosses from an Old Manse, 405–21.)*

## Publication History

The first three sections—"At Home," "A Flight in the Fog," and "A Fellow Traveller"—were first published in the *New-England Magazine* in November 1834 (VII, 352–58) under the heading "The Story Teller. No. I."; "The Village Theatre" section was first published in the December 1834 issue (VII, 449–59) as "The Story Teller. No. II.," with "Mr. Higginbotham's Catastrophe" as an integral part and no attribution given for either contribution. "Passages from a Relinquished Work" does not, however, include "Mr. Higginbotham's Catastrophe" because Hawthorne extracted it from "The Village Theatre" section and included it, on its own, in the 1837 *Twice-told Tales* (*CE, X, 579–80*).

Seventeen years later when Hawthorne was preparing a second edition of *Mosses from an Old Manse* in 1854, he asked his editor, James T. Fields, to look in the *New-England Magazine* for the years when Park Benjamin was its editor for "the beginning, and the conclusion of the 'Itinerate Storyteller.'" Fields found "Story Teller No. I" and "II" and added them to the 1854 *Mosses* as they are reproduced in the Centenary Edition (*CE, XI, 395*). (See publication history of "The Devil in Manuscript" and 202.)

## Circumstances of Composition, Sources, and Influences

As the opening sections of Hawthorne's third projected collection, *The Story Teller*, "Passages" was probably written in the fall and winter of 1832. The original concept of the wandering storyteller is found in "The Seven Vagabonds," a story Hawthorne wrote several years earlier, the exact circumstances of which are alluded to in the "At Home" segment of "Passages." (See circumstances of composition for "The Seven Vagabonds.") The summer trips Hawthorne took through New England and New York State between 1825 and 1832 undoubtedly provided the background for both works while the evening Bible class he attended on a Connecticut trip in 1830 (272:143) probably suggested the vocation for the storyteller's traveling companion, a young preacher who holds a Bible class immediately before the stage recitation of "Mr. ·Higginbotham's Catastrophe." Irving's *Sketch Book* is a likely source for the pattern Hawthorne chose to follow in developing his idea from the earlier "Seven Vagabonds" into a longer work in which the itinerant novelist's adventures would be interspersed with travel sketches and the tales he told along the way (11:131–46; *CE, IX, 492*).

Goldsmith is referred to as a prototype for the title character in the work itself; Goldsmith furnishes "the example of one illustrious itinerant in the other hemisphere . . . who planned and performed his travels through France and Italy, on a less promising scheme" (*408.5–8*). The allusion is probably to Goldsmith's adventures as recounted in the story of George Primrose in Goldsmith's novel, *The Vicar of Wakefield*.

## Relationship with Other Hawthorne Works

"Fragments from the Journal of a Solitary Man" is "the conclusion of the 'Itinerant Storyteller'" that Hawthorne referred to in the letter quoted above; in it, the protagonist, now dead, tells through his journal the sad ending to the adventures begun in the gay and carefree spirit of "Passages" and foreshadowed in "The Seven Vagabonds." The exact nature of the projected *Story Teller* between its beginnings in "Passages" and its conclusion in "Fragments" as it was submitted to Samuel Goodrich in 1834 has been guessed at by several scholars (11; 514; 204; 43), but all reconstructions reveal unexplainable shifts in point of view, contradictions in time and plot, and incongruous extremes in tone and subject matter. Specifically which stories and sketches belonged to the original collection remains conjectural, but most experts agree that the fifteen other pieces published in the *New-England Magazine* between November 1834 and December 1835 qualify as authentic *Story Teller* components. Of these, "The Devil in Manuscript," with its Oberon protagonist, is most closely related to the beginning and conclusion of the series, although it is presented as a tale about the storyteller figure rather than in the first-person framework of "The Story Tellers No. I" and "II." Of the other works usually accepted as originally belonging to *The Story Teller*, six are travel sketches—"My Visit to Niagara" (*CE, XI*), the three sections of "Old News" (*CE, XI*), and the two sections of "Sketches from Memory" (*CE, X; CE, XI*); two are essays—"A Rill from the Town-Pump" (*CE, IX*) and "Graves and Goblins" (*CE, XI*); and the remainder are tales—"The Gray Champion," "Wakefield," "The Ambitious Guest,"

"The White Old Maid," "The Vision in the Fountain" (all in *CE, IX*), and "Young Goodman Brown" (*CE, X*).

"The May-Pole of Merry Mount" has also been related to "Passages" in the sharp contrast each provides between stern Puritanism and frivolous mirth-making (232:108). The conjunction in the Merry Mounters' story is foreshadowed in the storyteller's imaginative vision of "the puritanic figure of my guardian standing among the fripperies of the theater . . . and eyeing me with stern rebuke. His image was a type of the austere duty, and they of the vanities of life" (*421.3–8*).

## Interpretations and Criticism

"Passages" has been interpreted from a psychologically biographical perspective by Normand in a chapter called "Oberon and the Story Teller" in which he emphasizes Hawthorne's wanderlust and love for the vagabond's life during his bachelor years (355:25–46). Baym also examines the *Story Teller* era, but she sees Hawthorne as closest to his protagonist in his desire to escape the conventional professions by engaging in a literary career (43:39–52). Baym interprets "The Story Teller" as "a moral and psychological tale about authorship." She equates Oberon's flight from his Puritanical guardian, Parson Thumpcushion, with Hawthorne's withdrawal from reality justified by his belief that a writer can enrich his transcription of reality only by detaching himself from it. Another critic reads into Hawthorne's conception of the itinerant novelist's travels his "conception of himself as somewhat a Western writer" who explores new frontiers (193:78).

The fragmented nature of "Passages," due to its chaotic publication history, has made most readers agree with its author when he said he "cared little for the stories, afterwards." Whether, as Hawthorne adds, they "had in their orginal place in the 'Storyteller' a greater degree of significance" has been questioned (106:32), but "Passages" has fared somewhat better critically than some of its scattered sequels. Adkins calls its dramatic situation admirably fitting for the story assigned to it (11:144), which suggests to Centenary Edition readers that they should reinsert "Mr. Higginbotham's Catastrophe" from the *Twice-told Tales* volume to its original position, three paragraphs before the end of "The Village Theatre," to experience Hawthorne's intended effect. The most valuable aspect of "Passages" remains the autobiographical insights it offers.

# XXXIX

# Peter Goldthwaite's Treasure

(*Centenary Edition, Volume IX, Twice-told Tales*, 383–406.)

## Publication History

This story was first published in the fall of 1837 in *The Token and Atlantic Souvenir* (pp. 37–65) dated 1838 and attributed to the author of *Twice-told Tales*. The four other works written by Hawthorne in the same edition appeared anonymously. A revised estimate, made in 1975, of Hawthorne's income from *The Token* theorizes that editor Samuel Goodrich never paid for the 1838 *Token* contributions, although Hawthorne had expected to receive the same pay as in 1837, that is, $1 per page, or $29 (250). The story was collected in the second volume of the second edition of *Twice-told Tales* in 1842 (*CE, IX, 573–74*).

## Circumstances of Composition, Sources, and Influences

"Peter Goldthwaite's Treasure" was probably written in the winter or early spring of 1837 (84:22). An obliquely related germ appears in the notebook entries made between October 25, 1835 and August 31, 1836: "A man, perhaps with a persuasion that he shall make his fortune by some singular means, and with an eager longing so to do, while digging or boring for water, to strike upon a salt-spring" (*CE, VIII, 15.27–16.2*). A year later, the summer before Hawthorne wrote Peter Goldthwaite's story, he recorded his observations on the ruins of General Knox's estate in Maine:

> It was not forty years, since this house was built, and Knox was in his glory; but now the house is all in decay, while, within a stones throw of it, is a street of neat, smart, white edifices of one and two stories, occupied chiefly by thriving mechanics.... The descendants are all poor; and the inheritance was merely sufficient to make a dissipated and drunken fellow of the one of the old General's sons, who survived to middle age. (*67.24–68.1*)

Although Peter is portrayed more sympathetically than Knox's "dissipated and drunken son," their situations are similar, and the "brick block" pro-

posed by Peter's old partner has much in common with the row of me-
chanics' houses that stood on Knox's former estate grounds (455:lxxvii–
viii). The Deliverance Parkman House, on the eastern corner of North
and Essex streets in Salem, has also been suggested as the original for
the Goldthwaite mansion, primarily because its occupants were reputed
to have had ancestors who, like Peter's grandfather, practiced alchemy
(84:22).

Several well-known folk motifs are incorporated into Tabitha's explanations to Peter of how his grandfather acquired his fortune, among them
the pact with the devil, the cursed house, and the money that disinte-
grates when a mortal touches it. A folklorist's study of the tale proposes
the New Hampshire legend of Jonathan Moulton's affair with the Devil
as a possible source (148:156–57).

## Relationship with Other Hawthorne Works

"Peter Goldthwaite's Treasure" is most closely related to *The House of
Seven Gables*. One reader has called the story "an important testing
ground" for the novel (75). Similarities in characterizations, setting, and
theme are clearly evident. Hepzibah and Clifford are, like Peter, descendants who have inherited a decrepit mansion. In each story, the influence
of the past is undesirable, and the present is cheerfully accepted at the
end (455:lxviii). Hidden treasures help shape the houses as "visionary
structures" (422), while the houses themselves serve as symbols—in the
story, of Peter's mind; in the novel, of Hepzibah's heart (75; 247:112).

To Martin, John Brown, as "the man of practicality," and Peter, as
"the man of imagination," illustrate one of Hawthorne's effective methods for confronting "themes that define the specific nature of his work"
(308:24–25). By presenting "bifurcated or fragmented characters who
complement each other in the totality of an individual tale," Hawthorne
achieves the latitude he needs. Variations include Warland as contrasted
to the Hovenden family in "The Artist of the Beautiful," and the children and mother of "The Snow-Image" as opposed to the infamously
commonsensical father.

"Peter Goldthwaite's Treasure" resembles the four other moralized
fictions Hawthorne wrote between 1837 and 1840 ("Sylph Etherege,"
"The Lily's Quest," "Edward Fane's Rosebud," and "The Threefold Destiny"), all of which celebrate "the common highway of life" (43:55–56).
In each, the unregulated imagination is viewed as a danger that leads to
separation, increasing subjectivity, and insanity.

## Interpretations and Criticism

On May 5, 1850, Hawthorne found this story (and "The Shaker Bridal") in a London newspaper at the Salem Athenaeum. Piqued by the boldness of the English pirates who had published it "as original," he wrote in his notebook: "The English are ten times as unscrupulous and dishonest pirates as ourselves. However, if they are poor enough to perk themselves in such false feathers as these, Heaven help them! I glanced over the stories, and they seemed painfully cold and dull" (*CE, VIII, 493.6–10*). Admittedly, such a casual and reactionary critique carries minimal validity, and yet, as far as "Peter Goldthwaite's Treasure" is concerned, Hawthorne's denigrating self-assessment has not been contested. Doubleday attributes Hawthorne's dissatisfaction to an exaggerated ideal, impossible to fulfill. The story itself, however, is credited with "an interesting allegorical scheme," one that contributes satisfactorily to a satire on financial speculations, appropriately reflecting the contemporaneous depression of 1837 (149:243).

As with many of Hawthorne's minor stories, this one is significant as a reflector of the motifs and techniques that are more completely realized in other works. In the case of "Peter Goldthwaite's Treasure," the story's worth is best discovered in *The House of Seven Gables*.

# XL
# The Prophetic Pictures

(*Centenary Edition, Volume IX, Twice-told Tales*, 166–82.)

## Publication History

This story was first published in the fall of 1836 in *The Token and Atlantic Souvenir* (pp. 289–307) dated 1837, with no attribution. Samuel Goodrich, the editor, paid $108 for the eight pieces written by Hawthorne in this issue; assuming that the pay was based on a per-page rate, "The Prophetic Pictures" earned its author a little over $19. It was included, with four other contributions from the same *Token*, in Hawthorne's first collection, *Twice-told Tales*, in 1837 (*CE, IX, 569, 497*).

## Circumstances of Composition, Sources, and Influences

The note that Hawthorne added to this story establishes both its source and its approximate composition date. The note states: "This story was suggested by an anecdote of Stuart related in Dunlap's History of the Arts of Design" (*166*). This identifies the painter, Gilbert Stuart, as a prototype for the nameless artist and points to the first part of 1836 as the probable date of composition since that was when Hawthorne twice withdrew Dunlap's book from the Salem Athenaeum (149:109; 108:601; 511:365). The anecdote that the footnote refers to is like Hawthorne's story in that the painter is able to see an inherent insanity in his subject's features which is confirmed by future events. It reads:

> Lord Mulgrave employed Stuart to paint the portrait of his brother, General Phipps, previous to his going abroad. On seeing the picture, which he did not until it was finished, Mulgrave exclaimed, "What is this?—this is very strange!" and stood gazing at the portrait. "I see insanity in that face," was the brother's remark. The General went to India, and the first account his brother had of him was that of suicide from insanity. He had gone mad and cut his throat. It is thus that the real portrait-painter dives into the recesses of his sitter's mind, and displays strength or weakness upon the surface of his canvass. (William Dunlap, *History of the Rise and Progress of the Arts of Design in the United States*, I, 187, as cited in 149:111–12)

Two scholars have suggested that John Smibert (1688–1751) may have been the model for Hawthorne's painter because the time and setting of the story and the character's personal history are more in keeping with Dunlap's account of Smibert (I, 27) than of Stuart (149:109; 511:366). The reference to Governor Burnet's portrait (*169–70*) establishes the time of the story as 1728 (William Burnet was made governor of Massachusetts in 1728 and died in 1729); Smibert was responsible for the "best portraits" of the magistrates of New England who lived between 1725 and 1751. Like the artist in the story, he was a man of impressive learning, educated in Europe, and one of the first collectors of paintings in America.

But whether Stuart or Smibert provided the ostensible outline for the painter of the prophetic pictures, self-portraiture has been acclaimed as the most significant factor in that character's portrayal (47:135; 385; 455:lxi; 511:366). The cold aloofness and penetrating powers of observation that mark the painter are characteristic, according to Stewart, of the dispassionate and analytical entries Hawthorne made in his notebooks (455:lxi–lxii). A revealing example occurs in the passage in which Hawthorne describes the "shrewd, crafty, insinuating" side of his friend, Jonathan Cilley, with a sense of satisfaction that he is able to perceive beyond the "wonderful tact" of his old college-mate's surface appearance (*CE, VIII, 61–63*). The painter is also one whose all-consuming artistic involvement had "insulated [him] from the mass of human kind"; consequently, "his heart was cold; no living creature could be brought near enough to keep him warm" (*178.27–32*). When Hawthorne created this artist-painter in 1836, he, as an artist-writer, had devoted eleven years of his life, since his graduation from Bowdoin College in 1825, to his work. He calls the room in his mother's Salem home where he spent those years a "lonely" and "haunted chamber." During a visit there in 1840, he writes to his fiancee, Sophia Peabody, "Here I have written many tales . . . and here my mind and character were formed. . . . And sometimes . . . it seemed as if I were already in the grave with only life enough to be chilled and benumbed" (458:36). The painter's cold isolation is clearly a reflection of Hawthorne's own fears, however tempered his recollection may be by his desire to contrast his new-found happiness with his former loneliness.

The most apparent literary influence in this story is the Gothic novel. "The Prophetic Pictures" incorporates several of its conventions: a work of art with extraordinary powers, an authoritative and attractive villain mysteriously allied with evil forces, a terror-evoking prophecy that is fulfilled, and a populace prone to attribute what it cannot understand to supernatural causes (47:68–69; 152; 149:109–10; 298:100). One specific detail borrowed from Ann Radcliffe's *Mysteries of Udolpho* is the heavy silk curtain used to hide the portraits from view and, at the dramatically climactic moment, to unveil them (47:124; 149:110).

Other literary works that have been suggested as possible factors are "The Memoirs of Martinus Scriblerus" and Sir Walter Scott's *The Bride of Lammermoor*. The first chapter of the latter offers an instance of a sketch, similar to the one in the story, that reveals a future scene in the lives of its subjects (149:112–13); the former, which was a joint effort by Pope, Swift, and other members of the Scriblerus Club in London during the last year of Queen Anne's reign, presents Scriblerus as one who could write a person's life from his physiognomy. "The Memoirs" also attacked the acquisition of knowledge that had no practical social value, one of the implications in Hawthorne's assertion that the painter's learning and skill were ultimately ineffectual (108).

## Relationship with Other Hawthorne Works

As Hawthorne's first story to deal directly with the problem of the artist, "The Prophetic Pictures" is a forerunner of "The Artist of the Beautiful," the work generally conceded to be his most comprehensive statement on the subject. The two tales invite comparisons; the analyses that have resulted are remarkably varied. While one reader concludes that the painter and Owen Warland are both dedicated Romantic idealists equally indifferent to the human side of emotion (47:119), another believes that Hawthorne's depiction of Owen ignores the danger that the artist's power poses for others, and that the painter is, therefore, a more complete representation of Hawthorne's attitude toward the artist and his role in society (144:188–89). As a rule, however, "The Artist of the Beautiful" is considered not only the better story, but a more mature and fully developed statement of the problems of the artist (52:134; 309:74). One comparison asserts that the point of both stories is that the artistic vision differs from the vision of other humans only in degree, not in kind (188:44). Such a distinction is, at best, irrelevant since Hawthorne's purpose is clearly to show how the artist's sensibility sets him apart from other men. "Drowne's Wooden Image" is another instance of the same phenomenon. In Drowne's case, however, Hawthorne reverses the alienating effects of art by making the wood-carver's genius dependent on the power of love (47:127). When his inspiration departs, he again becomes a "normal" member of society, something that Owen and the painter cannot do precisely because they are different from the bulk of mankind.

Hawthorne's canon offers a gallery of other artistlike characters who, like the painter, are detached observers. Among them are Oberon of *The Story Teller* pieces, the "spiritualized Paul Pry" of "Sights from a Steeple," Holgrave of *The House of Seven Gables*, Kenyon of *The Marble Faun*, and—the most similar of the parallels—Coverdale of *The Blithdale Romance* (32:133–49; 38; 385:45; 455:lxii–lxiii). In one study, Coverdale is viewed as an empirically conceived version of the anonymous painter with his prophetic powers demystified (127:155). Chillingworth, Rappaccini, Aylmer of "The Birthmark," and Ethan Brand are more explicitly manipulative observers who share the painter's renown for learning (32:133; 385; 431:220–22), while Gervayse Hastings of "The Christmas Banquet" conforms to the coldness and aloofness that characterize this type (38; 385:48–49).

## Interpretations and Criticism

Two themes, only tangentially related, dominate this story: the dichotomy of the artist's position in society and the concept of character as fate. Although both the painter, who exemplifies the first, and the subjects of his portraits, Walter and Elinor Ludlow, who embody the second, are central to the tale, most readers see the depiction of the artist as Hawthorne's primary concern. In one analysis, the story is a "negative-Romantic" portrayal in which the painter, precisely because of the purity of his aim as an artist, risks the danger of a damning amoralism that is in conflict with the Puritan standards of humility and duty (47:122–26). In another, the story is just as much a condemnation of the Puritans' intolerance of art as it is of the Leonardo da Vinci-like artist whose ego overrules all other considerations except those of his art (447:73–70). Others concur that the artist dominates the story, but they object to that emphasis for formalistic reasons. According to Martin, the two themes are thereby never effectively integrated (309:73–74), while Doubleday protests that the closing moral, because it does not emerge from the action, contributes to an "unsure" authorial intent that mars the tale's denouement (149:116). On the other hand, Dichmann deems the conclusion an appropriate statement of the unbridgeable abyss between the cold demands of the absolute values of art and the warm compromises of human affection. The moral becomes, in this reading, the author's admission that he cannot reconcile the spiritual nature of artistic creation with the evil that may result from it (144).

Because the story squarely confronts the danger that the artist's role can isolate and dehumanize the artist himself, that issue presents few

interpretative problems. What remains unclear, however, is how dangerous the artist's power may be for others. For example, one reading goes
so far as to suggest that the painter may be the "guilty medium" for a
"malignant fatality" (27:xi–xii). If Walter saw the sketch of himself
stabbing Elinor, the painter could be held responsible for implanting such
a suggestion in Walter's mind, but the story simply states that Walter
had come near enough to have seen the sketch when Elinor did, but
that Elinor "could not determine whether it had caught his eye" (*176.9–
10*). It is the "madman" (*181.32*) Walter who equates the painter with
Fate (*182.5*), and his judgment at that point is, at best, unreliable. The
closing moral (that foreknowledge is powerless to change the future) does
arise from Elinor's unwillingness to give up Walter in spite of the painter's
warning. It also appears to vindicate the painter.

An early Hawthorne admirer, Henry James, adapted the point of view
and the interior drama of the painter in "The Prophetic Pictures" to his
short story, "The Liar" (253.5; 400.5). Since then, however, some critics,
such as Doubleday and Martin, have dealt pejoratively with Hawthorne's
early artist-story, although only Bewley dismisses it as "a very poor
story . . . [with] little intrinsic interest" (52:134). A few praise it (47:126;
144); one applauds its perfect balance of idea and symbol (447:73); and
a highly respected anthology uses it as one of ten Hawthorne stories
chosen to represent his contribution to American literature (131.2:724–
30). "The Prophetic Pictures" does illustrate several distinctive Hawthornian features: foreshadowing to create suspense, ambiguity to suggest
supernatural possibilities, a view of evil as a pervasive and insidious
reality, the portrayal of appearances as an unreliable and deceptive facade,
and a concern with the artist's relationship to society. The editor's note
suggests that the story offers some autobiographical insights as well
(131.2:724). Hawthorne openly expresses his disapproval of "confessional" literature in "The Old Manse":

> So far as I am a man of really individual attributes, I veil my
> face; nor am I, nor have ever been, one of those supremely
> hospitable people, who serve up their own hearts delicately fried,
> with brain-sauce, as a tidbit for their beloved public. (*CE, X,
> 33.1–5*)

His assertion is true; this story is one of the few exceptions. In it, Hawthorne, the young, unknown writer living in a seclusion dominated by
his work, expresses his private hopes and fears; like the artist in his story,
he seeks to use his skills to reveal ultimate truth, but at the same time
he, too, risks the cold isolation and the possibility of becoming, however

blindly, an agent of the devil, especially in the light of his Puritan heritage. Such revelations compensate for whatever faults "The Prophetic Pictures" may have formalistically; in many respects, the story serves as a prophetic picture of Hawthorne's canon, clearly auguring its themes, techniques, and faults.

# XLI
# Rappaccini's Daughter

(*Centenary Edition, Volume X, Mosses from an Old Manse*, 91–128.)

## Publication History

This story was first published in December 1844 in the *United States Magazine and Democratic Review* (XV, 545–60) under Hawthorne's own name. It was titled "Writings of Aubepine" (French for *hawthorn*), with "Rappaccini's Daughter" as the interior title. (The easily identifiable pseudonym was bestowed many years earlier by a Mr. Schaeffer who taught Hawthorne French during the summer he spent in Maine in 1837.) Extant correspondence establishes Hawthorne's pay from the magazine's editor, John L. O'Sullivan, at approximately $22.50, less than one third of what the standard magazine rate of $5 per page would have netted. (See publication history of "The Christmas Banquet.")

"Rappaccini's Daughter" was collected in *Mosses from an Old Manse* in 1846 without the preface which was inserted again in the 1854 edition for Ticknor, Reed, and Fields. The preface was probably deleted in the first collection because of its last sentence, which pays tribute to O'Sullivan, who was also a personal friend, and to the *Democratic Review* under the guise of *Le Revue Anti-Aristocratique* and its editor, Comte de Bearhaven. Hawthorne's need for a political appointment to relieve his serious financial situation in 1846 made it prudent for him to omit what might have been interpreted as a partisan reference. His dismissal from the Custom House in 1849 on the basis of the literary reviews that he wrote for the Salem Democratic newspaper confirms his assessment of the political climate of the times. In 1854, as the American consul in Liverpool, England, and with his friend Franklin Pierce as President, he could reinsert the preface without fear of recrimination. According to the textual editor of the Centenary Edition, the 1846 text of this story received more "stylistic revisions" in 1854 than any other piece in the new edition, but he attributes this to Hawthorne's interest in it rather than to any drastic change in conception. One reader detects a shift in emphasis in one of the revisions. Beatrice's speech is changed from "The words of Beatrice Rappaccini's lips are true from the heart outward" to "The words of Beatrice Rappaccini's lips are true from *the depths* of the heart outward" (*107.11*; my italics); the addition is interpreted as part of Hawthorne's effort to clarify his allegorical intent (171). The Centenary Edition follows the 1854 text. (*CE, VIII, 46.18*; *CE, X, 523, 549–51, 574*; *CE, XI, 379–80*)

## Circumstances of Composition, Sources, and Influences

This story was written between mid-October and mid-November of 1844 (323:32). Julian Hawthorne records that when his father was writing "Rappaccini's Daughter" at the "Old Manse," he read the unfinished manuscript to his wife: " 'But how is it to end?' she asked him, when he laid down the paper; 'is Beatrice to be a demon or an angel?' 'I have no idea!' was Hawthorne's reply, spoken with some emotion" (223:I, 36). The suggestion has been made that during this discussion, Sophia may have been consulted about the Italian names used in the story. She had studied Italian as a girl, and the meaning of the names in Italian is significant. For example, *guastaconti* means "a meddler into affairs," an appropriate surname to assign to Giovanni, whose attempt to "cure" Beatrice results in her death (379). What is more important biographically, however, is the conviction with which the estrangement of the individual is portrayed, a power that has been attributed in part to the author's realization of how perilously close he had come to such a fate himself before he had found his "place in the world" as Sophia's husband. The earliest expression of this obsessive theme in Hawthorne's work has been traced to "The Devil in Manuscript," his most clearly autobiographical piece (455:lxii). Beatrice's dilemma may also be a reflection of Sophia's sheltered years as a semi-invalid in the loving but "misdirected care of her solicitous mother" (231:142), while Giovanni's failure to save Beatrice or himself is a tragic reversal of Nathaniel's and Sophia's happiness together (33:64; 346:155–56).

The earliest germ for the story appears in Hawthorne's notebook in 1839 in the form of a quotation: " 'A story there passeth of an Indian king that sent unto Alexander a fair woman, fed with aconite and other poisons, with this intent complexionally to destroy him!'—*Sir T. Browne*" (*CE, VIII, 184.1–4*). Its source is Sir Thomas Browne's *Pseudoxia Epidemica* (or *Vulgar Errors*), Book VII, chapter 17, except that Hawthorne omits the phrase, "either by converse or copulation," between "intent" and "complexionally" (455:lxxi; *CE, VIII, 601*; 171). A note to Browne's work added by Dean Wren, which Hawthorne may have seen, states that the Portuguese were killed by copulation with the women of the "eastern islands" (482:555, n.90). Baglioni tells Giovanni the story of Alexander the Great and the poisonous Eastern maiden, but he adds a "sage physician" who warns and saves Alexander in his version (*117.1-11*). The notebooks reveal a more general concept that is reflected in several other works as well as in a passage entered between October 27, 1841 and January 23, 1842: "To symbolize moral or spiritual disease of the body;— thus, when a person committed any sin, it might cause a sore to appear on the body;—this to be wrought out" (*CE, VIII, 222.13–14*). A more specific analogue is the entry made between June 1, 1842 and July 27, 1844:

> Madame Calderon de la B (in Life in Mexico) speaks of persons who have been inoculated with the venom of rattle-snakes, by pricking them in various places with the tooth. These persons are thus secured forever after against the bite of any venomous reptile. They have the power of calling snakes, and feel great pleasure in playing with and handling them. Their own bite becomes poisonous to people not inoculated in the same manner. Thus a part of the serpent's nature appears to be transfused into them. (*CE, VIII, 238.12–20*)

Not only does Beatrice follow the pattern of inoculation, immunization, and contagion, but the poisonous flowers are described as creeping "serpent-like along the ground" (455:lxxi). Analogues for the flowering shrub and for the purple hand imprinted on Giovanni's wrist have also been found in Mme. Calderon's book (452). Another notebook entry, also undated but appearing on the page immediately preceding the Calderon account, has been proposed as the allegorical key to Beatrice's portrayal:

> The human Heart to be allegorized as a cavern; at the entrance there is sunshine, and flowers growing about it. You step within, but a short distance, and begin to find yourself surrounded with a terrible gloom, and monsters of divers kinds; it seems like Hell itself. You are bewildered, and wander long without hope. At last a light strikes upon you. You press towards it yon, and find yourself in a region that seems, in some sort, to reproduce the flowers and sunny beauty of the entrance, but all perfect. These are the depths of the heart, or of human nature, bright and peace-ful; the gloom and terror may lie deep; but deeper still is this eternal beauty. (*CE, VIII, 237.17–28*)

Beatrice's role follows the three levels of the heart-cavern analogy: her external beauty parallels the sunny, flower-strewn entrance, her poison-ousness parallels the hellish monsters a short distance within, and her pure goodness parallels the perfection and light in the depths. The revision noted above in the publication history appears to sharpen this image

(171). Two other entries made during the  Old Manse years are related to Rappaccini's role in the story: "A moral philosopher to buy a slave, or otherwise get possession of a human being, and to use him for the sake of experiment, by trying the operation of a certain vice on him" (*CE, VIII, 237.7–9*) and "The Unpardonable Sin might consist in a want of love and reverence for the Human Soul. . . . Would not this, in other words, be the separation of the intellect from the heart?" (CE, VIII, *251.12–19*). Rappaccini's portrayal, however, is complicated by his good intentions and the equally uncertain intentions of his rival, Dr. Baglioni.

In addition to the literary sources reflected in the notebook germs, the story itself contains several literary allusions, beginning in the first paragraph with a reference to Dante and Italy's "great poem." Hawthorne's deliberate evocation of *The Divine Comedy* and his use of the name Beatrice, which is synonymous in Dante's writings with ideal feminine goodness and beauty, serve to foreshadow Beatrice Rappaccini's ultimate purity and Giovanni's upcoming test of faith (304:61). The predicament of Hawthorne's Beatrice and the failure of Giovanni's faith are used as ironic and tragic contrasts to the prototypes these characters originally appear to follow (304:69; 309:94), while a Dantean kind of self-inflicted damnation overtakes all the major characters except Beatrice (346:146). Another Italian artist alluded to in the story is Benvenuto Cellini, who created the silver vase that holds Baglioni's antidote. Cellini's *Autobiography* reveals that he first made his silver vases for a surgeon reputed to have had little success in curing his patients in spite of his "great sagacity." This *Autobiography* may also have provided some of the Italian names in the story (304:66).

More typical of Hawthorne are the biblical allusions to Eden and Adam (509; 500:124) and the reference to classical mythology used in the description of the garden. Among the dense foliage is the vine-shrouded "statue of Vertumnus" (*95.18*). According to Ovid's *Metamorphoses* (XIV, 623 ff.), Vertumnus is the vegetation god who invaded the isolated garden of the beautiful nymph Pomona, won her heart, and stole her away (384; 509). One passage in Book IX of *Paradise Lost* (393–95) may have suggested the Vertumnus and Eden conflation; Milton describes Eve, in her gardening capacity, as being "likeliest" to Vertumnus' beloved Pomona (509). Another passage in Book III (351–63) has been cited as a source for the flower and fountain imagery (265:328), while Giovanni's portrayal can be interpreted as a deliberate reversal of Milton's version of Eve's part in the fall (304:68; 288).

The most consistently recognized echoes are those from Book II, Canto XII of Spenser's *Faerie Queene* with reverberations of the dangerous Acrasia and the luxuriant Bower of Bliss resounding throughout Hawthorne's description of Beatrice and her unnatural garden, most specifically in the "sculptured portal," the central fountain of pure water, and the erotic plants (186:101–02; 288; 304:69; 509). Spenser's description of his villain Archimago in Book I has also been credited with influencing Hawthorne's description of Rappaccini (456:200–01).

Several nineteenth-century Romantic and Gothic works offer parallels that directly or indirectly may have helped shape this story. Among them are Keats's *Lamia* (22; 436); Shelley's *The Cenci* (170; 523); two stories by E. T. A. Hoffman, "Datura Fatuosa" (298:109) and "The Sandman" (100); Godwin's *St. Leon* (379); Mary Shelley's *Frankenstein* (379); and Maturin's *Melmoth the Wanderer* (298:109). The Gothic conventions themselves—isolated castles, victimized maidens, and patriarchal villains with mysterious powers—also influenced this story (152; 186:100–01). By overturning the expectations of these sources, Hawthorne adapts them to his ironical purpose (186:101).

Nineteenth-century nonliterary sources have also been suggested. George Rapp, an experimenter in alchemy and botany whose controversial commune featured a symbolic garden, could have contributed to the conception of Rappaccini (145), while many of the widespread opinions of Hawthorne's age about hybridization are discernible in the garden's description (56). Erasmus Darwin's account of the Upas tree in *The Botanical Garden* is another possible source (411).

## Relationship with Other Hawthorne Works

This story has most often been linked to "The Birthmark," published the year before, because of their thematic and structural similarities. In both, a beautiful young woman becomes the victim of a misguided scientist-idealist who ostensibly loves her. Beatrice and Georgiana are cast as spiritual guides who attempt to lead their heroes to fulfillment (447:148), and both subject themselves to death, but not without remarkable assertions of selfhood in the face of overwhelming male domination (513). Beatrice's poison parallels Georgiana's birthmark; neither can live without her flaw. Beatrice's identification with Georgiana's hand-shaped birthmark is strengthened by the purple handprint left on Giovanni's wrist by Beatrice's touch. Both have been interpreted as symbols of carnality or sexuality as well as of original sin and humanity's inherent imperfection (42:37). The role of a blinded idealist who pursues scientific knowledge to gain control over other humans characterizes Beatrice's father and Aylmer, Georgiana's husband; it extends to include "Ethan Brand" as well. Some see the three as tragic heroes whose "unpardonable sins" are rooted in the desire for good (45:90; 186:99–100; 333); others emphasize their coldly intellectual experimentation (32:71; 455:lxxiv) and liken them to "essentially immoral" modern atomic scientists (181:424). Warren considers the three stories companion pieces (511:367), but Waggoner rejects the *libido sciendi* classification for "Rappaccini's Daughter" primarily because he perceives Beatrice's role, not Rappaccini's, as pivotal (500:114–19).

"The Artist of the Beautiful" is the other story with which "Rappaccini's Daughter" and "The Birthmark" are most often associated. Franklin classifies them as "Hawthorne's three complete works of science fiction" (191:9). In them, the line between Art and Science is eliminated; the two pursuits merge into one. Warland, Rappaccini, and Aylmer are artist-scientists striving to create artistic alternatives to nature (191:9, 19). Other stories that depict man's attempt to play creator include "Drowne's Wooden Image" and "Feathertop" (379). In the art-science fantasies, the materialistic and earthly forces appear to overpower the imaginative aspirations of mankind: Old Peter Hovenden's "cold and scornful laugh" (475.17–18), Baglioni's triumphant mockery, and Aminidab's "hoarse. chuckling laugh" (56.5) sound the same derisive note at the conclusion of each (32:131; 186:100; 304:59). These same three stories, all written at the Old Manse in Concord between July 1842 and October 1845 and collected in *Mosses* after 1845, also incorporate aspects of the heart-as-cavern allegory as outlined in the notebook entry discussed above (*CE, VIII, 237.17–28*).

"Rappaccini's Daughter" has also been heralded as a kind of testing ground for what is generally considered to be Hawthorne's greatest work, *The Scarlet Letter,* written six years later. Sin, its complex effects, and the impossibility of separating evil from good dominate both pieces (129; 212; 236:136–37). The novel, like the story, uses physical symptoms of the body to exemplify moral conditions (455:lxxi). Rappaccini foreshadows Chillingworth's age, stature, professional interests, and intellectual prowess; both are satanic in their monomaniacal pursuit of control over other humans (3; 333:212; 455:1–li). Giovanni is an earlier version of the weak Dimmesdale who is equally self-righteous in his sinfulness and just as overwhelmed by the exotic beauty of the dark woman in his life (115:135; 288). It is, ultimately, this dark heroine who dominates both pieces.

Beatrice emerges not only as a prototype for Hester but as Hawthorne's seminal temptress, an ambivalent love-object that, according to Rahv, Hawthorne wants to destroy and glorify at the same time (383). Zenobia in *The Blithedale Romance* and Miriam in *The Marble Faun* are two other manifestations of this type of woman. Their physical characteristics are identical, and all four are intellectually accomplished and remarkably self-aware of their human potential (115:130–31; 304:55; 383; 455: lix-lx). Because Hawthorne's portrayal of these impassioned and essentially rebellious women is always ambivalent, he has been accused of renewing, in the fate he assigns to each, the persecution of the Salem witches (383:370). Beatrice's situation, like that of Miriam, echoes the Beatrice Cenci legend of incest and victimization of an innocent daughter (33:62; 523). Priscilla in *The Blithedale Romance* is a different kind of childhood victim whose life is also dominated by a male manipulator; the medium's veil that keeps Priscilla isolated is comparable to Beatrice's poison (32:110; 455:lxxv; 521).

Another aspect of "Rappaccini's Daughter" that points to the novels is the "window-scene" device, used in the story initially to emphasize Giovanni's perspective; both *The Blithedale Romance* and *The House of Seven Gables* incorporate "window scenes" to good advantage (268). The love between Holgrave and Phoebe in the latter novel has been suggested as a parallel to the situation between Giovanni and Beatrice and to a similar situation between Kenyon and Hilda in *The Marble Faun*. The common denominator is an incipient love prepared for by isolation and associated with a flower (265).

Because "Rappaccini's Daughter" confronts Hawthorne's most fundamental moral concerns, it necessarily echoes the themes expressed in earlier stories. Giovanni's mistake is most like that of "Young Goodman Brown" and of Hooper in "The Minister's Black Veil": he places too high a reliance on his subjective view of reality, and he is unable to accept the mixture of good and evil that characterizes mankind (29; 371; 445; 500:120). Like Edith and Edgar in "The May-Pole of Merry Mount," Giovanni and Beatrice are faced with the "fall" into the human condition, but Giovanni lacks the psychological maturity to accept it (29).

## Interpretations and Criticism

"The most difficult of Hawthorne's stories"—such is Fogle's assessment of "Rappaccini's Daughter" (186:91), and few of the circa seventy other readers whose interpretations are reflected in this review would disagree. Their very number attests to the complexities in the story, while their conflicting conclusions complicate the situation further. Each of the four main characters has been seen alternately as admirable or reprehensible, heroic or villainous, or as fancifully ideal or ironically grotesque. Rappaccini is a tragic hero (45) intent on defending God's estate (288) and protecting his daughter (421; 333:212; 265; 346). Or he is a devil (7.5; 455:50; 447:93) whose lust for power (255:159–60) drives him to supersede God's creation (18). Baglioni is a well-intentioned benevolent friend (9) and the voice of the "normal conscience" (27). Or he is a diabolical, malevolent murderer (62; 194; 288; 346; 421; 445), at best a bungler whose motives are seriously suspect (33; 236; 186; 309). Even the star-crossed lovers, who emerge in most readings with Beatrice as the pure and selfless innocent victim (33; 32; 186; 265; 280; 346; 403; 445; 447; 500) and Giovanni as the inadequate, shallow, faithless lover (9; 29; 124; 186; 191; 216; 265; 309; 330.5; 346; 403; 400; 445; 509; 521; 238), occasionally reverse roles with one reader giving precedence to Beatrice's poisonousness (40), another to Giovanni's good "common sense" (301).

Several typically Hawthornian attributes contribute to and help to explain such a paradoxical array of responses. The first, and most crucial, is his handling of point of view; the second, and most apparent, is his unique kind of symbolic allegory; and the third, and most pervasive, is his ambivalence, a vacillation firmly rooted in a basic psychological and philosophical duality.

Point of view is listed as the first of these factors because it is in this fundamental aspect of form, in a subtle yet highly significant shift in perspective, that many of the interpretative problems lie. In the opening sentence of the tale proper, Giovanni is established as the subject of the story, and it is from his viewpoint that the garden and the other characters are initially described and the incidents in the plot are developed. The reader is presented with some objective facts that help to shape and assess Giovanni's character, but primarily the reader's sensibilities parallel Giovanni's and change, with his, between accepting the sensory evidence of Beatrice's poisonousness and the intuitive feeling that she is pure and good. The dilemma is a valid one for the first thirty pages of the thirty-seven-page story, but at this point, in the middle of a paragraph that reviews Giovanni's "dark surmises," the perspective shifts to an authoritative, omniscient point of view that informs the reader, but not Giovanni, that it would be a mistake to trust one's senses. The authorial voice unequivocally states, "There is something truer and more real, than what we can see with the eyes, and touch with the finger (*120.18–20*). Two pages later this authority verifies beyond doubt that "the real Beatrice was a heavenly angel" (*122.30–31*). The uninitiated reader could easily overlook the actual source of the confirmation and assume that Giovanni shares the benefit of this insight. Those readers who have identified and analyzed the manipulation of the narrative structure have not approved of it. McCabe considers the abandonment of Giovanni's mediating consciousness as the "one unsatisfactory element" in an otherwise "compelling work of art" (317), while Ross calls the intrusion of an outside superior knowledge "a serious flaw" that undercuts the reader's identification with Giovanni and makes for an inept resolution of the conflict (402). Waggoner, without specifically referring to point of view, assesses the plot as a series of controlled revelations of Beatrice's full character (500:115–24). Hawthorne's shift may be a part of this "controlled revelation," or it may be an arbitrary change inserted after he had decided to make Beatrice an angel and not a devil. (His indecision is discussed under circumstances of composition, above.) In either case, the reader who is aware of the privileged communication between author and reader will be better able to grasp Giovanni's dilemma.

The author's sleight of hand with viewpoint is significant in another way as well. It demonstrates and confirms one of the story's dominant themes—the unreliability of sensory perceptions. Several readers have discussed Giovanni's "quick fancy," a phrase Hawthorne uses to denote the faculty that receives and combines sense impressions (304:64). Most have condemned Giovanni for not being able to transcend his physical senses (509; 317; 304; 9; 309), but Franklin points out that the issue of whether Giovanni perceives Beatrice accurately is ultimately irrelevant. Giovanni's perception is a trick intended to momentarily delude the reader in the same way that Baglioni's and Rappaccini's "science" deludes all three men in the story. They "mistake the actual for the real" (191:20–23). Without the authorial intercessions, the reader would too. If the narrative is directly calculated to "egregiously deceive," as Franklin claims, the change in point of view may not be a blunder but a case of the form skillfully echoing the content and reinforcing one of the themes.

The second factor that contributes to this story's interpretative difficulties is the allegorical "meaning" that it embodies. For the reader who defines allegory as a consistent set of symbols used to signify a second series of referents with exact correspondence, "Rappaccini's Daughter" is hopelessly "inconsistent" (519:28–32) and finally unsatisfactory as "pure allegory" (500:124). Such a rigid allegorical formula cannot be made to fit the multitude of conflicting literary allusions with which the story abounds. Each legend that it invokes suggests a different set of identifying symbols and a corresponding reversal in role assignments. For example, the biblical analogue proposes Beatrice as the temptress Eve who leads Giovanni to his fall; the Dantean model makes her the Italian, idealized Beatrice who leads her beloved to Paradise; and the Ovidian myth suggests that Giovanni as Vertumnus will rescue her instead. (See sources and influences, above.) These kinds of contradictions pose no problem for another set of readers who accept a broader definition of allegory. For them, allegory is a symbolic mode that thrives on irony and enigma. One such reader claims that "the confusion in the symbolism" aids this kind of fiction (135). Another commends Hawthorne for integrating a continuum of legendary allusions (236). Honig believes Baglioni's mixed motives add a dimension lacking in the antecedent legends and enhance the ironic character portrayals throughout the story (236:134–37). One explanation for Hawthorne's ambiguous allegory is that he could no longer accept the firm beliefs on which Spenser and Bunyan based their "allegory of certainty"; in following their manner but not their convictions, Hawthorne produces an "allegory of doubt" (50).

Unbelief provides a shaky foundation for allegory, but readers have nevertheless attempted allegorical approaches to "Rappaccini's Daughter." Edenic parallels are the most common, undoubtedly because the story itself asks, "Was this garden, then, the Eden of the present world?—and this man [Rappaccini], was he the Adam?" (*96.17–20*). The rhetorical question has been answered in diverse ways. Rappaccini could be the old Adam (Beatrice, like Eve, is created from him and for him); this would make Baglioni the serpent, who seduces and betrays, and Giovanni a second Adam who falls again (288). Giovanni's sin would be directly linked to his inability to accept Beatrice as a postlapsarian Eve. Or Rappaccini could be not Adam, but a kind of false God wielding his power over a perversely re-created Adam and Eve in an unnatural Paradise of his own making (186:99; 18). If Giovanni is Adam, his offering Beatrice the antidote could be interpreted as the temptation of the apple, a situation that reverses the Miltonic emphasis on Eve as temptress (304). Or Giovanni might simply be Adam after the fall in a "lost Eden Paradise" that he cannot redeem because of his un-Christian selfishness (136).

Two other allegorical schemes have also been applied, one involving folklore, the other science. The former centers on the principals in the fairy tale—a prince and princess, a good fairy and an evil one. Like the counterparts in the biblical versions, the identities reverse and confuse their roles. Beatrice is the bewitched Princess-in-Distress, but she is not rescued by the Knight-Errant (Giovanni) because he fails the test (the poison); Rappaccini is the Wicked Enchanter, but he is partially good; and Baglioni, who tries to conteract the spell with a magic potion (the antidote), is as much an Evil Counselor as a good fairy (186:102; 346:148). The self-contradictions, once more, underscore Hawthorne's ironic intent by forcing the reader to reshape his original expectations. As an allegory of science, the story yields, in one reading, a more clearly defined series of correspondences. Rappaccini is the experimental scientist, the garden is his laboratory. Beatrice is the new scientific generation; Giovanni, traditional education; and Baglioni, conservative science (400).

This neatly assigned scheme has been severely criticized as arbitrary and irrelevent (115). One reader completely rules out the notion that the doctors in the story are meant to represent science because they display none of the objectivity associated with the medical profession even in Hawthorne's day (485).

Perhaps the most telling commentary on "Rappaccini's Daughter" as allegory is Hawthorne's own reaction in 1854, ten years after he had written it. In preparing the *Mosses* collection for a new edition, Hawthorne writes to his publisher, James T. Fields: "Upon my honor, I am not quite sure that I entirely comprehend my own meaning in some of these blasted allegories" (*CE, X, 549-50*). Since reinsertion of the preface to "Rappaccini's Daughter" is one of the changes Hawthorne specifically mentions in this letter, and since the preface refers to "an inveterate love of allegory" (*91.18-19*) as part of the author's problem, we can rightfully assume that this story is one of the "blasted allegories" that confuses its author as it does many of its readers.

The third factor that contributes to the multitude of interpretations is the ambivalence in Hawthorne himself, especially in his attitude toward women and sex. Beatrice is declared an angel, yet her physical poisonousness is never denied. Crews believes that Beatrice's "poison" is her sexuality and that Giovanni's vacillations between lustful fantasy and the ideal of sexless virtue reflect Hawthorne's own contradictory feelings (115:116-35).

Much in the story itself is imbued with sexual connotations. The cross-hybridization of the plants in the garden is called "adultery" (*110. 17*), and the flowers are described as passionate, fierce, gorgeous, and unnatural (*110.10*). This prurient interest in the commingling of vegetable species establishes some clearly incestuous innuendos in the story (56). When Giovanni feels "like a brother" (*113.13*) to Beatrice, he is complying with Rappaccini's vicariously incestuous scheme (115; 170; 181: 420). Beatrice's attachment to her father has been viewed as unnatural too (56; 170; 238; 512.5; 523). More obvious, but in equally perverse terms, is the sexually seductive effect Beatrice has on Giovanni. The accidental touch of her hand thrills "through Giovanni's fibres" (*114.3*), yet they never touch, caress, or kiss one another (*116.5-6*). Giovanni's "ardent southern temperment" rises "to a higher fever-pitch" that burns like love and shivers like horror (*105.14-23*). The implications and contradictions suggest a Puritanical fascination with the forbidden, something simultaneously attractive and dangerous.

Giovanni's confusion, and by inference Hawthorne's too, has been attributed to a variety of factors—to his immature and destructive Puritanical fears (238), to his perverted notions of sex (519; 62), to an infantile narcissism (29), and to the corrupted nature of post-lapsarian man whose response to feminine beauty is tainted with lust (509). One maverick reading claims that Beatrice's poison is not sexuality but repression and that the antidote kills her because it is an aphrodisiac (301). Most readers, however, view Beatrice as innocent, not repressed; she is usually deemed guiltless of whatever sexual enticements she unconsciously embodies for Giovanni (115; 186; 500; 509; 62; 238). Hawthorne himself, however, is not so sure of her blamelessness. (See circumstances of composition, above, for his emotion-laden admission that he did not know whether Beatrice was to be a demon or an angel in the end. Also see his paradoxical portrayal of other exotically beautiful dark women, under relationship with other Hawthorne works, above.) It is precisely his mixed response to his own creation in the very process of creating her that creates the duality in the finished work.

Only slightly less ambivalent are Hawthorne's philosophical and sociological positions in this story. Science, faith, and morals play key roles, and all are riddled with ambiguity. The two scientists are in some ways admirable (Rappaccini is unselfishly devoted to science, his experiment intended to protect his daughter; Baglioni is concerned about the health and welfare of an old friend's son), yet both have mixed motives (Rappaccini, pride; Baglioni, jealousy) and both fail (Rappaccini misjudges what will bring his daughter happiness; Baglioni's interference results in Beatrice's death—a testament to the dangers of inept scientists). That is, Baglioni fails unless he deliberately plans Beatrice's death, in which case the issue becomes a moral one. Here, too, no clearcut demarcations exist. Do Rappaccini's good intentions make it permissible for him to play God? Does Baglioni interfere because he envies Rappaccini? Or if the antidote is simply an example of his incompetence, is he morally culpable for his mistake? Giovanni's mistake is a question more of faith than of morals. In spite of the overwhelming condemnations of faithlessness heaped on Giovanni, few readers will deny that Hawthorne makes his test an almost impossible one. Fogle says that Hawthorne's intention is to invent the greatest possible human dilemma (186:97); in this respect, Hawthorne succeeds, but his "hero," a very *human* human being, fails—and the reader who is aware of the limitations of Giovanni's "knowledge" cannot help but temper his condemnation with compassion. What results, on the issue of blind faith, is more ambivalence.

Other kinds of attempts have been made to explain these recurring thematic ambivalences. Dauber, while admitting to the tautology of his approach, accounts for Hawthorne's attempt to link two contradictory stories in a single printed text by claiming the complete absence of authorial purpose. By eliminating any intention of his own, Hawthorne creates a fiction that affirms itself (127:25–36). More traditionally oriented readers find an explanation in Hawthorne's habitual moderation, in his penchant for "the middle way" (162; 380). In this context, Rappaccini's scientific idealism and Beatrice's moralistic idealism are extremes countered by Baglioni's scientific conventionalism and Giovanni's skeptical materialism (304; 170). The situation is further complicated by the ever-present intermingling of good and evil in all humanity; each of the four main characters is such a moral mix. The very nature of man since the Fall negates total perfection and mandates an understanding of humanity's shortcomings. Further ambivalence develops, however, because Hawthorne's acceptance of these flaws is an uncomfortable one. He does not always want to take "the middle way." In the introduction to "Rappaccini's Daughter" he describes himself as occupying "an *unfortunate* position between the Transcendentalists" and "the great body of pen-and-ink men who address the intellect and sympathies of the multitude" (*91.6–10*, my italics). Nowhere more clearly does this "unfortunate" middle position manifest itself than in the ambiguous fabric of "Rappaccini's Daughter." The Transcendental ideals of Beatrice (and the pseudo-Transcendental and elitist hopes of Rappaccini) are pitted against the materialistic skepticism of the multitude outside the garden (represented by Baglioni and Giovanni). Hawthorne buffets himself, his characters, and his readers in the question-infested "middle" world. Several readers interpret Baglioni's final mocking speech as the triumph of the mediocre over the exceptional, but the victory is at best a fleeting and earthly one. Apparently, one is damned (physically and emotionally) for pursuing one's ideals and damned (spiritually and eternally) for abandoning them.

These complexities are part of the story's virtues, but in "Rappaccini's Daughter" an excess of virtues is an integral fault. A surfeit of significances results in too many meanings that ultimately defy coherent analysis (186:92; 304:55). Positive appraisals are, nevertheless, the rule. The story has been hailed as an excellent example of Hawthorne's "mature art" (186:101) and likened as well to his "great early fiction" (9). James was sufficiently impressed with it to suspend his dislike of allegory long enough to single it out for praise twice, once as "representing the highest point that Hawthorne reached" in his "stories of fantasy and allegory," and a second time as an example of Hawthorne's "deeper psychology" (241:44, 51). Waggoner classifies it among "the best of Hawthorne's tales," those that "convey the kind of knowledge poetry conveys, in symbolic terms not essentially different from those poetry uses" (500: 125.) Other readers also commend its symbolism. Special acclaim is often directed at the poison and the fountain as central symbols for man's corrupted nature (62:153; 171; 265:329; 346:148; 509:11; 500:112–17).

The exception to the rule is Warren who objects to the symbolism as "false" because "the physical and the psychic do not correspond" (511:356). Fogle also finds Beatrice's symbolism "puzzling," but by using the fountain as a symbol for her heavenly nature and the purple shrub for her earthly aspect, he is able to reconcile the apparent discrepancies; as the poisonous flower is fed by the pure water of the fountain, Beatrice's true nature is nurtured by a spiritually pure and eternal grace (186:93–98; 171; 265; 403).

One reader offers a worthwhile insight into the bewildering array of conflicting interpretations that Hawthorne's polysemous symbolism has generated. After charting his way through more than forty critiques published between 1950 and 1974, Ayo concludes that each reader constructs the tale's social reality according to his own values and concerns (33). Another commentary, published two years after Ayo's review, confirms his observation and serves as a case in point. In an era of feminist consciousness and activism, Beatrice's role as a victim of male exploitation is seen as the story's central issue; her "femaleness" explains why her father, lover, and professional rival project their fears, obsessions, and unhealthy desires onto her and succeed, in the end, in sacrificing her to their selfish wills (62).

What contemporary problem will next be illuminated by this eclectically applicable story remains to be seen. In his day, James found in it (according to several Jamesian devotees) some of the themes and characters for his *Turn of the Screw* (407) and *Washington Square* (34; 294; 238). In the middle of the twentieth century, Ocavio Paz used it as a basis for his drama *La Hija de Rappaccini* (1953), transforming it from a Christian allegory of dualism to a surrealistic search for a Buddhist unity (451). One modern reader notes the parallel elements between "Rappaccini's Daughter" and H. Rider Haggard's *She* as evidence that a Jungian analysis of Hawthorne's story would confirm Beatrice as a classic anima symbol (254). Another equates the view of science's moral dilemma expressed in the story with the doubts held by the responsible scientists of the atomic age (174). Josipovici's assessment of the "modernism" of "Rappaccini's Daughter" appears to be correct. Approaching the work from a post-Romantic European perspective, he commends Hawthorne's search for "the right objective correlative" (253). If reader response is any indication, Hawthorne's search is a successful one.

# XLII
# Roger Malvin's Burial

*(Centenary Edition, Volume X, Mosses from an Old Manse, 337–60.)*

## Publication History

This story was first published in 1831 in the *Token* (pp. 161–88) dated 1832 with no attribution (*CE, X, 578*). It is one of the four stories that Samuel Goodrich, the editor, persuaded Hawthorne to let him use in the 1832 *Token* after Hawthorne was unable to find a publisher for *Provincial Tales*, the projected collection of which they were a part (*CE, IX, 487–90*). How much Hawthorne was paid is not definitely known. Goodrich had earlier offered Hawthorne $35 for one of the other stories in the group. If Hawthorne was paid for all four stories at the proposed rate, which amounted to approximately 75¢ a page, his pay for "Roger Malvin's Burial" would have been $21 (207). However, another estimate of Hawthorne's income from the *Token* rules out any payment at all for these contributions (250:106). This story was reprinted in the *United States Magazine and Democratic Review* (XIII, 186–96) in August 1843 (*CE, X, 578*). Since it was not customary to charge for reprints, it is unlikely that John L. O'Sullivan, who edited the *Democratic Review* and was a close friend of Hawthorne's, was asked to pay anything (*CE, X, 505, n.18*). The reprint was used as printer's copy when the story was collected in *Mosses from an Old Manse* in 1846 (*CE, X, 537*).

## Circumstances of Composition, Sources, and Influences

This story was probably written between 1827 and 1829. That it was completed by December 20, 1829, is certain since it was one of the *Provincial Tales* that Hawthorne sent to Goodrich on that date (11:127–28). It may have been begun as early as 1827 when Hawthorne first withdrew John Farmer's and Jacob B. Moore's *Collections, Topographical, Historical, and Biographical* (Concord, N. H., 1822–24) from the Salem Athenaeum (360). Farmer's and Moore's *Collections* contains several accounts of Lovewell's Fight, also known as Lovell's Fight, that parallel the version that Hawthorne uses as the historical basis for his story. The incident was a raid in the spring of 1725 on the Pequawket Indian tribe by a small company of colonists from Dunstable, Massachusetts, with Captain John Lovewell in command. In southwestern Maine, close to the New Hampshire border, at what is now Fryeburg, the colonists were ambushed by the Indians and suffered a devastating defeat. Hawthorne could have heard stories about the battle during the boyhood summers he spent in Raymond, Maine, which is only twenty-eight miles from Fryeburg. He also could have known about the Fryeburg commemoration of the battle in 1825, the year in which he was a senior at Bowdoin College in Brunswick, Maine. One of his classmates, Henry W. Longfellow, wrote a centennial ode and recited it at the commemoration. Lovewell's Fight was also recorded in several histories of New England that Hawthorne is known to have read, but the details that he incorporates into his story seem to have come from three sources included in the *Collections* volumes. The first is *Historical Memoirs of the Late Fight at Piggwacket* by Thomas Symmes, which was written in 1725 and describes three instances of wounded men left unattended in the forest by the band of returning raiders (I, 25–34, cited in 360:314–16). The second is a ballad, later attributed to Thomas C. Upham, which describes two of the wounded survivors in melodramatic terms: Frye, "bloody and languishing," falls on Farwell's breast as he pleads with Farwell to go on without him (I, 34–36, cited in 360:316–17). The third is an article entitled "Indian Troubles at Dunstable" by J. B. H. (probably Joseph Bancroft Hill), which describes the parting between Farwell and another combatant, Davis, in almost the same terms that Hawthorne uses when he describes the parting between Roger and Reuben. J. B. H. writes:

> Farwell was . . . shot through the belly. He survived the contest two or three days, and with one Eleazer Davis, from Concord, attempted to reach home. . . . Though his case was hopeless, Davis continued with and assisted him till he became so weak as to be unable to stand, and then, at Farwell's earnest entreaties that he would provide for his own safety, left him to his fate. Previous to this he had taken Farwell's handkerchief and tied it to the top of a bush that it might afford a mark by which his remains could the more easily be found. After going from him a short distance, Farwell called him back and requested to be turned upon the other side. This was done, and was the last that was known of him. Davis reached Concord in safety. (II, 306, cited in 296:530)

Doubleday rightly calls this "a startling example of how intimately a tale may be related to a source in Hawthorne's work" (149:193).

Hawthorne may also be making reference to source material that he knew about but chose to ignore when he introduces the story by explaining: "Imagination, *by casting certain circumstances judiciously into the shade*, may see much to admire in the heroism of a little band, who gave battle to twice their number in the heart of the enemy's country" (*337.5–8*, italics added). One of the circumstances he is referring to is most probably the bounty of £100 paid by the Massachusetts General Court for every Indian scalp the colonists brought in (52.3:358; 125; 149:192, n.12; 461:283). When Hawthorne goes on to explain that because of "history and tradition . . . the captain of a scouting party of frontier-men has acquired as actual a military renown, as many a victorious leader of thousands" (*337.15–18*), he appears to be aware of how history, myth, and popular sentiment distorted and transformed the band of fortune hunters, who failed miserably in their bold attempt to scalp Indians for profit, into patriotic heroes (53.3:364; 461:280–86; 125).

Roger's surname is probably also related to the historical source material; Symmes' *Memoirs* uses the name of Malvin, which is a variant spelling of the name of two of Lovewell's band, Eleazor and David Melvin of Concord (360:315). The other names in the story, however, have been traced to biblical sources. The most convincing biblical analogue is Reuben, son of Jacob and brother of Joseph, in Genesis 27–50, who, like Hawthorne's Reuben, is compelled to leave a loved one in a situation of danger, to break a promise to his father, and then to live a lie for an extended period of time. Both suffer from feelings of guilt, and each of them experiences a deterioration in his worldly well-being and relationship with others (461:291–92; 472:92–94). The parallels proposed between Cyrus in Isaiah 40–48 and Dorcas in Acts 10:36–42 are less persuasive, although a passage from Isaiah is echoed in one sentence that describes Reuben Bourne as he stands over his dead son, Cyrus: "Then Reuben's heart was stricken, and the tears gushed out like water from a rock" (*360.13–14*). In the biblical verse, Cyrus is regarded as a redeemer of the Israelites who "led them through the deserts; he caused the water to flow out of the rock for them; he clave the rock also, and the waters gushed out" (Isaiah 48:21). Thompson believes that the conjunction of names and the parallel wording are conclusive proof that Hawthorne made conscious use of the material in Isaiah relating to Cyrus, the Redeemer (472:94). Stock sees another close biblical relationship between this story and covenant theology—directly in the story of Saul in I Samuel 18 and the Abraham-Isaac myth in Genesis 12–24, especially chapter 22, and indirectly through a sermon of Cotton Mather's which deals, in part, with the consequences of Lovell's fight. Mather's sermon could have suggested the tree as a symbol and the sacrifice of the son as a part of the action, although the Puritan dogma emerges, in Hawthorne's hands, with decidedly ironic overtones (461:287–96; see interpretations below).

Another influence that is reflected in the fundamental situation of this story is the tradition, dating back to ancient Rome and early Greece, that appropriate rites for the dead are a compelling duty. One reader cites as a source the Lemuria, an ancient Roman ceremony in which families appeased the spirits of their dead who were hostile because they had not been buried with due rites (319). While the obligation of the living to bury the dead properly plays a definite part in Reuben's feelings of guilt, the timing of the act of expiation to coincide with the dates specified for the Lemuria rite, that is, between the ninth and thirteenth of May, cannot be used as evidence because the historical accounts established the date of the battle as May 8 and of the subsequent death of some of the wounded survivors as several days later. The date of Reuben's expiation, which he acknowledges by saying, "The twelfth of May! I should remember it well" (*354.32*), is, of course, chosen to coincide with the anniversary of the day on which Reuben left the dying Malvin in the forest. Nevertheless, the "atmosphere of primitive superstition" that can be traced to ancient civilizations does permeate the story (319:322). In fact, the reference to the Indian superstitions about the importance of "the rites of sepulture" (*344.33*) reinforces the mythic and folkloric associations.

An admittedly conjectural source is explored by another reader who suggests that this story itself may be "a sort of expiatory ritual" whereby Hawthorne attempts to assuage the guilt carried over from childhood when he imagined that an unspoken wish had murdered his father who subsequently died at sea (406:16). Reuben's role as a disobedient son and his attempt at expiation also parallel the circumstances of one incident which is described in Boswell's *Life of Johnson*. Johnson is reputed to have recalled:

> 'Once indeed . . . I was disobedient; I refused to attend my father to Uttoxeter-market. Pride was the source of that refusal. A few years ago, I desired to atone for this fault; I went to Uttoxeter in very bad weather, and stood for a considerable time bareheaded in the rain, on the spot where my father's stall used to stand. In contrition I stood, and I hope the penance was expiatory.' (Boswell's *Life of Johnson*, pp. 372–73, as quoted in 406:12)

Another father-son relationship with expiation as a theme is evident in *The Ramayana*, a work in Hindu literature that was popular among the Transcendentalists of Hawthorne's day. A more specific parallel can be found in one of its incidents, known as "The Tale of the Hermit Son," in which a young man is mistaken for an animal and hurt unintentionally

(470). *The Ramayana*, like Johnson's explanation of his Uttoxeter penance, is proposed as a possible influence on "Roger Malvin's Burial."

## Relationship with Other Hawthorne Works

As one of the four definitively established *Provincial Tales*, this story has generic ties with "My Kinsman. Major Molineux," "The Gentle Boy," and "The Wives of the Dead" (*CE, IX, 487–90*). Other stories that have been included as part of the projected collection are "Alice Doane's Appeal," "Young Goodman Brown," "The Gray Champion," and "The May-Pole of Merry Mount" (11:127–31; 84:12–13; 10; 514). "Roger Malvin's Burial" has been thematically associated with various groupings of these stories, and a few less likely candidates, on several grounds—as based on American colonial history (11:129), as depicting the transition from childishness and adolescence to maturity (10), as exemplifications of the Puritan spirit (514), and as portraying imagination in action as a destructive or alienating force (43:34). It is one of five of these stories that begin with a paragraph of historical background but then overturn the verisimilitude of history by creating a less tangible and more subjective vision of reality (43:32; 147:7, n.12; 500:91). It is one of four of them that involve a quest for a home or a search for a parent (304: 38–53). And it shares with two of them, "Alice Doane's Appeal" and "My Kinsman," the feelings of guilt that arise from one's relationship to a father (115:44–95; 500:97). The former offers a close parallel to Reuben's symbolic parricide of Roger in the parricidal fantasy experienced by Doane (115:55, n.10; 406:15–16). Pearce believes that these three stories, plus "The Gentle Boy," are variations of what he calls the Molineux theme, that is, the imputation simultaneously of guilt and of righteousness through history. However, he deems "Roger Malvin's Burial" to be the least compelling of the four (368:146–52).

"My Kinsman" is also like "Roger Malvin's Burial" and another of these early stories, "Young Goodman Brown," in that all three have protagonists who undergo journeys that have startling psychological implications (398:40; 115:105, n.5). Hawthorne did not include these three early stories in his first collection, *Twice-told Tales*. While theories as to why he rejected them differ, readers generally agree that they are among the most preferred of his works today (*CE, IX, 524*; 43:54; 149.5).

"Young Goodman Brown," while usually considered the better of the two, has been compared to "Roger Malvin's Burial" on several other counts as well. Both stories have a circular structure and in each a blighted man comes out of the forest initiated into guilt (146:6; 115:94;

500:92). The latter aspect is also evident in *The Scarlet Letter*, not only in the similar tree and light imagery used to describe the forest (53.8: 182–84), but also in the secret guilt that torments Dimmesdale. Like Reuben, Dimmesdale finds that his sin of concealment, which stems from a subtle, unconscious pride, torments him all the more when he becomes the object of unmerited praise (53.8:182; 149:195; 455:xlvii; 500:95). This kind of secret guilt that feeds on intense introspection is also part of the characterization of Roderick in "Egotism" and Hooper in "The Minister's Black Veil" (32:96–97; 455:xlvii). Two pieces, "Fancy's Show Box" (*CE, IX, 220–26*) and "The Haunted Mind" (*CE, IX, 304–09*), shed light on Hawthorne's concept of conscience and further explore the subject of self-judged offenses (43:68–69; 406:14). One reader traces a development from Reuben's interiorized and unexpressed guilt through Dimmesdale's public confession to the release Hilda finds in the confessional in Rome in *The Marble Faun* (173). The fixation on the past that is a part of many of Hawthorne's guilt-stricken protagonists assumes equally overwhelming proportions in "The Hollow of the Three Hills," "Sylph Etherege," and "The White Old Maid" (189:5, 12). The last of these displays the same uncanny motif of the double and the unexplained repetition that marks "Roger Malvin's Burial" (352). A later story, "Ethan Brand," also follows a similar return pattern as Reuben's, including an eighteen-year cycle that may have biblical origins (524). The rock gravestone that forms a kind of symbolic center for Reuben's story has been likened to the pillory that dominates *The Scarlet Letter* (147:8) and to the maypole that acts as a focal point in "The May-Pole of Merry Mount" (79:4).

The ironic readings of "Roger Malvin's Burial" that attribute Reuben's torment and final desperate act to the influence of Calvinistic theology make this story one of a group that attacks Puritanism and the figure of an exacting vengeful Providence that Puritanism embodies. "The Ambitious Guest" comes closest in depicting an omnipotent God without mercy, but each of the guilt-obsessed characters discussed above testifies to the psychological ravages of the Calvinistic emphasis on sin. "The Gentle Boy," "The Man of Adamant," and "Alice Doane's Appeal" present pejorative views of Puritanism in action, while an ambivalence that has been interpreted ironically marks the depiction of Puritans in many of the other historical works. Among these are "Endicott and the Red Cross," the four Province-House legends, *The Scarlet Letter*, "Main Street," and even the ostensibly pro-Puritan "Gray Champion." For some readers the irony in many of these works, as in "Roger Malvin's Burial," is also directed at history itself and at the process by which the facts of the past, which are not always heroic or admirable, are transformed into patriotic myth.

## Interpretations and Criticism

The interpretative question that demands initial attention in this most bewildering of Hawthorne's stories is easily pinpointed: why does Reuben shoot his son? The answer, however, is a different matter, and as complex (some might say confused) as anything in Hawthorne's canon. The final sentence appears to establish the shooting as an effective expiatory act, but this conclusion provides more questions than answers. Does Reuben kill Cyrus so that he will be able to pray again? If so, why should murdering a son be atonement? And why should atonement be necessary? A different set of questions is necessary to clarify another fundamental issue in the story, that is, whether Reuben kills Cyrus intentionally or accidentally. The passage that describes the shooting (Doubleday calls it "the crux of the tale") contains some basic contradictions. Reuben is supposed to have fired "with the instinct of a hunter and the aim of a practised marksman," yet his aim is directed at "the motion of some object behind a thick veil of undergrowth" and he knows his wife and son are in the immediate vicinity (*356.17–19*). Under these circumstances, an experienced hunter would have held his fire. Doubleday concludes that "the statement hardly makes sense"; it is "a failure in technique . . . a merely bewildering statement . . . a wrong narrative tack" (149:197). The interpretative questions are thus compounded by critical judgments. Is the story simply a failure? Or do Hawthorne's intentions, conscious or otherwise, account for the paradoxes?

Not surprisingly, considering the provocative nature of the questions raised by this story, readers have provided explanations for all of the unresolved elements. One of the most convincing solutions to the interpretative puzzle is the psychological one: Reuben is insane. According to Crews, the killing is not accidental, although it is unconsciously motivated. Reuben is suffering from a guilt complex brought on by the selfish motives that influenced his decision to leave Roger in the forest. The guilt is reinforced by his subsequent inability to reveal the truth to Dorcas or to anyone. The destructive obsession grows until he convicts himself of patricide. Reuben's belief "that a supernatural voice had called him onward" (*356.8*) is a delusion fostered by the unconscious compulsion that he must punish himself by shooting his son (115:80–95). Waggoner says he is killing "the symbolic extension of himself" (500:97). Crews elaborates Bourne's unconscious stratagems further: at the same time that

Reuben projects his own guilty self into Cyrus, he changes places with the accusing Roger (115:88). One reader suggests that Cyrus is guilty of unconsciously desiring to repeat Reuben's patricide (189:51–52), but many identify Cyrus with what is best in Reuben. The text states: "The boy was loved by his father, with a deep and silent strength, as if whatever was good and happy in his own nature had been transferred to his child" (*351.15–18*). Cyrus is, therefore, a supreme sacrifice of what Reuben loves most (32:97). Another reader equates the destruction of Cyrus with Reuben's elimination of his own childishness (10:49–50). It is hardly surprising that the latter finds such an interpretation "uncomfortable." Equally jarring is the view that Cyrus' death is an act of revenge on Roger's spirit: Reuben resents Roger for having used rational arguments to lead him into sin, this use being a favorite device of the devil's and suggesting that Roger may be functioning in that role; Reuben retaliates by killing Cyrus and leaving Roger without posterity (169). However widely these Freudian-based readings may differ on details, they agree in principle. When Reuben murders his son and feels good about it, he has gone completely mad (418).

Equally convincing is the interpretation that "Roger Malvin's Burial" presents an ironic view of Hawthorne's Puritan heritage. Reuben's sacrifice is the atonement exacted by the Calvinist's vengeful God; Hawthorne is showing what it means to be a New England Puritan who fails to obey the harsh rule of an authoritarian Father, no matter how inadvertently the disobedience comes about. In Donahue's words, "In order to pray all Reuben has to do is become isolated, lose his material and spiritual prosperity, and kill his only son. Consciously or unconsciously Hawthorne's dark imagination . . . his fear of the price of expiation . . . have betrayed him into irony" (146:19). The cruelty and sadism of the situation are heightened by the empathy with which Reuben's dilemma is depicted. In choosing life over death, he unknowingly chooses an unhappy future to be climaxed by the grim necessity of having to destroy the one part of that life that he found any joy in—his son.

Several readers have identified Reuben as a figure who embodies Original Sin in the full Calvinistic sense (280:55; 146:14; 500:94), but all do not detect the irony that Donahue does. Waggoner, whose reading conjoins Oedipal theories and primitive religious myth with creedal Christianity, traces Reuben's guilt to a chain of previous wrong choices made with good intentions but guided by a "fatal necessity," all of which suggests a close parallel to the nature of Original Sin, which all men inherit through no immediate fault of their own (500:94). One reader appears to accept Reuben's killing of Cyrus as a morally acceptable act designed to bring Reuben the same peace alloted to Malvin after his self-sacrifice eighteen years earlier. According to Stock, Reuben's sin was a lack of faith that kept him from attempting to keep his promise because he could not believe that he would be led to Malvin's remains. Stock theorizes that Hawthorne would have called the workings of Reuben's unconscious mind the workings of Providence because by following this "call" he is redeemed (461:293–94).

Such a literal theological reading is effectively undercut by two leading Hawthorne scholars, Doubleday and Crews. The latter accounts for the biblical allusions, on which the Cyrus-as-redeemer readings rely heavily, by assigning them the role of placing in bold relief, by way of contrast, the pathological nature of Reuben's case. Crews observes: "The story's ending is heretical, to put it mildly: Reuben's alleged redemption has been achieved through murder, while the guilt from which he has thereby freed himself stemmed from an imaginary crime . . . the idea of divine care is cruelly mocked" (115:93). Doubleday, who has some doubts about Crews' kind of psychological interpretation for the story, nevertheless echoes Crews' denouncement: "The concept of Cyrus's death as somehow a necessary sacrifice is certainly in no way Christian; at the center of Christian belief is the assurance of a full, perfect, and sufficient sacrifice once offered for the sins of the whole world" (149:200).

While the most compelling of the theological asseverations remain the ironically tinged ones, Calvinist theology is not the only target that has been suggested for this story. Several readers believe "Roger Malvin's Burial" holds satiric implications for American history as well. Daly sees Reuben's story as an example in microcosm of how sordid historical events can be transformed into chivalric myth. Hawthorne's purpose is to suggest that the same kind of "heroicizing" fantasy that results in Reuben's lie can be seen as operative on the facts of history. By using a historical incident of questionable validity (see source studies, above), Hawthorne encourages his readers to become as wary about the chivalric myths of the American past as Reuben should have been about accepting the undeserved role of hero that was foisted on him (125). Naples, like Daly, sees this story as a parable not only for the American public but for American historians as well; more specifically, Naples directs her discussion toward historians of the American frontier (351). She examines the image of the frontier in the story and echoes Fussell's charge that Hawthorne's romanticizing of the pioneering West is essentially a parody intended to shatter some of the myths of the West as a new world free from the problems of the past (193:75–77).

The frontier as metaphor is explored by another reader who sees a series of figurative parallels that center on the frontier image (189:5–6): the frontier-as-mode (a created territory between history and fiction) parallels the frontier-as-background (the geographical region where civilization meets wilderness), which, in turn, parallels the frontier-as-psychological setting (where consciousness and unconscious impulses· meet), which also parallels the frontier-as-action (where the past encounters the present). Another extended metaphorical reading involves Reuben's journey into the depths of the wilderness to find Malvin's body as an allegorical mirror for Reuben's descent into the dark wilderness of his own heart. Hawthorne effectively uses the figure of shooting through a veil when he has Reuben shoot at something moving behind "a thick veil of undergrowth"; the game that Reuben had wandered in search of is his own cowardly falseness, which had been hidden from him by a thick veil of self-deception (522).

The two major symbols in this story are the oak tree and the rock; both are introduced immediately after the opening paragraph which provides the historical background, and they reappear together in the final climactic paragraph. The oak tree is identified with Reuben physically and psychologically. It first appears as a "young and vigorous sapling" (*338.12–13*) on the spot where Reuben, also young and vigorous, leaves Malvin, after tying a bloodstained handkerchief to its topmost branch. Eighteen years later, both man and tree are blighted, the oak, in its "upper part . . . the very topmost bough" where the handkerchief had been tied (*357.7–8*), and the man in a similar "upper part," that is, in his soul or mind, where his vow to Malvin is indelibly marked. Hawthorne affirms the parallel when he calls both tree and man "blighted" (*357.7*; *360.15*). The "excess of vegetation" that fringes the trunk almost to the ground suggests a growth of a lower kind; in Reuben, an excess of sinfulness or deceit. The falling of the withered bough from the tree at the moment of Reuben's expiation corresponds to the falling away of the curse from Reuben, who then finds he can pray again. One reader feels that the burial theme, which is emphasized by the shattering and falling of the bough over the dead, is effaced by the violent death of Cyrus (396). Donahue calls the falling of the bough of "the blasted oak, messenger of death" one of the "most artistic touches in a beautifully conceived story" (146:17). Crews thinks the symbolic meaning may be "too obvious" (115:94), but Birdsall applauds the passage, declaring that, in this final image, "all of the meanings which the tree has heretofore suggested are brought together with one masterful stroke" (53.8:185). The rock has received less attention, although several readers have conjectured about the significance of the "inscription in forgotten characters" that Hawthorne mentions each time he describes it (*338.11–12*; *356.27–28*). The rock suggests "the graven tablets of the Old Testament" (53.8:183–84); it is explicitly a gravestone and implicitly an altar (500:92); it is the kind of place in Christian, Hebrew, and pagan tradition that would be appropriate for a blood offering (146:16). The physical, figurative, and allusive development of the rock as a symbol is most completely analyzed by Carlson, who traces it from its role as a figurative tombstone at whose base the wounded Reuben and Malvin rested, through its appointed place serving as a milestone, a stepping-stone, a touchstone, a lodestone, and an altar stone, until it finally appears in the last paragraph as an actual tombstone, a marker for the bones of Malvin and the corpse of young Cyrus that lie at its base (79).

"Roger Malvin's Burial" has also been analyzed stylistically by a reader who uses a generative-tranformational grammar to show that Reuben's helplessness is embodied in the grammatical constructions that Hawthorne uses to portray his dilemma. Hawthorne's syntax repeatedly makes Reuben a grammatical object, especially in sentences containing a personified psychological abstraction, such as "moral cowardice." The reader more fully apprehends Reuben's passivity, and the fact that he is being acted upon by psychological forces he cannot understand and external circumstances beyond his control, as a result of the grammatical position he is given in which he is also being acted upon (264).

The array of interpretations attest to the popularity that this story enjoys. Josipovici attributes the appeal to its "modernism," an attribute that he describes as a post-Romantic stand characterized by skepticism, a concern for psychological truths, and an interest in depicting compulsive behavior (253). A tally of the interpretative and critical responses quickly establishes a pattern that confirms Josipovici's assessment. Those who pursue a psychological approach praise the story; in it they find "Hawthorne's best insight and highest art" (115:95). Those who read it ironically, with a heightened awareness of its skeptical overtones, also praise it; they see it as "one of the most polished of Hawthorne's short stories, one of the ones most rewarding of close reading" (146.1). But those who attempt a traditionally conservative approach—especially historical or moral—do not praise it; for them, it is a tale "blurred in focus" (368:147), one that fails because of problems with narrative coherence and conscious intent (149:199–200).

As if in confirmation of his admiration of Hawthorne's "deeper psychology," Henry James numbers "Roger Malvin's Burial" among "the most original" of Hawthorne's tales (241:51, 44). Readers new to Hawthorne are invariably fascinated by both the psychology and the originality. The questions that the story raises do not disturb the critical equilibrium of the average reader; rather, they challenge his imaginative response. Reuben's predicament, because it raises the specter of unintentional sin, filial disobedience, irrational guilt, and unconscious compulsion, touches the psyche of every human who, however faintly, has felt a subtle pang of guilt without fully understanding why.

# XLIII
# The Seven Vagabonds

(*Centenary Edition, Volume IX, Twice-told Tales*, 350–69.)

## Publication History

This story was first published in 1832 in the *Token and Atlantic Souvenir* (pp. 49–71) dated 1833 as the work of the author of "The Gentle Boy" (*CE, IX, 573*). Along with the other two Hawthorne pieces in this edition, "The Canterbury Pilgrims" and the biographical sketch, "Sir William Pepperell," "The Seven Vagabonds" was probably intended for publication in the annual from its inception, unlike the four stories from the aborted "Provincial Tales" collection inserted by *Token* editor Samuel Goodrich the preceding year, or the pieces published after 1833 that were part of the projected "Story-Teller" collection. Hawthorne was paid, at the most, an average of $1 per page for the twenty-seven contributions he made to the *Token*, making his earnings from "The Seven Vagabonds" an approximate $23. (*CE, IX, 487–97*).

Hawthorne added this work to the second volume of the second edition of *Twice-told Tales* in 1842 with one notable change, the deletion of the following passage:

> I hardly know how to hint, that, as the brevity of her gown displayed rather more than her ancles, I could not help wishing that I had stood at a little distance without, when she stept up the ladder into the wagon. (*CE, IX, 630*)

The question of whether Sophia Peabody objected to her fiancé's description of the wish to peek under the skirts of the "pretty maid" in the story, or whether, by 1841, Hawthorne himself was sensitive to its impropriety, has not been definitively settled; however, authorial authority for the changes has been established by C. E. Frazer Clark's discovery of the 1833 *Token* used for the printer's copy of the 1842 edition. The annotations are "incontestably" in Hawthorne's own hand (88).

## Circumstances of Composition, Sources, and Influences

"The Seven Vagabonds" was probably written in the fall of 1830 after

Hawthorne's return from his summer trip to Connecticut with his uncle, Samuel Manning (84:14). A letter, assigned to 1830, describes some of the "many marvelous adventures" he met with on the way from New Haven to Deerfield and their plan, "with our faces northward," to push "on to Canada." The itinerary parallels that of the story's narrator, as does the variety of people he encounters—for example, "a very polite and agreeable gentleman, whom I afterward discovered to be a strolling tailor of very questionable habits" (272:143–44). Warren's assessment of Hawthorne's "shrewd, but by no means unkindly, observations of his fellows" equates "The Seven Vagabonds" with the effective realism of the sketches and the *American Notebooks* and supports the theory that the observations and experiences of Hawthorne's 1830 summer holiday provided the basis for this story (511:358–59).

The following passage from "The Story Teller No. I," collected as "Passages from a Relinquished Work" in *Mosses from an Old Manse*, establishes "The Seven Vagabonds" as either an early attempt at an introductory sketch for the *Story Teller* collection (*CE, IX, 492*) or as the germ of the itinerant-novelist concept that developed into it (43:50):

> The idea of becoming a wandering story teller had been suggested, a year or two before, by an encounter with several merry vagabonds in a showman's wagon, where they and I had sheltered ourselves during a summer shower. (*CE, X, 407–08*)

## Relationship with Other Hawthorne Works

In addition to its relationship to *The Story Teller*, "The Seven Vagabonds" has been compared to "My Kinsman, Major Molineux" in its initiation theme and to a group of stories and sketches whose narrative pattern is based on a procession of characters in a controlled setting (242). These include such works as "The Canterbury Pilgrims" and "The Christmas Banquet." The showman's puppet theater and the young couple's mahogany showbox in "The Seven Vagabonds" are two examples of another favorite device, one that reappears almost twenty years later as the Dutch Jew's diorama box in "Ethan Brand" and as the pictorial exhibition put on by the narrator in "Main Street."

## Interpretations and Criticism

Although one of Hawthorne's lesser-known stories, "The Seven Vagabonds" was singled out by Henry James in 1879 as one of the "delicate, dusky flowers in the bottomless garden of American journalism" possessing "something essentially fresh and new" (241:44).

Three twentieth-century critics have interpreted it, with a variety of nuances, as a statement about the artist in society. Janssen concludes that art and life come together in the story at the expense of one or the other (242); Baym agrees that the artist is presented as alienated from life but emphasizes a changing pattern in Hawthorne's attitude as his career progresses (43:50); and Fussell finds a surrogate to the indigenous artist in the Penobscot Indian, one of the seven vagabonds, who, although ironically reduced to basket-weaving and archery, remains the representative modern hero. Fussell also interprets the narrator's free mind and restless spirit as part of America's "pioneering syndrome" and analyzes Hawthorne's attraction to unpopulous pockets of the East, such as the "rocky, woody, watery back settlement" in "The Seven Vagabonds," as an attempt to transform New England into a prototype of the West (193: 70–78).

Another of the vagabonds in the story, the wandering mendicant and prophet, whom Hawthorne describes as having "a love of deception for its own sake, a shrewd eye and keen relish for human weakness and ridiculous infirmity, and the talent of petty fraud," has been proposed as a source for Melville's *The Confidence Man* (269).

In its content and style, "The Seven Vagabonds" captures much of one phase of Hawthorne's young manhood. It acts as an effective companion piece to the *American Notebooks* (511:358–59) and offers the reader who intends to study Hawthorne's works in depth a portrait of the artist as a more social and less somber young man.

# XLIV

# The Shaker Bridal

(*Centenary Edition, Volume IX, Twice-told Tales, 419–25.*)


## Publication History

This story was first published in the fall of 1837 in the *Token and Atlantic Souvenir* (pp. 117–25) dated 1838 with no attribution (*CE, IX, 574*). A reprint of it in the *Salem Mercury* on October 11, 1837 credits it to Miss Sedgewick, as do reprints in the *American Traveler* on October 20 and in the *Pittsfield Sun* on November 16. On October 31, the *Salem Gazette* included a notice "to correct a mistake, which seems to be universal"; the announcement identified the story as the work of "our townsman, the author of 'Twice-told Tales'" (*CE, IX, 513, n.61*). The probable basis for attributing the piece to Catherine M. Sedgewick was her previous use of the Shakers in *Redwood* in 1824 (149:138). Based on Hawthorne's income from the 1837 *Token*, he should have been paid $1 per page, or $9, for "The Shaker Bridal," but he may never have received payment of any kind for it. (See publication history of "Sylph Etherege," one of the other 1838 *Token* pieces.) There is no likelihood that the newspapers paid for "The Shaker Bridal" either, since it was not customary to pay the author for reprints (*CE, IX, 499*). The story was included in the 1842 edition of *Twice-told Tales*.


## Circumstances of Composition, Sources, and Influences

Although not published until six years later, "The Shaker Bridal" was probably written in the fall of 1831 at about the same time that Hawthorne wrote his other Shaker tale, "The Canterbury Pilgrims" (84:15; 205:457; 274:83). On August 17, 1831, Hawthorne wrote to his sister, Louisa, describing his visit to the Shaker village at Canterbury, New Hampshire, with his uncle, Samuel Manning. His account, in which he jokingly suggested the possibility of his joining the sect (149:139; 205; 274:83), contradicts the somber picture of the Shaker community that he depicts in his fiction. (See circumstances of composition for "The Canterbury Pilgrims" for the text of the letter and a review of Hawthorne's contacts with the Shakers.)

The implicit condemnation of many of the sect's doctrines and practices that Hawthorne incorporates in "The Shaker Bridal" appears to have been based on Thomas Brown's *An Account of the People Called Shakers*, a book that Hawthorne borrowed from the Salem Athenaeum on August 27, 1831, ten days after his letter to his sister (205). Brown's emphasis in the book on the Shakers' "terrible desire to destroy all natural ties" is reflected in Hawthorne's description of the elders who had severed their relationships with their families (*423–24*). Many of the details in the tale of the sect's history and customs also parallel Brown's description; for example, the general low level of intelligence that Hawthorne attributes to the group (*422.17–18*) contradicts the impression he recorded in his letter to Louisa and follows Brown's assessment.

The structure of the story, with its focus on one event of a few moment's duration, may have been modeled on Sir Walter Scott's practice of using a single, highly wrought incident at strategic intervals in his novels (149: 245–46).

## Relationship with Other Hawthorne Works

Hawthorne wrote only two stories about the Shakers, this one and "The Canterbury Pilgrims"; the number of times that they have been discussed together attests to the similarities they share in theme and structure as well as subject matter. The pilgrims on their way to the Shaker community in "The Canterbury Pilgrims" parallel the experience of Adam Colburn and Martha Pierson before they join the Shakers, while Josiah and Miriam in the former story project the kind of hope for a reaffirmation of human affection that Martha is forced to relinquish at the end of "The Shaker Bridal." (See "The Canterbury Pilgrims" for a more detailed analysis of how the two stories complement one another.) Because the focus of "The Shaker Bridal" is on the community itself instead of on prospective and former members, the fanaticism of Father Ephraim and the other elders is depicted more explicitly, thereby linking the Shakers directly with Hawthorne's other religious extremists such as Digby in "The Man of Adamant" and both the Quakers and the Puritans in "The Gentle Boy" (205:463; 274:75; 309:71; 447:85). The judgment of the Puritan women in *The Scarlet Letter* who thought Hester should be punished more severely are other examples (162:40).

The conclusion, with Martha "like a corpse in its burial clothes," dead "at the feet of her early lover," links the story with "The Wedding Knell," which also conjoins a shroud and a marriage ceremony (274:83; 309:71). Two additional stories that center on unkept trysts and wasted lives are

"The White Old Maid" and "Edward Fane's Rosebud" (280:58). A less obvious resemblance groups "The Shaker Bridal" with "Roger Malvin's Burial" and "Young Goodman Brown"; in each, the male protagonist's obsession results in the unhappiness of the woman who loves him (43:57).

"The Shaker Bridal" is most like the best-known works, however, in two characteristic ways. It condemns those who violate the sanctity of human affection—one of the author's most persistent themes—and it concentrates on one representative scene that effectively communicates past and future associations.

## Interpretations and Criticism

In May 1850 Hawthorne came across an unauthorized reprint of "The Shaker Bridal" (and "Peter Goldthwaite's Treasure") in a copy of London's *Metropolitan Magazine* at the Salem Athenaeum. He recorded his reaction in his notebook: "I glanced over the stories, and they seemed painfully cold and dull" (*CE, VIII, 493.5–6*). Considering the marked differences between the two stories and the casual perusal indicated, Hawthorne's unfavorable remark seems to have been prompted more by his wish to deprecate the "unscrupulous and dishonest pirates . . . poor enough to perk themselves in such false feathers as these" (*CE, VIII, 493.7–10*) than by an objective appraisal of the stories themselves.

Although Hawthorne's other Shaker story has attracted more critical attention, "The Shaker Bridal" has been favorably viewed when it has been noticed. One reader calls it "an illustration of the remarkable technical skill of Hawthorne's early work," an accomplishment in economy and restraint seldom achieved in the first half of the nineteenth century (149:140–41). Another has singled out the savagely ironic ring of Father Ephraim's blindly self-righteous "blessing" in the penultimate paragraph as an effective technique for expressing a terror "as strong as anything in Hawthorne's writings" (282:58). The irony of the celibate "marriage" ceremony that culminates with Martha's death is another notable aspect (149:139–40; 205:458; 282:58), especially because Hawthorne relies on the situation's ironic implications to convey its moral, rather than on the explicit didactic statements that often mar many Hawthorne stories for modern readers (43:57; 511:363). The self-damning evidence of the Shakers' denial of life convincingly speaks for itself.

# XLV

# The Snow-Image: A Childish Miracle

(*Centenary Edition, Volume XI, The Snow-Image, 7–25.*)

## Publication History

This story first appeared in print under Hawthorne's own name in *The Memorial* (pp. 41–58), a volume which was published in 1851 in New York by George P. Putnam to memorialize Mrs. Fanny Osgood. However, on November 1, 1850 the editor, Rufus W. Griswold, printed "The Snow-Image," duly attributed to Hawthorne, in the *International Miscellany of Literature, Art, and Science* (I, 537–43). The publisher of *The Memorial* permitted Griswold to print the story in the *International* before its official publication, presumably to promote the forthcoming book. Griswold had offered Hawthorne $50 for a contribution to *The Memorial*; in a letter dated August 23, 1850, Hawthorne asked James T. Fields, who happened to have "The Snow-Image" in his possession, to give it to Griswold. As late as January 30, 1851, Hawthorne had not received payment in spite of a request from Fields to Griswold emphasizing that the money was "important" to Hawthorne just then. (Although *The Scarlet Letter* had been hailed as a critical success after its publication on March 16, 1850, Hawthorne was still hard pressed financially.) No record of payment has been found, but Hawthorne's willingness to send "Feather-top" to the *International* in December 1851 suggests that he finally did get paid. That same month saw the publication of Hawthorne's last major collection, with "The Snow-Image" as the opening title story. The original manuscript is the only known preserved one for the *Snow-Image* collection; it is now in the Henry Huntington Library and was used as the copy text for the Centenary Edition (*CE, XI, 386–87, 420, 427–28*).

## Circumstances of Composition, Sources, and Influences

An undated notebook entry made between October 25, 1836, and July 5, 1837 offers the earliest hint for this story:

> To describe a boyish combat with snowballs, and the victorious leader to have a statue of snow erected to him. A satire on

ambition and fame to be made out of this idea. It might be a child's story. (*CE, VIII, 29.9–12*)

But the form the story finally took reflects the author's observations, over a decade later, of his own children, Una and Julian, upon whom Violet and Peony are obviously modeled. His wife, Sophia, is undoubtedly also reflected in the loving mother who kept "a strain of poetry . . . alive amid the dusty realities of matrimony and motherhood" (*7.20–23*), but Hoeltje's suggestion that Mr. Lindsey is a humorously satirized self-portrait is more conjectural. Hoeltje attributes the closing moral about the dangers of benevolence to Hawthorne's earlier disillusionment with Brook Farm and interprets the snow image's demise as a triumph for the materialism that Hawthorne, as the head of a family, found himself forced to accept (231:276–77). The parallel between the fictional household and the author's is reinforced by Mr. Lindsey's closing call to Dora to bring in some towels; Dora was the name of the family servant who was with the Hawthornes throughout the Salem years (*CE, VIII, 398.5, 651*).

Available evidence suggests two equally probable dates of composition for the story in its final form: either the winter of 1848–49, in Salem, or the spring of 1850, just before or shortly after the move to Lenox. The earlier composition date is supported by several factors. A notebook entry made after March 16 but before September 17, 1849 suggests that the story had already been written by then: "The same children who make the little snow-girl shall plant dry sticks &c and they shall take root and grow; immortal flowers &c" (*CE, VIII, 287.3–5*). Julian Hawthorne reports "a dim impression" of "The Snow-Image" as read aloud to him during the fall of 1848 (223:I, 330). It is also possible that this was one of the "half dozen shorter" stories Hawthorne had originally intended for the projected collection, *Old Time Legends*, of which *The Scarlet Letter* was to have been the central tale. It could have been part of the manuscript he sent to Fields on January 15, 1850, which would explain Fields referring to it in August 1850 as having been "intended for another purpose" (*CE, XI, 384–86*). However, the long interval between this earlier composition date and the publication date makes 1850 more "probable," according to Crowley. He thinks "the chances are slight that Hawthorne would have withheld from publication for three years so polished a story" and concludes that Hawthorne more likely wrote it between finishing *The Scarlet Letter* and beginning *The House of Seven Gables*, that is, between February 3, 1850 and August 1850 (*CE, XI, 386*).

Although Tieck has been suggested as a possible but indirect influence on the mingling of the real and the imaginary in "The Snow-Image" (311), most readers recognize the concerns and characterizations in this story as typically Hawthornian, especially the implications about the plight of the imaginative artist in a materialistically oriented world. Leavis believes Hawthorne is exposing his own predicament as an artist in a bourgeois society (275:61–62); Hoffman concludes that "the unfeeling insensitivity of the hardware merchant" typifies the contemporaneous attitude toward art (232:170).

## Relationship with Other Hawthorne Works

"The Snow-Image" has most often been likened to "The Artist of the Beautiful" because both stories dramatize the conflict between imagination and common sense (275:61; 309:26–27). When the practical Mr. Lindsey overrides his wife's and children's acceptance of the snow maiden's true nature, with the result that she is brought into the house and melts away, he joins the Peter Hovenden family as a destroyer of the creations of the imagination (47:85; 232:170; 483.5:114; 309:150–51). The imaginative creation is again equated with the evanescent and the fragile, but, according to Baym, without the corrective irony of "The Artist of the Beautiful" and with the "same fastidious attitude toward actuality" that underlies "The Great Stone Face" (43:118–19).

Mr. Lindsey is also like the dull and unexciting John Brown of "Peter Goldthwaite's Treasure," except that Brown saves Peter from financial ruin while Mr. Lindsey is in no way redeemed (309:150–51); his good intentions serve but to illustrate how misguided and dangerous "men of benevolence" and their "philanthropic purposes" (*25.13–15*) can be. The earlier story, "Earth's Holocaust," (280:56) and the subsequent novel, *The Blithedale Romance*, make similar pronouncements about "do-gooders" and reformers.

Steward suggests that Priscillla of *The Blithedale Romance* and the snow image are both related to Hawthorne's sylphlike maidens, exemplified by the title character in "Sylph Etherege." In the novel, Priscilla makes her first appearance in a snowstorm, prompting the narrator to think of her as "some desolate kind of creature, doomed to wander about snow-storms" and tempted momentarily by the ruddiness of the window-panes "into a human dwelling." More specifically, she is later described as "this shadowy snow-maiden, who, precisely at the stroke of midnight, shall melt away . . . in a pool of ice-cold water" (455:lviii–lix). Axelsson points out two additional parallels between "The Snow-Image" and "Sylph Etherege": the characters of Mr. Lindsey and Mrs. Gosvenor, Sylph's guardian, are alike in their lack of imaginative sympathy, and both stories end with reality the victor in its contest with ideality (32:152, 169).

In "The Custom-House," which, according to one of the above esti-mates, was written about the same time as "The Snow-Image," Hawthorne uses snow images as symbolic of "the forms which fancy summons up." He thinks them capable of being converted into men and women if "a heart and sensibilities of human tenderness" are communicated to them. This is precisely what the children and the mother in "The Snow-Image" do, and what the father does not do (275:62). The mother's sewing has been interpreted as a related symbol for the achievements of the imagina-tion, an accomplishment similar to Hester's needlework in *The Scarlet Letter* (6:317). The novel's use of narrative centers of consciousness has also been linked to a similar technique in "The Snow-Image" (15).

This story's transformation theme, invariably associated with stories about art, is also found in "The Prophetic Pictures," "The Artist of the Beautiful," "Drowne's Wooden Image," "Feathertop," and *The Marble Faun* (391; 47:79, 84–85). The parallel that echoes the Pygmalion motif most closely is "Drowne's Wooden Image"; both stories portray a mys-terious kind of miracle in which a sculpture appears to come to life.

## Interpretations and Criticism

In the earliest available review of "The Snow-Image," which appeared in April 1852 in *Graham's Magazine* (XL, 443), E. P. Whipple calls it "one of those delicate creations which no imagination less ethereal and less shaping than Hawthorne's could body forth" (118:238). Over a century later, Waggoner addresses himself to essentially the same attri-butes ("the tender fancies, the whimsical sentiments" of an author who casts himself as a "man of sensibility"), but his assessment evokes less favorable connotations; he couples the story with "Little Daffydowndilly" as examples of a phase that "skirts perilously close to what today seems sentimentality" (500:3). In 1976, Baym's objections to the "sentimental, stereotypical" portrayals of the mother and the children confirm Wag-goner's misgivings, but her condemnation does not stop here. She sees "a crudely and carelessly conceived work" beneath the story's "delicately articulated surface"; her quarrel is primarily with the failure to acknowledge that the father, whose obtuseness is ridiculed, is the breadwinner who supports the protected world in which his family's imagination flourishes (43:118).

The otherwise negligible critical attention bestowed on "The Snow-Image" between 1852 and 1976 would appear to corroborate these doubts and complaints were it not for some notable exceptions. No less a figure than Henry James calls it "a little masterpiece" (241:51), while Leavis judges it to be "the finest" of the artist stories. She specifically objects to its being treated as "playful" or "a fairy tale," considering it the equivalent of James's stories about writers (275:61). Anderson, on the other hand, admires it as a vehicle for Hawthorne's judicious sense of human limitations. Plaudits are given for Mrs. Lindsey's characterization; caught between her alliance with her children and their creative imagination on one side and her allegiance to her husband and his practical good intentions on the other, she is both aware of her dilemma and conscious of her limitations (23:564–65). The mother's portrayal is also favorably reviewed in the one article devoted exclusively to this story, although Abel pays no attention to her moral dilemma, concentrating instead on her needlework as a symbol of feminine creativity. His principal concern is to explore the perception-reality theory that is at the heart of the situation; the story is "an allegory expressing the differences between the realities seen by an idealist and a materialist" (6:331).

In the light of the deluge of articles generated by some of the short stories, "The Snow-Image" remains a neglected stepchild, commented upon peripherally and condescendingly, if at all. It is seldom anthologized, rarely cited, and almost never praised. Yet among those who have somehow managed to discover it, it evokes strong responses and raises provocative and universal questions: How "real" are childhood fantasies? Can they survive in the "real" world? Can the differences between dreamers and pragmatists be resolved? Are good intentions necessarily good? These "real" issues underlie its fairy-tale aura, for in spite of Leavis' objections to that classification, "The Snow-Image" is a fairy tale in the best sense of the word. Its deceptively simple characters and instinctively recognizable Pygmalion motif mark it as a vehicle for the kind of fantasy that reveals archetypal truths.

# XLVI

## Sylph Etherege

(*Centenary Edition, Volume XI, The Snow-Image,* 111–19.)

### Publication History

"Sylph Etherege" was first published in the fall of 1837 in the *Token and Atlantic Souvenir* (pp. 22–32) dated 1838 with no attribution (*CE, XI, 429*). The editor, Samuel Goodrich, who stood to benefit from keeping Hawthorne anonymous, inserted four other pieces, but acknowledged only one, "Peter Goldthwaite's Treasure," as the work of the author of *Twice-told Tales*, which had been published the preceding spring. Based on Hawthorne's income from the 1837 *Token*, he should have been paid $1 a page, or $11 for "Sylph Etherege," but a 1975 reevaluation of Hawthorne's income from *The Token* theorizes, on the basis of Goodrich's notoriety for financial chicanery and the lack of an extant record of payment, that Hawthorne was never paid for his 1838 *Token* contributions (250). Of these five pieces, "Sylph Etherege" is the only one Hawthorne did not include in his 1842 edition of *Twice-told Tales*. It was not until 1851, when, at the author's request, editor James T. Fields had "got together all the Token articles for the new vol. of Tales," that it was included in Hawthorne's last collection, *The Snow-Image* (*CE, XI, 389–90*).

### Circumstances of Composition, Sources, and Influences

This story was probably written in the winter of 1837 in order to meet the standard June deadline for assembling *The Token*. It follows the pattern of the Gothic romance in the tradition of Ann Radcliffe and parallels her most famous novel, *The Mysteries of Udolpho*, in several specific ways: the heroine is a delicate maiden of acute sensibility who becomes the ward of a distantly related older woman; the unsuspecting guardian collaborates with the ominous yet attractive villain, and a miniature plays a key role in the story's development.

## Relationship with Other Hawthorne Works

"Sylph Etherege" offers early models for two of Hawthorne's recurrent character types, the villain with evil designs against innocent girls and the vulnerable, fragile heroine. The former includes Butler in *Fanshawe* and Walter Brome in "Alice Doane's Appeal"; the latter, Alice Vane in "Edward Randolph's Portrait" and Leslie Fay in "The Lily's Quest," but vestiges of Edgar Vaughan and Sylph Etherege are most notable in Matthew Maule of *The House of Seven Gables* and in his victim, Alice Pyncheon, who, like Sylph, escapes her persecutor by wasting away and finally dying. Westervelt and Priscilla form a similar twosome, especially in her physical frailty when she arrives at Blithedale (455:xlix–1, lviii–lix). The Gothic convention of a portrait with unusual powers links this story with two others written during the same period, "The Prophetic Pictures" and "Edward Randolph's Portrait," and with Colonel Pyncheon's portrait in *The House of Seven Gables*.

## Interpretations and Criticism

One passage in this story has occasionally been quoted to document Hawthorne's aesthetic theory. In describing his heroine's appearance, he writes, "it was like the original loveliness in a painter's fancy, from which the most finished picture is but an imperfect copy" (*112.2–4*). This statement has been interpreted as the author's acknowledgement of the importance of the Platonic ideal (47:44; 188:41).

The story as a whole, however, has been ignored. Hawthorne's rejection of it for the *Twice-told Tales* collection appears to have set the pattern for its subsequent critical history. Durr uses it as a contrast to the ironic counterpoise found in Hawthorne's successful stories; he brands it a failure on two counts, its "all of a piece" structure and its sentimentality (156:494–95). Other reviewers, and all anthologists, overlook it entirely. It is innocuous enough to avoid controversy and too insipid to warrant commendation. It fits best in the *Token* where its unabashed sentimentality made it indistinguishable from the annual's other pallid offerings.

# XLVII

# The Threefold Destiny: A Faery Legend

*(Centenary Edition, Volume IX, Twice-told Tales, 472–82.)*

## Publication History

"The Threefold Destiny" was first published in March 1838 in the *American Monthly Magazine* (XI, 228–35) under the pseudonym, Ashley Allen Royce. It was the last story the magazine's editor, Park Benjamin, published for Hawthorne, marking the end of a relationship fraught with disappointment for Hawthorne, who held Benjamin responsible for the breakup of his projected collection, *The Story Teller*. However, because Benjamin had written favorably about Hawthorne's writings in a review of the *Token* for 1836 (dated 1837), Hawthorne contributed two new pieces to Benjamin in 1838 (a biographical sketch of Thomas Green Fessenden in January, in addition to "The Threefold Destiny"), probably intending to mend relations further. Intentions notwithstanding, the review of *Twice-told Tales* that appeared in the same issue with "The Threefold Destiny" was ambivalent rather than laudatory, damning the author with faint praise and calling for American writers "of a hardier and more robust kind." As was the case with the segments of *The Story Teller* published by Benjamin, Hawthorne received no pay for his new contributions, not even in the intangible form of a propitious critique. The story was collected in the second edition of *Twice-told Tales* in 1842, appearing as the last selection in the second volume (*CE, IX, 509–10, 576*).

## Circumstances of Composition, Sources, and Influences

This story was probably written in December 1837 or January 1838 (84:25; *CE, VIII, 593*). The following undated notebook entry, very generally related to its theme, can be presumed to have been recorded on or soon after December 6, 1837, the date that appears three entries before it:

> A man will undergo great toil and hardship for ends that must be many years distant,—as wealth or fame,—but none for an end that may be close at hand,—as the joys of heaven. (*CE, VIII, 166.22–24*)

Part of another entry in the same group, seven items later is also incorporated in the story: "An ornament to be worn about the person of a lady—as a jewelled heart" (CE, VIII, 167.14–15). This becomes the token by which Ralph Cranfield is to recognize his true love. An earlier note, entered between August 22 and October 7, 1837, parallels the closing moral, although the plot is changed significantly and Faith Egerton does not join her young man in his search:

> A young man and girl meet together, each in search of a person to be known by some particular sign. They watch and wait a great while for that person to pass. At last some casual circumstance discloses that each is the one that the other is waiting for. Moral, —that what we need for our happiness is often close at hand, if we knew but how to seek for it. (CE, VIII, 153.9–15)

One analogue for this story is established by the author in its opening paragraph. The tale is, he says, "an allegory, such as the writers of the last century would have expressed in the shape of an eastern tale," but he has set it among "New England personages and scenery" in an endeavor "to give a more life-like warmth than could be infused into those fanciful productions" (472.7–14). The eighteenth-century Eastern tale it resembles most is Samuel Johnson's *Rasselas*, because the paramount idea in both works is the foolishness of impossible goals and far-flung searches and the need to compromise to find fulfillment (188:75–78).

A more subtly indicated, yet undeniably evident, source for the mode and technique of "The Threefold Destiny" is Spenser's *Faerie Queene*. Jones presents a detailed analysis of the Spenserian basis, especially as openly displayed in the story's first paragraph, "literally a miniature critical preface" in which Hawthorne outlines his intentions of following "the spirit and mechanism of the faery legend" (472.3–4), and in its second paragraph, which is a "fictional presentation of the journey-to-faery-land theme" (247:108–09).

## Relationship with Other Hawthorne Works

In starting with a moral idea for an allegory and working out its substantiation, "The Threefold Destiny" follows the same pattern as "The Birthmark" and "Ethan Brand" and is closely associated with those stories that have analogues in the Eastern tale, such as "The Lily's Quest," "David Swan," and "Fancy's Show Box" (149:70).

It has also been called a companion piece to "The Ambitious Guest" because its protagonist, like the title character in the earlier story, "from his youth, felt himself marked out for a high destiny" (*473.17–18*). Stein interprets both stories as versions of the Faustian theme of overweening ambition, but deems them experiments with limited dramatic impact because they result in moral platitudes rather than philosophical truths (447:72–73). A later, more effective Faust-oriented story, "Ethan Brand," repeats a motif found in "The Threefold Destiny"; the worldwide search for both Cranfield and Brand ends where it began, in the place of their birth and boyhood, although with decidedly different climaxes.

Stewart points out the similarity between Faith Egerton in this story and the Faith in "Young Goodman Brown," the nameless girl in "David Swan," and Eve in "The New Adam and Eve." While all are "very lightly sketched," they display the same "cheerfulness, prettiness, and . . . simple-minded domesticity" as Susan in "The Village Uncle," the proto-type who develops into Phoebe of *The House of Seven Gables* and Hilda of *The Marble Faun* (455:lvi).

## Interpretations and Criticism

"The Threefold Destiny" has been used to demonstrate Hawthorne's concept of allegory; that is, the theory that the moral content of a story and not its symbolic mode makes it an allegory (188.75). In another context, it illustrates the author's celebration of the "common highway of life" at this point in his career (43:55). Certainly no better example of the glorifica-tion of the everyday norm can be found than Cranfield's willingness to accept the task of schoolmaster in place of his earlier dreams of being a king, a general, or a prophet.

Other than being useful for such specialized purposes, this story has a current critical rating which is revealed, indirectly but accurately, in the historical commentary for *Twice-told Tales.* Crowley, in an attempt to explain the reasons behind Park Benjamin's negative review of the 1837 edition, attributes part of his dissatisfaction as stemming from "having been given nothing more substantial" than "The Threefold Destiny" for publication in his magazine (*CE, IX, 509, n.57*). This lightweight quality has elicited more comment than any other feature of this story. One critic calls the tale a "pat, little moralized legend" (188:75); another, a "feeble" attempt at balancing lifelike warmth and allegory (149:7).

In the face of the insignificance generally accorded the story, Henry James's praise of "The Threefold Destiny" as evincing "in a degree dis-tinctly appreciable . . . an original element in literature" is surprising (241:44). Perhaps James was responding to a theme that appealed to him, one that he would eventually incorporate in his own short story,

"The Beast in the Jungle." James's John Marcher, like Cranfield, searches long and far for the sign that will signal his high destiny. Hawthorne develops his plot so that in the end, "the wild dreamer was awake at last" (*481.33*). James's "wild dreamer" does not "awake" until his "Faith," May Bartram, is dead and no compromise is possible. In spite of its trite moral and conventional happy ending, "The Threefold Destiny" may have fulfilled its destiny by helping to shape one of James's best "unlived life" stories.

# XLVIII

## The Village Uncle:
## An Imaginary Retrospect

*(Centenary Edition, Volume IX, Twice-told Tales, 310–23.)*

### Publication History

This story was first published as "The Mermaid: A Reverie" in 1835 with no attribution (*CE, IX, 572*). The *Token*'s editor, Samuel Goodrich, also inserted "The Haunted Mind" and "Alice Doane's Appeal" in the same annual gift book without any signatures (*CE, IX, 493*). A note from Goodrich establishes $46 as the price paid by Charles Bowen, the publisher, for three pieces in the following year's *Token* (*CE, IX, 497*). Based on this figure, the approximate average would have been $1 per page, and the story should have netted Hawthorne $15.

Hawthorne added this work in the second volume of the second edition of *Twice-told Tales* in 1842 with several noteworthy changes. He retitled it, replaced Chatham harbor with Boston harbor, omitted one reference to the mermaid's lost fins and another to her sister's name, Hannah, and deleted the following passage::

> Oh, Susan the sugar heart you gave me, and the old rhyme—
> 'When this you see, remember me'—scratched on it with the point of
> your scissors! Inscriptions on marble have been sooner forgotten,
> than those words shall be on that frail heart. (*CE, IX, 628*)

The reason for these changes and who was responsible for them—Hawthorne's sister Elizabeth, his fiancée, Sophia Peabody, or Hawthorne himself—remains conjectural. (See source discussion, below.)

### Circumstances of Composition, Sources, and Influences

"The Village Uncle" was probably written in the fall or winter of 1833–34 after Hawthorne's return from one of the summer trips he was accustomed to taking each year while he was living with his mother and sisters in Salem between 1825 and 1838. According to his sister Elizabeth, the story is based on "a sojourn of two or three weeks at Swampscott" in 1833 (223:I, 127–28). Samuel Adams Drake, a folklorist writing in 1884, also places the scene at this typical New England fishing village situated along the hard sand-beaches and between the rocky headlands of Nahant Bay, Massachusetts (154:102–104).

Elizabeth Hawthorne establishes a biographical prototype for Susan in a shopgirl Hawthorne met during his Swampscott stay. A newly discovered manuscript, originally adapted and somewhat revised by Julian Hawthorne in his parents' biography, reads:

> Susan kept a little shop—he said she was one of [the] "resident aristocracy" of the place. She gave him a pink sugar heart, and I suppose he gave her something of equal value. He ate the heart. Her father was a fisherman, and he met him afterwards in Salem, selling his fish, but the man did not speak to him. . . . Susan's sister lived at John Forrester's, and so the affair became known. He never would tell us her name. He called her The Mermaid. He said she was pretty, but her great charm was what the French term *espieglerie*. (89:12)

Hawthorne's story supports his sister's statement, as does the deleted passage about the sugar heart. The incident has been called Hawthorne's "first serious love affair" (89:14); a literal reading of one passage in the mermaid's description certainly affirms such a hypothesis:

> How was it, Susan, that you talked and acted so carelessly, yet always for the best, doing whatever was right in your own eyes, and never once doing wrong in mine, nor shocked a taste that had been morbidly sensitive till now? (*CE, IX, 316*)

The revised version of the story, coming as it does near the end of Hawthorne's long engagement to Sophia and just months before their wedding, reinforces such a reading, although one reader theorizes that "if the matter had been a touchy one it presumably would have been suppressed altogether" (*CE, IX, 544*). Another reader believes that the change of title was due to an artistic shift in focus (284:206–07).

The possibility exists of a relationship between the Susan in this story and Hawthorne's early story "Susan Grey," part of the *Seven Tales of My Native Land* which he burned after becoming exasperated at his inability to get them published (11:121–26). His sister remembered the stories as being about witchcraft and the sea; they had as their motto "We are seven," from Wordsworth's poem (272:134). "The Village Uncle" is set in a sea-fishing village and has a Wordsworthian air about it; however, since the *Seven Tales* project was abandoned in 1822, more than ten years earlier, "The Village Uncle" could only have incorporated echoes of his former "Susan" story.

The well-established source of Spenser's *Faerie Queene* is credited with contributing the "journey-to-faery-land" motif on which the imaginary retrospect is based (247:111–12). The dream conception in the story has been traced to a similar technique used in one of Charles Lamb's essays, "Dream Children" (487:152–54). Contemporaneous reviewers often cited Hawthorne's likeness to Lamb (178:76, 92, 113), and the sketchlike nature of "The Village Uncle," its mix of humor and pathos, and its gently ironic rhetoric are very much in the style of the celebrated essayist. On August 26, 1833, Hawthorne did withdraw a volume of Lamb's *Elia* essays from the Salem Atheneum (259:54), and a striking parallel does exist in the descriptions, in both pieces, of the persona's final failing vision of the limitations of what might have been (487: 152–54).

Oral folklore tradition, transmitted to Hawthorne during his Swampscott stay, is probably the principal source for the sailors' yarns and sea lore Hawthorne attributes to the two uncles in the story (232:102–04; 154:104). When the narrator inherits his predecessor's role as village storyteller, he includes another major strand of native tradition also derived from raw folk materials, a local spectral legend of "the dripping corpse" of a drowned young man seen on the pathway to his bride's dwelling (148:152).

## Relationship with Other Hawthorne Works

Susan is in many ways a prototype for Phoebe in *The House of Seven Gables*. Like her, Susan is "a frank, simple, kindhearted, sensible, and mirthful girl" who works in a shop selling "gingerbread men and horses, picture-books and ballads, small fish-hooks, pins, needles, sugar-plums and brass thimbles (*CE, IX, 316*). Even Phoebe's freckles belonged originally to Hawthorne's "mermaid" (455:lxvii). Stewart classifies both Susan and Phoebe as belonging to the "wholesome New England" type of Hawthorne heroine, one who is cheerful, pretty, self-reliant, and essentially domestic. Others include Ellen Langton in *Fanshawe*, the girl in "David Swan," Faith in "Young Goodman Brown" and in "The Threefold Destiny," Eve in "The New Adam and Eve," and, to a degree, Hilda in *The Marble Faun* (455:lvi).

The identification of Susan with Phoebe and Hilda can be extended to encompass their respective roles as women who redeem their men, thus equating the village uncle with Holgrave and Kenyon (47:159–70). The village uncle has also been linked to the lonely and frustrated Oberon of *The Story Teller*, but the later story presents an alternative to the artist's life (47:136–47).

This story demonstrates other affinities with several pieces Hawthorne wrote later in his career. It is, like "The Old Apple Dealer," a study in the "moral picturesque" (487:150), and it shares a concern for balance between illusion and reality evidenced in 1851 in "The Snow-Image" and in 1852 in "Feathertop" (6:52). But the sketch "Footprints on the Sea-Shore" (*CE, IX, 451–62*), published in 1838 and based primarily on a notebook entry dated October 16, 1837 (*CE, VIII, 162–65*), bears the closest relationship. Although written at least four years after "The Village Uncle," it too is set in Swampscott, recapitulating a solitary day-long ramble on one of the beaches that skirt the town and repeating many of the images in the earlier story (284:209–11).

## Interpretations and Criticism

The appraisals extended to "The Village Uncle" are often colored by the critics' expectations. A folklore scholar calls it Hawthorne's "principal failure in this line" (232:102); an essay-oriented reader who is partial to realistic detail commends its "vivid concreteness" (487:154). Almost all critics see it as a commentary on the life of the artist, but considerable disagreement exists as to the nature of the commentary. One reader accepts the traditional interpretation that the village uncle represents the happier choice of an unspectacular but warm family life over the isolated and more difficult life of the artist and fits it into a pattern of concessions in Hawthorne's early career to what he presumed were his readers' views on the limitations of art and the imagination (43:61). Two readers detect a counterstatement underlying this explicit layer of meaning, one flatly denying its censure of the artistic life and reading it as a nostalgic reverie of yearning for lost possibilities (215), while another believes the life of the imagination has been happily fused with the life of everyday reality and that the village uncle represents the Transcendental ideal of the artist whose creativity finds fulfillment in life itself (284).

This story is little known even among readers who consider themselves familiar with Hawthorne's works. It reflects the conventional views that Hawthorne occasionally adopted in his writings, but Hawthorne's appeal is strongest when he ventures away from the conventional. The village uncle may have been content with the life he chose, but his story brings little satisfaction to today's readers, except perhaps as a revelation of what the young man, Hawthorne, may have thought of as the options open to him—domestic happiness or the life of a writer.

# XLIX

## The Vision of the Fountain

(*Centenary Edition, Volume IX, Twice-told Tales,* 213–19.)

### Publication History

According to the Centenary Edition, this story was first published in August 1835 in the *New-England Magazine* (IX, 99–104) as the work of the author of "The Gray Champion" (*CE, IX, 570*). However, Gross refers to an earlier version, published in the *New-England Magazine* for August 1834; this text opens with two paragraphs that were dropped when the story appeared in the August 1835 issue. The Centenary Edition does not include the two paragraphs nor does it acknowledge Gross's finding (211:104). For this story, as for the other pieces that were intended as part of *The Story Teller*, Hawthorne "got little or nothing as pay" (11:133; see publication history of "The Devil in Manuscript"). He included "The Vision," as it appeared in the 1835 magazine, in the 1837 *Twice-told Tales*. Although the rationale behind Hawthorne's choices for his first collection is still open to interpretation (120; 149:80; 43:69–71), today's critics would be unanimous in choosing "The Vision of the Fountain" as one of the stories least qualified to represent his artistry.

### Circumstances of Composition, Sources, and Influences

This story was written during the fall and winter of 1832–33 or 1833–34, when Hawthorne was working on *The Story Teller*. (See circumstances of composition for "Passages from a Relinquished Work.") Spenser's *Faerie Queene* (247:111–12), German romantic irony (305:285–86), and the sentimental gift-book fiction popular in the nineteenth century (211) have all been credited with influencing Hawthorne in the conception of this tale.

### Relationship with Other Hawthorne Works

The intermingling of actuality and fantasy, which marks almost all of the narratives from *The Story Teller* (43:47), is central to "The Vision of the Fountain," an account by and about a fifteen-year-old youth whose daydreams result in his mistaking the daughter of a country squire for the Naiad of a freshwater spring. This same element links the maiden of the fountain to Susan in "The Village Uncle" because the practical but idealized Susan finds a complement in the mythologized spirit who is also described as "a careful housewife" keeping her fountain clean and clear of debris (247:111–12). Hawthorne's use of mirror images in these two stories, and in a multitude of others, is related to the same dichotomy; Cowley interprets them as symbolic bridges between the inner and outer world (110).

"Monsieur du Miroir," the sketch devoted exclusively to the exploitation of the mirror image, is like "The Vision of the Fountain" in another way as well. Both follow a pattern of deliberate exaggeration and excessive expression. They, and such sketches as "P's Correspondence" and "A Virtuoso's Collection," appear to be exercises in ingenuity for its own sake. "Monsieur du Miroir" is also like "The Vision of the Fountain" in its self-mocking irony, an effect shared by "Graves and Goblins" and "Fragments from the Journal of a Solitary Man" (487:156–59).

## Interpretations and Criticism

In the most significant interpretation this story has received, Gross convincingly demonstrates that "The Vision of the Fountain" is a parody of the gift-book tale rather than an insipid example of the genre, as had been generally conceded. Hawthorne's satiric intentions have been overlooked because of the missing *Story Teller* frame and the deletion of the story's original first two paragraphs. When the story is seen as a part of the repertoire of a wandering young storyteller given to "an incorrigible levity of spirits" and when it is viewed as a tale intended for an audience of gift-book enthusiasts, the satiric possibilities become clear. The story verifies this audience through the narrator's direct references to the "sweet readers," "sweet ladies," and "sweet maids" he is addressing, while the target is illuminated by the extravagant sentiments phrased in gift-book jargon that he uses throughout the story, but most flagrantly in the two subsequently deleted paragraphs (211).

Those critics who interpret "The Vision" as romantic irony agree; others do not. Vance believes that the comic effect derives from a combination of humorous exaggeration and detachment achieved by taking two contradictory attitudes at the same time (487:159). His reading is similar to one by Marks, who contends that by presenting a carefully motivated possibility that the vision might be altogether the materialization of the young man's imagination, Hawthorne admits the charm of the thing that is contrary to what he asserts, even as he ridicules it (305:286). On the other hand, Baym finds "The Vision" an example of one of Hawthorne's weakest pieces, and Doubleday ignores it altogether in a volume devoted entirely to the critical study of the tales Hawthorne wrote between 1825 and 1838 (149).

When Hawthorne included this story in his first collection, he may have had several practical reasons for choosing it (120; 149:80; 43:69–71), but the fact that he omitted the original opening paragraphs appears to confirm his intention to eliminate its satiric edge. Without its ironic implications, it would be chosen by most readers today as one of the stories in *Twice-told Tales* least qualified to represent Hawthorne's artistry.

# L

# Wakefield

*(Centenary Edition, Volume IX, Twice-told Tales, 130–40.)*

## Publication History

This story was first published in May 1835 in the *New-England Magazine* (VIII, 341–47) as the work of the author of "The Gray Champion," a story that had appeared in the same journal the preceding January (*CE, IX, 569*). These two, and fifteen other pieces published in the *New-England Magazine* under Park Benjamin's editorship in 1834 and 1835, were a part of *The Story Teller*, a projected work that netted Hawthorne "little or nothing as pay." (See publication history of "The Devil in Manuscript.") Hawthorne included "Wakefield" in his first collection, the 1837 *Twice-told Tales*, placing it between "Little Annie's Rambles" and "A Rill from the Town Pump" for dramatic, if obvious, contrast (120).

## Circumstances of Composition, Sources, and Influences

As a part of *The Story Teller*, this story was probably written in the fall and winter of 1832–33 or 1833–34, although it fits awkwardly into Hawthorne's announced plan for the collection. The itinerant novelist was supposed to tell his stories before an audience, but the narrator of "Wakefield" repeatedly addresses his audience as "readers"; his tales were supposed to suit and reflect his listeners throughout the New England countryside, but "Wakefield" is set in London. It appears likely that this was one of the pieces first written as a separate unit and then incorporated into *The Story Teller* format (11:144). Consequently, "Wakefield" could have been written anytime between Hawthorne's return to Salem after graduation from Bowdoin College in 1825 and his submission of *The Story Teller* manuscript in 1834.

Hawthorne acknowledges the source for "Wakefield" in the opening words of the story: "In some old magazine or newspaper, I recollect a story. . . ." The outline, as he reviews it in the first paragraph of the piece, follows an account in William King's *Political and Literary Anecdotes of his Own Times* (1818) of an acquaintance named Howe who left his wife one morning after seven or eight years of marriage on the pretext of a business trip, not to return for seventeen years. According to King, "After he returned home, he never would confess, even to his most intimate friends, what was the real cause of such a singular conduct; apparently there was none" (as cited in 365). Hawthorne, who probably read King's anecdote in a periodical reprint, changes some details, omits others, but retains the emphasis on the husband's apparent lack of motivation. Howe changed his name, donned a black wig, and took a room in another part of London. Ten years later he made the acquaintance of his wife's neighbor and, dining with him once or twice a week, was able to look into his wife's room. During the last seven years of his self-imposed exile, he attended St. James Church every Sunday, sitting where he could see his wife without being seen himself (511:364–65). Hawthorne's Wakefield departs in the "dusk of an October evening" and finds an apartment "in the next street to his own," enabling him to ascertain his wife's subsequent illness and recovery. He buys a red wig, but Hawthorne does not allow him the social amenities of dining with a friend or attending church services. Instead, Hawthorne marks the tenth year of the separation by devising an anonymous face-to-face encounter with Mrs. Wakefield in a crowded street.

The outcast is a pervasive enough figure in Hawthorne's canon to explain why Dr. King's anecdote would appeal to him, but his decision to use it as a story germ may also have been influenced by two earlier and very popular pieces of American fiction. Both Washington Irving's "Rip Van Winkle" (1819) and William Austin's "Peter Rugg, the Missing Man" (1824) are stories about men who leave their places in the world (149:151). Some aspects of "Wakefield" suggest Hawthorne may have had them in mind. The seventeen-year absence in the anecdote becomes a twenty-year exile in keeping with Rip Van Winkle's sojourn. The closing moral seems more applicable to Peter Rugg, who never does return to his place in the universe, than to Wakefield, who, objectively at least, does.

## Relationship with Other Hawthorne Works

"Wakefield" has become, warranted or not (149:154), the source for the most quoted statement by Hawthorne on his most dominant theme: the horror of isolating oneself from humanity. The story closes with this moral:

> Amid the seeming confusion of our mysterious world, individuals
> are so nicely adjusted to a system, and systems to one another, and to

a whole, that, by stepping aside for a moment, a man exposes himself to a fearful risk of losing his place forever. Like Wakefield, he may become, as it were, the Outcast of the Universe. (*CE, IX, 140*)

This statement has been applied most often to "Ethan Brand" and to Chillingworth of *The Scarlet Letter* (232:186; 255:155–56; 315:287; 412:10), but it has also been used on such other "outcast" characters as Richard Digby of "The Man of Adamant," Mr. Hooper of "The Minister's Black Veil," and Roderick Elliston of "Egotism." A more limited subclassification, based on why a character isolates himself, groups Wakefield, because of his passive withdrawal, with Hepzibah Pyncheon of *The House of Seven Gables*, the title characters in "The White Old Maid" and "Old Esther Dudley," and the bridegrooms in "The Wedding Knell" and "The Shaker Bridal" (32:45–55).

Another kind of parallel links Wakefield to the narrator of "Night Sketches" (*CE, IX, 426–32*). Each takes a walk on a rainy night. Wakefield, who finds himself standing, chilled and wet, outside his home where he had earlier discerned a warm fire on the hearth, decides to go in and end his twenty-year exile. Because the narrator of "Night Sketches" expresses some of the primal doubts that trouble him, his experience offers the reader an insight into what might have prompted Wakefield's decision to return home at that unpremeditated moment. Like Wakefield, the narrator contrasts the "drear obscurity and chill discomfort" outside with the "warmth and cheerfulness" of his deserted fireside, but he adds, "I look upward, and discern no sky, not even an unfathomable void but only a black, impenetrable nothingness, as though heaven and all its lights were blotted from the universe" (*427.29–33*). In what the twentieth century would call existential terms, the narrator illuminates Wakefield's sudden and overpowering impulse to reassert his place in the universe.

Wakefield embodies another characteristic motif that is sometimes interwoven with the isolation theme (as does Chillingworth), that of the detached observer. The sketch, "Sights from a Steeple" (*CE, IX, 191–98*), entertains the prospect of being "a spiritualized Paul Pry" as "the most desirable mode of existence." He would enjoy "hovering invisible round man and woman, witnessing their deeds, searching into their hearts, borrowing brightness from their felicity, and shade from their sorrow, and retaining no emotion peculiar to himself" (*192.27–31*). Hawthorne makes Wakefield a living example of the dangers of such an undertaking (280:43). Holgrave of *The House of Seven Gables* and Kenyon of *The Marble Faun* are also detached observers, but Hawthorne does not condemn them to Wakefield's "social limbo" (412:10). Coverdale of *The*

*Blithedale Romance* is the most developed of this group; he is also the closest to Wakefield in his incapacity for moral growth and critical failure of personality (337). Holgrave, Kenyon, and Coverdale are all artist figures who, like the painter in "The Prophetic Pictures," are keen observers; Wakefield shares their cold aloofness but not their penetrating insights (455:lxi–lxiii). One reader observes that "Hawthorne denies almost too firmly that Wakefield is an artist; we sense the implication that *therefore* does his strange desertion of his wife seem most paradoxical" (47:178). Another view of Wakefield, as "Yankee Peddler become Babbitt," inadvertently confirms the antiartist relationship while it sets him up as a debased Dominicus Pike (from "Mr. Higginbotham's Catastrophe") whose sense of humor has degenerated into a crafty smile and a cruel practical joke (412:11).

This story has been linked with "Fancy's Show Box" for several reasons. Both pieces embody sets of speculative moral ideas (149:151), an attribute that leads one reader to classify them, with eight others, as works that are essentially essays and have been mislabeled "short stories" (510). Both works have also been used as evidence of Hawthorne's belief in free will (177), but not without dissenters. (See interpretations, below.)

Two studies have credited "Wakefield" with being a significant precursor to the methods Hawthorne uses in *The Scarlet Letter* (15; 483). The sequence of highlighted episodes that tell the story over its twenty-year span is an example in miniature of the technique Hawthorne incorporates into all his longer narratives (483:307).

## Interpretations and Criticism

In a critical age that has come to revere Kafka, the Kafka-like ambience of "Wakefield" has garnered it kudos from as impressive an international figure as Jorge Luis Borges (57:47–65). Deeming "Wakefield" superior to *The Scarlet Letter*, Borges notes the Kafkaesque "profound *triviality*" that marks Hawthorne's protagonist and his "world of enigmatic punishments and indecipherable sins." Borges says that " 'Wakefield' prefigures Kafka, but Kafka modifies and refines the reading of 'Wakefield' " (57: 56–57). Others have also suggested that Hawthorne be read like Kafka (412:7), but for most knowledgeable readers, Hawthorne's reliance on alternative explanations makes him radically different (512:112). In the case of "Wakefield," however, Hawthorne does not follow his usual pattern of offering a supernatural theory to contrast with a natural one; here, as in Kafka's surrealist perspective, the action is accepted and presented as a given entity. The reader is sure of what happens. What he is not sure of is why.

The "why" of the situation is what attracted Hawthorne to the anecdote in the first place. He wanted to imagine why the husband left; the story's interpreters have focused on why he returns—and what it all signifies. One extended analysis contends that Wakefield is psychologically incapable of making a decisive move to return home and, therefore, his return has to be accidental. Hawthorne makes it the result of an unexpected rainshower. Caught in the "iron tissue of necessity" (*136–37*), Wakefield has, in this reading, no volition whatsoever (412:10). Another reader agrees: Wakefield's unthinking involvement illustrates that life, far from being subject to the will, is a matter of obscurity and compulsion (47:26–27). On the other hand, one commentator maintains that Hawthorne "unfailingly reserved to man the initial moral choice" and that the "nigh-unalterable consequences" that follow are predicated on the initial conception, which is an act of free will. For him, Wakefield's return home exemplifies free will (177:976). For others, Wakefield has served to illustrate the danger of not asserting one's will (52:61); the need of a place within the community for individual fulfillment (255:159); the meaningless detachment that results when basic social ties are cut (343); the workings of the Chain of Being that impelled Wakefield to return to his assigned place in nature (313); and, in a discussion that suggests readers can identify more easily with Wakefield's indecision than with Hawthorne's more willful characters, the interplay of choice and necessity (149:154).

Even the ordinarily simple task of genre identification becomes complicated in "Wakefield." A leading Hawthorne scholar asks, "Is 'Wakefield' a sketch or a story?" (500:253) His colleagues reply in a variety of ways. Because a plot does evolve, the majority accept "Wakefield" as a tale. One reader accuses Hawthorne of not writing it, but of writing about it, thereby treating a tale as a sketch (203:76). Another distinguishes between the sketch (which involves the author and the reader) and the story (which involves the character, Wakefield), making the work a composite of the two (127:60). An anthology of short fiction, based on form, suggests through a series of questions that "Wakefield" is another kind of composite, a cross between a fable and a tale (197:60–61). Hawthorne's merger of forms has resulted, in another instance, in a newly coined genre, the "illustrated idea," a structure composed of an essaylike statement of concept followed by a dramatized illustration. This reader contends that since Hawthorne never intended "Wakefield" to be a short story, he should not be criticized "for not doing well what he never intended to do in the first place" (510).

Another structural aspect of the story that has aroused comment is the reunion scene—or rather, its omission. Critics are agreed that the climax occurs during the confrontation scene in the London crowd, but they do not all agree that Hawthorne was justified in not following Wakefield across the threshold of his home at the end. One reader thinks that Hawthorne fails "to make Wakefield's return to his wife convincing" (149:154); another complains about "a failure of development" (500:75). Others approve, accepting Hawthorne's omission as a matter of course because Wakefield's homecoming is not central to the moral purpose (511:365), and calling such a projected scene "gratuitous" (412:10).

The invariably contentious issue of ironic intent is also present in "Wakefield." Hawthorne's comment, "The happy event—supposing it to be such" (*140.4*), is a case in point. Some have read the passage literally, assuming that Hawthorne meant Wakefield's return to be the end of his isolation (313:285; 177:976); some have interpreted his attitude as sincerely noncommittal (511:365; 149:154); but some have detected a deliberate irony in the author's words, a sardonic echo to his earlier exclamation, "Stay, Wakefield! Would you go to the sole home that is left you? Then step into your grave" (32:55; 181:424; 412). Hawthorne's reference to Wakefield as "the Outcast of the Universe" in the closing words of the story substantiates the ironic readings. That Hawthorne's protagonists can be isolated while apparently participating in the human community is confirmed by the examples of "Young Goodman Brown" and Gervayse Hastings in "The Christmas Banquet."

Irony has also been identified in the "mock-heroic description of Wakefield's 'escape' " (156:490) and as a basic element in Wakefield's ego-centered appraisal of his situation (412:8). Wakefield does not realize his insignificance. Hawthorne highlights it: "It is perilous to make a chasm in human affections; not that they gape so long and wide—but so quickly close again!" (*133:30–32*).

The most subtle ironic implications are found in the conventions associated with statements of moral purpose. Hawthorne's introductory promise to deliver "a pervading spirit and a moral . . . done up neatly, and condensed into the final sentence" becomes suspect and invites an ironic reading when he adds "even should we fail to find them" (*131.11–13*). Hawthorne deals with his stated morals ironically in the romances (468:18); and in at least one other piece, "Night Sketches," the moral has been viewed as having nothing to do with the tale itself (483.5:53). In "Wakefield" Hawthorne delivers his moral neatly done up in the final sentence as promised even though, as he had anticipated might happen, he has failed to find it in the actual story. The husband in the newspaper account becomes "a loving spouse till death" (*130.21*), not "the Outcast of the

Universe" that Wakefield is in the closing moral. Is Hawthorne satirizing romantic fiction that distorts actuality for its own ends? Is he poking fun at himself for using a situation that fascinated him even when it only problematically illustrated the moral he saw inherent in it? The possibility that he may be doing both adds another interpretative dimension to "Wakefield."

Hawthorne's own years as a semirecluse have been alluded to as a factor in the author's protrayal of Wakefield's folly (111). A psychoanalytic reading equates Wakefield's schizoid tendencies with Hawthorne as well (30). Another article identifies Hawthorne with the narrator instead; it suggests that the technique of detached observation that Hawthorne uses reinforces that trait in Wakefield's portrayal and reveals it as one of the author's feared propensities (330). (This reader engages in a pedagogically sound exercise; he compares "Wakefield" with Melville's "Bartleby the Scrivener" to highlight some of the differences between Hawthorne and Melville.)

"Wakefield" has been credited with being a likely influence in Henry James's creation of John Marcher in "The Beast in the Jungle" and of Lambert Strether in *The Ambassadors* (337), and a possible influence in Eudora Welty's development of character and theme in "Old Mr. Marblehead" (479).

Prominent Hawthorne scholars have expressed serious reservations about "Wakefield"; it has been termed "a stunt" that does not represent Hawthorne at his best (149:151–52) and "a failure of creative energy" that results in "too great a burden of thought for so slight a framework" (500:98). In spite of these respected negative appraisals, readers continue to respond to it. One avid "Wakefield" admirer explains Hawthorne's modernity by calling Hawthorne's works "an ur-form of modern fiction" (412:7). The "crafty nincompoop" and his apprehensive narrator provide a touchstone for man's primal fear that his tenuously held place in the universe may be lost too. Perhaps it is at this mythic level that the ultimate appeal of "Wakefield" lies.

# LI

# The Wedding Knell

(*Centenary Edition, Volume IX, Twice-told Tales,* 27–36.)

## Publication History

"The Wedding Knell" was first published in 1835 in the *Token and Atlantic Souvenir* (pp. 113–24) dated 1836 as the work of the author of "Sights from a Steeple," a sketch published four years earlier in the same yearbook (*CE, IX, 565*). "The Minister's Black Veil" and "The May-Pole of Merry Mount" also appeared in the 1836 *Token*, a trio for which Hawthorne was paid $46 (*CE, IX, 495–97*). Based on this figure, "The Wedding Knell" netted Hawthorne $19. Hawthorne included this story in the 1837 *Twice-told Tales*. Its placement as the third selection in his first collection has been interpreted as a deliberate opening rhetorical device to present his works to the reading public in a way that would appeal to what he thought they wanted (43:72–74). The original manuscript, now in the Berg Collection, New York Public Library, reveals no significant editorial revisions (213) and was used as copy text for the Centenary Edition (*CE, IX, 546, 565*).

## Circumstances of Composition, Sources, and Influences

The publication of "The Wedding Knell" in Samuel Goodrich's annual the year after Hawthorne gave Goodrich his *Story Teller* manuscript makes this story another possible *Story Teller* fragment. (See publication history of "The Devil in Manuscript.") Such a conjecture is reinforced by Elizabeth Peabody's statement that Goodrich said he would buy some of the *Story Teller* stories for the *Token* (106:32) and by the fact that no letters (written between May 31, 1831 and September 23, 1836) from Goodrich asking Hawthorne for contributions have been found (*CE, IX, 494–96*). As a part of *The Story Teller*, "The Wedding Knell" would have been written in the fall and winter of 1832–33 or 1833–34; as an independent story, it might have been written anytime from his Bowdoin graduation in 1825 to the spring of 1835 when the 1836 *Token* was assembled to be ready for the 1835 Christmas market.

The two entries in *The American Notebooks* related to "The Wedding

Knell" do not help in establishing a composition date because the first appears about the time the story was published, between September 7 and October 25, 1835, and the second, still later, after October 25, 1836. Both seem to be only tangentially related to the story. The earlier one echoes the striking contrast between the aged widow's gaily attired bridal party and the appearance of the shrouded groom amidst a funeral procession. The second one refers more specifically to the same paradoxical conjunction:

> The world is so sad and solemn, that things meant in jest are liable, by an overpowering influence, to become dreadful earnest,— gaily dressed fantasies turning to ghostly and black-clad images of themselves. (*CE, VIII, 11.1–4*)

> Would it not be wiser for people to rejoice at all that they now sorrow for, and *vice versa*? To put on bridal garments at funerals, and mourning at weddings? For their friends to condole with them when they attained riches and honor, as only so much care added? (*CE, VIII, 24.8–12*)

The other two stories published in the same *Token* offer illustrations of the same concepts. "The May-Pole of Merry Mount" contrasts the gay "fantasies" of the Merry Mounters with the "black-clad images" of the Puritans, and "The Minister's Black Veil" conjoins funereal and bridal elements when Mr. Hooper performs a wedding ceremony while wearing his black veil. In fact, the authorial voice in the latter points out the similarity: "If ever another wedding were so dismal, it was that famous one, where they tolled the wedding knell" (*CE, IX, 43*).

Another story, "The Village Uncle," published the year before, has been proposed as an influence in suggesting the bride–shroud paradox (232:104). In it, the narrator briefly recounts a local spectral legend of a drowned bridegroom whose corpse had been washed up onto the pathway leading to his bride's dwelling.

But Hawthorne did not have to search out folklore for this motif; it was readily available to him as one of the Gothic traditions of the novel of terror in which the sepulchral chamber is often used as a meeting place for betrothed lovers. Lundblad finds a specific source for Hawthorne's bridegroom's macabre injunction: "Come, my bride! . . . Let us be married; and then to our coffins" (*34.14–16*). The summons is strikingly similar to the one whispered by the ghostly horseman in Burger's ballad, *Lenore*. Hawthorne's notebook reveals that he translated *Lenore* from the German in 1843, but whether almost a decade earlier he was familiar with Burger's poem directly or knew its device through one of its many imitations in the Gothic genre, he was clearly following the tradition (298:97–98).

Homan has located a passage from Cotton Mather's sermon, *Ornaments for the Daughters of Zion* (1692), that could well have served as a source for another of the motifs—Mrs. Dabney's vain pursuit of youth. The flower imagery used to describe the wedding procession is also suggested in the following lines:

> For an *old* Woman to flaunt it in a *youthful* Dress, is altogether as prodigious a Disorder, as for the *Flowers* of *May* to appear among the *Snows* of December. A *Summer-Dress* will not suit a *Winter Age.* The Aged shew themselves to be *twice Children,* indeed, if they go like *Children,* & not *put away childish Things.* For a Woman that knows herself near her *Winding Sheet,* still to affect a *Wedding Robe,* is a Lightness that nothing can be more uncomely. (Mather, p. 62, cited in 235)

## Relationship with Other Hawthorne Works

In addition to the similarities noted above shared by the three stories published in the 1836 *Token*, "The Wedding Knell" and "The May-Pole of Merry Mount" have been grouped with "The Shaker Bridal" as stories in which two polarities are merged in the single symbol of marriage. In the case of "The Wedding Knell," Mrs. Dabney's vanity merges with John Ellenwood's vindictiveness (188:121–22). A more significant matrimonial grouping has been proposed by Levin who traces the pattern of unkept trysts and wasted lives in "The Wedding Knell" and three other stories: "The Shaker Bridal," "The White Old Maid," and "Edward Fane's Rosebud" (280:58). Each of these juxtaposes unrequited love and death. Otherwise, the one story most often associated with "The Wedding Knell" is "Dr. Heidegger's Experiment," primarily because of the old widow's attempt to retain her youth (149:180; 221:406; 188:146, 169).

"The Wedding Knell" also shares a commitment to the "common highway of life" and a warning of the danger of stepping aside from it. Baym identifies this theme in the twelve other moralized fictions Hawthorne wrote between 1834 and 1840. The theory that separation leads to abnormal subjectivity and eventually to insanity helps to explain the shrouded bridegroom's eccentric behavior as it does that of the title characters in "The Man of Adamant," "The Minister's Black Veil," "Peter Goldthwaite's Treasure," and "Edward Fane's Rosebud," all of whom have lost contact with other minds and everyday actuality (43:55–56). With due respect to Stewart's prudent observation that "the idea of isolation is so pervasive in Hawthorne's works that the consideration of all possible examples would include almost all of his characters" (455:lxxi), "Wakefield is the one earlier example that demands specific mention as the original "Outcast of the Universe."

## Interpretations and Criticism

Without knowing the name of the author, Chorley singled out "The Wedding Knell" and its two Hawthorne companion pieces for praise in his review of the 1836 *Token* for the London *Athenaeum* (149:75). Edgar Allan Poe admired it too in his 1842 review of *Twice-Told Tales*, calling it "full of the boldest imagination—an imagination fully controlled by taste" (378:91–92). Since the sinister effects and grotesque subject matter are very similar to Poe's own techniques and themes, his approval is not surprising (511:364).

Twentieth-century critics have largely ignored the story, except as an illustration of the Gothic tale (54); in one instance it has been called "a fine example of Hawthorne's manipulation of the gothic to make an antigothic effect . . . managed with technical finesse" (43:73–74). But for most readers, the exaggerated Gothic touches are unhappily combined with an equally exaggerated change of heart in the sentimental conclusion. As pathetic as the bride and groom of the story are supposed to be, they are less "pathetic" than the marriage of the macabre and the maudlin attempted by Hawthorne in this least effectual of stories.

# LII

# The White Old Maid

(*Centenary Edition, Volume IX, Twice-told Tales, 370–82.*)

## Publication History

Originally titled "The Old Maid in the Winding Sheet," this story was
first published in the *New-England Magazine* in July 1835 (IX, 8–16)
as the work of the author of "The Gray Champion" (*CE, IX, 573*). As
one of the seventeen pieces by Hawthorne published in the *New-England
Magazine* under Park Benjamin's editorship in 1834 and 1835, "The
Old Maid" was part of the *Story Teller* collection, a project for which
Hawthorne "got little or nothing as pay." (See publication history of
"The Devil in Manuscript.") The author collected it in the second edition
of *Twice-told Tales* in 1842 as "The White Old Maid."

## Circumstances of Composition, Sources, and Influences

As a part of *The Story Teller*, this story was probably written in the fall
and winter of 1832–33 or 1833–34, although it fits awkwardly into the
dramatic structure of the adventures of the wandering novelist. (See
circumstances of composition of "Passages from a Relinquished work.")
Adkins suggests this as one of the pieces that might have been written as
a separate unit and then interjected into the *Story Teller* frame (11:144).
The similarities between "The Old Maid" and several stories Hawthorne
wrote before 1830 suggest it may have been written before *The Story
Teller*. In "The Hollow of the Three Hills," Hawthorne's first acknowledged tale, the description of the conscience-stricken lady who "as she
knelt down . . . laid her forehead on the old woman's knees" (*CE, IX,
201.7–9*) is very much like the mysteriously evil "stately dame . . .
fallen on her knees, with her forehead on the holy knees of the Old Maid"
(*381.31–33*). In both stories, the sinning women die in that penitent
posture, while the exact nature of their wrongdoing remains darkly ambiguous. Here, as in "The Wives of the Dead," another early tale, the
central characters are a pair of contrasting women. In addition, the
provincial seaport-town setting shared by "The Wives of the Dead" and
"The Old Maid" suggests the possibility that, like "The Wives of the

Dead," "The Old Maid" may have been one of the *Provincial Tales*, Hawthorne's second attempted collection. Such a theory would place the composition date in 1828 or 1829.

Like many of Hawthorne's early writing attempts, including the novel *Fanshawe* published in 1828 at his own expense and then suppressed, "The White Old Maid" incorporates many of the devices of the Gothic tradition. Van Doren complains of "a misdeed at the start which nothing in the tale elucidates" (490:88), thereby inadvertently highlighting one of the genre's conventions, the mysterious crime. Hawthorne was still using that motif three decades later in his last completed novel, *The Marble Faun*—and dissatisfied readers still wanted to know exactly what evil deed Miriam and the monk had committed. While the deserted old mansion in the story functions as another Gothic trapping, the ruined castle, it has also been traced to Lucifera's House of Pride in the first book of Spenser's *Faerie Queene* (247:111–12). Hawthorne's characterization of the "ancient lady" of magnificent dress and dignified figure who returns to the mansion to die follows the body-house analogy: she is "a stately ruin . . . with a look, at once, of pride and wretchedness" (*378.1–2*).

## Relationship with Other Hawthorne Works

The many tales and sketches indebted to the Gothic tradition, for example, "Alice Doane's Appeal" and "Graves and Goblins" (*CE, XI, 289–97*), are forerunners, with "The White Old Maid," of *The House of Seven Gables*, Hawthorne's American Gothic novel. More specifically, the family mansion in the story that has "some dispute about the right of inheritance" (*374.14–15*) foreshadows one of the themes of the novel, while the "fair, young . . . creature of hope and joy" who becomes the Old Maid is a prototype for Phoebe and Alice Pyncheon (247:111).

A Freudian analysis of Hawthorne's Gothic vision finds the common ground of two uncanny motifs, the double and unexplained repetition, in "The White Old Maid" and "Roger Malvin's Burial" (352), while a time-oriented study links the two stories, along with "Sylph Etherege," to an unfulfilled present due to a fixation on the past (189:5). A related phenomenon, frustrated love resulting in wasted lives, characterizes another group of stories associated with "The White Old Maid"—"The Wedding Knell," "The Shaker Burial," and "Edward Fane's Rosebud" (280:58).

Edith is also one of the contaminated characters feared by the crowds in Hawthorne's tales; the people stand "aside that her white garments might not wave against them" (*375.15–16*), just as they avoid contact with Mr. Hooper in "The Minister's Black Veil," Roderick Elliston in "Egotism," and Hester in *The Scarlet Letter* (20:45). However, the Old Maid has the distinction of being one of the few withdrawn characters Hawthorne never implicitly or explicitly criticizes or condemns (32: 50–51).

## Interpretations and Criticism

This story has been proposed as a source for William Faulkner's "A Rose for Emily" (36). From Hawthorne's opening scene, where Edith mourns her dead lover with "her head pillowed beside that of the corpse" (*371.14–15*), to the closing description of "a lock of hair, once sable, now discolored with a greenish mould" (*382.1–2*), the striking similarities attest to "The White Old Maid" as further evidence of Hawthorne's already established influence on Faulkner.

In its own right, "The White Old Maid" is usually considered one of Hawthorne's narratives "of a lesser order" (490:88), of little note except as an example of a "standard melodramatic gothic exercise" (43:48).

# LIII
# The Wives of the Dead

(*Centenary Edition, Volume XI, The Snow-Image,* 192–99.)

## Publication History

This story was first published in 1831 in the *Token* (pp. 74–82) dated
1832 with no attribution (*CE, XI, 430*). It was one of the tales Hawthorne had sent to Samuel Goodrich in December 1829 in the hope of
finding a publisher for them as a collection, which he planned to call
*Provincial Tales.* Shortly afterward, Hawthorne refused Goodrich's offer
to publish one of the pieces, "The Gentle Boy," for $35 in the *Token*,
but by May 1831, Hawthorne, who had become discouraged in his attempts to get the collection published, agreed to allow Goodrich to use
the stories. Although no record of the financial transaction has been found,
Hawthorne's pay for the four tales that Goodrich included in the 1832
*Token* has been estimated at $84, a figure based on the 75-cents-per-page
rate he was offered for "The Gentle Boy" (*CE, IX, 497*). This would
have netted Hawthorne an approximate $6.75 for "The Wives of the
Dead," but another estimate of Hawthorne's income from the *Token*
theorizes that Hawthorne finally let Goodrich have the four pieces for
nothing (250:106). Scholars do agree, however, that when "The Wives
of the Dead" was reprinted in July 1843 as "The Two Widows" in the
*U. S. Magazine and Democratic Review*, no payment was expected or
made. Since Hawthorne had allowed *Arcturus* to reprint his stories without charge in 1841, he would have extended the same courtesy to his close
friend, John L. O'Sullivan, who edited the *Democratic Review* (*CE, X,
505*).

   Hawthorne did not include "Wives of the Dead" in a collection until
1851 when his editors, James T. Fields and George Ticknor, were looking
for material to include in *The Snow-Image.* How they located the story
is not clear. Apparently Fields did not search as far back as the 1832
*Token* for uncollected pieces because the copy text for "My Kinsman,
Major Molineux," the other story in *The Snow-Image* that was originally
published with "The Wives of the Dead," had to be procured through
the help of *Literary World.* Since the correspondence makes no mention
of "The Wives of the Dead," Hawthorne may have supplied the copy
text himself from a clipping in his possession (*CE, XI, 390–91, 413–14*).

## Circumstances of Composition, Sources, and Influences

Although this story is usually considered to be one of the *Provincial Tales*, most of which were written in 1828 and 1829, it may have been written originally as part of *Seven Tales of My Native Land*, which would make its composition date considerably earlier, in 1824 or 1825. The little we know about Hawthorne's first attempt at a collection of stories centers on what his sister, Elizabeth, remembered about them; therefore, her recollection that "some of them related to witchcraft, and some to the sea" (272:134) becomes an important consideration. In Julian Hawthorne's account, she identifies one of the tales of witchcraft, "Alice Doane," by name (223:I, 124). In its revised version as "Alice Doane's Appeal," Hawthorne explains that it and one other were the only stories inadvertently to escape the fire in which he destroyed all his early work. Since we know that "Alice Doane" was part of *Seven Tales of My Native Land* and also one of the stories Hawthorne submitted to Goodrich as part of *Provincial Tales*, it becomes likely that the other early story that was not destroyed in the fire could have become a part of the subsequent collection, too. Of all the tales that have been proposed as belonging to the *Provincial Tales* group, "The Wives of the Dead" is the only one related to the sea. It becomes the best available candidate to represent one of the two types of stories specified in Elizabeth's description.

One reader has responded to "The Wives of the Dead" as a sea story since both it and the sketch "Footprints on the Sea-Shore" are evidence of the "inborn passion" for the sea transmitted to Hawthorne from his father, who was a sea captain all his life and died while on a voyage to Dutch Guiana (230).

## Relationship with Other Hawthorne Works

The possible connection between this story and *Seven Tales of My Native Land* has been explored above, possibly for the first time; its place in the *Provincial Tales*, however, has long been recognized by a majority of scholars, although they do not all agree on why, or on which other tales also belong. Baym limits the number to the four 1832 *Token* stories and "Alice Doane"; she believes that the view of reality that underlies all five tales is antithetical to historical facts. The four biographical sketches that Hawthorne wrote at about the same time offer a good example of his historical writing, a genre that he viewed as distinctly different from fiction. In the sketches, he presents actual events objectively; in "The Wives of the Dead" and the other *Provincial Tales*, he uses the American past not as history, but as a remote and shadowy meeting ground for the merger of the actual with the imaginary (43:29–37). Weber suggests that *Provincial Tales* was made up of seven stories, all of which examined the Puritan spirit (514:83). Adkins proposes a connection with American Colonial history as the criterion; he estimates as many as nine may have been in the series (11:127–30).

The similarity between "The Wives of the Dead" and two very early stories, "The Hollow of the Three Hills" and "An Old Woman's Tale," has also been noted, but only as an incidental example of the mingling of vision and actuality to be found in a great many of Hawthorne's stories (43:32). The similarity among the three is more specific in one respect; in each, the intermingling is carried to such an extreme that either the characters or the reader find it impossible to differentiate between the actual and the imaginary. For the lady who dies as a result of her three visions in "The Hollow of the Three Hills," her fantasies are real enough to kill her; the reader is not sure whether she dreamed the events, whether the old woman conjured them up, or whether the lady dies or faints at the end. For the couple who dream simultaneous dreams in "An Old Woman's Tale," the events that follow confirm the reality of the dream; the reader is forced to supply his own ending, thereby giving his imagination the final role in the resolution of the plot's reality. For "The Wives of the Dead," the confusion over what actually happens is clearly demonstrated in the criticism reviewed below.

One of Hawthorne's sketches, "The Haunted Mind," is closely related to all four of these early tales (404.5), but it offers some especially illuminating concepts for consideration of "The Wives of the Dead." The hypnogogic state which "The Haunted Mind" re-creates and explores presents the same kind of interplay between consciousness and dreams that "The Wives of the Dead" does. When the hypothetical "you" in the sketch breaks from "a sort of conscious sleep," gazes "wildly round the bed," and in the light of a flickering ember reassures himself by identifying the familiar furnishings of his room (*CE, IV, 307–08*), he is attempting to eliminate the confusion between reality and fantasy. When Margaret of "The Wives of the Dead" is trying to fall asleep, she looks over at the hearth and, in the light of a flickering lamp, sees the shadows of the two empty armchairs; she, too, is confirming a reality. Paradoxically, however, the knock that she experiences immediately afterward, which heralds the news of her husband's safety, makes what had been reality, not real— or what she currently perceives to be real, only a dream. With either interpretation, an inextricable fusion of reality and fantasy results. "The Haunted Mind" provides an explanation for Margaret's experience; sometimes, usually during the night "when the mind has a passive sensibility," the imagination becomes "a mirror, imparting vividness to all ideas, without the power of selecting or controlling them" (*CE, IX, 306.27–30*). Margaret, and Mary too, cannot differentiate between reality and its reflection in the mirror of the imagination; understandably, neither can the reader.

## Interpretations and Criticism

The ambiguity in the last sentence of "The Wives of the Dead" has resulted in a sharp difference of opinion about the interpretation of this story on a literal level. The sentence reads: "But her hand trembled against Margaret's neck, a tear fell upon her cheek, and she suddenly awoke" (*199*). If the "she" refers to Mary, who is arranging the sleeping Margaret's bedclothes, the events of the night are a dream, and the news that the women's husbands are still alive is not true. If the "she" is Margaret, then Mary's tear woke Margaret when it "fell upon her cheek," and both sisters can rejoice that their husbands are not dead.

The interpretation of the night's events as dreams has been explicated in detail by Lang. Since syntactically the "she" should refer to Mary, Hawthorne would have had to be a careless and clumsy writer to have meant his antecedent to be Margaret and to have ended his story with an unintentionally ambiguous sentence. The realistic interpretation calls for the improbable occurrence of two simultaneous resurrections after two simultaneous deaths; and the light imagery, which establishes the lamp of hope, confirms the dream interpretation on a literal level when both women receive their good news in its light. Finally, the story has more validity as a study in the resistance to but inevitable acceptance of death than as a reassuring placebo (270).

Confirmation for this reading has been found in the story's self-explanatory title (280:58) and in its light imagery, which captures the vivid yet vague aura of dreams (416:110–12). But Hawthorne employs, it has also been argued, a "what would happen if" approach to demonstrate the nature of human experience. The literal events have a deeper meaning discernible in the human solidarity achieved by the two women. If the emphasis is shifted to the differences between the two wives (Mary does not feel as alienated as Margaret), and if the central symbol is changed from the lamp of hope to the light of human sympathy, the ending may be read as one in which Mary "touches" Margaret, awakening her from the "darkness" of isolation (450).

Several other readers also interpret the experiences of the night as actual events. One notes that we should not have to assume "an entirely dishonest narrator" who says what is not true, and that the point of view used to describe the alleged dream sequences is not always that of the "dreamer." The tale is thus a study in the precariousness of human happiness, though there is a "pleasant dramatic irony" in Mary's reluctance to wake her sister, when Margaret is, in reality, as happy as she is (149:216). Another reader who dismisses the dream interpretations emphasizes the unreliable nature of reality—the women erroneously believe their husbands are dead, yet when they are told that the husbands are safe, they, at first, cannot believe what is true. She applauds Hawthorne's effective portrayal of the estranged vision and confused perceptions of the two grieving women (43:32).

On the whole, however, critical appraisals of "The Wives of the Dead" have been both niggling and niggardly. Crews ignores the story in his book-long Freudian analysis of Hawthorne's works (115), a lamentable oversight considering the ease with which the story lends itself to a psychoanalytic interpretation. Two young wives, facing a future without sexual gratification are awakened in the night and given news of their husbands' safe return, in one case by a former suitor, in the other by a fatherly townsman. Given such a situation, together with Hawthorne's dreamlike imagery and deliberately ambiguous handling, only the dismissal of the story as critically inferior can explain its not having been given more attention.

Yet, "The Wives of the Dead" stands up to the most rigorous structural analysis. Formalists have also ignored it, however, in spite of its unity and effective imagery. For example, the parallel structure of Margaret's and Mary's experiences is skillfully established; each is sleeping restlessly; each is awakened by someone outside; each hears that her husband is alive; each stops herself from waking the other. At the same time that this motif sets up a pattern of repetition and expectation, it also accentuates the differences in their perceptions and temperaments. The symbolism in the story, especially the lamp imagery, has been discussed, but primarily in the interest of supporting a thematic theory. The only reader who has taken adequate note of the literal and metaphorical function of the lamp is Carlson. She points out that the light motif structures the plot, underscores the attitude of each widow, and illustrates what an integral part of the story Hawthorne makes the scenic constituents (78.8).

The modernity of this story has been recognized. It has been called "more like the best *New Yorker* short fiction of the 1940's than like the fiction of Hawthorne's time" (149:216). Other virtues noted have been its timelessness (490:82), its "economy of material" (84:15), and its narrative technique, comparable to Henry James's masterpiece of ambiguity, *The Turn of the Screw* (271). Anyone who has had the opportunity to see how college students react to it can testify to the universality of its appeal. No one has yet, however, given "The Wives of the Dead" the full measure of critical approbation it deserves. It is in many ways as representative of the qualities that make Hawthorne readable today as is the celebrated "Young Goodman Brown."

# LIV

# Young Goodman Brown

(*Centenary Edition, Volume X, Mosses from an Old Manse, 74–90.*)

## Publication History

This story was first published in April 1835 in the *New-England Magazine* (VIII, 249–60) as the work of the author of "The Gray Champion" (*CE, X, 573*). Both stories are among the seventeen pieces that appeared during 1834 and 1835 in this periodical, all of which are thought to have been part of *The Story Teller*, a projected collection that never materialized. According to Hawthorne's sister-in-law, Elizabeth Peabody, he blamed Park Benjamin, the editor of the *New-England Magazine*, for cutting up *The Story Teller* and for the fact that he received "little or nothing" as pay. The standard rate was $1 a page, but no record of exact payment has been found (*CE, IX, 494, 499*). Hawthorne did not include "Young Goodman Brown" in either the 1837 or the 1842 edition of *Twice-told Tales*. It was collected in *Mosses from an Old Manse* in 1846.

## Circumstances of Composition, Sources, and Influences

Based on the generally accepted theory that "Young Goodman Brown" is one of the *Provincial Tales*, its date of composition was probably 1828 or 1829 (10; 11; 84:13). The supposition is that when Hawthorne did not succeed in finding a publisher for *Provincial Tales*, he incorporated some of its stories into his subsequent project, *The Story Teller*. Since "Young Goodman Brown" is, however, never specifically mentioned or identifiably described in any of the extant correspondence, it could have been written as late as March 1835, shortly before it appeared in print (84:56; 314:152–53).

Many sources and influences have been credited with helping to shape this relatively brief story. The most significant ones establish Hawthorne's debt to the historical actuality of the Salem witchcraft delusion of 1692 as he came to understand it through a variety of means. The witch folklore transmitted through oral tradition is difficult to document, yet during the course of growing up in the environs of Salem, Hawthorne had to have been exposed to some of the local folk beliefs. The devil's power to change his shape is one such superstition that is incorporated into the story (89.5; 148; 232:162; 359; 533:57–58). Written accounts that reflect the Puritan community before, during, and after the Salem witch trials provide a more tangible source for the material that forms the basis for the story. Allegedly factual reports of witches' Sabbaths were available to Hawthorne in the records of Essex County Court (101; 232:158; 359:65). C. W. Upham's book, *Lectures on Witchcraft* (Boston, 1831), also contains a detailed description (pp. 46–48, as cited in 359:65), although Upham's book was published after the earliest conjectured composition date, discussed above.

Historians such as Thomas Hutchinson (*History of Massachusetts Bay,* 1764), with whose work Hawthorne is known to have been familiar, included the Salem witch trials as a part of the social and political history of New England (89.5; 149:202–08). Cotton Mather also describes the trials in *Wonders of the Invisible World* (1693), providing at the same time the official Puritan dogma regarding witchcraft. The following excerpt clearly establishes the concepts from Mather that are subsumed in the structure of "Young Goodman Brown":

> The *Devil,* exhibiting himself ordinarily as a small *Black Man,* has decoy'd a fearful knot of proud, froward, ignorant, envious and malicious Creatures, to list themselves in his horrid Service, by entring their Names in a Book by him tendred unto them. These Witches . . . have met in Hellish Rendezvouzes [sic], wherein the Confessors do say, they have had their Diabolical Sacraments, imitating the Baptism and the Supper of our Lord. . . . But that which makes this Descent [of the Devil] the more formidable, is the *multitude* and *quality* of Persons accused of an Interest in this Witchcraft, by the Efficacy of the *Spectres* which take their Name and Shape upon them. . . . That the Devils have obtain'd the power, to take on them the likeness of harmless people. . . . (pp. 17–19, cited in 511:361–62)

The passage in the story that describes one of the witches participating in the satanic rite as "Martha Carrier, who had received the devil's promise to be queen of hell" (*86.27–29*) is taken almost verbatim from Mather's *Wonders* (149:204–05; 232:162; 359:65; 482:546). An earlier work by Cotton Mather, *Memorable Providences Relating to Witchcraft and Possessions* (1689), provides similar data and precepts defining the Puritan belief in witches. His *Wonders,* however, appears to have been written explicitly to justify the Salem trials and to convince Mather himself and the public that no defendant had been convicted solely on spectral evidence (94:357). In June 1692, a more explicit clarification of the specter question was issued by a group of Puritan clergymen; in a statement probably written by Cotton Mather himself, the devil is acknowledged as having the power to impersonate innocent people. The following year such evidence was ruled as inadmissable in the courts (149:207; 279). Levin makes the point that Brown, in his own mind, convicts the townspeople and Faith on the same kind of spectral evidence admitted in the earlier trials (279).

Another work by Mather, *Magnalia Christi Americana* (1702), records an incident during Governor Winthrop's visit at Plymouth in 1632 that might have suggested the ironic overtones in the title Hawthorne affixes to Brown's name; Mather reports the governor's disapproval of the use of the term *good-man* to describe an unregenerate man (397:218–19). The name Deacon Gookin, used for the churchgoer who accompanies the minister to the witches' Sabbath, has also been traced to Mather's *Magnalia* (I, 141–42, cited in 482:552), while Goody Cory (*79.15*) is one of the accused witches in *Wonders* (p. 166, cited in 482:552). A possible analogue for Brown's own name has been located in Samuel Sewall's *Diary* (p. 52, cited in 482:552). Goody Cloyse, the "very pious and exemplary dame" who taught Brown his catechism (*78.20–31*), is another of the accused witches whose name appears in the historical records (323.5).

An account of the trials that is bitterly critical of the Puritans is probably another source for the reference to Goody Cory as "that unhanged witch" (*79.15*). Robert Calef's *More Wonders of the Invisible World* (1692) presents a detailed account of the interrogation of Goody Cory by Hawthorne's ancestor, John Hathorne, before she was committed to Salem's prison (232:154). The reference in the story (*85.5–6*) to the affirmation by some "that the lady of the governor" (the wife of Sir William Phips) was among the Devil worshippers reflects a specific passage in Calef's book (149:204).

Another book, Deodat Lawson's *Christ's Fidelity* (1704), which is known to have been part of the Hawthorne family library, may also have influenced Hawthorne's portrayal of the psychological aberrations involved in the Salem witch delusion (94). The testimony of Joseph Ring, which is recounted in the appendix of Lawson's book, describes the phenomenon of forced transport to witch meetings; Ring's testimony, which also appears in Mather's *Wonders* in more pallid terms, could have provided the journey motif as well as the subjective nature of the experience Brown goes through during his night in the woods. Lawson's sermon, which makes up the bulk of the book, emphasizes the power of Satan and could have suggested to Hawthorne the ironies inherent in a theological position that inadvertently minimizes God's authority and strength. Lawson's sermon would have held personal implications for Hawthorne because it was originally delivered in Salem Village on March 24, 1692, when his ancestor, John Hathorne, conducted a vigorous interrogation of accused witches.

The source for the flying ointment "receipt" described by Goody Cloyse and the devil (79.16–18) is revealed in a brief article called "Witch Ointment," which appeared in the July 1836 issue of *The American Magazine of Useful and Entertaining Knowledge* while Hawthorne was its editor (86). The recipe in the article, which is almost identical to the one in the story, is attributed to Lord Bacon and can be found in one of his philosophical works, *Sylva Sylvarum* (X, 975). The efficacy of the formula has been verified by an experiment conducted in connection with Margaret Murray's *The Witch Cult of Western Europe* (Oxford, 1921); two of the ingredients—smallage, which is hemlock, and wolfsbane, which is aconite—were tested in controlled experiments and did produce the illusion of flight (232:167, n.21). The apparent substitution of one of Bacon's ingredients, "the fat of children digged out of their graves," with "the fat of a new-born babe" is traced to a tale by Cervantes called "El Cologuio de los Perros," or "The Conversation of the Dogs." In it, a witch discusses the common belief that witches anoint themselves with "the blood of infants which we strangle" (86:344). Cervantes is referred to specifically in the penultimate sentence of the *American Magazine* article:

> Cervantes, in one of his tales, seems to be of opinion that the oint-ment cast them into a trance, during which they merely dreamt of holding intercourse with Satan. If so, witchcraft differs little from a nightmare. (II, 470, cited in 86:343)

The equation of witchcraft with nightmare, a central concept in "Young Goodman Brown," can thus be ascribed to Cervantes. One reader believes that Hawthorne's depiction of the evils of witchcraft bears a closer rela-tion to the creed expressed by La Canizares, the witch in Cervantes' story, than to the New England version; Hawthorne's story is not concerned with the diabolical persecution of neighbors, which was an important element in the Salem witch trials, but rather with secret sin covered up by hypocrisy, which is what La Canizares emphasizes about herself as a full-fledged witch (86).

Like the rite that Brown witnesses, Cervantes' version of the witches' Sabbath suggests orgies of a sexual nature, an association Hawthorne could also have found in a more famous work in European literature, the *Walpurgisnacht* of Goethe's *Faust* (232:166). The prearranged nature of Brown's meeting also suggests a Faustian pact with the devil (181:425; 189:54; 377:387; 447:63).

In addition to the trappings of magic, moonlight, and blood that are a part of the Gothic conventions employed by Hawthorne in this story (152:255–56; 298:93–94; 482:557), other literary influences that have been identified include works by Spenser, Milton, and Shakespeare. Brown's devil is almost identical to Spenser's description of Archimago in Book I of *The Faerie Queene* (455:11), with additional parallels between Duessa and Goody Cloyse, between the Redcrosse Knight and Brown himself, and between the forest as a symbol of moral error in both works (276:461–63). The narrative pattern and some specific details from the ninth and tenth books of Milton's *Paradise Lost* have also been credited with providing the prototype against which Hawthorne could create his psychological reenactment of the fall of man. Hawthorne assigns Brown a dual role which combines the two separate falls of Adam and Eve into one; he also reverses the final rebirth phase of the myth to create an ironic commentary on Milton's "fortunate fall" (97; 315:284; 398:45). A parallel with Shakespeare's intent in the first two acts of *Macbeth* has also been noted; the transforming power and paralyzing deceptiveness of an evil thought out of control is dramatically charted in Brown's denouement as in Macbeth's (135).

One final influence that has only recently been given attention as operative on Hawthorne's work is the periodical market where Hawthorne knew many of his stories would be introduced to the reading public. Mathews suggests that Hawthorne's choice of subject matter could have been guided by the popularity of witchcraft stories with the magazine audiences. He proposes Whittier's "Powow Hill," a story which appeared in the *New-England Magazine* three years before "Young Goodman Brown," in May 1832, as a possible model; some of the circumstances in Whittier's story—a young man in the woods alone at night, a waiting bride, and a pagan ceremonial—are used by Hawthorne but with a decidedly different effect (314:152–53).

## Relationship with Other Hawthorne Works

From its position as Hawthorne's most highly praised short story, "Young Goodman Brown" is related to what is admirable in all his other works. Invariably, Hawthorne's most highly praised novel, *The Scarlet Letter*, is most often cited as a fitting companion piece for this story, and few would disagree that if only two of Hawthorne's works had to represent him at his most characteristic best, they should be *The Scarlet Letter* and "Young Goodman Brown." Both have been admired for their timeless universality, and both are firmly rooted in historicity, sharing a similar historical background—seventeenth-century Puritan New England—and a similar sociocultural theme—the effect of sin on individuals in the Puritan community. In these two works, Hawthorne effectively subsumes the cultural psychology of the nation in the individual psychology of the created characters of Brown, Hester, and Dimmesdale.

Hawthorne accomplishes this feat in much the same way in both pieces; they are alike in method as well as content. While some call this method allegorical (45:13–22), many prefer the less restrictive term *symbolic*. Pearce says both works are "symbolic history transformed into symbolist fiction" (370:230–38). Fiedler identifies a developmental relationship between the symbolism in the two; the story is "a piece of symbolic Gothicism whose promise is fulfilled . . . in *The Scarlet Letter*" (181:426). Two of the symbols used in these works, Dimmesdale's black glove (dropped on the scaffold during his night of mock penitence) and Faith's pink ribbon, afford insights into similarity of technique even as they illustrate subtle but significant differences in theological perspectives. Abel contrasts the symbolic meaning of the black glove—faith troubled by doubt—with that of the pink ribbon—doubt almost despairing of faith (2). Because the glove is merely a dislocated detail while the displaced ribbon betokens an entire subversion of morality, the former symbolizes Dimmesdale's plight and the corresponding state of Boston moral consciousness in the 1640s, while the latter represents Brown and the state of mind of Salem Village during the witchcraft delusion of 1692.

Many readers have compared the two works, but, as illustrated above, the similarities are almost always highlighted by very significant differences. This is true of the division between town and forest on which both are structured (275:36), of the conflict between head and heart which Hester resolves but Brown never does (394), and of the "insidious whispers of the bad angel" which Hester (in chapter 5) hears and resists but which Brown heeds, to the lifelong detriment of his happiness (166; 149:210–11; 520). One reader contrasts Hester's "fortunate fall" (and that of Donatello in *The Marble Faun*) with Brown's refusal to complete his initiation into evil (123:52–53).

When Brown is compared to Dimmesdale, however, the parallels are more consistent. This is especially clear in chapter 20, entitled "The Minister in a Maze," which Doubleday calls "almost another version" of "Young Goodman Brown" (149:211). Dimmesdale, like Brown, experiences inexplicable evil impulses, wonders if he has made a contract with the devil in the forest, thinks he sees a witch who greets him as an ally, and returns to town with a new and bitter kind of knowledge.

Brown and Dimmesdale are, in this Calvinistic knowledge of sin that overwhelms and isolates them, very much like Hooper in "The Minister's

Black Veil" (127:109; 270:89–92; 275:49–50). Crews considers all three men to be sexual escapists; Hooper and Brown proceed from sexual fear to obsession and misanthropy, and all are related to the most grotesque and openly pathological of Hawthorne's escapists, Digby in "The Man of Adamant" (115:96–116). Brown's arrogant isolation is much like Digby's self-righteous retreat to his cave (97:293, n.17; 420:194–205), as is Hooper's self-confining image of himself as the only one with a fully developed awareness of sin. This quartet—Brown, Hooper, Digby, and Dimmesdale—illustrates for many readers the devastating effects that Calvinism can have. One reader includes Reuben Bourne in "Roger Malvin's Burial" as another victim of Puritan dogma (146). Each of these stories has been interpreted as an ironic attack on Puritanism in spite of the absence of any such directly stated intent.

Those readers who believe Hawthorne meant his portrayal of Puritans to be self-incriminating relate all his Puritan stories to the guilt he felt over his ancestors' part in the persecutions recorded during the early history of Puritan New England. This theory links "Young Goodman Brown" directly to the pieces in which Hawthorne openly expresses his disapproval of his Puritan heritage. His most explicit statements appear in "Main Street," "The Custom-House," and "Alice Doane's Appeal." One clearly anti-Puritan story which deals with the Puritans' persecution of the Quakers rather than of witches, is "The Gentle Boy," but it, like almost all of Hawthorne's works, has some ambivalent passages that can be construed as approving. On the other hand, the heroic rendition of the Puritan presence in "Endicott and the Red Cross" is marred with some decidedly pejorative details. "The May-Pole of Merry Mount" is a good example of how ambivalent Hawthorne can be in his portrayal of the Puritans, yet it, too, has been suggested as a corollary to the anti-Puritanism of "Young Goodman Brown" because it serves as a comparison which illustrates how much more destructive Endicott's iron rigidity can be when it is directed against the Puritans themselves (232:152). It is as if, having whetted their appetite for destruction on the Quakers and Merry Mounters, the Puritans turn on themselves. The pagan rites that Brown witnesses in the forest bear a resemblance to the pagan sensuality and collective evil which characterize the dances and rituals of "The May-Pole" (533), although one reader sees the witches' Sabbath as a parody of both the Merry Mounters' pagan paradise and the Christian sacraments (232:168).

The wizard-devil and the witches who participate in the demonic rite populate many of Hawthorne's other writings in a variety of forms. A witch plays a key role in one of his earliest stories, "The Hollow of the Three Hills," and in the last short story he ever wrote, "Feathertop"

(232:155; 315:161–62; 359:63–67). The wizard in another early story, "Alice Doane's Appeal," is a prototype for Brown's devil, who, in turn, prefigures such satanic old men as Rappaccini in "Rappaccini's Daughter," Chillingworth in *The Scarlet Letter*, and Westervelt in *The Blithedale Romance* (455:1). In Westervelt's case, the stick he carries confirms his origin; it bears a striking resemblance to the devil's staff in "Young Goodman Brown" (455:lvii). Instances of infernal imagery reminiscent of the demonic ritual in this story occur in "The Devil in Manuscript," "Earth's Holocaust," "Ethan Brand," and in the characterization of Aminidab in "The Birthmark" (123; 97:293).

Two male characters who may be added to the group of sexual escapists to which Brown is assigned are Giovanni in "Rappaccini's Daughter" and Aylmer in "The Birthmark" (115:116). Both of their stories appear in the *Mosses* collection with Brown's, although Brown's was created at least a decade earlier. Giovanni shares Brown's lack of trust and his inability to see beyond surface appearances (32:92–93); one reader calls both of them "victims of Fancy" (97:288, n.12). Aylmer is like Brown in his insistence on perfection; neither can be content without a wholly ideal woman (232:168). The three stories are also linked by three symbols—Faith's pink ribbon, Georgiana's crimson birthmark, and Beatrice's purple plant; each can be interpreted as symbolizing woman's physical nature and her attendant earthly imperfections (397:224). Because they cannot accept human fraility, all three men transform the dreams they experience into nightmarish reality (227). For one reader, Brown's compromise, in which he neither fully accepts nor fully denies his wife, is a wiser choice than Giovanni's or Alymer's (397:224).

The short story most often likened to "Young Goodman Brown" is "My Kinsman, Major Molineux" because both deal with an initiatory experience conceived in terms of a journey where reality and dream interact (10; 45:21; 81; 115:104; 232:168; 398:40; 500:92). The stories were probably written about the same time, and both are usually considered part of the *Provincial Tales* project (10; 11). Both protagonists undergo a fantasylike experience that follows a classic Oedipal pattern and both emerge permanently altered (115:104), but the similarity ends there. Readers disagree as to the degree of maturity achieved by Robin, but most assess his future as brighter and more hopeful than the one Hawthorne assigns to Brown.

"Roger Malvin's Burial," also thought to be one of the *Provincial Tales*, follows a journey motif with similar Oedipal overtones. Like "Young Goodman Brown," it is dominated by an obsession with secret sin, but the theme of hidden guilt is to be found in many of Hawthorne's works. It is most prominent in *The Scarlet Letter*, "The Minister's Black Veil," and "The Hollow of the Three Hills," all mentioned above, plus in "Egotism," "Fancy's Show Box," and "The Haunted Mind."

The other pervasive motif is isolation, and most of the secret sinners suffer isolation as well as guilt. Brown is especially like Gervayse Hastings of "The Christmas Banquet" in this respect because both of them hide their desolation behind the facade of a fulfilled life (255:170–71). Brown is also like Wakefield, who risks permanent isolation by deliberately leaving his place in the moral universe (309:93). Brown, however, finds he can never regain it, thereby providing a more appropriate exemplum for the "Wakefield" story than its title character does.

"Young Goodman Brown" is also a dream tale, which links it to the "it was only a dream" ending of "The Celestial Rail-road," the dream as a foreshadowing device in "The Birthmark" and "Rappaccini's Daughter," and the dreamlike state of Robin in "My Kinsman, Major Molineux" (227). Comparable dream imagery is present in "The Hollow of the Three Hills" and "The Wives of the Dead," but it is in "Alice Doane's Appeal" that the similarity is strongest. The psychological implications of Leonard Doane's nightmare experience are closely related to Brown's Oedipal-haunted revelations during his night in the forest.

## Interpretations and Criticism

In a 1972 review of the critical history of this story, one reader conjectures that "Young Goodman Brown" "has provoked perhaps more discussion than any other short story in American literature" (60:15). A 1976 bibliography of secondary studies on "Young Goodman Brown" published between 1845 and 1975 appears to confirm the estimate; it lists over 400 entries (444). These 400 items cover an intimidating array of responses that pursue every possible interpretative nuance, from esoteric theological dogma to technically precise but scientifically complex psychoanalytical theories. Yet the story that has generated this critical furor remains available on its own terms to anyone who reads it, and the questions that it raises are fundamentally simple ones. Why does Brown go into the forest? What happens to him there? Why does he emerge a permanently embittered man? The ambivalence that Hawthorne openly deploys in the telling makes it possible for each reader to project his particular sensibilities and attitudes into the answers to these questions. In the sense that all responses to literature have an intrinsic value, such personalized answers are valid enough. But even the most devoted formalist, however firmly he may be committed to the principle that the work must speak for itself, should be willing to admit that, in the case of "Young

Goodman Brown," the wealth of adjunct interpretations—historical, sociological, religious, semantic, and psychological—can be used profitably to
widen and enrich each individual's apprehension of the story.

The answers to the three basic questions proposed are shaped by a
fundamental decision which each reader makes about Brown: either he
is to blame for what happens or he is a victim.

The most convincing "victim" interpretation is proposed by the historicists. They maintain that Brown is a victim of Puritanism. Levin,
Cohen, and Colacurcio lead the critical contingent that emphasizes the
importance of the historical background and the relevance of the specific
theological controversy and the ecclesiological practices that were a part
of Salem Village in 1692 (94; 97:295–96; 101; 279). Like the Salemites
who were sufficiently convinced of the guilt of witches to condone their
executions, Brown is deluded into accepting spectral evidence as conclusive proof of his neighbors' depravity. Although the courts subsequently
ruled that the devil could impersonate innocent people and that, therefore, the appearance of an individual at a witches' Sabbath could not be
used as proof of witchcraft, the records show that many were convicted
on the basis of such evidence. The emphasis that Calvinist theologians
placed on the power of the devil, on the innate depravity of man, and on
predestination combine to convince Brown that the devil is right when he
proclaims, "Evil is the nature of mankind" (88.3). Brown comes to the
grim conclusion that redemption for the majority is impossible.

Readers of the same persuasion have pursued various aspects of this
anti-Puritan position. Mathews believes that Brown exemplifies the Calvinistic doctrine of Antinomianism, which insists on salvation by faith,
with good works only a by-product of divine grace. As a result of Brown's
conviction that he is one of the elect, he does not hesitate to expose himself to the devil. His resultant passive cynicism demonstrates the ineffectuality of the Antinomian principles of faith (312). Connolly emphasizes
foreordination of the damned as the Puritan doctrine responsible for
Brown's misanthropy. Brown does not lose his faith; rather, he realizes
fully for the first time the horrible consequences of its teachings (102).
Stein stresses the power that the Puritan religion ascribes to Satan; as a
result of Brown's Calvinistic indoctrination, he is deceived into believing
that the devil's sovereignty is comparable to God's (447:61). Miller suggests that the witches Brown sees in the forest are real. They illustrate
the hypocrisy that the narrow and rigorous tenets of Puritanism encourage,
while Brown is the self-righteous and sanctimonious product of his Puritan
upbringing (334). Johnson appraises Brown's "descent into Hell" as a
mock version of the Puritan's second covenant with God; the promised
justification is never realized because Brown cannot admit he is as de-

praved as the others (243). Bell qualifies the anti-Puritan position somewhat. Brown is not a reflection of Hawthorne's overall judgment of New
England Puritanism; he is a "forceful example" of the "falling-off from
the manhood of the first generation," an illustration of the mentality of
the second and third generation Puritans whom Hawthorne describes in
"Main Street" as "a race of lower and narrower souls than their progenitors had been" (46:76–81). Hoffman makes the point that Hawthorne's
presentation is a double one; he is criticizing his Puritan forebears,
but he is also presenting their belief in witches as valid for them. For
Hawthorne the alleged witches simply share in the general guilt of mankind as all men do; he is more concerned with the sins perpetrated against
them. It is this guilt, bequeathed to him by his witch-hunting ancestor,
John Hathorne, that Hawthorne assumes as his own. This makes the story
an expiation as well as a judgment (232:156). In a very real way, Hawthorne is as much a "victim" of Puritanism as Brown is.

Another persuasive "victim" rationale is offered by the psychologists:
Brown is a sick man with a diseased mind who cannot help what he sees
in the forest or his reaction to it. As Lang pithily observes, "If we are
sane, we do not hold our neighbors responsible for what they do in our
dreams" (270:1). Crews, Male, and Hoffman spearhead the Freudian
interpretations. Brown's problem stems from "his insistence upon seeing
Faith more as an idealized mother than as a wife" (115:96–106), an
attitude clearly revealed in Brown's assurance to himself that "after this
one night, I'll cling to her skirts" (*75.12–13*). The night's journey is essentially a vicarious and lurid sexual adventure that ends in a "fiery orgy of
lust," but the experience turns out to be more than Brown can handle.
He is psychologically incapable of accepting the sexual aspects of Faith's
womanhood. He retreats from it by rejecting her (304:76–80). The sexual
overtones of the story are also delineated in the forbidden knowledge that
the devil shares with the communicants at the witches' Sabbath (*87.10–23*).
The knowledge is primarily of a sexual nature, and Brown's overreaction
is attributed to his carnal knowledge of his wife. The presence of his father
suggests the legacy of original sin as well. Adultery and original sin are
conjoined in what Hoffman calls an "unmistakeable" inference in the
story: "old Brown has had carnal knowledge of Goody Cloyse" (232:
159–63). Robinson follows a similar tack in tracing the etymology of the
term *good-man* to its archaic meaning of "husband." He too identifies
the shared passion of Brown's marriage as the source of Brown's guilt
complex (397). Rohrberger echoes Crews's diagnosis of mother fixation,
citing as evidence Brown's call to Faith, the mother figure, just before the
climax of the pagan rite (*88.21–22*). She applies the Freudian theory that
a belief in the devil represents "repressed wishes . . . derived from the

infantile Oedipus situation." In normal growth, the child comes to accept
the sexuality of his parents and to eliminate the hostility he feels toward
his father by incorporating the image of the father with his own self-image.
Brown fails to reach this reconciliation, and he never achieves psychological maturity or stability (398:46–47).

In spite of the impressive evidence amassed by the historical and psychological critical camps that supports the contention that Brown is a
dupe or a neurotic but not a sinner, another group of readers maintains
that the story itself, taken on its own imagistic and thematic terms, establishes Brown as an evil man who is solely responsible for all that happens
to him. What he sees in "the heart of the dark wilderness" (83.19) is a
reflection of his own "heart of darkness" and not a spectral display (240).
His sinfulness leads him to consider all others sinful, and his warped
vision causes him to misjudge humanity (326; 520). The complex symbol
patterns establish his "bedevilment" as self-inflicted; his wife symbolizes
the faith that he rejects; the journey into the forest is an inward journey
into the blackness of his soul; and the devil signifies his darker, doubting
side. All three sets of symbols work together to chart a pattern that points
to his own nature as the source of his despair (505). He willfully mistakes his illusions for realities in his desire for self-punishment (107)
because it is the awareness of his own innate depravity that shapes his
outlook (202.8). If he listens to the "bad angel," he does so of his own
free will (166); he answers the devil's summons (60); and though the
devil enslaves him with wily half-truths, he chooses to listen (189:56).
The decision to leave Faith and to go into the forest, whatever irrational
drive prompts it, is indisputably his own (309:92). Cohen calls that
decision the one irrevocable fall in the story, out of which spring Brown's
impenitence and despair (97:291–94). One reader accuses Brown of
lacking not faith or hope, but charity; without "the greatest of these"
he condemns others to damnation and himself to misery (144.5). All of
these accusatory readers appear to have left the story with the same outlook that Brown had when he left the forest; they are as stern, sad, darkly
meditative, and distrustful as Brown himself.

Another group of readers, who can be classified in a general way as
archetypalists, reverse the moralistic position. Brown emerges a troubled
man not because he succumbs to evil but because he resists it. He refuses
to complete his initiation into evil; he stops short of receiving "the mark
of baptism" that would make him one of the "partakers of the mystery
of sin" (88.13–15). Adams says that Brown "should have fallen . . . should
have accepted the devil's destructive knowledge, which might have led
eventually to rebirth. By refusing he has caught himself in the trap of an
absolute and static isolation" (10:56). Dahl hypothesizes that Brown's

gloom and estrangement may be explained by his not having participated in the "communion" of his race or in the humanizing knowledge of sin (123:52–53). Rohrberger adds a mythic dimension to her Freudian interpretation by conjoining the pattern of an initiatory rite toward maturation with Christian symbolism (398:39–47). The network of correspondences that exist in the Christian myth (God's relationship to the devil, Christ as the son of God, the Holy Mother as the Church) are applied to the symbols in the story, with Faith paralleling the Virgin Mary and Brown functioning in some ways as Christ, in others as Adam. The stick that looks like a wiggling snake suggests the serpent in Eden, but the rebirth phase of the Adamic myth is reversed. One reader, in comparing "Young Goodman Brown" with Coleridge's *The Rime of The Ancient Mariner*, assesses Brown's final state as a partial rebirth that turns out to be, in fact, a stillbirth (78.5). Cohen's Miltonic analysis traces a similar pattern of reversed rebirth, but he attributes the reversal directly to Hawthorne's understanding of how the witchcraft hysteria had perverted the Christianity of the Puritans of Salem (97). Rohrberger's emphasis is philosophical rather than historical; the major symbolic implication is that evil is a necessary part of good. Christ had to descend into Hades before he could emerge victorious; death must precede rebirth; but Brown refuses to complete the initiatory cycle. He cannot accept the evil with the good. He chooses instead to believe that whatever is evil must be wholly evil, thereby eliminating the good and elevating evil to a position of dominance and supremacy. Paulits also proposes Christ as an analogue for Brown; like Christ, Brown is tempted and resists—but not strongly enough because of his ambivalence (366).

A small minority choose to view this story as national myth, that is, as a historical allegory in which Brown represents young America (193: 83–84; 344; 405). The motif is again a failed journey of initiation, but on a broader scale. Brown's penetration into the dark forest is analogous to the colonists' advance into the western frontier. Like the immature nation he symbolizes, Brown is naive and inexperienced, but his response to the fiery ordeal he faces in the unexplored territory reveals not so much innocence as inadequacy. He fails to complete his passage to maturity, signaling a similar unhappy fate for his national counterpart.

Stylistic concerns dominate a final contingent of readers who concentrate on how the story operates and the correspondence between method and message. Levy, for example, finds that the allegorical structure conflicts with Hawthorne's analysis of Brown's consciousness, especially in the dual portrayal of Faith as a character and as an allegorical concept. Hawthorne advances the proposition that there is no necessary relationship between the demand for faith and its availability; he reinforces this proposition by formulating the problem of faith within the limits of an allegorical mode that cannot contain it (285.5). Stoehr, on the other hand, sees Hawthorne's emblematic technique as less allegorical than hypothetical. In using the "as if" reality of a folktale, Hawthorne's mimesis involves not an imitation of nature but a re-creation of the supernatural through natural emblems. Stoehr, too, deduces a thematic purpose: Hawthorne issues warnings that his "creative imitations" are supposed truths and that taking the symbolic burden of an emblem literally can be destructive of faith (463). Clark also believes that this story examines and reflects upon the storytelling process itself. Hawthorne transforms data via imagination into historical fiction. This process points to the "gloomy truth that is the main theme of the tale"—literary artistry and all other essentially devotional commitments, whether familial or religious, are impure (89.5). Narrative technique is Liebman's principal concern; he identifies three narrative devices ("diverting ambiguity," "dilatory exposition," and "dissimulated narration"), all of which make the reader the central character by giving him the same choices that Brown has (290). Paulits believes ambivalence rather than ambiguity solves the intent of the story, both as dominant motif and as device. Brown continually vacillates between two diametrically opposed feelings, first about his wife's presence among the sinners, and then about the morals of his neighbors. Because he rejects the knowledge of sin, the ambivalence can never be resolved. His conviction of evil alternates with his desperate need for a confirmation of good, and he can neither break away from his wife and neighbors nor enjoy his life amidst them (366).

The best and most complete stylistic analysis of "Young Goodman Brown" remains Fogle's. He shows how Hawthorne combines ambiguity of meaning with clarity of technique to achieve "that reconciliation of opposites which Coleridge considered the highest art." The clarity which counterbalances the hazy multiple possibilities of theme is embodied in the structure and style—in the simple plot (the adventures of one night in the forest); in the foreshadowing of the opening paragraph (the talk of dreams, Brown's ironic confidence, the pink ribbons which are specifically mentioned three times); in the balance of episodes and scenes (the encounter with Goody Cloyse, who anticipates the appearance of "a nice young man to be taken into communion tonight," followed by the encounter with Deacon Gookin, who is looking forward to "a goodly young woman to be taken into communion"); in the contrast set up between town and forest, day and night, good and evil, appearance and reality; in the parallel opposition between the red of the fire and the black of the night, and between the multitude around the fire at the witch meeting and the damp and chill solitude of the "awakening"; and finally in the ironic detachment and formal gravity with which the bizarre and grotesque incident is recounted (186:15–32).

The one symbol that has received the most attention is the pink ribbon. Almost every reader who discusses the story has something to say about it—or them. Boudreau says the confusion over the singular or plural form is "symptomatic of a general misreading about the pink ribbons." In a detailed review of how the pink ribbons have been interpreted by the cynical camp, who read them as evidence of Faith's sinfulness, and by the Pollyannaists, who see them as vindicating her innocence, Boudreau concludes that Hawthorne has left the reader as much in the woods about Faith as he has about Brown (60). Readers have adapted the symbolism of the pink ribbons to their respective views so that the ribbons have served to convey such diverse abstractions as feminine passion (397:223), the airy texture and pastel infancy of Brown's religious faith (312), and the psychological state of man between the scarlet of total depravity and the white of innocence (180). A few readers have objected to the use of the ribbons: Matthiessen is bothered because "it is an abstraction pretending to be something else" and because its "literal insistence . . . short-circuits the range of associations" (315:284–85). But for most, the pink ribbons are an example of Hawthorne's artistry. Cohen admires and discusses at length how Hawthorne uses them as links in the story's construction, at the beginning and ending, and as part of the spectral apparatus leading up to Brown's psychologically perverted vision of truth (94:360–61).

The other aspect that has elicited discussion is the question of whether Brown had "fallen asleep in the forest and only dreamed a wild dream" (*89.15–16*). Hawthorne answers his apparently rhetorical question himself: "Be it so, if you will" (*89.17*). He clearly says that it does not matter because it is the effect of the experience and not its nature that is relevant. Readers have nevertheless explored the implications of the dream alternative. One suggests that since there is no clear-cut indication of when the dream begins, Brown's opening conversation with Faith may be part of the dream (397:223). The psychologically oriented readers and the historicists describe the dream, respectively, as the hallucinations of a diseased mind and the spectral display that the Puritans believed the devil had the power to simulate. Some have corroborated it as a literal dream (430:113–14; 97:283); one is convinced that Brown actually experienced the events (239), and another traces a modulation from physical fact to the symbolic penetration of a universal unconscious (503:124–30).

Any story that can generate the volume of response represented in the foregoing survey must be a powerful piece of literature. Melville's comments on "Young Goodman Brown" in his review of *Mosses* expressed surprise—and profound pleasure—that a simple little tale whose title suggests it as a "supplement to 'Goody Two Shoes' " should turn out to be as "deep as Dante" (332:123). Another contemporaneous reader called it the most "exquisitely managed" tale of the supernatural in American literature (513.5:133). Poe, on the other hand, disliked its allegorical intent and advised its author to escape "from the mysticism of his Goodman Browns" (378.1:150), while another mid-nineteenth-century reader found it practically unintelligible, with nine out of ten of its readers incapable of apprehending its moral (157.5:139–40).

Although twentieth-century readers have not unanimously endorsed "Young Goodman Brown" either, an overwhelming number have exhausted superlatives in their efforts to praise it adequately. The few negative responses appear insignificant amidst the multitude of accolades. One reader finds the authorial attitude lacking in compassion (239); another, whose book is devoted to en masse debunking, chooses to find fault with the story's "language of empty exaggeration" (203:73–74). The editors of two short-story collections have objected to its last paragraph as anticlimactic and artistically damaging; they say the dramatic impact would have been stronger if Hawthorne had let the incidents tell their own story (202.8:38; 445.5). Over a half-century earlier, Henry James chose that very passage to quote in full with the comment, "There is imagination in that" (241:49). Some have specifically defended the conclusion as necessary (1) and ironically powerful (397:224). On the Brown"; they are more prone to extol its virtues aggressively. Fiedler says whole, however, readers are not on the defensive about "Young Goodman it is "the most perfect in form and tone" of Hawthorne's tales (181:426). For Matthiessen, it is "Hawthorne's imagination . . . at its most delicately masterful" (315:283). Many consider it not only the best of Hawthorne, but the best of all American short stories. Others extend the critical horizons further. Leavis thinks it is more impressive than the *Walpurgesnacht* scene in Joyce's *Ulysses* (275:37). Male calls it "one of the world's great short stories" (304:76), and Abcarian suggests it may be "one of the finest . . . ever written" (1:343). It is without a doubt the best-known of Hawthorne's short stories in America and internationally as well. In combining historicity and universality (500:125), it transports each reader simultaneously to seventeenth-century New England and to the unexplored depths of his own soul. What he finds there may be of his own making, but the journey is the kind of interior exploration triggered by great works of literature. In "Young Goodman Brown," as in *The Scarlet Letter*, Hawthorne qualifies himself as a writer of works of genius.

# Bibliography

## Primary Sources

Charvat, William, Roy Harvey Pearce, Claude M. Simpson, Fredson Bowers, Matthew J. Bruccoli, and L. Neal Smith, eds. *The Centenary Edition of the Works of Nathaniel Hawthorne.* Columbus: Ohio State Univ. Press. Vol. I: *The Scarlet Letter,* 1962. Introd. William Charvat. Vol. II: *The House of the Seven Gables,* 1965. Introd. William Charvat. Vol. III: *The Blithedale Romance; Fanshawe,* 1964. Introd. Roy Harvey Pearce. Vol. IV: *The Marble Faun: Or, The Romance of Monte Beni,* 1968. Introd. Claude M. Simpson. Vol. V: *Our Old Home: A Series of English Sketches,* 1970. Introd. Claude M. Simpson. Vol. VI: *True Stories from History and Biography,* 1972. Introd. Roy Harvey Pearce. Vol. VII: *A Wonder Book; Tanglewood Tales,* 1972. Vol. VIII: *The American Notebooks,* 1972. Ed. Claude M. Simpson. Vol. IX: *Twice-told Tales,* 1974. Ed. J. Donald Crowley. Vol. X: *Mosses from an Old Manse,* 1974. Ed. J. Donald Crowley. Vol. XI: *The Snow-Image; Uncollected Tales,* 1974. Ed. J. Donald Crowley.

## Secondary Sources

1. Abcarian, Richard. "The Ending of 'Young Goodman Brown.'" *Studies in Short Fiction,* 3 (1966), 343–45.

2. Abel, Darrel. "Black Glove and Pink Ribbon: Hawthorne's Metonymic Symbols." *New England Quarterly,* 42 (1969), 163–80.

3. ————. "The Devil in Boston." *Philological Quarterly,* 32 (1953), 366–81.

4. ————. "Le Sage's Limping Devil and 'Mrs. Bullfrog.'" *Notes and Queries,* 198 (1953), 165–66.

5. ————. "The Theme of Isolation in Hawthorne." *Personalist,* 32 (1951), 42–59, 182–90.

6. ————. "'A Vast Deal of Human Sympathy': Idea and Device in Hawthorne's 'The Snow Image.'" *Criticism,* 12 (1970), 316–32.

7. Abernathy, P. L. "The Identity of Hawthorne's Major Molineux." *American Transcendental Quarterly,* 31 (1976), 5–8.

7.5. Adams, John F. "Hawthorne's Symbolic Gardens." *Texas Studies in Literature and Language,* 5 (1963), 242–54.

8.  Adams, Joseph D. "The Societal Initiation and Hawthorne's 'My Kinsman, Major Molineux': The Night Journey Motif." *English Studies Colloquium* (East Meadows, N.Y.), 1 (1976), 1–19.

9.  Adams, Richard P. "Hawthorne: The Old Manse Period." *Tulane Studies in English*, 8 (1958), 115–51.

10. ––––––. "Hawthorne's Provincial Tales." *New England Quarterly*, 30 (1957), 39–57.

11. Adkins, Nelson F. "The Early Projected Works of Nathaniel Hawthorne." *Papers of the Bibliographical Society of America*, 39 (1945), 119–55.

12. ––––––. "Notes on the Hawthorne Canon." *Papers of the Bibliographical Society of America*, 60 (1966), 364–67.

13. ––––––. "Hawthorne's Democratic New England Puritans." *Emerson Society Quarterly*, 44 (1966), 66–72.

14. Allen, M. L. "The Black Veil: Three Versions of a Symbol." *English Studies*, 47 (1966), 286–89.

15. ––––––. "Hawthorne's Art in his Short Stories." *Studi Americani* (Roma), 7 (1961), 9–41.

16. Allen, Margaret V. "Imagination and History in Hawthorne's 'Legend of the Province-House.' " *American Literature*, 43 (1971), 432–37.

17. Allison, Alexander W. "The Literary Contexts of 'My Kinsman, Major Molineux.' " *Nineteenth-Century Fiction*, 23 (1968), 304–11.

18. Alsen, Eberhard. "The Ambitious Experiment of Dr. Rappaccini." *American Literature*, 43 (1971), 430–31.

19. Altschuler, Glenn C. "The Puritan Dilemma in 'The Minister's Black Veil.' " *American Transcendental Quarterly*, 24, supp. 1 (1974), 25–27.

20. Anderson, D. K., Jr. "Hawthorne's Crowds." *Nineteenth-Century Fiction*, 7 (1952), 39–50.

21. Anderson, George K. *The Legend of the Wandering Jew.* Providence: Brown Univ. Press, 1965.

22. Anderson, Norman A. " 'Rappaccini's Daughter': A Keatsian Analogue." *PMLA*, 83 (1968), 271–83.

23. Anderson, Quentin. "Henry James and the New Jerusalem." *Kenyon Review*, 8 (1946), 515–66.

24. Ano, Fumio. "The Mischianza Ball and Hawthorne's 'Howe's Masquerade.' " *Nathaniel Hawthorne Journal*, 4 (1974), 231–35.

25. Arner, Robert D. "Hawthorne and Jones Very: Two Dimensions of Satire in 'Egotism; or, The Bosom-Serpent.' " *New England Quarterly*, 42 (1969), 267–75.

26. ––––––. "The Legend of Pygmalion in 'The Birthmark.' " *American Transcendental Quarterly*, 14 (1972), 168–71.

27. Arvin, Newton. *Hawthorne.* Boston: Little, Brown, 1929; rpt. New York: Russell & Russell, 1961.

28. ——————. *Hawthorne's Short Stories.* 1946; rpt. New York: Vintage-Knopf, 1955.

29. Askew, Melvin W. "Hawthorne, the Fall, and the Psychology of Maturity." *American Literature,* 34 (1962), 335–43.

30. ——————. "The Wounded Artist and his Work." *Kansas Magazine* (1961), 73–77.

31. Autrey, Max. "Hawthorne's Study in Clay." *Xavier University Studies,* 11 (1972), 1–5.

32. Axelsson, Arne. *The Links in the Chain: Isolation and Interdependence in Nathaniel Hawthorne's Fictional Characters.* Stockholm, Sweden: Uppsala Univ., 1974.

33. Ayo, Nicholas. "The Labyrinthine Ways of 'Rappaccini's Daughter.' " *Research Studies* (Washington State Univ.), 42 (1974), 56–69.

34. Babiiha, Thaddeo Kitasimbwa. "James's *Washington Square*: More on the Hawthorne Relation." *Nathaniel Hawthorne Journal,* 4 (1974), 270–72.

35. Barnes, Daniel R. "The Bosom Serpent: A Legend in American Literature and Culture." *Journal of American Folklore,* 85 (1972), 11–22.

36. ——————. "Faulkner's Miss Emily and Hawthorne's Old Maid." *Studies in Short Fiction,* 9 (1972), 373–78.

37. ——————. " 'Physical Fact' and Folklore: Hawthorne's 'Egotism; or, The Bosom Serpent.' " *American Literature,* 43 (1971), 117–21.

38. Baxter, Annette K. "Independence vs. Isolation: Hawthorne and James on the Problem of the Artist." *Nineteenth-Century Fiction,* 10 (1955), 225–31.

39. Baxter, David J. " 'The Birth-mark' in Perspective." *Nathaniel Hawthorne Journal,* 4 (1974), 232–40.

40. Baym, Nina. "Hawthorne's Gothic Discards: *Fanshawe* and 'Alice Doane.' " *Nathaniel Hawthorne Journal,* 4 (1974), 105–15.

41. ——————. "The Head, the Heart, and the Unpardonable Sin." *New England Quarterly,* 40 (1967), 31–47.

42. ——————. "Nathaniel Hawthorne." In *American Literary Scholarship: An Annual/1971.* Durham, N.C.: Duke Univ. Press, 1973, pp. 24–40.

43. ——————. *The Shape of Hawthorne's Career.* Ithaca, N.Y.: Cornell Univ. Press, 1976.

44. Becker, Isadore H. "Tragic Irony in 'Rappaccini's Daughter.' " *Husson Review,* 4 (1971), 89–93.

45.  Becker, John E. *Hawthorne's Historical Allegory*. New York: Kennikat Press, 1971.

46.  Bell, Michael Davitt. *Hawthorne and the Historical Romance' of New England*. Princeton, N.J.: Princeton Univ. Press, 1971.

47.  Bell, Millicent. *Hawthorne's View of the Artist*. New York: New York State Univ. Press, 1962.

47.5.  Benoit, Raymond. "Hawthorne's Psychology of Death: 'The Minister's Black Veil.' " *Studies in Short Fiction*, 8 (1971), 553–60.

48.  Bercovitch, Sacvan. "Diabolus in Salem." *English Language Notes*, 6 (1969), 280–85.

49.  ———. "Endicott's Breastplate: Symbolism and Typology in 'Endicott and the Red Cross.' " *Studies in Short Fiction*, 4 (1967), 289–99.

50.  Berek, Peter. *The Transformation of Allegory from Spenser to Hawthorne*. Amherst, Mass.: Amherst College Press, 1962.

51.  Bewley, Marius. *The Complex Fate: Hawthorne, Henry James and Some Other American Writers*. London, 1952; rpt. New York: Gordian Press, 1967.

52.  ———. *The Eccentric Design: Form in the Classic American Novel*. New York: Columbia Univ. Press, 1959.

53.  ———. "Hawthorne and 'The Deeper Psychology.' " *Mandrake*, 2 (1956), 366–73.

53.3.  Bickford, Gail H. "Lovewell's Fight, 1725–1958." *American Quarterly*, 10 (1958), 358–66.

53.8.  Birdsall, Virginia Ogden. "Hawthorne's Oak Tree Image." *Nineteenth-Century Fiction*, 15 (1960) 181–85.

54.  Birkhead, Edith. *The Tale of Terror: A Study of the Gothic Romance*. London: Constable, 1921.

55.  Blair, Walter. "Nathaniel Hawthorne." In *Eight American Authors: A Review of Research and Criticism*. Ed. James Woodress. New York: Norton, 1971, pp. 85–128.

56.  Boewe, Charles. "Rappaccini's Garden." *American Literature*, 30 (1958), 37–49.

56.6.  Booth, Edward Townsend. "New Adam and Eve in an Old Manse." In *God Made the Country*. New York: Knopf, 1946, pp. 202–19.

57.  Borges, Jorge Luis. "Nathaniel Hawthorne." In *Other Inquisitions 1937–1952*. Trans. Ruth L. C. Simms. Austin: Univ. of Texas Press, 1964, pp. 47–65.

58.  Boswell, Jackson Campbell. "Another Generation of Vipers." *English Language Notes*, 14 (1976), 124–31.

59. ————. "Bosom Serpents before Hawthorne: Origin of a Symbol." *English Language Notes,* 12 (1975), 279–87.

60. Boudreau, Gordon V. "The Summons of Young Goodman Brown." *Greyfriar: Siena Studies in Literature,* 13 (1972), 15–24.

61. Brennan, J. X. and Seymour L. Gross. "The Origin of Hawthorne's Unpardonable Sin." *Boston University Studies in English,* 3 (1957), 123–29.

62. Brenzo, Richard. "Beatrice Rappaccini: A Victim of Male Love and Horror." *American Literature,* 48 (1976), 152–64.

63. Bridge, Horatio. *Personal Recollections of Nathaniel Hawthorne.* 1893; rpt. New York: Haskell House, 1968.

64. Brill, Lesley W. "Conflict and Accommodation in Hawthorne's 'The Artist of the Beautiful.'" *Studies in Short Fiction,* 12 (1975), 381–86.

65. Brodwin, Stanley. "Hawthorne and the Function of History: A Reading of 'Alice Doane's Appeal.'" *Nathaniel Hawthorne Journal,* 4 (1974), 116–28.

66. Broes, Arthur T. "Journey into Moral Darkness: 'My Kinsman, Major Molineux' as Allegory." *Nineteenth-Century Fiction,* 19 (1964), 171–84.

67. Brooks, Cleanth and Robert Penn Warren. *Understanding Fiction.* New York: Crofts, 1943, pp. 104–06. Rpt. in *A Casebook on the Hawthorne Question.* Ed. Agnes McNeill Donahue. New York: Crowell, 1963, pp. 185–88.

68. Brown, Dennis. "Literature and Existential Psychoanalysis: 'My Kinsman, Major Molineux' and 'Young Goodman Brown.'" *Canadian Review of American Studies,* 4 (1973), 65–73.

69. Brown, E. K. "Hawthorne, Melville, and 'Ethan Brand.'" *American Literature,* 3 (1931), 72–75.

70. Brubaker, B. R. "Hawthorne's Experiment in Popular Form: 'Mr. Higginbotham's Catastrophe.'" *Southern Humanities Review,* 7 (1973), 155–66.

71. Bruccoli, Matthew J. "Negative Evidence about 'The Celestial Railroad.'" *Papers of the Bibliographical Society,* 58 (1964) 290–92.

72. Brumm, Ursula. *American Thought and Religious Typology.* Trans. John Hoagland. New Brunswick, N. J.: Rutgers Univ. Press, 1970.

73. Burhans, C. S. "Hawthorne's Mind and Art in 'The Hollow of the Three Hills.'" *Journal of English and Germanic Philosophy,* 60 (1961), 286–95.

74. Bush, Sargent, Jr. "Bosom Serpents before Hawthorne: The Origins of a Symbol." *American Literature,* 43 (1971), 181–99.

75.    ——————. " 'Peter Goldthwaite's Treasure' and *The House of Seven Gables.*" *Emerson Society Quarterly*, 62 (1971), 35–38.

76.    Cameron, Kenneth Walter. "Background of Hawthorne's 'The Canterbury Pilgrims.' " *Emerson Society Quarterly*, 13 (1958), 41–45.

77.    ——————. *Genesis of Hawthorne's "The Ambitious Guest."* Hartford, Conn.: Transcendental Books, 1955.

78.    Cantwell, Robert. *Nathaniel Hawthorne: The American Years.* New York: Rinehart, 1948.

78.5.  Cargas, Harry J. "The Arc of Rebirth in 'Young Goodman Brown.' " *New Laurel Review*, 4 (1975), 5–7.

78.8.  Carlson, Patricia Ann. "The Function of the Lamp in Hawthorne's 'The Wives of the Dead.' " *Southern Atlantic Bulletin*, 40 (1975), 62–64.

79.    ——————. "Image and Structure in Hawthorne's 'Roger Malvin's Burial.' " *Southern Atlantic Bulletin*, 41 (1976), 3–9.

80.    Carnochan, W. B. " 'The Minister's Black Veil': Symbol, Meaning, and the Context of Hawthorne's Art." *Nineteenth-Century Fiction*, 24 (1969), 182–92.

81.    Carpenter, Richard C. "Hawthorne's Polar Explorations: 'Young Goodman Brown' and 'My Kinsman, Major Molineux.' " *Nineteenth-Century Fiction*, 24 (1969), 45–56.

82.    Cervo, Nathan A. "The Gargouille Anti-Hero: Victim of Christian Satire." *Renascence*, 22 (1970), 69–77.

83.    Chamber, Jane. "Two Legends of Temperance: Spenser's and Hawthorne's." *Emerson Society Quarterly*, 20 (1974), 275–79.

84.    Chandler, Elizabeth Lathrop. *A Study of the Sources of the Tales and Romances Written by Nathaniel Hawthorne before 1853.* Manasha, Wis.: George Banta, 1926.

85.    Cherry, Fannye N. "A Note on the Source of Hawthorne's 'Lady Eleanore's Mantle.' " *American Literature*, 6 (1935), 437–39.

86.    ——————. "The Sources of Hawthorne's 'Young Goodman Brown.' " *American Literature*, 5 (1934), 342–48.

87.    Clark, C. E. Frazer, Jr., ed. *The Love Letters of Nathaniel Hawthorne, 1839–1863.* 1907; rpt. Washington, D. C.: NCR Microcard, 1972.

88.    ——————. "New Light on the Editing of the 1842 Edition of *Twice-told Tales.*" *Nathaniel Hawthorne Journal*, 2 (1972), 91–139.

89.    ——————. "The Susan 'Affair.' " *Nathaniel Hawthorne Journal*, 1 (1971), 12–17.

89.5.  Clark, James W., Jr. "Hawthorne's Use of Evidence in 'Young Goodman Brown.' " *Essex Institute Historical Collections*, 111 (1975), 12–34.

90. Clayton, Laurence. " 'Lady Eleanore's Mantle': A Metaphorical Key to Hawthorne's 'Legends of the Province-House.' " *English Language Notes*, 9 (1971), 49–51.

91. Clive, Geoffrey. "The Teleological Suspension of the Ethical in Nineteenth-Century Literature." *Journal of Religion*, 34 (1954), 75–87.

92. Cochran, Robert W. "Hawthorne's Choice: The Veil or the Jaundiced Eye." *College English*, 23 (1962), 342–46.

93. Coffey, Dennis G. "Hawthorne's 'Alice Doane's Appeal': The Artist Absolved." *Emerson Society Quarterly*, 21 (1975), 23–40.

94. Cohen, B. Bernard. "Deodat Lawson's *Christ's Fidelity* and Hawthorne's 'Young Goodman Brown.' " *Essex Institute Historical Collections*, 104 (1968), 349–70.

95. ————. " 'The Gray Champion.' " *Folio*, 13 (1948), 11–12.

96. ————. "Hawthorne's 'Mrs. Bullfrog' and *The Rambler*." *Philological Quarterly*, 32 (1953), 382–87.

97. ————. "*Paradise Lost* and 'Young Goodman Brown.' " *Essex Institute Historical Collections*, 94 (1958), 282–96.

98. ————, ed. *The Recognition of Nathaniel Hawthorne: Selected Criticism since 1828*. Ann Arbor: Univ. of Michigan Press, 1969.

99. ————. "The Sources of 'The Ambitious Guest.' " *Boston Public Library Quarterly*, 4 (1952), 221–24. Rpt. in *Writing About Literature*. Chicago: Scott, Foresman, 1963, pp. 104–09.

100. Cohen, Hubert I. "Hoffmann's 'The Sandman': A Possible Source for 'Rappaccini's Daughter.' " *Emerson Society Quarterly*, 18 (1972), 148–53.

101. Colacurcio, Michael J. "Visible Sanctity and Specter Evidence: The Moral World of Hawthorne's 'Young Goodman Brown.' " *Essex Institute Historical Collections*, 110 (1974), 259–99.

102. Connolly, Thomas E. "Hawthorne's 'Young Goodman Brown': An Attack on Puritanic Calvinism." *American Literature*, 28 (1956), 370–75.

103. ————. "How Young Goodman Brown Became Old Badman Brown." *College English*, 24 (1962), 153.

104. ————, ed. *Nathaniel Hawthorne: "Young Goodman Brown."* Columbus, Ohio: Charles E. Merrill, 1968.

105. Connors, Thomas E. " 'My Kinsman, Major Molineux': A Reading." *Modern Language Notes*, 74 (1959), 229–302.

106. Conway, Moncure D. *Life of Nathaniel Hawthorne*. London: Walter Scott, 1895.

107.   Cook, Reginald. "The Forest of Goodman Brown's Night: A Reading of Hawthorne's 'Young Goodman Brown.'" *New England Quarterly,* 43 (1970), 473–81.

108.   Cooke, Alice Lovelace. "The Shadow of Martin Scriblerus in Hawthorne's 'The Prophetic Pictures.'" *New England Quarterly,* 17 (1944), 597–604.

109.   ——————. "Some Evidence of Hawthorne's Indebtedness to Swift." *University of Texas Studies in English,* 18 (1938), 140–62.

110.   Cowie, Alexander. *The Rise of the American Novel.* New York: American Books, 1951.

111.   Cowley, Malcolm. "Hawthorne in the Looking Glass." *Sewanee Review,* 56 (1948), 545–63.

112.   ——————. "Hawthorne in Solitude." *New Republic,* 109 (1948), 19–23.

113.   ——————. "The Hawthornes in Paradise." *American Heritage,* 10 (1958), 30–35, 112–15.

114.   ——————. *The Portable Hawthorne.* New York: Viking, 1948.

115.   Crews, Frederick C. *The Sins of the Fathers: Hawthorne's Psychological Themes.* New York: Oxford Univ. Press, 1966.

116.   Crie, Robert D. "'The Minister's Black Veil': Mr. Hooper's Symbolic Fig Leaf." *Literature and Psychology,* 17 (1967), 211–17.

117.   Cronkhite, G. Ferris. "The Transcendental Railroad." *New England Quarterly,* 24 (1951), 306-28.

118.   Crowley, J. Donald, ed. *Hawthorne: The Critical Heritage.* New York: Barnes & Noble, 1970.

119.   ——————. "Nathaniel Hawthorne's *Twice-told Tales*: A Textual Study." *Dissertation Abstract,* 25 (Ohio State Univ., 1964), 7242.

120.   ——————. "The Unity of Hawthorne's *Twice-told Tales.*" *Studies in American Fiction,* 1 (1973), 35–61.

121.   Curran, Ronald T. "Irony: Another Thematic Dimension to 'The Artist of the Beautiful.'" *Studies in Romanticism,* 6 (1966), 34–45.

122.   Dahl, Curtis. "The American School of Catastrophe." *American Quarterly,* 11 (1959), 380.

123.   ——————. "The Devil is a Wise One." *Cithara,* 6 (1967), 52–58.

124.   Daly, Robert J. "Fideism and the Allusive Mode in 'Rappaccini's Daughter.'" *Nineteenth-Century Fiction,* 28 (1973), 25–37.

125.   ——————. "History and Chivalric Myth in 'Roger Malvin's Burial.'" *Essex Institute Historical Collections,* 109 (1973), 99–115.

126.   Dameron, J. Lasley. "Hawthorne and Blackwood's Review of Goethe's *Faust.*" *Emerson Society Quarterly,* 19 (1960), 25.

127. Dauber, Kenneth. *Rediscovering Hawthorne*. Princeton, N. J.: Princeton Univ. Press, 1977.

128. Dauner, Louise. "The 'Case' of Tobias Pearson: Hawthorne and the Ambiguities." *American Literature*, 21 (1950), 464–72.

129. Dauphin, Vernon A. "Religious Content in Hawthorne's Works." *Southern University Bulletin*, 46 (1959), 115–23.

130. D'Avanzo, Mario. "The Literary Sources of 'My Kinsman, Major Molineux': Shakespeare, Coleridge, Milton." *Studies in Short Fiction*, 10 (1972), 121–36.

131. Davidson, Edward H. *Hawthorne's Last Phase*. New Haven, Conn.: Yale Univ. Press, 1949.

131.2. ––––––, ed. "Nathaniel Hawthorne." In *Major Writers of America*. Ed. Perry Miller. New York: Harcourt, Brace, & World, 1962, I, 683–792.

131.5. Davidson, Frank. "Hawthorne's Hive of Honey." *Modern Language Notes*, 61 (1946), 14–21.

132. ––––––. "Hawthorne's Use of a Pattern from the *Rambler*." *Modern Language Notes*, 63 (1948), 545–58.

133. ––––––. "Thoreau's Contributions to Hawthorne's *Mosses*." *New England Quarterly*, 20 (1947), 535–42.

134. ––––––. "Voltaire and Hawthorne's 'The Christmas Banquet.'" *Boston Public Library Quarterly*, 3 (1951), 244–46.

135. ––––––. "'Young Goodman Brown': Hawthorne's Intent." *Emerson Society Quarterly*, 31 (1963), 68–71.

136. Davis, Joseph. "The Myth of the Garden: Nathaniel Hawthorne's 'Rappaccini's Daughter.'" *Studies in the Literary Imagination*, 2 (1969), 3–12.

137. Davis, Richard Beale. "Hawthorne, Fanny Kemble, and 'The Artist of the Beautiful.'" *Modern Language Notes*, 70 (1955), 589–92.

138. Davison, Richard Allan. "The Villagers and 'Ethan Brand.'" *Studies in Short Fiction*, 4 (1967), 260–62.

139. DeHayes, R. "Charting Hawthorne's Invisible World." *CEA Critic*, 27 (1965), 5–6.

140. Delaune, Henry M. "The Beautiful of 'The Artist of the Beautiful.'" *Xavier University Studies*, 1 (1961), 94–99.

141. Deming, Robert H. "The Use of the Past: Herrick and Hawthorne." *Journal of Popular Culture*, 2 (1968), 278–91.

142.    Dennis, Carl. "How to Live in Hell: The Bleak Vision of Hawthorne's
        'My Kinsman, Major Molineux.' " *The University Review*,
        37 (1971), 250–58.

143.    Devlin, James E. "A German Analogue for 'The Ambitious Guest.' "
        *American Transcendental Quarterly*, 17 (1973), 171–74.

144.    Dichmann, Mary E. "Hawthorne's Prophetic Pictures."
        *American Literature*, 23 (1951), 188–202.

144.5.  Dickson, Wayne. "Hawthorne's 'Young Goodman Brown.' "
        *Explicator*, 29 (1971), 44.

145.    Dobbs, Jeannine. "Hawthorne's Dr. Rappaccini and
        Father George Rapp." *American Literature*, 43 (1971), 427–30.

146.    Donahue, Agnes McNeill. " 'From Whose Bourn No Traveller Returns':
        A Reading of 'Roger Malvin's Burial.' " *Nineteenth-Century Fiction*,
        18 (1963), 1–19.

147.    ————. " 'The Fruit of That Forbidden Tree': A Reading of
        'The Gentle Boy.' " In *A Casebook on the Hawthorne Question*.
        Ed. Agnes McNeill Donahue. New York: Crowell, 1971, pp. 158–70.

148.    Dorson, Richard M. "Five Directions in American Folklore."
        *Midwest Folklore*, 1 (1951), 149–65.

149.    Doubleday, Neal Frank. *Hawthorne's Early Tales: A Critical Study*.
        Durham, N. C.: Duke Univ. Press, 1972.

149.5.  ————. "Hawthorne's Estimate of His Early Work."
        *American Literature*, 37 (1966), 403–09.

150.    ————. "Hawthorne's Inferno." *College English*, 1 (1940), 658–70.

151.    ————. "Hawthorne's Satirical Allegory." *College English*,
        3 (1942), 325–37.

153.    ————. "The Theme of Hawthorne's 'Fancy's Show Box.' "
        *American Literature*, 10 (1938), 341–43.

154.    Drake, Samuel Adams. *A Book of New England Legends and
        Folk Lore in Prose and Poetry*. Boston: Little, Brown, 1906.

155.    Durr, Robert Allen. "Feathertop's Unlikely Love Affair."
        *Modern Language Notes*, 72 (1957), 492–93.

156.    ————. "Hawthorne's Ironic Mode." *New England Quarterly*,
        30 (1957), 486–95.

157.    Dusenbery, Robert. "Hawthorne's Merry Company: The Anatomy of
        Laughter in the Tales and Short Stories." *PMLA*, 82 (1967), 285–88.

157.5.  Dutton, Samuel W. "Nathaniel Hawthorne." *New Englander*,
        5 (1847), 56–69. Rpt. in 118, pp. 135–40.

158.   Dwight, Sheila. "Hawthorne and the Unpardonable Sin."
       *Studies in the Novel,* 2 (1970), 449–58.

159.   Eberwein, Jane Donahue. "Temporal Perspective in 'The Legends of
       the Province-House.'" *American Transcendental Quarterly,*
       14 (1972), 41–45.

160.   Edgren, C. Hobart. "Hawthorne's 'The Ambitious Guest':
       An Interpretation." *Nineteenth-Century Fiction,* 10 (1955), 151–56.

161.   Ehrenpreis, Anne Henry. "Elizabeth Gaskell and Nathaniel Hawthorne."
       *Nathaniel Hawthorne Journal,* 3 (1973), 89–119.

162.   Eisinger, Chester E. "Hawthorne as Champion of the Middle Way."
       *New England Quarterly,* 27 (1954), 27–52.

163.   Elder, Marjorie J. *Nathaniel Hawthorne: Transcendental Symbolist.*
       Athens: Ohio Univ. Press, 1969.

164.   Elias, Helen L. "Alice Doane's Innocence: The Wizard   Absolved."
       *Emerson Society Quarterly,* 62 (1971), 28–32.

165.   England, A. B. "Robin Molineux and the Young Ben Franklin:
       A Reconsideration." *Journal of American Studies,* 6 (1972), 181–88.

166.   Ensor, Allison. "'Whispers of the Bad Angel': A *Scarlet Letter*
       Passage as a Commentary on Hawthorne's 'Young Goodman Brown.'"
       *Studies in Short Fiction,* 7 (1970), 467–69.

167.   Erisman, Fred. "'Young Goodman Brown': Warning to Idealists."
       *American Transcendental Quarterly,* 14 (1972), 156–58.

168.   Erlich, Gloria C. "Deadly Innocence: Hawthorne's Dark Women."
       *New England Quarterly,* 41 (1968), 163–79.

169.   ––––––. "Guilt and Expiation in 'Roger Malvin's Burial.'"
       *Nineteenth-Century Fiction,* 26 (1972), 377–89.

170.   Evans, Oliver. "Allegory and Incest in 'Rappaccini's Daughter.'"
       *Nineteenth-Century Fiction,* 19 (1964), 185–95.

171.   ––––––. "The Cavern and the Fountain: Paradox and Double
       Paradox in 'Rappaccini's Daughter.'" *College English,*
       24 (1963), 461–63.

172.   Fairbanks, Henry G. "Hawthorne Amid the Alien Corn."
       *College English,* 17 (1956) 263–68.

173.   ––––––. "Hawthorne and Confession." *Catholic Historical Review,*
       43 (1957), 38–45.

174.   ––––––. "Hawthorne and the Atomic Age." *Revue de l'Universite
       d'Ottawa,* 31 (1961), 436–51.

175.   ––––––. "Hawthorne and the Machine Age." *American Literature,*
       28 (1956), 155–63.

176. ———————. "Man's Separation from Nature: Hawthorne's Philosophy of Suffering and Death." *Christian Scholar*, 42 (1959), 51–63.

177. ———————. "Sin, Free Will, and 'Pessimism' in Hawthorne." *PMLA*, 71 (1956), 975–89.

178. Faust, Bertha. *Hawthorne's Contemporaneous Reputation: A Study of Literary Opinion in America and England, 1828–1864.* New York: Octagon Books, 1968.

179. Feeney, Joseph J., S. J. "The Structure of Ambiguity in Hawthorne's 'The May-Pole of Merry Mount.' " *Studies in American Fiction*, 3 (1975), 211–16.

180. Ferguson, J. M., Jr. "Hawthorne's 'Young Goodman Brown.' " *Explicator*, 28 (1969), 32.

180.5. Fick, Leonard J. *The Light Beyond: A Study of Hawthorne's Theology.* Westminster, Md.: Newman Press, 1955.

181. Fiedler, Leslie. *Love and Death in the American Novel.* New York: World, 1960. Revised ed. New York: Stein and Day, 1966.

182. Fields, James T. *Yesterdays with Authors.* Boston: Osgood, 1872; rpt. New York: AMS Press, 1970.

183. Fisher, Marvin. "The Pattern of Conservatism in Johnson's *Rasselas* and Hawthorne's Tales." *Journal of the History of Ideas*, 19 (1958), 173–96.

184. Flanagan, John T. and Arthur P. Hudson. *Folklore in American Literature.* Evanston Ill.: Row, Peterson, 1958.

185. Fletcher, Angus. *Allegory: The Theory of a Symbolic Mode.* Ithaca, N. Y.: Cornell Univ. Press, 1964.

186. Fogle, Richard Harter. *Hawthorne's Fiction: The Light and the Dark.* Rev. ed. Norman: Oklahoma Univ. Press, 1964.

187. ———————. "Weird Mockery: An Element of Hawthorne's Style." *Style*, 2 (1968), 191–202.

188. Folsom, James F. *Man's Accidents and God's Purposes: Multiplicity in Hawthorne's Fiction.* New Haven, Conn.: College and Univ. Press, 1963.

189. Fossum, Robert H. *Hawthorne's Inviolable Circle: The Problem of Time.* Deland, Fl.: Everett/Edwards, 1972.

190. Foster, Charles. "Hawthorne's Literary Theory." *PMLA*, 57 (1942), 241–54.

191. Franklin, Howard Bruce. *Future Perfect: American Science Fiction of the Nineteenth Century.* New York: Oxford Univ. Press, 1966.

192. Friedrich, Gerhard. "A Note on Quakerism and *Moby Dick*: Hawthorne's 'The Gentle Boy' as a Possible Source." *Quaker History*, 54 (1965), 94–102.

193.  Fussell, Edwin. *Frontier: American Literature and the American West.* Princenton, N. J.: Princeton Univ. Press, 1965.

194.  Gale, Robert L. "Rappaccini's Baglioni." *Studi Americani*, 9 (1964), 83–87.

195.  Gallagher, Edward J. "History in 'Endicott and the Red Cross.' " *Emerson Society Quarterly*, 50, supp. (1968), 62–55.

196.  ––––––. "Sir Kenelm Digby in Hawthorne's 'The Man of Adamant.' " *Notes and Queries*, 17 (1970), 15–16.

197.  Gardner, John and Lennis Dunlap. *The Forms of Fiction.* New York: Random House, 1962.

198.  Gargano, James W. "Hawthorne's 'The Artist of the Beautiful.' " *American Literature*, 35 (1963), 225–30.

199.  Gautreau, Henry W., Jr. "A Note on Hawthorne's 'The Man of Adamant.' " *Philological Quarterly*, 52 (1973), 315–17.

200.  Geist, Stanley. "Fictitious Americans: A Preface to 'Ethan Brand.' " *Hudson Review*, 5 (1952), 199–211.

201.  Gibbens, Victor E. "Hawthorne's Note to 'Dr. Heidegger's Experiment.' " *Modern Language Notes*, 60 (1945), 408–09.

202.  Gilkes, Lillian B. "Hawthorne, Park Benjamin, S. G. Goodrich: A Three-Cornered Imbroglio." *Nathaniel Hawthorne Journal*, 1 (1971), 83–112.

202.5.  Goodman, Paul. *The Structure of Literature.* Chicago: Univ. of Chicago Press, 1954.

202.8.  Gordan, Caroline, and Allen Tate. "Nathaniel Hawthorne: 'Young Goodman Brown.' " In *The House of Fiction: An Anthology of the Short Story.* New York: Charles Scribner's Sons, 1960, pp. 27–39.

203.  Green, Martin. *Re-appraisals: Some Commonsense Readings in American Literature.* New York: Norton, 1965.

204.  Gross, Seymour L. "Four Possible Additions to Hawthorne's 'Story Teller.' " *Papers of the Bibliographical Society of America*, 51 (1957), 90–95.

205.  ––––––. "Hawthorne and the Shakers." *American Literature*, 29 (1958), 457–63.

206.  ––––––. "Hawthorne's 'Alice Doane's Appeal.' " *Nineteenth-Century Fiction*, 10 (1955), 232–36.

207.  ––––––. "Hawthorne's Income from *The Token.*" *Studies in Bibliography*, 8 (1956), 236–38.

208.  ––––––. "Hawthorne's 'Lady Eleanore's Mantle' as History." *Journal of English and Germanic Philology*, 54 (1955), 549–54.

209.    ――――. "Hawthorne's 'My Kinsman, Major Molineux':
History as Moral Adventure." *Nineteenth-Century Fiction*, 24 (1969),
45–56.

210.    ――――. "Hawthorne's Revisions of 'The Gentle Boy.'"
*American Literature*, 26 (1954), 196–208.

211.    ――――. "Hawthorne's 'Vision of the Fountain' as a Parody."
*American Literature*, 27 (1955), 101–05.

212.    ――――. "Prologue to *The Scarlet Letter*: Hawthorne's Fiction to
1850." In *A Scarlet Letter Handbook*. Belmont, Calif.: Wadsworth,
1960, pp. 1–14.

213.    ――――, and Alfred J. Levy. "Some Remarks on the Extant
Manuscripts of Hawthorne's Short Stories." *Studies in Bibliography*,
14 (1961), 254–57.

214.    Grossman, James. "Vanzetti and Hawthorne." *American Quarterly*,
22 (1970), 902–07.

215.    Gupta, R. K. "Hawthorne's Treatment of the Artist."
*New England Quarterly*, 45 (1972), 65-80.

216.    Gwynn, Frederick L. "Hawthorne's 'Rappaccini's Daughter.'"
*Nineteenth-Century Fiction*, 7 (1952), 217–19.

217.    Halligan, John. "Hawthorne on Democracy: 'Endicott and the
Red Cross.'" *Studies in Short Fiction*, 8 (1971), 301–07.

218.    Harding, Walter. "Another Source for Hawthorne's 'Egotism; or,
The Bosom-Serpent.'" *American Literature*, 40 (1969), 537–38.

219.    Haskell, Raymond I. "The Great Carbuncle." *New England Quarterly*,
10 (1937), 533–35.

220.    ――――. "Sensings and Realizations on Reading 'The Great
Stone Face.'" *Education*, 43 (1923), 544–50.

221.    Hastings, Louise. "An Origin for 'Dr. Heidegger's Experiment.'"
*American Literature*, 9 (1938), 403–10.

222.    Havighurst, Walter. "Symbolism and the Student." *College English*,
16 (1955), 429–34, 461.

223.    Hawthorne, Julian. *Nathaniel Hawthorne and his Wife: A Biography*.
2 vols. Cambridge, Mass.: Osgood, 1884, 1885. Variously reprinted.

224.    Hawthorne, Manning. "Aunt Ebe: Some Letters of
Elizabeth M. Hawthorne." *New England Quarterly*, 20 (1947), 214.

225.    Hawthorne, Nathaniel. "Letter to his sister Louisa dated August 17,
1831." *Essex Institute Historical Collections*, 75 (1939), 125–28.

226.    Heilman, Robert B. "Science as Religion." *South Atlantic Quarterly*,
48 (1949), 573–83.

227. Herndon, Jerry A. "Hawthorne's Dream Imagery."
*American Literature*, 46 (1975), 538–45.

228. ––––––, and Sidney P. Moss. "The Identity and Significance of the German Jewish Showman in Hawthorne's 'Ethan Brand.' "
*College English*, 23 (1962), 362–63.

229. Hilton, Earl R. "Hawthorne, the Hippie, and the Square."
*Studies in the Novel*, 2 (1970), 425–39.

230. Hoeltje, Hubert H. "Captain Nathaniel Hawthorne: Father of the Famous Salem Novelist." *Essex Institute Historical Collections*, 89 (1953), 329–56.

231. ––––––. *Inward Sky: The Heart and Mind of Nathaniel Hawthorne.*
Durham, N. C.: Duke Univ. Press, 1962.

232. Hoffman, Daniel G. *Form and Fable in American Fiction.*
New York: Oxford Univ. Press, 1961.

233. ––––––. "Myth, Romance, and the Childhood of Man."
In *Hawthorne Centenary Essays.* Ed. Roy Harvey Pearce.
Columbus: Ohio State Univ. Press, 1964, pp. 197–219.

234. Holaday, Clayton A. "Re-examination of 'Feathertop' and RLR."
*New England Quarterly,* 27 (1954), 103–05.

235. Homan, John J. "Hawthorne's 'The Wedding Knell' and Cotton Mather." *Emerson Society Quarterly*, 43 (1966), 66–67.

236. Honig, Edwin. *Dark Conceit: The Making of Allegory.*
Evanston, Ill.: Northwestern Univ. Press, 1959.

237. Horne, Lewis B. "The Heart, The Hand, and 'Birthmark.' "
*American Transcendental Quarterly*, 1 (1969), 38–41.

238. Hovey, Richard B. "Love and Hate in 'Rappaccini's Daughter.' "
*Univ. of Kansas City Review*, 29 (1962), 137–45.

239. Humma, John B. " 'Young Goodman Brown' and the Failure of Hawthorne's Ambiguity." *Colby Library Quarterly*, 9 (1971), 425–31.

240. Hurley, Paul J. "Young Goodman Brown's 'Heart of Darkness.' "
*American Literature*, 37 (1966), 410–19.

241. James, Henry. *Hawthorne.* New York: Harper, 1879. Variously reprinted.

242. Janssen, James G. "Hawthorne's Seventh Vagabond: 'The Outsetting Bard.' " *Emerson Society Quarterly,* 62 (1971), 22–28.

243. Johnson, Claudia D. " 'Young Goodman Brown' and Puritan Justification." *Studies in Short Fiction*, 11 (1974), 200–03.

244. Johnson, W. Stacy. "Hawthorne and *The Pilgrim's Progress.*"
*Journal of English and Germanic Philology*, 50 (1951), 156–66.

245.    —————. "Sin and Salvation in Hawthorne." *Hibbert Journal*,
       50 (1951), 39–47.

246.    Jones, Bartlett C. "The Ambiquity of Shrewdness in 'My Kinsman,
       Major Molineux.' " *Midcontinent American Studies Journal*,
       3, (1962), 42–47.

247.    Jones, Buford. "The *Faery Land* of Hawthorne's Romances."
       *Emerson Society Quarterly*, 48 (1967), 106–24.

248.    —————. " 'The Man of Adamant' and the Moral Picturesque."
       *American Transcendental Quarterly*, 14 (1972), 33–41.

249.    Jones, Priscilla M. "Hawthorne's Mythic Use of Puritan History."
       *Cithara*, 12 (1972), 59–73.

250.    Jones, Wayne Allen. "The Hawthorne Goodrich Relationship and a
       New Estimate of Hawthorne's Income from *The Token*."
       *Nathaniel Hawthorne Journal*, 5 (1975), 91–140.

251.    —————. "New Light on Hawthorne and the Southern Rose."
       *Nathaniel Hawthorne Journal*, 4 (1974), 31–46.

252.    Joseph, Brother, F. S. C. "Art and Event in 'Ethan Brand.' "
       *Nineteenth-Century Fiction*, 15 (1960), 249–57.

253.    Josipovici, G. D. "Hawthorne's Modernism." *Critical Quarterly*,
       8 (1966), 351–60.

253.5.  Kane, Robert J. "Hawthorne's 'The Prophetic Pictures' and
       James's 'The Liar.' " *Modern Language Notes*, 65 (1950), 257–58.

254.    Karrfalt, David H. "Anima in Hawthorne and Haggard."
       *American Notes and Queries*, 2 (1964), 152–53.

255.    Kaul, A. N. "Nathaniel Hawthorne: Heir and Critic of the Puritan
       Tradition." In *The American Vision: Actual and Ideal Society in
       Nineteenth-Century Fiction*. New Haven, Conn.: Yale Univ Press,
       1963, pp. 139–213.

256.    Kelly, Richard. "Hawthorne's 'Ethan Brand.' " *Explicator*,
       28 (1970), 47.

257.    Kern, Alexander. "Hawthorne's 'Feathertop' and R.L.R."
       *PMLA*, 52 (1937), 503–10.

258.    —————. "The Sources of Hawthorne's 'Feathertop.' "
       *PMLA*, 46 (1931), 1253–59.

259.    Kesselring, M. L. "Hawthorne's Reading, 1828–1850."
       *Bulletin of the New York Public Library*, 53 (1949), 55–71, 121–38,
       173–94.

260.    Kesterson, David B. "Nature and Hawthorne's Religious Isolationists."
       *Nathaniel Hawthorne Journal*, 4 (1974), 196–208.

261. ———–. "Nature and Theme in 'Young Goodman Brown.'"
*Dickinson Review*, 2 (1970), 42–46.

262. Kim, Yong-Chol. "A Note on 'My Kinsman, Major Molineux.'"
*The English Language and Literature* (Korea), 19 (1966), 85–88.

263. Kjorven, Johannes. "Hawthorne and the Significance of History."
In *American Norvegica: Norwegian Contributions to American Studies*. Phildelphia: Univ. of Pennsylvania Press, 1966, pp. 110–60.

264. Kligerman, Jack. "A Stylist Approach to Hawthorne's 'Roger Malvin's Burial.'" *Language and Style*, 4 (1974), 188–94.

265. Kloeckner, A. J. "The Flower and the Fountain: Hawthorne's Chief Symbols in 'Rappaccini's Daughter.'" *American Literature*, 38 (1966), 323–36.

266. Kozckowski, Stanley J. "'My Kinsman, Major Molineux' as Mock Heroic." *American Transcendental Quarterly*, 31 (1976), 20–21.

267. Krumpelmann, J. T. "Hawthorne's 'Young Goodman Brown' and Goethe's 'Faust.'" *Die Neueran Sprachen*, 5 (1956), 516–21.

268. Kuhlmann, Susan. "The Window of Fiction." *CEA Critic*, 30 (1967), 15–16.

269. Lang, Hans-Joachim. "Ein Argerteufel bel Hawthorne und Melville: Quellenutersuchung zu *The Confidence Man*." *Jahrbuch fur Amerikastudien*, 12 (1967), 246–51.

270. ———–. "How Ambiguous is Hawthorne?" *Freie Gesellschaft* (1962), 195–220. Rpt. in *Hawthorne: A Collection of Critical Essays*. Ed. A. N. Kaul. Englewood Cliffs, N. J.: Prentice-Hall, 1966, pp. 86–98.

271. ———–. "The Turns in *The Turn of the Screw*." *Jahrbuch fur Amerikastudien*, 9 (1964), 111–28.

272. Lathrop, George Parsons. *A Study of Hawthorne*. Boston: Osgood, 1876.

273. Lathrop, Rose Hawthorne. *Memories of Hawthorne*. Boston: Houghton Mifflin, 1897. Rpt. New York: AMS Press, 1969.

274. Lauber, John. "Hawthorne's Shaker Tales." *Nineteenth-Century Fiction*, 18 (1963), 82–86.

275. Leavis, Q. D. "Hawthorne as Poet." *Sewanee Review*, 59 (1951), 180–205, 426–58. Rpt. in *Hawthorne: A Collection of Critical Essays*. Ed. A. N. Kaul. Englewood Cliffs, N. J.: Prentice-Hall, 1966, pp. 25–63.

276. Leibowitz, Herbert A. "Hawthorne and Spenser: Two Sources." *American Literature*, 30 (1959), 459–66.

277. Lesser, Simon O. *Fiction and the Unconscious*. New York: Random House, 1957.

278.    Levin, David. *In Defense of Historical Literature.* New York: Hill and Wang, 1967.

279.    ––––––. "Shadows of Doubt: Specter Evidence in Hawthorne's 'Young Goodman Brown.'" *American Literature,* 34 (1962), 344–52.

280.    Levin, Harry. *The Power of Blackness: Hawthorne, Poe, and Melville.* New York: Alfred A. Knopf, 1958.

281.    Levy, Alfred J. "'Ethan Brand' and the Unpardonable Sin." *Boston University Studies in English,* 5 (1961), 185–90.

282.    Levy, Leo B. "Hawthorne and the Sublime." *American Literature,* 37 (1966), 391–402.

283.    ––––––. "Hawthorne's Middle Ground." *Studies in Short Fiction,* 2 (1964), 56–60.

284.    ––––––."The Mermaid and the Mirror: Hawthorne's 'The Village Uncle.'" *Nineteenth-Century Fiction,* 19 (1964), 205–11.

284.5.    ––––––. "The Problem of Faith in 'Young Goodman Brown.'" *Journal of English and Germanic Philology,* 74 (1975), 375–87.

285.    ––––––. "The Temple and the Tomb: Hawthorne's 'The Lily's Quest.'" *Studies in Short Fiction,* 3 (1966), 334–42.

286.    Lewisohn, Ludwig. *Expression in America.* New York: Harper, 1932.

287.    Liebman, Sheldon W. "Ambiguity in 'Lady Eleanore's Mantle.'" *Emerson Society Quarterly,* 58 (1976), 97–101.

288.    ––––––. "Hawthorne and Milton: The Second Fall in 'Rappaccini's Daughter.'" *New England Quarterly,* 41 (1968), 521–35.

289.    ––––––. "Moral Choice in 'The May-Pole of Merry Mount.'" *Studies in Short Fiction,* 11 (1974), 173–80.

290.    ––––––. "The Reader in 'Young Goodman Brown.'" *Nathaniel Hawthorne Journal,* 5 (1975), 156–67.

291.    ––––––. "Robin's Conversion: The Design of 'My Kinsman, Major Molineux.'" *Studies in Short Fiction,* 8 (1971), 443–57.

292.    Litzinger, Boyd. "Mythmaking in America: 'The Great Stone Face' and *Raintree County.*" *Tenn. Studies in Lit.,* 8 (1963), 81–84.

293.    Loggins, Vernon. *The Hawthornes: The Story of Seven Generations of an American Family.* New York: Columbia Univ. Press, 1951.

294.    Long, Robert Emmet. "James's *Washington Square*: The Hawthorne Relation." *New England Quarterly,* 46 (1973), 573–90.

295.    ––––––. "The Theatre of Political Moralism: Lowell, Hawthorne, and Melville." *Modern Poetry Studies,* 1 (1970), 207–24.

296.    Lovejoy, D. S. "Lovewell's Fight and Hawthorne's 'Roger Malvin's Burial.'" *New England Quarterly,* 27 (1954), 527–31.

297.   Lowell, Robert. *The Old Glory*. New York: Farrar, Straus and Giroux, 1968.

298.   Lundblad, Jane. *Nathaniel Hawthorne and the European Literary Tradition*. Cambridge: Harvard Univ. Press, 1947.

299.   Lynch, James J. "The Devil in the Writings of Irving, Hawthorne, and Poe." *New York Folklore Quarterly*, 8 (1952), 111–31.

300.   ————. "Structure and Allegory in 'The Great Stone Face.' " *Nineteenth-Century Fiction*, 15 (1960), 137–46.

301.   Lyttle, David. "Giovanni! My Poor Giovanni." *Studies in Short Fiction*, 9 (1972), 147–56.

302.   Maddocks, Melvin. "Rituals: The Revolt against the Fixed Smile." *Time*, 96 (1970), 42–43.

303.   Male, Roy R. " 'From the Innermost Germ': The Organic Principle in Hawthorne's Fiction." *English Literary History*, 20 (1953), 218–36.

304.   ————. *Hawthorne's Tragic Vision*. Austin: Univ. of Texas Press, 1957.

305.   Marks, Alfred H. "German Romantic Irony in Hawthorne's Tales." *Symposium*, 7 (1953), 274–305.

306.   ————. "Two Rodericks and Two Worms: 'Egotism; or, The Bosom Serpent' as Personal Satire." *PMLA*, 74 (1959), 607–12.

307.   Markus, Manfred. "Hawthorne's 'Alice Doane's Appeal': An Anti-Gothic Tale." *Germanisch-Romanische Monatsschrift*, 25 (1975), 338–49.

308.   Martin, Terence. "The Method of Hawthorne's Tales." In *Hawthorne's Centenary Essays*. Ed. Roy Harvey Pearce. Columbus: Ohio State Univ. Press, 1964.

309.   ————. *Nathaniel Hawthorne*. New York: Twayne, 1965.

310.   Marx, Leo. *The Machine in the Garden*. New York: Oxford Univ. Press, 1964.

311.   Matenko, Percy. "Tieck, Poe, and Hawthorne." In *Ludwig Tieck and America*. Chapel Hill: Univ of North Carolina Press, 1954, pp. 71–88.

312.   Mathews, James W. "Antinomianism in 'Young Goodman Brown.' " *Studies in Short Fiction*, 3 (1965), 73–75.

313.   ————. "Hawthorne and the Chain of Being." *Modern Language Quarterly*, 18 (1957), 282–94.

314.   ————. "Hawthorne and the Periodical Tale: From Popular Lore to Art." *Papers of the Bibliographical Society of America*, 68 (1974), 149–62.

315.   Matthiessen, F. O. *American Renaissance: Art and Expression in the Age of Emerson and Whitman*. New York: Oxford Univ. Press, 1941.

316.    Maxwell, Desmond E. S. "The Tragic Phase: Melville and Hawthorne." In *American Fiction: The Intellectual Background*. New York: Columbia Univ. Press, 1963.

317.    McCabe, Bernard. "Narrative Technique in 'Rappaccini's Daughter.'" *Modern Language Notes*, 74 (1959), 213–17.

318.    McCall, Dan E. "'I Felt a Funeral in My Brain' and 'The Hollow of the Three Hills.'" *New England Quarterly*, 42 (1969), 432–35.

319.    McCullen, Joseph T., Jr. "Ancient Rites for the Dead and 'Roger Malvin's Burial.'" *Southern Folklore Quarterly*, 30 (1966), 313–22.

320.    ––––––. "Influences on Hawthorne's 'The Artist of the Beautiful.'" *Emerson Society Quarterly*, 50 (1968), 43–46.

321.    ––––––. "'Young Goodman Brown': Presumption and Despair." *Discourse*, 2 (1959), 145–57.

321.5.  ––––––, and John C. Guilds. "The Unpardonable Sin in Hawthorne: A Re-examination." *Nineteenth-Century Fiction*, 15 (1960), 221–37.

322.    McDonald, John J. "Longfellow in Hawthorne's 'The Antique Ring.'" *New England Quarterly*, 46 (1973), 622–26.

323.    ––––––. "The Old Manse Period Canon." *Nathaniel Hawthorne Journal*, 2 (1972), 13–39.

323.5.  McDowell, Tremaine. "Nathaniel Hawthorne and the Witches of Colonial Salem." *Notes and Queries*, 166 (1934), 152.

324.    McElderry, B. R., Jr. "The Transcendental Hawthorne." *Midwest Quarterly*, 2 (1961), 307–23.

325.    McElroy, John. "The Brand Metaphor in 'Ethan Brand.'" *American Literature*, 43 (1972), 633–37.

326.    McKeithan, Daniel M. "Hawthorne's 'Young Goodman Brown': An Interpretation." *Modern Language Notes*, 67 (1952), 93–96.

327.    ––––––. "Poe and the Second Edition of Hawthorne's *Twice-told Tales*." *Nathaniel Hawthorne Journal*, 4 (1974), 257–69.

329.    McMurray, William. "Point of View in Howell's *The Landlord at Lion's Head*." *American Literature*, 34 (1962), 207–14.

330.    McNamara, Leo F. "Subject, Style, and Narrative Technique in 'Bartleby' and 'Wakefield.'" *Michigan Academician*, 3 (1971), 41–46.

330.5.  McPherson, Hugo A. *Hawthorne as Myth-Maker: A Study in Imagination*. Toronto: Univ. of Toronto Press, 1969.

331.    Mehta, R. N. "'Mr. Higginbotham's Catastrophe': An Unusual Hawthorne Story." In *Indian Essays in American Literature in Honor of Robert E. Spiller*. Ed. Sujit Mukherjee. Bombay: Popular Prakashan, 1969.

332. Melville, Herman. "Hawthorne and His Mosses." *Literary World*, 1850. Reprinted in 118, pp. 111-25.

333. Miller, James E., Jr. *Quests Surd and Absurd*. Chicago: Univ. of Chicago Press, 1967.

334. Miller, Paul W. "Hawthorne's 'Young Goodman Brown': Cynicism or Meliorism?" *Nineteenth-Century Fiction*, 14 (1959), 255–64.

335. Mills, Bariss. "Hawthorne and Puritanism." *New England Quarterly*, 21 (1948), 78–102.

336. Monteiro, George. "The Full Particulars of the Minister's Behavior According to Hale." *Nathaniel Hawthorne Journal*, 2 (1972), 173–82.

337. ————. "Hawthorne, James and the Destructive Self." *Texas Studies in Literature and Language*, 4 (1962), 58–71.

338. ————. "Hawthorne's Emblematic Serpent." *Nathaniel Hawthorne Journal*, 3 (1973), 134–42.

339. ————. "Hawthorne's 'The Minister's Black Veil.' " *Explicator*, 22 (1963), 9.

340. ————. "A Nonliterary Source for Hawthorne's 'Egotism; or, The Bosom Serpent.' " *American Literature*, 41 (1970), 575–77.

341. Moore, L. Hugh. "Hawthorne's Ideal Artist as Presumptuous Intellectual." *Studies in Short Fiction*, 2 (1965), 278–83.

342. Morrow, Patrick. "A Writer's Workshop: Hawthorne's 'The Great Carbuncle.' " *Studies in Short Fiction*, 6 (1969), 157–64.

343. Morsberger, Robert E. "Wakefield in the Twilight Zone." *American Transcendental Quarterly*, 14 (1972), 6–8.

344. ————. "The Woe that is Madness: Goodman Brown and the Face of the Fire." *Nathaniel Hawthorne Journal*, 3 (1973), 177–82.

345. Moss, Sidney P. "The Mountain God of Hawthorne's 'The Ambitious Guest.' " *Emerson Society Quarterly*, 47 (1967), 74–75.

346. ————. "A Reading of 'Rappaccini's Daughter.' " *Studies in Short Fiction*, 2 (165), 145–56.

347. Moyer, Patricia. "Time and the Artist in Kafka and Hawthorne." *Modern Fiction Studies*, 4 (1958), 295–306.

348. Mumford, Lewis. *Herman Melville*. New York: Literary Guild of America, 1929, pp. 145–47.

349. Murphy, Morris. "Wordsworthian Concepts in 'The Great Stone Face.' " *College English*, 23 (1962), 364–65.

350. Napier, Elizabeth R. "Aylmer as 'Scheidekunstler': The Pattern of Union and Separation in Hawthorne's 'The Birthmark.' " *Southern Atlantic Bulletin*, 41 (1976), 32–35.

351.    Naples, Diane C. " 'Roger Malvin's Burial'—a Parable for Historians?" *American Transcendental Quarterly*, 13 (1972), 45–49.

352.    Newlin, Paul A. " 'Vague Shapes of the Borderland': The Place of the Uncanny in Hawthorne's Gothic Vision." *Emerson Society Quarterly*, 67 (1972), 83–96.

353.    Newman, Franklin B. " 'My Kinsman, Major Molineux': An Interpretation." *Univ. of Kansas City Review*, 21 (1955), 203–12.

354.    Newman, Lea Vozar. "Anti-Historicism in Hawthorne's 'Legends of the Province-House.' " In *Northeast Modern Language Association Conference Program*. 8–10 April 1976. Burlington: Univ. of Vermont, p. 74.

355.    Normand, Jean. *Nathaniel Hawthorne: An Approach to an Analysis of Artistic Creation*. Trans. Derek Coltman. Cleveland, Ohio: Case Western Univ. Press, 1969.

356.    Orians, G. Harrison. "The Angel of Hadley in Fiction: A Study of the Source of Hawthorne's 'The Gray Champion.' " *American Literature*, 4 (1932), 257–69.

357.    ——————. "Hawthorne and 'The Maypole of Merry Mount.' " *Modern Language Notes*, 53 (1938), 159–67.

358.    ——————. "Hawthorne and Puritan Punishments." *College English*, 13 (1952), 424–32.

359.    ——————. "New England Witchcraft in Fiction." *American Literature*, 2 (1930), 54–71.

360.    ——————. "The Sources of 'Roger Malvin's Burial.' " *American Literature*, 10 (1938), 313–18.

361.    ——————. "The Sources and Themes of Hawthorne's 'The Gentle Boy.' " *New England Quarterly*, 14 (1941), 664–78.

362.    Pancost, David W. "Evidence of Editorial Additions to Hawthorne's 'Fragments from the Journal of a Solitary Man.' " *Nathaniel Hawthorne Journal*, 5 (1975), 210–26.

363.    Pandeya, Prabhat K. "The Drama of Evil in 'The Hollow of the Three Hills.' " *Nathaniel Hawthorne Journal*, 5 (1975) 177–81.

364.    Pattison, Joseph C. " 'The Celestial Railroad' as Dream-Tale." *American Quarterly*, 20 (1968), 224–36.

365.    Paul, Louis. "A Psychoanalytic Reading of Hawthorne's 'Major Molineux': The Father Manqué and the Protégé Manqué." *American Imago*, 18 (1961), 279–88.

366.    Paulits, Walter J. "Ambivalence in 'Young Goodman Brown.' " *American Literature*, 41 (1970), 577–84.

367.    Pauly, Thomas H. " 'Mr. Higginbotham's Catastrophe': The Story

Teller's Disaster." *American Transcendental Quarterly*, 14 (1972), 171–73.

368.   Pearce, Roy Harvey. *Historicism Once More: Problems and Occasions for the American Scholar*. Princeton, N.J.: Princeton Univ. Press, 1969.

369.   ––––––. "Robin Molineux on the Analyst's Couch: A Note on the Limits of Psychoanalytic Criticism." *Criticism*, 1 (1959), 83–90.

370.   ––––––. "Romance and the Study of History." In *Hawthorne's Centenary Essays*. Ed. Roy Harvey Pearce. Columbus: Ohio State Univ. Press, 1964.

371.   Pebworth, Ted-Larry. "The Soul's Instinctive Perception: Dream, Actuality, and Reality in Four Tales from Hawthorne's *Mosses from an Old Manse*." *South Central Bulletin*, 23 (1963), 18–23.

372.   Pederson, Glenn. "Blake's Urizen as Hawthorne's 'Ethan Brand.' " *Nineteenth-Century Fiction*, 12 (1958), 304–14.

373.   Perry, Bliss. "Hawthorne at North Adams." In *The Amateur Spirit*. Boston: Houghton Mifflin, 1904.

374.   Peterich, Werner. "Hawthorne and the *Gesta Romanorum*: The Genesis of 'Rappaccini's Daughter' and 'Ethan Brand.' " In *Kleine Bertrage Zue Amerikanischen Literature–geschite*. Heidelberg: Carl Winter, 1961, pp. 11–18.

375.   Pfeiffer, K. G. "The Prototype of the Poet in 'The Great Stone Face.' " *Research Studies of the State College of Washington*, 9 (1941), 100–08.

376.   Plank, Robert. "Heart Transplant Fiction." *Hartford Studies in Literature*, 2 (1970), 102–12.

377.   Pochmann, Henry A. "Nathaniel Hawthorne." In *German Culture in America: Philosophical and Literary Influences, 1600–1900*. Madison: Wisconsin Univ. Press, 1957, pp. 381–88.

378.   Poe, Edgar Allan. "Review of *Twice-told Tales*." *Graham's Magazine*, 20 (April, May 1842), 254, 298–300. Reprinted in 118, pp. 84–85, 87–94.

378.1.   ––––––. "Tale Writing–Nathaniel Hawthorne." *Godey's Lady's Book*, 35 (November 1847), 252–56. Reprinted in 118, pp. 141–50.

379.   Pollin, Burton R. " 'Rappaccini's Daughter': Sources and Names." *Names*, 14 (1966), 30–35.

380.   Price, Sherwood R. "The Heart, the Head and 'Rappaccini's Daughter.' " *New England Quarterly*, 27 (1954), 399–403.

381.   Prosser, Michael H. "A Rhetoric of Alienation as Reflected in the Works of Nathaniel Hawthorne." *Quarterly Journal of Speech*, 54 (1968), 22–28.

382.   Quinn, James and Ross Baldessarini. "Literary Technique and

Psychological Effect in Hawthorne's 'The Minister's Black Veil.' "
*Literature and Psychology*, 24 (1974), 115–23.

383.   Rahv, Phillip. "The Dark Lady of Salem." *Partisan Review*,,
8 (1941), 362–81.

384.   Rawls, Walton. "Hawthorne's 'Rappaccini's Daughter.' " *Explicator*,
15 (1957), 47.

385.   Reed, Amy Louise. "Self-Portraiture in the Works of Nathaniel
Hawthorne." *Studies in Philology*, 23 (1926), 40–54.

386.   Reed, P. L. "The Telling Frame of Hawthorne's 'Legends of the
Province-House.' " *Studies in American Fiction*, 4 (1976), 105–11.

387.   Rees, John O., Jr. "Hawthorne's Concept of Allegory:
A Reconsideration." *Philological Quarterly*, 54 (1975), 494–510.

388.   Reeves, George, Jr. "Hawthorne's 'Ethan Brand.' " *Explicator*,
14 (1956), 56.

389.   Regan, Robert. "Hawthorne's 'Plagiary': Poe's Duplicity."
*Nineteenth-Century Fiction*, 25 (1970), 281–98.

390.   Reid, Alfred S. "Hawthorne's Humanism: 'The Birthmark' and
Sir Kenelm Digby." *American Literature*, 38 (1966), 337–51.

391.   –––––– "The Role of Transformation in Hawthorne's Tragic
Vision." *Furman Studies*, 6 (1958), 9–20.

392.   Reilly, Cyril A. "On the Dog's Chasing His Own Tail in 'Ethan Brand.' "
*PMLA*, 68 (1953), 975–81.

393.   Ringe, Donald A. "Hawthorne's Night Journeys." *American
Transcendental Quarterly*, 10 (1971), 27–32.

394.   ––––––. "Hawthorne's Psychology of the Head and Heart."
*PMLA*, 65 (1950), 120–32.

395.   ––––––. "Teaching Hawthorne to Engineering Students."
*Emerson Society Quarterly*, 25 (1961), 24–26.

396.   Robillard, Douglas. "Hawthorne's 'Roger Malvin's Burial.' " *Explicator*,
26 (1968), 56.

397.   Robinson, E. A. "The Vision of Goodman Brown: A Source and
Interpretation." *American Literature*, 35 (1963), 218–25.

398.   Rohrberger, Mary. *Hawthorne and the Modern Short Story*. Paris:
Mouton, 1966.

399.   Rose, M. "Theseus Motif in 'My Kinsman, Major Molineux.' "
*Emerson Society Quarterly*, 47 (1967), 21–23.

400.   Rosenberry, Edward H. "Hawthorne's Allegory of Science:
'Rappaccini's Daughter.' " *American Literature*, 32 (1960), 39–46.

400.5. ――――――. "James's Use of Hawthorne in 'The Liar.' " *Modern Language Notes*, 76 (1961), 234–38.

401. Ross, Morton L. "Hawthorne's Bosom Serpent and Mather's *Magnalia*." *Emerson Society Quarterly*, 47 (1967), 13.

402. ――――――. "What Happens in 'Rappaccini's Daughter.' " *American Literature*, 43 (1971), 366–45.

403. Rossky, William. "Rappaccini's Garden or the Murder of Innocence." *Emerson Society Quarterly*, 19 (1960), 98–100.

404. Russell, John. "Allegory and 'My Kinsman, Major Molineux.' " *New England Quarterly*, 40 (1967), 432–40.

404.5. St. Armand, Barton Levi. "Hawthorne's 'Haunted Mind': A Subterranean Drama of the Self." *Criticism*, 13 (1971), 1–25.

405. ――――――. " 'Young Goodman Brown' as Historical Allegory." *Nathaniel Hawthorne Journal*, 3 (1973), 183–97.

406. Salomon, Louis B. "Hawthorne and his Father: A Conjecture." *Literature and Psychology*, 13 (1963), 12–17.

407. Samuels, Charles T. "Giovanni and the Governess." *American Scholar*, 37 (1973), 655–78.

408. Sanders, Charles. "A Note on Metamorphosis in Hawthorne's 'Artist of the Beautiful.' " *Studies in Short Fiction*, 4 (1966), 82–83.

409. Scanlon, Laurence E. "That Very Singular Man, Dr. Heidegger." *Nineteenth-Century Fiction*, 17 (1962), 253–63.

410. Schechter, Harold. "Death and Resurrection of the King: Elements of Primitive Mythology and Ritual in 'Roger Malvin's Burial.' " *English Language Notes*, 8 (1973), 201–05.

411. Scherting, Jack. "The Upas Tree in Dr. Rappaccini's Garden: New Light on Hawthorne's Tale." *Studies in American Fiction*, 1 (1973), 203–07.

412. Schiller, Andrew. "The Moment and the Endless Voyage: A Study of Hawthorne's 'Wakefield.' " *Diameter*, 1 (1951), 7–12. Rpt. in *A Casebook on the Hawthorne Question*. Ed. Agnes McNeill Donahue. New York: Crowell, 1971, pp. 111–16.

413. Schneider, Herbert W. "The Democracy of Hawthorne." *Emory Univ. Quarterly*, 22 (1966), 123–32.

414. Scholl, Diane G. "Robert Lowell's *Endecott and the Red Cross*." *Christianity and Literature*, 22 (1973), 15–28.

415. Schriber, Mary Sue. "Emerson, Hawthorne and 'The Artist of the Beautiful.' " *Studies in Short Fiction*, 8 (1971), 607–16.

416. Schubert, Leland. *Hawthorne, the Artist: Fine Art Devices in Fiction*. Chapel Hill: North Carolina Univ. Press, 1944.

417. Schulz, Dieter. "'Ethan Brand' and the Structure of the American Quest Romance." *Genre*, 7 (1974), 233–49.

418. ———. "Imagination and Self-Improvement: The Ending of 'Roger Malvin's Burial.'" *Studies in Short Fiction*, 10 (1973), 183–86.

419. Schwartz, Joseph. "'Ethan Brand' and the Natural Goodness of Man: A Phenomenological Inquiry." *Emerson Society Quarterly*, 39 (1965), 78–81.

420. ———. "Three Aspects of Hawthorne's Puritanism." *New England Quarterly*, 36 (1963), 192–208.

421. Scott, Arthur L. "The Case of the Fatal Antidote ('Rappaccini's Daughter' Reexamined—with Apologies to Edgar Allan Poe)." *Arizona Quarterly*, 11 (1955), 38–43.

422. Scoville, Samuel. "Hawthorne's Houses and Hidden Treasures." *Emerson Society Quarterly*, 71 (1973), 61–73.

423. Secor, Robert. "Hawthorne's 'The Canterbury Pilgrims.'" *Explicator*, 22 (1963), 8.

424. Shaw, Peter. "Fathers, Sons, and the Ambiguities of Revolution in 'My Kinsman, Major Molineux.'" *New England Quarterly*, 49 (1976), 559–76.

425. Shelton, Austin J. "Transfer of Socio-Historical Symbols in the Interpretation of American Literature by West Africans." *Phylon*, 26 (1965), 372–79.

426. Shroeder, John W. "Alice Doane's Story: An Essay on Hawthorne and Spenser." *Nathaniel Hawthorne Journal*, 4 (1974), 129–34.

427. ———. "Hawthorne's 'Egotism; or, The Bosom Serpent' and its Sources." *American Literature*, 31 (1959), 150–62.

428. ———. "Hawthorne's 'The Man of Adamant': A Spenserian Source-Study." *Philological Quarterly*, 41 (1962), 744–56.

429. ———. "Sources and Symbols for Melville's *Confidence-Man*." *PMLA*, 66 (1961), 363–80.

430. ———. "'That Inward Sphere': Notes on Hawthorne's Heart Imagery and Symbolism." *PMLA*, 65 (1950), 106–19.

431. Shulman, Robert. "Hawthorne's Quiet Conflict." *Philological Quarterly*, 47 (1968), 216–36.

432. Smith, David E. "Bunyan and Hawthorne." In *John Bunyan in America*. Bloomington: Indiana Univ. Press, 1966, pp. 45–89.

433. Smith, Julian. "Coming of Age in America: Young Ben Franklin and Robin Molineux." *American Quarterly*, 17 (1985), 550–58.

434. ———. "Hawthorne and a Salem Enemy." *Essex Institute Historical Collections*, 111 (1966), 299–302.

435.   ——————. "Hawthorne's 'Legends of the Province-House.' "
       *Nineteenth-Century Fiction*, 24 (1969), 31–44.

436.   ——————. "Keats and Hawthorne: A Romantic Bloom in Rappaccini's
       Garden." *Emerson Society Quarterly*, 42 (1966), 8–12.

437.   Smith, Nolan E. "Another Story Falsely Attributed to Hawthorne:
       'The First and Last Dinner.' " *Papers of the Bibliographical Society of
       America*, 65 (1973), 172–73.

438.   Smyth, Albert H. "Hawthorne's 'Great Stone Face.' "
       *The Chautauquan*, 31 (1900), 75–79.

439.   Sokoloff, B. A. "Ethan Brand's Twin." *Modern Language Notes*,
       73 (1958), 413–14.

440.   Solensten, John M. "Hawthorne's Ribald Classic: 'Mrs. Bullfrog'
       and the Folktale." *Journal of Popular Culture*, 7 (1973), 582–88.

441.   Spencer, Benjamin T. "Criticism: Centrifugal and Centripetal."
       *Criticism*, 8 (1966), 139–54.

442.   Stallman, Robert W., and R. E. Watters, eds. *The Creative Reader*.
       New York: Ronald Press, 1954.

443.   Stanton, Robert. "Hawthorne, Bunyan and the American Romances."
       *PMLA*, 71 (1956), 155–65.

444.   ——————. "Secondary Studies on Hawthorne's 'Young Goodman
       Brown,' 1845–1975: A Bibliography." *Bulletin of Bibliography*,
       33 (1976), 32–44, 52.

445.   Stavrou, C. N. "Hawthorne's Quarrel with Man." *Personalist*,
       42 (1961), 352–60.

445.5. Stegner, Wallace, and Mary Stegner, eds. *Great American Short
       Stories*. New York: Basic Books, 1957.

446.   Stein, William Bysshe. " 'The Artist of the Beautiful': Narcissus and
       the Thimble." *American Imago*, 18 (1961), 35–44.

447.   ——————. *Hawthorne's Faust: A Study of the Devil Archetype*.
       Gainesville: Univ. of Florida Press, 1953.

448.   ——————. "The Parable of the AntiChrist in 'The Minister's Black
       Veil.' " *American Literature*, 27 (1955), 386–92.

449.   ——————. "Teaching Hawthorne's 'My Kinsman, Major Molineux.' "
       *College English*, 20 (1958), 83–86.

450.   Stephenson, Edward R. "Hawthorne's 'The Wives of the Dead.' "
       *Explicator*, 25 (1967), 63.

451.   Sterne, Richard Clark. "Hawthorne Transformed: Octavio Paz's
       *La Hija de Rappaccini*." *Comparative Literature Studies*,
       13 (1976), 230–39.

452.     ———. "A Mexican Flower in Rappaccini's Garden: Madame Calderon de la Barca's *Life in Mexio* Revisited." *Nathaniel Hawthorne Journal*, 4 (1974), 277–79.

453.     ———. "Puritans at Merry Mount: Variations on a Theme." *American Quarterly*, 22 (1974), 846–48, 58.

454.     Stewart, Randall. *American Literature and Christian Doctrine.* Baton Rouge: Louisiana State Univ. Press, 1958.

455.     ———, ed. *The American Notebooks by Nathaniel Hawthorne.* New Haven, Conn.: Yale Univ. Press, 1932.

456.     ———. "Hawthorne and the *Faerie Queene.*" *Philological Quarterly*, 12 (1933), 196–206.

457.     ———. "Melville and Hawthorne." *South Atlantic Quarterly,* 51 (1952), 436–46.

458.     ———. *Nathaniel Hawthorne:* A *Biography.* New Haven, Conn.: Yale Univ. Press, 1948.

458.1.   ———. "Recollections of Hawthorne by his Sister, Elizabeth." *American Literature*, 16 (1945), 316–31.

459.     Stibitz, E. Earle. "Ironic Unity in Hawthorne's 'The Minister's Black Veil.' " *American Literature*, 34 (1962), 182–90.

460.     Stock, Ely. "The Biblical Context of 'Ethan Brand.' " *American Literature*, 37 (1965), 115–34.

461.     ———. "History and the Bible in Hawthorne's 'Roger Malvin's Burial.' " *Essex Institute Historical Collections*, 100 (1964), 279–96.

462.     ———. "Witchcraft in 'The Hollow of the Three Hills.' " *American Transcendental Quarterly*, 14 (1972), 31–33.

463.     Stoehr, Taylor. " 'Young Goodman Brown' and Hawthorne's Theory of Mimesis." *Nineteenth-Century Fiction*, 23 (1969), 393–412.

464.     Stone, Edward. "The Two Faces of America." *Ohio Review*, 13 (1972), 5–11.

465.     Stott, Jon. "Hawthorne's 'My Kinsman, Major Molineux' and the Agrarian Ideal." *Michigan Academician*, 4 (1973), 197–203.

466.     Stovall, Floyd. "Contemporaries of Emerson." In *American Idealism.* Norman: Oklahoma Univ. Press, 1943, pp. 55–78.

467.     Strandberg, Victor. "The Artist's Black Veil." *New England Quarterly*, 41 (1968), 567–74.

468.     Stubbs, John Caldwell. *The Pursuit of Form: A Study of Hawthorne and the Romance.* Urbana: Univ. of Illinois Press, 1970.

469.     Taylor, J. Golden. *Hawthorne's Ambivalence toward Puritanism.* Logan: Utah State Univ. Press, 1965.

470. Tharpe, Jac. "Hawthorne and Hindu Literature." *Southern Quarterly*, 10 (1973), 107–15.

471. Thompson, W. R. "Aminidab in Hawthorne's 'The Birthmark.' " *Modern Language Notes*, 70 (1955), 413–15.

472. ――――. "Biblical Sources of Hawthorne's 'Roger Malvin's Burial.' " *PMLA*, 77 (1962), 92–96.

473. ――――. "Patterns of Biblical Allusions in Hawthorne's 'The Gentle Boy.' " *South Central Bulletin*, 22 (1962), 3–10.

474. ――――. "Theme and Method in Hawthorne's 'The Great Carbuncle.' " *South Central Bulletin*, 21 (1961), 3–10.

475. Thorner, Horace E. "Hawthorne, Poe, and a Literary Ghost." *New England Quarterly*, 7 (1934), 146–54.

476. Thorpe, Dwayne. " 'My Kinsman, Major Molineux': The Identity of the Kinsman." *Topic*, 18 (1969), 53–63.

477. Travis, Mildred K. "Of Hawthorne's 'The Artist of the Beautiful' and Spenser's 'Muiopotmos.' " *Philological Quarterly*, 54 (1975), 537.

478. ――――. "Hawthorne's 'Egotism' and 'The Jolly Corner.' " *Emerson Society Quarterly*, 63 (1971), 13–18.

479. ――――. "A Note on 'Wakefield' and 'Old Mr. Marblehall.' " *Notes on Contemporary Literature*, 4 (1974), 9–10.

480. Turner, Arlin. "Elizabeth Peabody Reviews *Twice-told Tales*." *Nathaniel Hawthorne Journal*, 4 (1974), 75–84.

481. ――――. *Hawthorne as Editor: Selections from his Writings in the American Magazine of Useful and Entertaining Knowledge.* Baton Rouge: Louisiana State Univ. Press, 1941.

482. ――――. "Hawthorne's Literary Borrowings." *PMLA*, 51 (1936), 543–62.

483. ――――. "Hawthorne's Method of Using His Source Material." In *Studies for W. A. Read*. Baton Rouge: Louisiana State Univ. Press, 1940.

483.5. ――――. *Nathaniel Hawthorne: An Introduction and Interpretation.* New York: Barnes and Noble, 1961.

484. Turner, Frederick W., III. "Hawthorne's Black Veil." *Studies in Short Fiction*, 5 (1968), 186–87.

485. Uroff, M. D. "The Doctors in 'Rappaccini's Daughter.' " *Nineteenth-Century Fiction*, 27 (1972), 61–70.

486. Vahanian, Gabriel. "Nathaniel Hawthorne: The Obsolescence of God." In *Wait Without Idols*. New York: George Braziller, 1964, pp. 49–71.

487. Vance, William L. "The Comic Element in Hawthorne's Sketches." *Studies in Romanticism*, 3 (1964), 144–60.

488.   Van Der Beets, Richard, and Paul Witherington. "My Kinsman,
       Brockden Brown: Robin Molineux and Arthur Mervyn." *American
       Transcendental Quarterly*, 1 (1969), 13–15.

489.   Vanderbilt, Kermit. "The Unity of Hawthorne's 'Ethan Brand.' "
       *College English*, 24 (1963), 453–56.

490.   Van Doren, Mark. *Nathaniel Hawthorne.* New York: William Sloane,
       1949.

491.   Van Leer, David M. "Aylmer's Library: Transcendental Alchemy in
       Hawthorne's 'The Birthmark.' " *American Transcendental Quarterly*,
       25 (1975), 211–20.

492.   Van Winkle, Edward S. "Aminadab, the Unwitting 'Bad Anima.' "
       *American Notes and Queries*, 8 (1970), 131–33.

493.   Vernon, John. "Melville's 'The Bell Tower.' " *Studies in Short Fiction*,
       7 (1973), 26–76.

494.   Vickery, John B. "The Golden Bough at Merry Mount."
       *Nineteenth-Century Fiction*, 12 (1957), 203–14.

495.   Voigt, Gilbert P. "The Meaning of 'The Minister's Black Veil.'
       *College English,* 13 (1952), 337–38.

496.   Von Abele, Rudolph. "Baby and Butterfly." *Kenyon Review*,
       15 (1953), 280–92.

497.   ––––––. *The Death of the Artist: A Study of Hawthorne's
       Disintegration.* The Hague: Nijhoff, 1955.

498.   Wagenknecht, Edward. *Nathaniel Hawthorne: Man and Writer.*
       New York: Oxford Univ. Press, 1961.

499.   Waggoner, Hyatt Howe. "Art and Belief." In *Hawthorne's Centenary
       Essays.* Ed. Roy Harvey Pearce. Columbus: Ohio State Univ. Press,
       pp. 167–95.

500.   ––––––. *Hawthorne: A Critical Study.* Rev. ed. Cambridge, Mass.:
       Belknap Press, 1963.

501.   ––––––. "Hawthorne's 'Canterbury Pilgrims': Theme and Structure."
       *New England Quarterly*, 22 (1949), 373–87.

501.5. ––––––. "Nathaniel Hawthorne." *UMPAL*, 23. Minneapolis:
       Minnesota Univ. Press, 1962.

502.   ––––––. *Nathaniel Hawthorne: Selected Tales and Sketches.*
       3rd ed. New York: Holt, Rinehart and Winston, 1970.

503.   Walcutt, Charles Child. "The Idle Inquiry." In *Man's Changing
       Masks: Modes and Methods of Characterization in Fiction.*
       Minneapolis: Univ. of Minnesota Press, 1966, pp. 124–30.

504.   Wallins, Roger P. "Robin and the Narrator in 'My Kinsman, Major
       Molineux.' " *Studies in Short Fiction,* 12 (1975), 173–79.

505. Walsh, Thomas F., Jr. "The Bedevilling of Young Goodman Brown." *Modern Language Quarterly*, 19 (1958), 331–36.

506. ——————. "Character Complexity in Hawthorne's 'The Birth-mark.'" *Emerson Society Quarterly*, 23 (1961), 12–15.

507. ——————. "Hawthorne: Mr. Hooper's 'Affable Weakness.'" *Modern Language Notes*, 74 (1959), 401–06.

508. ——————. "Hawthorne's Satire in 'Old Esther Dudley.'" *Emerson Society Quarterly*, 22 (1961), 31–39.

509. ——————. "Rappaccini's Literary Garden." *Emerson Society Quarterly*, 19 (1960), 9–13.

510. ——————. "'Wakefield' and Hawthorne's Illustrated Ideas: A Study in Form." *Emerson Society Quarterly*, 25 (1961), 29–35.

510.5. Warren, Austin. "Hawthorne's Reading." *New England Quarterly*, 8 (1935), 480–97.

511. ——————. *Nathaniel Hawthorne: Representative Selections.* New York: American Book, 1934.

512. ——————. *Rage for Order.* Chicago: Chicago Univ. Press, 1948.

512.5. Wasserstrom, William. "The Spirit of Myrrha." *American Imago*, 13 (1956), 455–72.

513. Webb, Jane Carter. "The Implications of Control for the Human Personality: Hawthorne's Point of View." *Tulane Studies in English*, 21 (1974), 57–66.

513.5. Webber, Charles Wilkins. "Hawthorne." *American Whig Review*, 1846. Reprinted in 118, pp. 126–34.

514. Weber, Alfred. *Die Entwicklung Der Rahmenerzahlungen Nathaniel Hawthorne's "The Story Teller" und Andere Fruhe Werke.* Berlin: Ehrich Schmidt, 1973.

515. Webner, Helene L. "Hawthorne, Melville and Lowell's *The Old Glory*." *Re: Arts and Letters*, 4 (1973), 1–17.

516. Wentersdorf, Karl P. "The Genesis of Hawthorne's 'The Birthmark.'" *Jahrbuch fur Amerikastudien*, 8 (1963), 171–86.

517. Werge, Thomas. "Thomas Shepard and Crevecoeur: Two Uses of the Image of the Bosom Serpent before Hawthorne." *Nathaniel Hawthorne Journal*, 4 (1974), 236–39.

518. West, Harry C. "The Sources for Hawthorne's 'Artist of the Beautiful.'" *Nineteenth-Century Fiction*, 30 (1975), 105–11.

519. West, Ray B. and R. W. Stallman, eds. *The Art of Modern Fiction.* New York: Rinehart, 1949.

520.  Whelan, Robert Emmet, Jr. "Hawthorne Interprets 'Young Goodman Brown.' " *Emerson Society Quarterly*, 62 (1971), 2–4.

521.  ———. " 'Rappaccini's Daughter' and Zenobia's Legend." *Research Studies* (Washington State Univ.), 39 (1971), 47–52.

522.  ———" 'Roger Malvin's Burial': The Burial of Reuben Bourne's Cowardice." *Research Studies* (Washington State Univ.), 37 (1969), 112–21.

523.  White Robert L. " 'Rappaccini's Daughter,' *The Cenci,* and the Cenci Legend." *Studi Americani*, 14 (1968), 63–86.

524.  White, William A. "Hawthorne's Eighteen Year Cycle: Ethan Brand and Reuben Bourne." *Studies in Short Fiction*, 6 (1969), 215–18.

525.  Williams, J. Gary. "History in Hawthorne's 'The Maypole of Merry Mount.' " *Essex Institute Historical Collections*, 108 (1972), 173–89.

526.  Wilson, James D. "Incest and American Romantic Fiction." *Studies in the Literary Imagination*, 7 (1974), 31–50.

527.  Wilson, Rod. "Further Spenserian Parallels in Hawthorne." *Nathaniel Hawthorne Journal*, 2 (1972), 195–201.

528.  Winkelman, Donald A. "Goodman Brown, Tom Sawyer, and Oral Tradition." *Keystone Folklore Quarterly*, 10 (1965), 43–48.

529.  Wood, Clifford A. "Teaching Hawthorne's 'The Celestial Railroad.' " *English Journal*, 54 (1965), 601–05.

530.  Woodward, R. H. "Automata in Hawthorne's 'Artist of the Beautiful' and Taylor's 'Meditation 56.' " *Emerson Society Quarterly*, 31 (1963), 63–66.

531.  Wycherley, H. Alan. "Hawthorne's 'The Minister's Black Veil.' " *Explicator*, 23 (1964), 11.

532.  Yagyu, Nozomu. "Hawthorne's Concept of Original Sin as Seen in 'The Birthmark.' " *Eibungaku Tenbo* (Meiji Gakuin Univ., Japan), 1 (1962), 1–6.

533.  Yates, Norris. "Ritual and Reality: Mask and Dance Motifs in Hawthorne's Fiction." *Philological Quarterly*, 34 (1955), 56–70.

533.5.  Yoder, R. A. "Hawthorne and His Artist." *Studies in Romanticism*, 7 (1968), 193–206.

534.  Ziff, Larzer. "The Artist and Puritanism." In *Hawthorne's Centenary Essays*. Ed. Roy Harvey Pearce. Columbus: Ohio State Univ. Press, 1964, pp. 245–69.

535.  Zivley, Sherry. "Hawthorne's 'The Artist of the Beautiful' and Spenser's 'Muiopotmos.' " *Philological Quarterly*, 48 (1969), 134–37.